400
-
Pol
619

PRAI

THE PEOPL

THE GREEN MOVEMENT AND THE STRUGGLE FOR IRAN'S FUTURE

"In bringing together these essential texts from and about Iran's Green movement, Nader Hashemi and Danny Postel have opened the door for critical engagement with one of the most significant social movements in the Middle East today." —*Orhan Pamuk*

"The editors of this collection have put together an extraordinary resource to help further the development of democracy and social justice in Iran. It brings together vital contributions to the debate about Iran's future and invites all those concerned with this future to become active participants in its definition." —*David Held, London School of Economics & Political Science*

"This anthology illuminates the ethical demands at the core of Iran's Green Movement, one of the most vibrant and promising social forces on the global horizon. *The People Reloaded* plunges us into a defining conflict of modern political history: how nonviolent democratic resistance might succeed in the face of a repressive regime. Defeat often seems inevitable and change never seems to come fast enough. And then, all of a sudden, the dam bursts, time accelerates and nothing can stop it. This welcome volume provides an anatomy of how this process is unfolding in Iran today, whatever its eventual outcome." —*Simon Critchley, New School for Social Research*

"Words, yes, words and justice and bodies—that's all the Iranian human earthquake called the Green Movement has had on its side from the start of its peaceful insurrection. The bodies have been beaten and jailed and persecuted and the justice is a long time coming, but the words, the indispensable words that have always been at the heart of that country's history, the words are finally available in one crucial and moving and thought-provoking book. Here is proof—as if Gandhi needed proof, as if King needed proof—that the people of Iran will prevail." —*Ariel Dorfman*

"*The People Reloaded: The Green Movement and the Struggle for Iran's Future* includes very insightful, informative, and original brief analyses by outstanding Iran specialists such as Asef Bayat, Ervand Abrahamian, Fred Halliday, Reza Aslan, Juan Cole, and Robin Wright. Readers may take their pick among numerous readable articles from inside and outside Iran and find new and varied views that shed much light on the genesis, development, and future of this important movement."
—*Nikki Keddie, author of* Modern Iran:
Roots and Results of Revolution

"For all those who are interested in the new shapes of democracy in our world, and who felt deep solidarity with the Iranian protests last year, and horror at their suppression, this collection offers precious insights into the historical sources and future potentials of this great movement." —*Charles Taylor, McGill University*

"The events of June 2009 marked a turning point in Iranian politics. This timely collection of essays and articles is of capital importance not only for all those who take an interest in Iranian affairs, but also for students of democratization and of social movements."
—*Houchang E. Chehabi, Boston University*

"This anthology on the Iranian Green Movement is the most impressive collection of writings on one of the most inspiring and democratic movements of our time. This volume is a rare resource for anyone who is interested in the understanding of post-Islamist social movements."
—*Ali Mirsepassi, New York University*

THE
PEOPLE RELOADED

THE GREEN MOVEMENT AND THE STRUGGLE FOR IRAN'S FUTURE

Edited by Nader Hashemi and Danny Postel

MELVILLEHOUSE
BROOKLYN, NEW YORK

THE PEOPLE RELOADED

© 2010 Nader Hashemi and Danny Postel
First Melville House printing: December 2010

Melville House Publishing
145 Plymouth Street
Brooklyn, NY 11201
www.mhpbooks.com

ISBN: 978-1-935554-38-7

Page 440 is an extension of this copyright page.

Printed in the United States of America

1 2 3 4 5 6 7 8 9 10

Library of Congress Cataloging-in-Publication Data

The people reloaded : the green movement and the struggle for Iran's future /
edited by Nader Hashemi and Danny Postel.
   p. cm.
Includes bibliographical references and index.
ISBN 978-1-935554-38-7
   1. Green movement--Political aspects--Iran. 2. Iran--Politics and govern-
ment--1997- 3. Political participation--Iran. 4. Democracy--Iran. I. Hashemi,
Nader, 1966- II. Postel, Danny.
GE199.I7P46 2010
322.4'40955--dc22
                              2010046822

THOSE WHO STOOD UP FOR TOLERANCE
Hafez

May days of love's reunions be remembered
May those days be remembered, may they always be remembered.
My mouth is poisoned by the bitterness of grief;
May the toasts of those happy drinkers be remembered.
Although my comrades are free from remembering me,
I remember them all constantly.
Though I'm captured and bound by this misery,
May the attempts of those who stood up for tolerance be remembered.
Even though a hundred rivers constantly flow from my eyes,
Zayanderud irrigates for those who make gardens, may it be remembered.
From now on the secret of Hafez will remain unspoken.
Have pity on those who must keep secrets; may that be remembered.

CONTENTS

PART II
BEYOND "WHERE IS MY VOTE?"—A GREEN VISION TAKES SHAPE

PART III
CONFRONTING SETBACKS, RETHINKING STRATEGY

PART IV
A LUTA CONTINUA: THE GREEN MOVEMENT'S SECOND YEAR AND THE STRUGGLE FOR IRAN'S FUTURE

INTRODUCTION

Nader Hashemi and Danny Postel

The study of democracy is not an exact science. It is always difficult to pinpoint the precise moment that triggers the seismic shift which fundamentally alters the direction of a society's political development. This is because the factors that affect democratization are numerous and cannot easily be reduced to a single variable or dramattic event.[1] Notwithstanding this truism, future historians of democracy will likely look back on the month of June 2009 as the period when the struggle for democracy in Iran underwent a momentous transformation, shifting the entire country's political trajectory and sealing the fate of the Islamic Republic of Iran in the process.

At the beginning of June 2009, Iran was in the midst of its tenth presidential election campaign since the 1979 revolution. Voter enthusiasm was high and the country was engulfed in a peaceful public debate about the future of Iran. As it had done in the past, the Iranian regime loosened political restrictions in the lead-up to a national election in order to encourage a high voter turnout and bolster the regime's sagging legitimacy. Judging from the number of people who attended political rallies and the increased interest in the American-style presidential debates, this tactic seemed to be working. In the final two weeks of the election, the campaign of the leading reformist candidate, Mir Hossein Mousavi, picked up steam. It was bolstered by an effective grassroots effort to mobilize civil society as well as the mood of "anybody but Ahmadinejad" that was especially prevalent among Iran's middle class and burgeoning population of young people.[2]

As the June 12 election day approached, the political expectations of voters who sided with the opposition were extremely modest. The maximum hope was that the direction of the Islamic Republic could be steered away from the reckless domestic and foreign policies of

Mahmoud Ahmadinejad and toward a more measured approach, similar to what the country had experienced during the first term of Mohammad Khatami's reformist presidency (1997–2001). Deep structural transformation was not on the agenda. But, following the official announcement of Ahmadinejad's supposed landslide victory at the polls—which many regarded, and continue to regard, as a *coup d'état*—the remaining days of June were filled with cries of "Where is my vote?" and massive state-sanctioned repression (embodied by the violent death of Neda Agha Soltan). Criticism of Ahmadinejad was gradually replaced with chants of "Death to the Dictator" and a repudiation of the political and religious authority of Ali Khamenei, Iran's Supreme Leader. Iranian political culture had qualitatively changed in ways that would shape the political destiny of the country for many months and years to come. Central to this story is the rise of Iran's Green Movement (*Jonbesh-e sabz Iran*).

What is Iran's Green Movement? What sort of creature is this social force that appeared—indeed, exploded—on the streets of Tehran and other Iranian cities in the summer of 2009?

The late sociologist Charles Tilly defined a social movement as a series of contentious performances, displays and campaigns by which ordinary people make collective claims on the state.[3] A social movement is different from an organization like a political party, which typically has a clear leadership structure. A social movement is a more amorphous phenomenon, at least at its inception. Iran's Green Movement is a case in point.

The movement has varyingly been described by journalists, sociologists, historians, and political philosophers as an "Iranian-style *intifada*" (Robert Fisk), a "great emancipatory event" (Slavoj Žižek), a "grassroots civil rights movement" and as "something quite extraordinary, perhaps even a social revolution" (Hamid Dabashi).[4]

What are its precise origins, the nature of its vision and the scope of its demands? Is it reformist or revolutionary, or perhaps "refolutionary" as Timothy Garton Ash has suggested?[5] What is its structure? Does it have leaders? Is it horizontal rather than vertical, or some combination of both? Is it more of a network than organizational in form? In his contribution to this volume, longtime Iran observer Gary Sick likens the movement to a ganglion:

> Rather than a hierarchy flowing down from one or more individuals at the top, or even the classic cell structure of a clandestine organization, the Iranian opposition most resembles a ganglion, a tangled bundle of nerve cells where each part of the system is constantly and instantly in touch with all other parts.

In thinking about the Green Movement, one wonders whether existing categories and paradigms are even adequate, or if new ones are required to make sense of this dynamic phenomenon. Are we witnessing a replay of Iran's 1979 revolution? Or is Iran's 1906 Constitutional Revolution, as Ali Ansari has argued, a better framework to make sense of recent events?[6] "This movement is ahead of our inherited politics, floating ideologies or mismatched theories," Dabashi observes. "We need to adjust our lenses and languages in order to see better."[7]

Some have already asked, is the Green Movement now dead? Or only dormant? Has it lost its footing? Has it gone underground? Is it metamorphosing? Re-designing its strategy? What impact has it had on Iran's political landscape? What does it portend for Iran's future?

These questions have surrounded discussion of the Green Movement since its emergence. In recent months, the Movement has been declared dead by people of varying political orientations and ideological agendas—everyone from the commissars of the Islamic Republic to certain Western leftists to the *Realpolitik* power couple Flynt and Hillary Mann Leverett. While the Leveretts are very much creatures of the US foreign policy establishment—they have worked for the CIA, the National Security Council and the State Department—they enjoy an unfortunate cachet among many peace activists who support the couple's call for the US to engage Iran. It is not with this position that we take issue, but rather with the Leveretts' specious and toxic case against the Green Movement, which has confused many well-intentioned peace activists.[8]

If the Green Movement is really dead and relegated to the dustbin of history, someone needs to tell this to Iran's ruling oligarchy. Over a year after the stolen presidential election—long after the movement was declared dead—the Iranian regime continues to wage open war against it. In late August 2010, orders were issued by Iran's Ministry of Culture and Islamic Guidance to all domestic media and news agencies banning any mention of the names, photographs or statements of Mir Hossein Mousavi, Mehdi Karoubi and Mohammad Khatami, in order to "create a calm atmosphere in society and in the public mind."[9] At the same time, leading clerical hardliners such as Ayatollahs Mohammad Taqi Mesbah Yazdi and Ahmad Jannati, backed by the Minister of Intelligence, Heydar Moslehi, brought new charges of treason against the Green Movement. This time the preposterous accusation was that the movement had taken a billion dollars from the US (and the promise of 50 billion more), via the Saudis, in order to topple the Islamic Republic.[10] While this was happening, a "Green Sedition Festival" was held, replete with posters comparing the Green Movement to the Mujahideen-e Khalq, an extremist cult widely detested by Iranians (and now backed by American neoconservatives). Meanwhile, Khamenei has claimed to be the "representative of the Prophet Muhammad and the 12th [Shia] Imam on Earth" and issued a new fatwa demanding total obedience.[11]

Which one is it? The Islamic Republic proclaims the death of the Green Movement and yet goes to extraordinary lengths to criminalize it, stamp it out and conduct a campaign of repression against its leaders and adherents. But if the movement is in fact extinct, why all the strenuous efforts and elaborate measures to kill it?

What these various foes of the Green Movement—the Islamic Republic, certain Western leftists and the Leveretts—are actually saying is that they *want* the movement to be dead.[12] At the same time, though, there are many who harbor no ill will towards Iran's Greens but merely wonder about its state of play. In the first days, weeks and months following the June 12 election, the whole world watched as millions of Iranians took to the streets to protest the officially announced results. The silent rally of June 15, 2009 at Azadi (Freedom) Square in Tehran attracted one of the largest crowds not only in Iran's history, but quite possibly in world history. In his contribution to this volume, the eminent historian Ervand Abrahamian describes the occasion as follows:

> Around a million people heeded the call—the conservative mayor of the capital put the number at three million. The scene was reminiscent of the rallies held in the same square during the 1979 revolution.... The rally drew all kinds of protesters: old and young, professionals and workers, bazaaris and students, women wearing sunglasses and headscarves as well as those with the full-length chador. Lines of protesters five miles long converged on the square from the better-off northern districts as well as from the working-class southern ones.

Street protests continued throughout the summer and autumn of 2009. They were met with paroxysms of brutality as the Islamic Republic's repressive security apparatus went into overdrive, its forces attacking peaceful demonstrators, killing dozens and injuring hundreds. Hoping to crush the growing movement and deter further expressions of dissent, the state arrested virtually every leader, journalist or activist associated with or even sympathetic to the Green Movement, filling its prisons—in which, we soon learned, crimes of a truly horrifying nature were systematically committed. Stalinist-style show trials were conducted. Iran witnessed a full-blown reign of terror.[13]

And yet the movement endured and even expanded. In December 2009, during the holy day of Ashura, the streets of many Iranian cities were rocked with protests, many of them confrontational and some involving skirmishes with police. The Green Movement was not merely alive, but appeared to be growing even more defiant. Protesters no longer chanted about the stolen election. The chants and placards had shifted focus to the very foundation and future of politics in Iran.

But the Islamic Republic's repressive machinery responded in full force, crushing protests, rounding up and jailing yet more of the movement's partisans. In a special report by Amnesty International, the state of human rights in Iran was described as "the most severe period of repression since the end of the revolutionary period."[14]

The next stage of confrontation was set for February 11, 2010—the thirty-first anniversary of the 1979 Islamic Revolution. The Green Movement had been consistently denied a permit to demonstrate, so their strategy was to subvert state-approved demonstrations by encouraging its supporters to take to the streets with peaceful pro-democracy slogans. There was never any central coordinating committee. Small networks of activists mobilized supporters by word of mouth, using cell phones and the Internet. Aware that the momentum was shifting and that the existing repression and state-sanctioned violence was unable to quell the protests, the Iranian regime resorted to a new tactic—targeted assassinations and executions.

In late December 2009, Mir Hossein Mousavi's nephew, Ali Habibi-Mousavi, was mysteriously shot dead on a quiet side street near the home of his in-laws. Friends and family reported that he had received death threats throughout the previous week. The Tehran police described his death as a "targeted assassination" while *Kayhan* newspaper (run by the office of the Supreme Leader) and the head of the Basij militia blamed Mousavi himself for the murder.[15] Two weeks later a University of Tehran physics professor, Masoud Ali Mohammadi, was killed by a remote control bomb blast outside his home in north Tehran. While not a prominent critic of Ahmadinejad, he was among 240 professors who signed a letter expressing support for Mousavi, and he openly defended student protests after the sacking of their dormitory.[16] No suspects were named in either case but the message sent to Green Movement was clear.

To ensure that it was fully received, on January 28, 2010 the regime executed two political prisoners, Mohammad Reza Ali Zamani and Arash Rahmanipour, who had been arrested before the election. After a closed-door trial, a revolutionary court convicted them of "propaganda against the system," "insulting the holy sanctities" and "gathering and colluding with intent to harm national internal security."[17] The following day, the influential chairman of Iran's Guardian Council, Ayatollah Ahmad Jannati, delivered a Friday sermon that was broadcast on state radio in which he publicly *praised* these executions and encouraged the head of the judiciary to execute more political prisoners. "I thank the judiciary chief for executing two rioters and urge him to execute others if they do not give up such protests," Jannati told worshippers at Tehran University.[18] A few days later, Ebrahim Raisi, a senior judiciary official, announced that "nine others will be hanged soon. The nine, and the two who were hanged on Thursday, were surely arrested in the recent riots and had links to anti-revolutionary groups."[19]

The protests of February 11 did not materialize. Severed communication links, mass arrests, an enormous security presence and threats of executions won the day. Busloads of regime loyalists were brought to Tehran and others were enticed by free food or fear for their government jobs. As "Mr. Verde" writes in this volume, it was a Pyrrhic victory for the Iranian regime:

> And here comes the problem: this year's events were less like celebrating a revolution that freed the country from tyranny and dictatorship and more like a tyrannical dictatorship celebrating its continued survival.... From the start of the post-election protests, the regime has been adamant that the protesters were few in number and did not have a real agenda except causing chaos and mayhem.... If the protesters are so few in number and so insignificant, there is no reason for such a heavy security presence. How to resolve this contradiction? Either the regime knows that opposition is widespread or we are witnessing a totalitarian regime in action.[20]

Since then, street demonstrations have been fewer and further between, but the Green Movement soldiers on. Iran has moved steadily from an authoritarian regime to a neo-totalitarian one. Power is now concentrated in the hands of what Scott Peterson has called "the new leadership troika—the Revolutionary Guard, the Supreme Leader, and Ahmadinejad and his neoconservative cabal."[21] The state which they control attempts to regulate all facets of public life, the private lives of citizens are under constant surveillance, and the security forces operate with impunity. This repressive context notwithstanding—including physical attacks and raids on the homes of Green Movement leaders— the movement continues its principled defense of democracy and human rights by regularly issuing defiant statements and proclamations, and by giving courageous interviews which are circulated on the Internet and eagerly consumed by their supporters. Some of the most important statements and interviews have been selected for this volume, including the all-important Green Movement Charter issued on the first anniversary of the movement's founding.[22]

While events in the aftermath of June 2009 have severely damaged the legitimacy of the Iranian regime and significantly narrowed its base of support, it is important that we do not exaggerate the internal balance of power. While the Greens have deep roots in Iranian society, their strategy of nonviolent resistance within the framework of the law suggests that, to quote Hamid Dabashi's apt formulation, the struggle for democracy in Iran will be "a marathon, not a 100-meter sprint."[23] We are still far from witnessing a demise of the Islamic Republic of Iran, for several reasons. Iran is a rentier state, which means it pays its bills from the sale of oil rather than through taxation. This gives the regime a significant degree of autonomy from society, which immunizes it from popular pressure, while also fueling an extensive patron-client network that allows the regime to buy the allegiance of millions of people whose livelihood is tied to its survival. The transference of large sections of the economy into the hands of the Islamic Revolutionary Guard Corps (IRGC) figures centrally in this same process, as they in turn provide a forceful guarantee for the regime's durability.[24]

Beyond this fact, the Islamic Republic retains ideological support in some poorer, rural areas of the country where people are more religiously pious and more dependent on the state-controlled media instead of the Internet or satellite TV. Furthermore, there exists a loyal set of hardcore devotees who have internalized the regime's propaganda line that the Green Movement is foreign-funded, that Iran's domestic problems are caused by the machinations of the United States, Britain and Israel, and that Supreme Leader Ali Khamenei is God's representative on earth. Exact figures on the size of this core group of loyal supporters are difficult to ascertain, but they are significant and many of them are willing to lay down their lives for the Supreme Leader if called upon.[25]

Finally, the Islamic Republic retains control of key institutions of the state that pertain to the means of violence, the administration of justice, and economic production. There is little evidence that this control has significantly weakened. If and when it does—particularly if the much-discussed strikes by oil workers or defections from the Revolutionary Guard materialize—it will mark a turning point for the regime. At least twenty-eight members of Iran's Ministry of Foreign Affairs have already resigned their posts, several of them openly citing the post-election crackdown as a reason and publicly siding with the Green Movement. Could this be a sign of things to come?[26]

The movement draws its support from a cross-section of Iranian society—the country's sizable educated and middle classes as well as working-class Iranians (particularly trade unionists), and overwhelming support from Iran's intellectuals, students, women's groups, and especially the country's youth, who comprise two-thirds of the population. A myth that has made the rounds of the Western Left has it that the Green movement is a creature of the privileged elite while Ahmadinejad is a hero of the downtrodden masses. This is a crass and lazy distortion, one that is invoked in bad faith with the purpose of disparaging the movement. In her essay "This Magic Green Bracelet" in these pages, the Iranian journalist Nasrin Alavi provides a healthy corrective to this ritual incantation:

A simple glance at the background of Iran's prominent student leaders tells you that, by and large, they are not the children of affluent citizens of north Tehran, but instead come from provincial working-class families or are the children of rural schoolteachers and clerks. The Western media cliché of an opposition limited to the urban upper class belies the current realities. These future leaders of Iran commonly hail from the very heartland of Ahmadinejad's purported support base.

By far the movement's biggest asset is that it has already won an overwhelming ideological victory against the regime. In the realm of political ideas, the battle is over, and Iran's clerical oligarchs know it: witness the number of university deans and professors who have been fired, the number of journalists and intellectuals who have been jailed and the number of newspapers that have been forcibly closed.[27]

Today the guardians of the Islamic Republic cannot tolerate an open debate or exchange of ideas about events that have occurred since June 2009 or, more broadly, about Iran's political and human rights records over the past thirty years. Nothing terrifies the regime more. An open public discussion about Khomeini's theory of political rule, *velayat-e faqih* (the rule of the Islamic jurist), or even a consideration of the merits of democracy and secularism, can land citizens in prison. Newspaper censorship, satellite television interruptions, website blocking and, most revealingly, the mass arrest of nearly every leading Iranian dissident and human rights activist—all of whom have been jailed for nonviolent political dissent—speaks to the extreme paranoia of the Islamic Republic. What this reveals is that while militarily powerful, the regime is ideologically weak.[28]

The roots of this important ideological victory can be traced to the rise of the reform movement in the 1990s. It was during this period, due primarily to the work of Iran's religious intellectuals, that Iranian political culture experienced a transformation in which the basic principles of liberal democracy and an indigenous understanding of "Islamic secularism" emerged and sank deep roots into civil society. This phenomenon underpins and informs the Green Movement today.[29]

The period of reform during the late 1990s is also the immediate framework needed to understand the Green Movement. While several of the contributors to this volume rightly note that Iran's struggle for democracy is over 100 years old, the current movement is directly tied to debates and transformations that emerged during Khatami's reformist presidency which itself can be traced back to the democratic ideals of the 1979 Islamic Revolution. The title of this book, *The People Reloaded*, is drawn from one of the essays that speaks to this point—the continuity of democratic struggle within Iran, particularly in the post-revolutionary period. According to Morad Farhadpour and Omid Mehrgan:

> The expression 'people reloaded' tries to capture this sense of repetition without mere imitation. For thirty years, the regime has claimed that freedom and, more recently, justice have been realized, praising the Iranian people for their political commitment and courage. Now people are taking these claims literally, calling the regime's bluff. People are trying to redeem the lost hopes and aspirations of the revolution, as they did once before by electing Khatami in 1997. But this time, we are much more resolute and creative.

Furthermore, the rise of the Green Movement in Iran has engendered an extraordinary flourishing in the intellectual and artistic spheres both within Iran and in the Iranian diaspora. There has been an explosion of thinking and writing on the movement, visible in essays, blogs, listservs, Facebook groups, academic conferences and general acts of solidarity. Iran's political culture has been deeply affected and for the first time since the 1979 Revolution, a new unity of purpose is visible among Iranians around the world.

Within Iran, prominent actors, filmmakers, musicians and sports personalities have demonstrated their support for the Green Movement. These include leading members of Iran's national soccer team, who wore green arm bands at a World Cup qualifying match; the internationally celebrated filmmaker Jafar Panahi, the arrest of whom led to the mobilization of the global film industry who petitioned for his release, and Mohammed-Reza Shajarian, the critically-acclaimed traditional Persian singer and musician, who demanded the government cease broadcasting his music and announced that his voice belongs to all the people of Iran. In August 2010 the moderate daily, *Mardom Salari*, published a list of prominent poets, actors, singers and other celebrities who have were banned from appearing on television because they sided with the opposition.[30] Those who claim that politically the Green Movement was an ephemeral moment in Iranian history have missed its enduring cultural effects.

Among Iranian expatriates, the Green Movement has both brought together Iranians from different ideological currents and has politicized many others who until recently remained aloof from political engagement. Among the most vibrant new forums to have emerged in this context is the web-based program The Week in Green (www.weekingreen. org). Hosted by Hamid Dabashi, the show features Persian and English interviews (with subtitles in the other language) of activists, writers, artists and scholars who explore various dimensions of the Green Movement. With viewers all over the world, The Week in Green has become an intellectual and political hub for news and reflection on the Green Movement. The archives of the program (all available online) offer a treasure trove of material and illuminate the intellectual renaissance that has taken shape since the emergence of the Movement. This book includes two interviews from the program, notably those of Cornel West and Akbar Ganji.

In conclusion, this book seeks to capture an important moment in Iran's history. It provides an intellectual and political road map to understanding the tumultuous events that have rocked the Islamic Republic since June 2009. In this volume, we have collected some of the best writing and political analyses of the first year of the Green Movement written by leading scholars, intellectuals and activists interested in and engaged with the struggle for democracy in Iran, including key documents, statements and interviews from prominent voices within the country. It is by no means an exhaustive or comprehensive collection; rather, it is a selective one that provides valuable historical and political context. In the end, it seeks to impress the reader with the importance of recent developments and what they portend for the future of Iran, the Middle East and indeed, the entire world.

November 2010

PART I

DEMOCRACY IS IN THE STREETS:
THE BIRTH OF A MOVEMENT

WHY ARE THE IRANIANS DREAMING AGAIN?

Ali Alizadeh

June 18, 2009

Iran is currently in the grip of a new and strong political movement.[1] While this movement proves that Ahmadinejad's populist techniques of deception no longer work inside Iran, it seems they are still effective outside the country. This is mainly due to thirty years of isolation and mutual mistrust between Iran and the West which has turned my country into a mysterious phenomenon for outsiders. In this piece I will try to confront some of the mystifications and misunderstandings produced by the international media in the last week.

In the first scenario the international media, claiming impartiality, insisted that the reformists provide hard objective evidence in support of their claim that the June 12 election has been rigged. But despite their empiricist attitude, the media missed obvious facts due to their lack of familiarity with the socio-historical context. Although the reformists could not possibly offer any figures or documents, because the whole show was single-handedly run by Ahmadinejad's ministry of interior, anyone familiar with Iran's recent history could easily see what was wrong with this picture.

It was the government that reversed the conventional and logical procedure by announcing a fictitious total figure first—in four stages— and then fabricating figures for each polling station, something that is still going on. This led to many absurdities: Mousavi received fewer votes in his hometown of Tabriz than Ahmadinejad; Karoubi's total vote was less than the number of people active in his campaign; Rezaee's votes shrank by a hundred thousand between the third and fourth stages of announcement; blank votes were totally forgotten and only hastily added to the count when reformists pointed this out; and finally

3

the ratio between all candidates' votes remained almost constant in all four stages of announcement (63, 33, 2 and 1 percent).

Moreover, as in any other country, the increase in turnout in Iran's elections has always benefited the opposition and not the incumbent, because it is rational to assume that those who usually don't vote, i.e. the silent majority, only come out when they want to change the status quo. Yet in this election Ahmadinejad, the representative of the status quo, allegedly received ten million votes more than what he got in the previous election.

Finally, Ahmadinejad's nervous reaction after his so-called victory is the best proof for rigging. He shut down SMS networks and the whole of country's mobile phone network, arrested more than one hundred leading political activists, blocked access to Mousavi's and many other reformists' websites and unleashed violence in the streets. But if all this is not enough, the bodies of more than seventeen people who were shot dead and immediately buried in unmarked graves should persuade all those "objective-minded" observers.

In the second scenario, gradually unfolding in the last few days, the international media implicitly shifted its attention to the role of the Internet and social networking sites (Twitter, Facebook, YouTube, etc.). The implication is that millions of illiterate, conservative villagers have in fact voted for Ahmadinejad and that the political movement is mostly limited to the educated middle classes in North Tehran. While this simplified image is more compatible with the media's comfortable position toward Iran in the last thirty years, it is far from reality. The recent political history of Iran does not confirm this image. For example, Khatami's victory in 1997, despite his absolute lack of any economic promises and his focus instead on liberal civic demands, was made possible by the polarization of society into people and the state. Khatami could win only by embracing people from all different classes and groups, villagers and urban people alike.

There is no doubt that new media and technologies have been playing an important role in the movement, but it seems that the cause and the effect are being reversed in the picture painted by the media. First of all, it is the existence of a strong political determination, combined with a lack of basic means of communication and discourse, which has led the movement to creatively test every other channel and method. Mousavi's paper was shut down on the night of the election, his frequent requests to talk to people on state TV have been rejected, his official website is blocked, and physical contact with his supporters is kept to a minimum by prolonged periods of house arrest (with the exception of his appearance at the march on June 15, which drew over a million people).

Second, due to considerable pressure placed on foreign journalists inside Iran, these technological tools have come to play a significant role in sending the messages and images of the movement to the outside world. However, the creative self-organization of the movement uses myriad methods and channels, many of them simple and traditional, depending on their availability: shouting "Death to the dictator" from rooftops, calling landlines, at the end of one rally chanting the time and place of the next one, and physically standing on the street and distributing news to every passing car. Western societies have created a cyber-fantasy by labeling this movement a "Twitter revolution." Such a label completely misses the reality of the people who are shot dead, injured or endangered by non-virtual bullets.

What is more surprising in the midst of this media frenzy is the blindness of the Western left to the political dynamism and energy of our movement. The causes of this blindness oscillate between the misgivings about Islam (or the Islamophobia of the hyper-secular left) and the confusion made by Ahmadinejad's fake anti-imperialist rhetoric (his alliance with Hugo Chavez, perhaps, who after all was the first to congratulate him). It should be emphasized that Ahmadinejad's economic policies fall to the right of the IMF. He advocates cutting subsidies in a radical way, more privatization than any other post–1979 government (by selling the country to the Revolutionary Guards), and an inflation and unemployment rate which have brought the low-income sections of society to their knees. It is in this regard that Mousavi's politics needs to be understood in contradistinction from both Ahmadinejad and the other reformist candidate, Karoubi.

While Karoubi went for the liberal option of dividing people into identity groups with different demands (women, students, intellectuals, ethnicities, religious minorities, etc.), Mousavi emphasized the universal demands of "people" who wanted to be heard and counted as political subjects. This subjectivity, emphasized by Mousavi during his campaign and fully incarnated in the rallies of the past few days, is constituted by political intuition, creativity and recollection of the 1979 revolution (no wonder that people so quickly reached political maturity, best manifested in the abstention from violence in their silent demonstrations). Mousavi's "people" are easily, and forcibly, distinguished from Ahmadinejad's anonymous masses who depend on state charity. Mousavi's people, the collective that appears at the rallies, include religious women covered in chador walking hand in hand with westernized young women who are usually prosecuted for their appearance; war veterans in wheelchairs alongside young boys for whom the Iran–Iraq war is only an anecdote; and members of the working class who sacrifice their daily salary to participate in the rally next to the middle classes. This story is not limited to Tehran. Shiraz, Isfahan, Tabriz and Urumiyeh are also part of this movement, and other cities are joining with a predictable delay (as was the case in the 1979 Revolution).

History will prove who the real participants of this movement are, but meanwhile we are faced with a new, non-classical and unfamiliar radical politics. Will the Western left get it right this time?

CULTURAL JIU-JITSU AND THE IRANIAN GREENS

Charles Kurzman

On June 12, 2009, the day of Iran's presidential election, we knew something was wrong when the government shut down the opposition's election-monitoring system.[1] This system used cell phones and text messages to allow election monitors across the country to communicate with the opposition's headquarters, tally up votes, and take note of any irregularities that they may have observed.

Electronic media have been one of the backbones of the Green Movement in the past year. They have been periodically vulnerable to this kind of interruption, but the movement has found ways to sidestep barriers. One example is Mir Hossein Mousavi's Facebook page.[2] That may sound funny—a presidential candidate in Iran with a Facebook page. But, in fact, it has become a major source for information for the Green Movement, along with many other websites. After the official campaign website, www.mirhossein.com, was shut down, the Facebook page remained because it was out of the reach of the Iranian government. The page continues to be one of the central ways for the Green Movement to distribute information.

The election results were released the next day in a hurried manner, before the end of the required three-day waiting period, elevating suspicions that the whole thing had been rigged. Within two weeks, on June 24, precinct-level electoral results were made available from the Ministry of the Interior's website for anybody to download and analyze. If fraud occurred, as I assume it did, it was quite well done. The precinct-level data shows few signs of manipulation. This is not to say that manipulation didn't occur, simply that there are no smoking guns in this particular ream of data.

The electoral results showed that the incumbent Iranian president,

Left: Presidential candidate Mir Hossein Mousavi's Facebook
page. Right: Protester in Iran, June 2009.

Mahmoud Ahmadinejad, won a huge victory throughout the entire
country, even in regions assumed to be opposition strongholds. Mousavi
received a majority vote in only two provinces, West Azerbaijan in the
far northwest and Sistan and Baluchistan in the far southeast, inhabited
primarily by ethnic minorities.[3]

Many Iranians regarded the election results with suspicion, and
widespread protests began the following day. These protests were spontaneous at first. It took everyone by surprise, including the opposition,
that people were willing to go out into the streets and publicly identify
themselves as supporters of the opposition in the face of great potential
danger.

"*Ra-ye man koo*?" the protesters asked. Sometimes their signs—
many of them printed on their home computers—included the English
translation, "Where is my vote?" in an appeal to international audiences.
Koo is a slang word for "where," instead of the standard word *koja*, so
the slogan might be translated as "Where's my vote at?" This slogan reflects the demographics of the Green Movement, whose principle base
is educated young people. This is a significant segment of the Iranian
population, given the vast expansion of the Iranian educational system
under the Islamic Republic. In the 1970s, during the last years of the
Pahlavi monarchy, around 5 percent of college-age youths went to college; today the figure is 31 percent.[4] The change was especially dramatic
for girls, who came to outnumber boys in secondary schools in 1996,
primary schools in 1999, and higher education in 2001.[5] Educated young

women are at the forefront of movements for social and political reform in Iran.

News photographers recognized this role during the election protests and seemed to over-represent good-looking female protesters, generally with some hair showing. This may be because sex sells, but it may also be because women's participation in Middle East politics runs counter to the Western image of the repressed Muslim woman and feeds into the Western desire to liberate Muslim women. Here the women are themselves, standing up for the right to show several inches of hair, wearing trendy sunglasses and a face scarf to avoid being identified— not the *niqab*, the devout Islamic face-covering that so upsets many Westerners, but a strategic use of an Islamic symbol for the purpose of challenging a government that claims a monopoly on Islamic symbols.

In a similarly media-savvy move, the Mousavi campaign draped its posters and campaign paraphernalia in emerald green, a color strongly associated with Islam. All it took was a small green ribbon for Iranians to convey, subtly but effectively, their support for the opposition.

These moves find an analogy in the Asian martial art jiu-jitsu. According to the International Ju-Jitsu Federation, this "gentle art," or the "art of subtleness," does "not aim to neutralize power with power but rationally absorb an attack and convert that energy to the opponent's own detriment." Similarly, the Green Movement used the power, the rituals and the history of the Islamic Republic against the leaders of the Islamic Republic.

The phrase "political jiu-jitsu" was first popularized by Gene Sharp, an American theorist of nonviolent activism who was influenced by the techniques of direct action pioneered by Mahatma Gandhi and Martin Luther King, Jr.[6] Sharp sought to apply these techniques to American strategy in the Cold War. He aimed to create a system of nonviolent civil resistance that would deter or repel the Soviet invasion of the United States, by using the power of one's overlords against them.[7] Since the Cold War, Sharp has worked to promote nonviolent, pro-democracy protests around the world.[8] After the "color revolutions" in various

post-Communist states over the last several years, the Iranian government became concerned that Gene Sharp and others were promoting
a similar sort of revolution in Iran. He was the subject of a scathing
television program broadcast on an official regional network in Iran,
which was then copied and translated by MEMRI TV, an Israeli-based
organization that seeks out clips of extremists in the Middle Eastern
media and makes them widely available. In this particular program, an
animatronic version of Gene Sharp—identified in the broadcast as a
"theoretician of civil disobedience and velvet revolutions"—sits at a table
with animatronic versions of a CIA official, George Soros—the founder
of the pro-democracy Open Society Institute—and John McCain, who
was running for president of the United States at the time but was mis-
identified in the broadcast as a White House official. The animatronic
figures have an amusing chat about how they're trying to overthrow the
regime in Iran.[9]

After the June 2009 presidential election, the Iranian government
became particularly concerned that Gene Sharp's website—sections of
which contained material in Persian—was being accessed in Iran and
used to promote civil disobedience. An article published by Fars News
Agency, a hardline pro-regime outlet, combined a plagiarized translation of an Associated Press article, about Gene Sharp and his theories
of non-violent resistance, with original material to establish supposed
links between Sharp and the Iranian opposition, along with the CIA, Israel and other alleged conspirators. According to this conspiracy theory,
the Iranian opposition had applied 100 of the 198 techniques of civil
disobedience that Gene Sharp had described in his latest publication, as
if protesters were going down a list and checking them off.[10]

Regardless of whether they got these tactics from Gene Sharp, from
models in Iran, or invented them on their own, the Iranian opposition
was very creative in its use of history, specifically the Islamic Revolution
of 1979, in order to make the point that the revolution itself had come
full circle and that a new revolution was underway. In 1979, the front
page of the popular newspaper *Ettela'at* boldly announced *"Shah raft,"*

Left: An animatronic cartoon of Gene Sharp broadcast on an official regional television network in Iran, Khuzestan TV, February 5, 2008.
Right: "Ahmadi Raft" (Ahmadinejad Is Gone).

the shah is gone. During the summer of 2009, a variety of mock versions of the newspaper began to appear in demonstrations. Instead of "*Shah raft*," the parody read, "*Ahmadi raft*," Ahmadinejad is gone, alongside a goofy portrait and various funny slogans.

The protesters of 2009 also resuscitated the technique of shouting "Allah-u-akbar," God is great, from the rooftops at night. The tactic is anonymous, therefore low-risk and difficult to repress, and it makes a very impressive presentation of popular grievances when carried out simultaneously all over the city.

Another technique borrowed from the Iranian Revolution of 1979, as well as many other movements around the world, was the erection of street barricades. They were not intended as real barriers, since they could be cleared in a few moments by bulldozers and, in any case, wouldn't stop officers on foot or on motorbikes. Rather, the barricades were symbolic acts of resistance—instances of dissent that provided inspiring visuals to fellow Iranians and communicated to the world, via cell-phone cameras and news photographers, the fact that resistance continues. The security forces played into the protesters' hands by showing up in black, swinging batons, with flak jackets that read "POLICE" in English on the back—the government must have bought the jackets in a hurry, in too much of a rush to ask the manufacturers to embroider them with Persian script.

Left: Barricades and police (with English-language jackets), Tehran, June 2009. Right: Black eye, green headband, Tehran, June 2009.

Another jiu-jitsu strategy of the Green Movement was to claim the Shia heritage of victimhood. Protesters showed off their bruises proudly—smiling for the cameras, holding up bloody clothes. Since the revolution of 1979, the Islamic Republic has claimed that a culture of victimhood is an essential strength of Iranian Islamic culture and that identification with ancient Shia victims was part of the reason that the shah's repression fueled the revolution rather than undermining it. The Green Movement used the same trope to claim that they, too, will not be dissuaded by violent repression.

Digital transmission amplifies the effects of these strategies. With cell-phone cameras in so many hands, protest movements in Iran and elsewhere are documented more quickly and more thoroughly than ever before. Almost every photograph of the Iranian demonstrations contains at least one person taking a picture, a self-referential, self-conscious record of their activities.[11] Thousands, perhaps millions, of photographs now reside in file-sharing websites that will be used to write the history of this period. The most famous of these images are drawn from the cell-phone video of the sniper shooting of Neda Agha-Soltan, taken just after she was shot by a sniper.[12] In half a minute, we watch Neda, as she became known around the world after the video went viral, fall and die. The video of her death is seen as a powerful symbol of the cruelty of the Iranian government toward unarmed protesters.

Aside from the power of the video itself, imagine the circumstances of its production. Somebody at this demonstration saw a person get shot, and within a second or two, he took out his cell phone, turned on the video function, and filmed the victim. He didn't take a quick picture and run away from the sniper. Instead, he walked toward Neda. There is no zoom function on standard cell-phone cameras, but by the final frame of the video, Neda's face almost fills the frame. Thus, the cameraman must have held his phone out just a couple feet from this dying woman. There's something cruel in that, but also something very media savvy—knowing that the close-up will maximize the impact of the image.

In the same municipal cemetery where the martyrs of the 1979 Revolution are buried, Neda's tomb immediately became a shrine. Iranians visited continually and placed flowers on it, as a site of symbolic resistance to the regime. In August 2009, on the fortieth day after Neda's death, the traditional mourning ceremony also harkened back to the revolution. The followers of Ruhollah Khomeini developed the idea of using the fortieth-day commemoration as a political protest in early 1978. They would turn the mourning ceremonies of slain protesters into demonstrations against the regime. If troops shot at these demonstrations and killed more protesters, the opposition had another excuse for mourning protests forty days later. This cycle continued until June 1978, when Khomeini's followers decided to put an end to it. They felt it was too dangerous, so they banned public demonstrations on the 40th mourning day for the martyrs of the previous demonstration.[13] Some observers credit this forty-day protest cycle of protests as the impetus behind the full-blown revolution, but in fact the revolutionary movement itself abandoned this tactic six months before the revolution succeeded in forcing out the monarchy. After coming to power, the Islamic Republic organized numerous fortieth-day mourning rallies for significant religious and political figures, or for martyrs of the war with Iraq, but these were always in support of the regime, not in the spirit of opposition that brought the technique into existence in 1978.

As a method of protest, fortieth-day mourning had all but disappeared until the Green Movement revived it in the summer of 2009. The opposition attracted hundreds, perhaps thousands of people to Neda's

Left: Fortieth-day mourning for Neda Agha-Soltan, July 30, 2009.
Right: Green money: "Ya Hossein, Mir Hossein," Fall 2009.

grave forty days after her death in a strong display of political solidarity. Mousavi himself allegedly drove past the grave in a car with tinted windows to be with them for a moment.

The Green Movement tried to co-opt other elements of state legitimacy as well. Oppositionists took paper money, replete with the iconography of the Islamic Republic, and stamped it with reformist slogans like *"Ya Hossein, Mir Hossein,"* "O Hossein, Mir Hossein." *"Ya Hossein"* is a religious phrase appealing to Prophet Mohammad's grandson Hossein, a central figure in Shia history and in the official ideology of the regime. The stamp associates this Hossein with Mir Hossein Mousavi—another form of jiu-jitsu.

Another public symbol of the regime is identification with the people of Palestine. The Green Movement used the annual observance of Quds Day—Jerusalem Day—as a venue for oppositional protest. The Green Movement explicitly identified this tactic as political jiu-jitsu: "Among the martial arts, jiu-jitsu is a way of fighting in which one fighter counters the opponent's attacks by deflecting the power of the opponent at minimum cost and using the attacks of the aggressor against him. Using symbols related to the Israel–Palestine problem may also be considered an example of this political jiu-jitsu, if the Greens take these legitimating symbols of the regime and make them delegitimating."[14] The Green Movement even took the iconic Palestinian cartoon character, Naji al-Ali's Handala, and dressed him up with a reformist green scarf,

Left: "This Year's Ashura—We're Going to Make It Green," December 27, 2009. Above: Naji al-Ali's Handala, a Palestinian icon, wearing a reformist green scarf.

identifying the Palestinian cause with the Iranian opposition, not the Iranian regime.

The Green Movement also set its sights on Ashura, a major ritual of the Shia religious calendar and the occasion for one of the most important demonstrations of the Iranian Revolution in December 1978. In web postings prior to Ashura in 2009, the opposition used the slogan, "This Year's Ashura—We're Going to Make It Green."[15] Similarly, for the anniversary of the Iranian Revolution on February 11, 2010, supporters of the Green Movement produced movie-style trailers to advertise the upcoming protests. In one of these short films, posted on YouTube and other video file-sharing sites, a calendar flips through the days beginning with the disputed election in June 2009 and ending on February 11, 2010, where the phrase "The End of Dictatorship" is superimposed in green on a photo from the revolutionary days of February 1979.[16]

Some activists hoped that the anniversary would bring about a decisive showdown with the regime, but that was not the case. In the end, the Green Movement seems scarcely to have touched the main pillars of power in Iran—the loyalty of the armed forces and paramilitaries, or the regime's oil income and other powerful economic institutions. Of course, there is no way to know how much damage the Green Movement's

Left: Calendar of revolution: "The End of Dictatorship," February 11, 2010. Right: Ahmadinejad election rally, early June 2009.

jiu-jitsu has inflicted upon the regime's popular support. Perhaps the movement is indeed a "sandpaper revolution," as Simon Critchley has termed it, slowly abrading the pillars of power.[17] In any case, as I have argued elsewhere, revolutions are unpredictable.[18]

I'd like to conclude by pointing out that the Green Movement does not enjoy unanimous support in Iran. Pro-regime forces still command a significant following, even among the younger generation. In one photo from an Ahmadinejad rally prior to the June 2009 presidential election, we see three women cheering, decked out with Ahmadinejad campaign stickers that read "*Dowlat, Ahmadi*"—"The state, Ahmadinejad"—associating support for the incumbent with support for the Islamic Republic itself. One of the women looks the part of an Ahmadinejad supporter— an older woman who we can imagine comes from a poorer, more religiously conservative neighborhood. But the other two women in the photo do not match this stereotype—they appear to be young, heavily made-up, possibly with nose jobs.[19] After showing this slide to a group of Iranian-Americans, an audience member informed me that these two women are well known in Iran—the government apparently trots them out in front of the cameras at pro-regime rallies, precisely to imply that trendy, well-to-do youths are not all in the opposition.

We don't know whether Mousavi would have won a truly fair election, one in which election monitors were not harassed and ballot challenges were given the hearing that Iranian law required. Two surveys conducted after the election showed that Iranian political sympathies

are almost evenly divided. Though we should be skeptical of telephone surveys on politically sensitive topics carried out during a major crackdown, these surveys gain credibility because they both report
the same correlation between individuals' level of education and their
political affiliation. In one survey, commissioned by the Toronto *Globe
& Mail*, 62 percent of respondents with less than a high school education said that they voted for Ahmadinejad, compared with 48 percent
of respondents with high school education and 38 percent of respondents with higher education.[20] The second survey, commissioned by
WorldPublicOpinion.org, a polling project associated with the University of Maryland, found very similar proportions: 67 percent of the less
educated said they voted for Ahmadinejad, compared with 50 percent
of respondents with high school education and 38 percent with higher
education.[21] If some of these responses were falsified out of fear of government repression, it seems unlikely that people with less education
consistently hid their views more than people with more education. In
effect, these polls suggest a considerable division in the Iranian population, implying that the political future of the country is up for grabs.
There appear to be sizeable constituencies both for and against reform,
enough to fuel the political jiu-jitsu of both sides.

THE GANDHIAN MOMENT

Ramin Jahanbegloo

June 20, 2009

Iran's Green movement has shaken the widespread image of Iranian society as violent. On the one hand, Iranian civil society has shown itself capable of manifesting its dissatisfaction with the officially declared election results—and its dissent more generally—in a nonviolent way, while on the other, the regime, surprised and surpassed by the scope of the protests, has dropped all formal pretentions to the rule of law and unleashed ferocious repression on the protestors. As such, what we have witnessed since the first demonstrations might very well be considered a major nonviolent movement in a Gandhian style. Affinities abound between the civil disobedience movement in Iran today and the successful nonviolent movements led by Gandhi in India in the 1920–1940s and Martin Luther King Jr. in the United States in the 1950–1960s.

In the minds of many Iranians, Mahatma Gandhi represents two different and contradictory characters. The first is the political Gandhi who fought against British colonialism and is the father of the modern Indian nation. This is the man whom Einstein lauded as "a leader of his people, unsupported by any outward authority, a politician whose success rests not upon craft nor mastery of technical devices, but simply on the convincing power of his personality." The second Gandhi is the Ashramic one, who is somewhere between a saint and a Messiah, who wore hand-spun khadi and was more of a mystic than a politician. This said, there is an important aspect of *satyagraha* (Gandhi's concept of truth) that makes it universally applicable as a method of action. It is commonly said that *satyagraha* is particular to Gandhi's cultural setting, one in which the concept of self-suffering and nonviolence are familiar. But it would be a mistake to reduce the Gandhian moment to purely cultural terms. The recent history of nonviolent action around the world has shown us clearly that *satyagraha* is a seed that can grow and flourish in other cultures and religions beyond the Indian and Hindu context. We can refer here to several successful experiences of *satyagraha* in the past fifty years. Among the followers of Gandhi in the twentieth century who successfully launched their own *satyagrahas* against racial, religious and economic injustice and struggled for human rights one could mention Khan Abdul Ghaffar Khan, Martin Luther King, Jr., Nelson Mandela, Lech Walesa, Vaclav Havel, Benigno Aquino, Aung San Suu Kyi, and Ibrahim Rugova.

Iran is not the first Muslim country to experience a Gandhian moment. Several decades before the Green Movement, there was Khan Abdul Ghaffar Khan of Pakistan, known as the Frontier Gandhi. He embodied Gandhi's claim that nonviolence infuses everyday politics with ethical values and prefigures a form of public life in which truthfulness undermines and eventually replaces tyranny. It is no accident that Khan Abdul Ghaffar Khan believed firmly in Islam as a religion of truth, love, and service to humanity. This is indeed fundamental to the whole mentality of nonviolence, with its active resistance to evil and its deep faith that justice will eventually win. Martin Luther King's world was built on these two principles. In him, we find a luminous instance of the Gandhian moment. For King, nonviolent resistance was the most effective weapon against a racist and unjust social system in the United States. Though King was deeply influenced by his black church heritage and by liberal Protestant Christianity, his two principal tactics of noncooperation and civil disobedience against racist laws in the U.S. were primarily influenced by Gandhi's concept of *satyagraha*.

To many observers, the idea of the Gandhian moment in a despotic society like Iran is a fairy tale. However, one could respond to this objection with the words of Gandhi himself: "The nonviolent technique does not depend for its success on the good will of the dictators... *Satyagraha* is never vindictive. It believes not in destruction but in conversion. Its failures are due to the weaknesses of the *satyagrahi*, not to any defect in the law itself." In other words, the policy of the weak or the coward is not worthy of the name of nonviolence. This reminds us that Gandhi regarded nonviolence not merely as a tactic but a spiritual way of life. As such, nonviolence is not just refusal to kill; it is a manifestation of love and truth as a force for positive social change.

It remains to be seen whether Iranian social movements could be committed wholly to the nonviolence of the brave, thereby realizing the Gandhian moment in Iran. It is clear that such a path is a daunting challenge for a society like Iran, where ends are valued above means and social actions tend to have no specific rules, ethos or moral grounding. That is why the relevance of Gandhi has been questioned time and again in the Iranian public sphere.

Intriguingly, however, many Iranians in the past months have walked silently and lit black candles. Others have worn green wristbands or ribbons and carried flowers. Gandhi chose a spinning wheel as a symbol of his idea of non-violence. A spinning wheel represented two different messages: it was the main instrument to protest against India's growing westernization and it was also a symbol of resistance to the British-made clothes that had replaced the Indian hand-made clothes. King evoked the language of dreams, appealing to American idels of equality and justice for all. Today, Mousavi has become the symbol of nonviolent protest in Iran, but the true hero of the Iran's democratic struggle is the emerging republican model of nonviolent resistance, which provides the clearest guideposts and vision for Iran's gradual transition to an open society.

In other words, there is common agreement among the demonstrators and activists that the main contradiction in contemporary Iran is the one between authoritarian violence and democratic nonviolence. This is due to the fact that the protest movement in Iran is nonviolent and civil in its methods of creating social change while also seeking an ethical dimension to Iranian politics. This judgment implies that Iranian civil society is ready to make a distinction between two approaches: searching for truth and solidarity versus lying and using violence. Today young Iranians couch their conversations about politics in a moral vo-cabulary. Regardless of how things ultimately turn out in the future, the Islamic Republic will never be the same again. Whether it compromises or resorts to totalitarian violence, it will be a weakened and discredited regime, less and less capable of preventing Iranian civil society's ad-vance towards a democratic state.

In the months and years ahead, we will have to wait and see how this dialectic between Iran's powerless, nonviolent truth-seekers and its powerful purveyors of violence and lies will work itself out. As such, the issue of whether the election results were rigged or not is now a second-ary issue. What is now at stake is something much deeper: a challenge to the legitimacy of violence in Iran. Gandhi once said: "You must be the change you wish to see in the world." The change we are witnessing in Iran is the change in the younger generation of Iranians, who have shown the world that they have enough maturity and tolerance to spark nonviolent change in Iran.

IRAN'S GREEN MOVEMENT AS A CIVIL RIGHTS MOVEMENT

Hamid Dabashi

June 22, 2009

In a short essay for the *New York Times*, Abbas Amanat, a scholar of nineteenth-century Iran at Yale University, asserted that what we are witnessing in the current crisis in Iran is "the rise of a new middle class whose demands stand in contrast to the radicalism of the incumbent President Ahmadinejad and the core conservative values of the clerical elite, which no doubt has the backing of a religiously conservative sector of the population."[1]

This learned position of a leading scholar very much sums up the common wisdom that Iranian expatriate academics are offering an excited public mesmerized by the massive demonstrations they witness on their television sets or computer screens and eager for some assistance in making sense of them.

In part because of these hurried interpretations, the movement that is unfolding in front of our eyes is seen as essentially a middle class uprising against a retrograde theocracy that is banking on backward, conservative, uneducated masses who do not know any better. The illiterate and "uncouth" masses provide the populist basis of Ahmadinejad's support, while the middle class demands an open-market civil society.

Highly educated, pro-Western, progressive Iranians are thus placed on Mir Hossein Mousavi's side, while backward villagers and urban poor are on the side of Ahmadinejad. The fact that in North America and Western Europe, unveiled and fluent English-speaking women are brought to speak on behalf of women demonstrators further intensifies the impression that if women are veiled or do not speak English fluently they must be Ahmadinejad supporters.

This deeply false dichotomy projects a flawed picture to the outside world. It is predicated on a very limited pool of expatriate academics putting their own spin on a movement that is quite extraordinary in Iranian political culture, one whose full dimensions have yet to be unpacked.

Given the structural limitations of a nascent democracy that is being crushed and buried in Iran under a particular interpretation of a Shiite juridical citadel, opposition to Ahmadinejad is fractured into the followers of three candidates with widely dissimilar economic programs and political positions.

Mousavi is a hardcore socialist in his economic platform and a social reformist in his politics. Mehdi Karoubi is far to the right of Mousavi in his economic neoliberalism and social conservatism. Mohsen Rezaee is even farther to the right of Karoubi in his social conservatism but to his left in his economic platform.

What above all challenges the interpretation of this event as a middle class revolt against "uncouth radicalism" is a crucial statistic that Professor Djavad Salehi-Isfahani, one of the most reliable Iranian economists in the US, provided in an article for the *New York Times*.[2] "Young people ages 15–29," Salehi-Isfahani reported, "make up 35 percent of the population but account for 70 percent of the unemployed." It is precisely these young people who are pouring into streets of Tehran and other major cities in support of Mousavi. How could this be a middle-class uprising if the overwhelming majority of its supporters are in fact jobless fifteen to twenty-nine-year-olds who still live with their parents, who cannot even afford to rent an apartment, let alone marry and raise a family, and join the middle class in an oil-based economy that is not labor-intensive to begin with?

Today, more than 63 percent of university entrants in Iran are women, but only 12 percent are part of the labor force. The remaining 51 percent are jobless, and the most visible aspect of these anti-Ahmadinejad demonstrations is that women visibly outnumber men. Why would all these jobless men and women participate in a strictly middle class uprising?

If one looks closely at Mousavi's campaign commercials, the presidential debates, and his social and economic platforms, we see that a sizable component of his supporters are indeed university students, young faculty and the urban intellectual elite—such as filmmakers, artists and the literati. But the fact is that a major Mousavi constituency is the urban poor and particularly the war veterans who have no respect for Ahmadinejad, believing he had an inglorious war record, but are full of unsurpassed admiration for Mousavi because of his role as a fiercely dedicated prime minister during the Iran–Iraq war of 1980–1988.

Conversely, there is a significant segment of the traditional middle class, the *bazaaris*, that has benefited from Ahmadinejad's economic policies of government-subsidized commodities and services, and thus supports him.

As for the "uncouth" among the Iranian peasantry, Eric Hooglund, a senior Iran scholar with decades of experience in rural areas, has recently said that when he hears reports that Ahmadinejad's support base is rural, he is left quite baffled. "Is it possible that rural Iran," he asks pointedly, "where less than 35 percent of the country's population lives, provided Ahmadinejad the 63 percent of the vote he claims to have won? That would contradict my own research in Iran's villages over the past 30 years, including just recently."[3]

The fact is that we really don't know how this uprising is going to pan out, and yet we seem to be in too much of a rush to assimilate it with inherited assumptions that may have lost their validity in face of this new reality. I am convinced that we are witnessing something quite extraordinary, perhaps even a social revolution that is overriding its economic roots. Although it shares many parallels to the 1979 Islamic Revolution, the situation today is much different. It is not clear that this movement sees itself as a revolution or will actually transmute into one.

Given the brutality it faces, the movement has no choice but opt for a method of nonviolent civil disobedience. The age of ideological warfare is over in Iran. If anything, this is the closest Iran has come to creating an event like the civil rights movement of the 1960s in the

United States. Precisely like that movement, its economic dimensions are couched in social demands.

We need to adjust our lenses and languages in order to see better, and there is no better adjustment than to watch, with caution, hope and sagacity, what is unfolding in front of us.

This movement is ahead of our inherited politics, floating ideologies or mismatched theories. We need to sit back and let this inspirational movement of a whole new generation of hope teach us courage and humility.

A SPECTER IS HAUNTING IRAN—
THE SPECTER OF MOSADDEGH

Stephen Kinzer

June 22, 2009

Despite efforts by Iran's leaders to keep photographers off the streets during post-election protests this month, many vivid images have emerged. The one shown here is the one I found most chilling, poignant and evocative.

By now, many outsiders can identify the man whose picture is on the right-hand side of this pro-

Protesters display pictures of former Prime Minister Mohammad Mossadeq alongside presidential candidate Mir Hossein Mousavi during demonstrations in Iran.

test sign. He is Mir Hossein Mousavi, the reported loser in this month's presidential election. The elderly gentleman in the other picture is unfamiliar to most non-Iranians. He and his fate, however, lie at the historical root of the protests now shaking Iran.

The picture shows a pensive, sad-looking man with what one of his contemporaries called "droopy basset-hound eyes and high patrician forehead." He does not look like a man whose fate would continue to influence the world decades after his death. But this was Mohammad Mossadeq, the most fervent advocate of democracy ever to emerge in his ancient land.

Above the twinned pictures of Mossadeq and Mousavi are the words, "We won't let history repeat itself." Centuries of intervention, humiliation and subjugation at the hands of foreign powers have decisively shaped Iran's collective psyche. The most famous victim of this intervention—and also the most vivid symbol of Iran's long struggle for democracy—is

Mossadeq. Whenever Iranians assert their desire to shape their own fate, his image appears.

Iranians began their painful and bloody march toward democracy with the Constitutional Revolution of 1906. Only after World War II did they finally manage to consolidate a freely elected government. Mossadeq was prime minister, and he became hugely popular for taking up the great cause of the day, the nationalization of Iran's oil industry. This move outraged the British, who had "bought" the exclusive right to exploit Iranian oil from a corrupt shah, and the Americans, who feared that allowing nationalization in Iran would encourage the political pursuits of leftists around the world.

In the summer of 1953 the CIA sent the intrepid agent Kermit Roosevelt—grandson of President Theodore Roosevelt, who believed Americans should "speak softly and carry a big stick"—to Tehran with orders to overthrow Mossadeq. He accomplished it in just three weeks. It was a vivid example of how easy it is for a rich, powerful country to throw a poor, weak one into chaos.

With this covert operation, the world's proudest democracy put an end to democratic rule in Iran. Mohammad Reza Shah Pahlavi returned to the Peacock Throne and ruled with increasing repression for a quarter of a century. His repression produced the explosion of 1979 that brought reactionary mullahs to power. Theirs is the regime that rules Iran today.

Carrying a picture of Mossadeq today means two things: "We want democracy" and "No foreign intervention." These demands fit together in the minds of most Iranians. Desperate as they are for the political freedom their parents and grandparents enjoyed in the early 1950s, they have no illusion that foreigners can bring it to them. In fact, foreign intervention has brought them nothing but misery.

The US sowed the seeds of repression in Iran by deposing Mossadeq in 1953, and then helped bathe Iran in blood by giving Saddam Hussein generous military aid during the Iran–Iraq war of the 1980s. Militants in Washington who now want the US to intervene on behalf of Iranian protesters either are unaware of this history or delude themselves into thinking that Iranians have forgotten it. Some of them, in fact, are the same people who were demanding just last year that the US bomb Iran—an act which would have killed many of the brave young protesters they now hold up as heroes.

America's moral authority in Iran is all but non-existent. To the idea that the US should jump into the Tehran fray and help bring democracy to Iran, many Iranians would roll their eyes and say, "We had a democracy here until you came in and crushed it!"

President Barack Obama seems to grasp this reality. During his recent speech in Cairo, without mentioning Mossadeq by name, he conceded that "in the middle of the Cold War, the United States played a role in the overthrow of a democratically elected Iranian government." Then, after the current electoral protests broke out, he avoided the hypocrisy of righteous indignation and confined himself to saying that "ultimately the election is for the Iranians to decide."

Anyone doubting the wisdom of those words should pay attention to the sprouting of Mossadeq pictures during protests in Iran. They mean: "Americans, your interventions have brought us tyranny and death. Stay home, keep your hands off and leave our country to us for a change."

SLAPS IN THE FACE OF REASON:
TEHRAN, JUNE 2009

Kaveh Ehsani, Arang Keshavarzian
and Norma Claire Moruzzi

June 28, 2009

The morning after Iran's June 12 presidential election, Iranians booted up their computers to find Fars News, the online mouthpiece of the Islamic Republic's security apparatus, heralding the dawn of a "third revolution." Many an ordinary Iranian, and many a Western pundit, had already adopted such dramatic language to describe the burgeoning street demonstrations against the declaration by the Ministry of Interior that Mahmoud Ahmadinejad, the sitting president, had received 64 percent of the vote to the 34 percent for his main challenger, Mir Hossein Mousavi. But the editors of Fars News were referring neither to the protests, as were the people in the streets, nor to the prospect that the unrest might topple the Islamic Republic, as were some of the more wistful commentators. Rather, the editors applied the label to their own attempt to radically realign Iranian politics. This realignment would complete the removal of the old guard, as did the "first" revolution of 1978–9, and consolidate the rule of inflexible hardliners, as did the "second revolution" symbolized by the US Embassy takeover of 1979.

Whatever history's verdict on the desiderata of Fars News, neither the institutional structure nor the political culture of the Islamic Republic will emerge unchanged from the crisis following the 2009 election. The stakes are nothing less than this: should the protesters persevere, the limited traditions of political and civil rights and citizen participation in the Islamic Republic may be considerably strengthened. Should Ahmadinejad and his supporters prevail instead, the political system in Iran may lose all remaining meaningful traits of a republic.

As in 1979, or in 1997 when the "reformist" cleric Mohammad Khatami captured the presidency, or in 2005 when Ahmadinejad won his own (highly contested) landslide victory, the Western media has been caught off guard by events on the Iranian stage. The crudest analysts insist upon seeing an epic battle between the government and "the people"—but neither of these actors is unitary. Others, writing from left, right and center, extrapolate theories from the supposed characteristics of the dramatis personae. Hence "the opposition," urban, educated, technologically savvy and broadly supportive of Mousavi, is said to be arrayed against the poor, exaggeratedly pious peasants and plebeians who back Ahmadinejad. Such interpretations are also far too simple. They fail to explain why the election campaign was so competitive and why the popular reaction became so virulent once the scale of the fraud employed by the regime to fix the election for Ahmadinejad became evident.

Through numerous rallies and other gatherings in the week before the election, the Mousavi campaign illustrated that it could mobilize many thousands of peaceful, enthusiastic supporters in Tehran and other major cities. This successful electioneering was a double-edged sword. On the one hand, it convinced an increasing number of Iranians that Ahmadinejad's victory was not a foregone conclusion. On the other hand, the prospect of a large turnout that included many disenchanted voters may have contributed to the hardliners' decision to manipulate the results to ensure victory.

More important in the long run may be the fact that the campaign broke the monopoly of the Iranian regime over the expression of political opinions in public spaces. For three decades, the Islamic Republic has managed for the most part to limit public displays of "politics" to pro-government mass demonstrations, while conducting the public's real business behind closed doors. Independent associations and trade unions, grassroots organizations and political groupings have been crushed. Notwithstanding the serious shortcomings of the reformist's program and political skills, the eight years of the Khatami government saw the emergence of a relatively independent press and the curtailment of direct state interference in the home and in the private behavior of citizens. Ahmadinejad and his ilk have tried mightily to roll back these changes.

In defiance of these efforts, a overwhelming number of citizens took advantage of the political opening provided by the 2009 campaign. By all accounts, Iranian citizens were deeply engaged in debate over the candidates right up until voting day. Numerous observers in Tehran and other cities report that political debates in public spaces, like Vanak Square or Enqelab Square, were substantive and civil, if impassioned. People who had been intimidated or demoralized, or who had considered their differences with Islamic Republic politicians of all stripes to be irreconcilable, began to poke their heads above the battlements. Artists, filmmakers, political activists, feminists and student groups across the ideological spectrum forged alliances and acknowledged common interests. Thirty-four Islamist and secular feminist groups coalesced to form the Women's Movement Convergence, with nearly 700 activists gathering to hammer out a common platform. A week before the election, the Convergence held a debate with the representatives of the reformist candidates in the Office of the Islamic Revolution's Women to assess which candidate would be most consistently committed to women's rights.[1]

In sum, the 2009 presidential election campaign was unique. Not even amid the ferment that presaged Khatami's sweeping triumph in 1997 was a candidate able to mobilize support across so many social boundaries and to be so inclusive of elements of the population that have been actively marginalized under the Islamic Republic. The effort at broad-based mobilization by non-incumbents was new, as was the degree of interplay between the political contestation roiling the ranks of "the regime" and the debates reverberating in "the street."

Slaps in the face of reason

In the early afternoon of June 13, the Ministry of Interior announced the final "result" of the election. The turnout was a record-setting 85 percent and Ahmadinejad had won with 63 percent of the vote, followed by Mousavi with 34 percent, and Rezaee and Karoubi earning a mere 2 percent and less than 1 percent, respectively. These figures were remarkably congruent with early morning returns released prior to the closure of some overseas polls and strangely consistent across all regions of the country.

For many Iranians, the dispute over this "result" is not simply about the outcome—Ahmadinejad's anointment as president—but about the basic election procedures and laws that were violated. Beyond this, many voters are insulted by the responses of both Ahmadinejad and Khamenei to the popular skepticism, with the president-select dismissing the protesters' misgivings as "dirt" and the Supreme Leader unaccountably averring that the entire nation is united behind the official tally. The cries of CIA and MI-6 manipulation are likewise a slap in the face of reason. The Tehran municipality, run by the conservative mayor Mohammad Bagher Ghalibaf, estimated the number of protesters in mid-June to be three million. These are not only the chic middle classes beloved by Western photographers. They are also the women in chadors, working-class youths and older people who are supposedly in thrall to the undying revolutionary fervor to which Ahmadinejad appeals.

Several examples will illuminate the reasons for the rampant disbelief in the June 12 "result." Unlike in previous elections, the Ministry of Interior authorized deployment of 14,000 mobile voting booths, making it very difficult for candidates to send monitors to observe the balloting at every booth. By some reports, some 14.5 million extra ballots were printed, and no clear system was in place to track them. When several polling stations in urban centers ran out of ballots, Mousavi supporters asked where the extra ballots were, but they could not be found and remain unaccounted for to date. Communication among campaign workers was hindered when the SMS messaging network was turned off and a website associated with the Mousavi campaign was shut down. The popular BBC Persian service was jammed to restrict the flow of information. In the evening of June 12, a Mousavi campaign building was raided by the authorities. Several volunteers were detained and released, then rearrested the next day.

Yet the clearest violation of the law was Mousavi and Karoubi's claim that their observers were not allowed to be present when ballots were counted and the ballot boxes sealed. By law and custom, these observers confirm that the boxes are empty before voting starts, and they are present during the vote count, sign the result sheet and take away a copy. They are also supposed to be present when the ballot boxes are finally sealed and sent to the Interior Ministry. A sixty-five-year-old monitor in charge of a station at a mosque in the modest, middle-class Yousefabad neighborhood of Tehran told local journalists, "Compared to previous elections, we had a huge turnout. Two years ago we had barely 400 votes at our station. This time, more than 2,000 voted. We closed the station and started counting the votes. By midnight we were done. Mousavi had 1,600 votes, Ahmadinejad approximately 300, and Karoubi and Rezaee each had around 150 or 200. We were in the process of filling out the forms and signing them when the announcement came that Ahmadinejad had won with two thirds of the votes!" Interviews by local journalists in and around the Shahid Mahallati neighborhood of northeast Tehran, where a vast quadrant of the city consists of gated communities for military families, Revolutionary Guards and intelligence personnel, indicated that even this stratum of the electorate was strongly divided in its choice of candidate.

Unlike in previous elections and despite the enormous voter turnout, the Ministry of Interior was quick to declare a victor, and the Supreme Leader officially congratulated Ahmadinejad before a final tally was released or the Guardian Council had time to review complaints. The composition of the ballot "results" generated its own sub-controversies. For instance, Karoubi supposedly received less than half a million votes (less than the number of spoiled ballots), when in 2005 he earned about 5 million votes, or 17 percent of the total vote. Oddly, the initial count did not include any ruined ballots. The Guardian Council was compelled to acknowledge that, according to the numbers that had been released, at least fifty voting districts had more than 100 percent turnout.

Since June 12, opposition candidates, Iranian journalists and independent researchers have marshaled a host of evidence that calls into question both the procedural fairness of the elections and the veracity of the result.[2] This evidence is so overwhelming that no impartial observer can credit the hardliners' protestations that the election was clean.

What lies ahead

During the campaign, opposition candidates repeatedly argued that Ahmadinejad had flaunted regulatory procedures in order to circumvent the constitutional checks and balances on the powers of the presidency. Today, it is apparent that this major campaign theme has been borne out in the election itself.

Supporters of Mousavi therefore had clear, ready-made language for protesting the election "result" on procedural grounds—and thus Ahmadinejad's retort that their outcry is mere sour grapes is completely off point. Using the network of civil society organizations and campaign workers that had taken shape starting in late May, the protesters disseminated information quickly and people congregated in front of the Ministry of Interior and in the squares that join the main thoroughfares in Tehran and other cities. The unprecedented mass protests have demonstrated that the ruptures among the political elite are in fact a reflection of deep discontent in the polity. Although Mousavi is the symbolic leader of the street movement, it is not at all clear that he is in charge. The strength of the street actions was their sheer size and spontaneity, yet it is plain as well that they have been partly organized around a common goal: the rule of law and the right of citizen participation. Opposition campaign workers and civil society activists have helped a great deal in choosing effective locations for the gatherings, as well as in promoting the tactic of silence and the ethic of inclusiveness and nonviolence.

Initial responses by leading hardline clerics, including Khamenei, and other political figures seemed to offer some opening for reconciliation among the factions. But Ahmadinejad, Khamenei and members of the Guardian Council, as well as state radio and television, rapidly turned against the protesters, trying at first to deny the extent of the outcry and then to denigrate it with flippancy, condescension and mindless conspiracy theory. Predictably, they soon brought to bear the coercive apparatus of the state in order to repress it.

Khamenei's Friday prayer sermon on June 19, and the ensuing violent crackdown, have ensured the further alienation of the population from the powers that be and have deepened the political divide in the governing class. Khamenei's decision to throw his personal clout behind Ahmadinejad, and thereby compromise the institutional neutrality of the Leader's position, is almost inexplicable in terms of long-term strategy for maintaining his position and the structure of the Islamic Republic. By aligning himself so strongly with a divisive extremist who has only a hammer for every Iranian nail, Khamenei has undermined his own authority—not only with the population but also with members of the political elite. He has done so irrevocably.

By openly condoning the shooting of civilians, the powers that be have crossed another red line. The fact that regime spokesmen and the state media are calling the protesters "terrorists" will only inflame Iranian opinion further. Meanwhile, the video clips showing the June 20 death of an unarmed young woman, Neda Agha-Soltan, at the hands of the authorities have given the protesters an unimpeachable martyr.

What is painfully clear is that violence and intimidation are the chosen methods of the new elite in its quest to monopolize the political sphere. This is a costly and risky strategy for everyone involved. As signaled by the Friday sermon of June 19, the Khamenei–Ahmadinejad alliance has turned its back on the two other tried-and-true methods of conflict management in the Islamic Republic: intra-elite negotiation and mass participation. The two men have shown little willingness to compromise with "the old guard" or to acknowledge the demands of the mass of Iranian citizens.

The problem now for the protest movement is to find a way to keep up the pressure while defusing the impact of state violence. Given that many of the movement's leaders and mid-level cadres are now in prison (and reportedly under torture), this will be no mean feat. The movement will probably conclude that protest should move off the streets, where violence is easier to employ and the flame of dissent itself burns hotter and more unsustainably. The state's escalation of violence has made the streets a site of confrontation rather than mobilization. In order to sustain the momentum, the movement will have to shift tactics and weave itself more tightly to the disgruntled factions of the power structure. Rafsanjani's faction is already making overtures in this direction. The political alternative would presumably be a series of lower-key and less dangerous, but increasingly costly, work stoppages, boycotts of state manufactures and strikes, maybe including general strikes, combined with intermittent street mobilizations, most likely on the monthly and annual anniversaries of protesters' deaths.

Such is the pattern of resistance that emerged during the revolution that overthrew the shah. Everyone in Iran is acutely aware of this pattern's significance, both practical and symbolic. Mousavi's supporters have appropriated a chant that animated the crowds in 1978 and 1979, and they call it out from the rooftops of their houses in the evenings: "Allah-u-akbar" resounds once again in Tehran—and, once again, the forces of political and social change have taken the religious invocation back from the state.

FEMINIST WAVES IN THE IRANIAN GREEN TSUNAMI?

Golbarg Bashi

June 29, 2009

As pictures of women, young and old, religious and non-religious, have plastered our Internet and TV screens, chanting and bleeding for a recount in what many Iranians believe has been a fraudulent presidential election, their extraordinary heroism and sheer numbers have awakened the international media to the sizable female presence in the Iranian Green Movement.

At this point, a poignant question might be where and what are the positions of Iranian feminists inside the country? They have been demanding their civil liberties for a long time. To what extent are they now participating in defining the goals and aspirations of the Green Movement?

Unknown to perhaps many outside Iran, the Iranian women's rights movement has been relentlessly expanding its demands for an end to gender discrimination in a country where women are treated like second-class citizens in the realm of family and penal law. Since the 1990s, various NGOs, magazines (such as *Zanan*), individual lawyers, and specific campaigns like One Million Signatures and Stop Stoning Forever have worked tirelessly and across ideological divides to publicize, mobilize and realize their specific demands for women's rights in the legal sphere. The women we see marching in the streets of Tehran, Shiraz and elsewhere did not grow like mushrooms out of nowhere. They are the robust children of decades of sustained grassroots struggle.

A Feminist Awakening (without the "F" word) has emerged slowly but surely in post-revolutionary Iran. Over 63 percent of university graduates are female in Iran, and unlike many other countries in the region,

Iranian women are visible in all areas of public life. They are lawyers, doctors, artists, publishers, journalists, bloggers, politicians, students and professors. In 2003, on a visit to Tehran and other major Iranian cities, I noticed that any given state radio news broadcast might feature an entire news team composed of women: Negin, Parvaneh, Sara, Fatemeh... This was often the rule and not the exception. But one should not paint an overly rosy picture of women in Iran. Only 12.3 percent are part of the public workforce, and for many marriage is the only gateway out of their parental home. The general unemployment rate is a staggering 30 percent, and this is a particularly acute problem among young women, who also face gender discrimination in the workforce. Furthermore, drug abuse, runaway girls, child labor (especially among Afghan refugees), prostitution and human trafficking of women and children in Iran are critical issues today because of the country's abysmal economic, immigration and gender-imbalanced policies and neglect.

During the presidential campaign of June 2009, Zahra Rahnavard, the wife of the Green Movement candidate Mir Hossein Mousavi, who is herself an accomplished painter, professor and former university chancellor, held her husband's hand and spoke to thousands of women about gender equality. Her presence prompted many women to vote for Mir Hossein Mousavi. Rahnavard had been removed from her administrative duties at Al-Zahra University, where she was the Vice Chancellor, when Ahmadinejad took over as president of Iran in 2005. Like many others, her story is one of a Muslim feminist who realized that the Islamic Republic was not fulfilling its religious, constitutional and international duties in protecting women's rights.

But Zahra Rahnavard is only the tip of the iceberg. In April 2009, weeks before the election of June 12, 2009, a coalition of influential women wrote a political charter that included the following statement:

> We—as members of the women's movement in Iran and as civil rights activists from diverse areas such as NGOs, political parties, campaigns, press and trade unions—have realized that there are many ways in which to achieve women's demands. When it is

necessary, we have stepped in unison with one another. Today, we have decided to form another coalition in which to present the demands of women within our country through the pivotal period and space of the presidential election. The only goal of this coalition is to declare women's demands. We neither support any specific candidate nor are we interfering in a citizen's right and decision to participate or not in the election.

However, this proposal was not signed by some of the most prominent members of the women's movement, namely secular feminists such as Parvin Ardalan and Sussan Tahmasebi. In her blog, Leila Mouri, one of the members of the Stop Stoning Forever Campaign who is now a student in the United States wrote:

I wish my friends in the women's rights movement would have been more active than before these days, and as a progressive social movement had a more pronounced presence in these crucial times. Perhaps they have the answer to some of the questions I have (e.g. have they joined these demonstrations just for their votes to be counted or are there other demands for which we have been fighting all these years), and which I am very eager to know. I very much hope the civil demands of women are not forgotten in the midst of all this.

Much ideological strife has divided the women's movement in Iran. But that hasn't stopped ordinary women from actively participating in the June 2009 pre- and post-election rallies. As history shows us, Iranian women have often been at the forefront of their country's democratic aspirations and social uprisings. They were the key to success for such iconic events as the Babi movement of the mid-nineteenth century, the Tobacco Revolt of the late nineteenth century, the Constitutional Revolution of the early twentieth century, and right down to the struggles for nationalization of the Iranian oil industry in the 1950s and ultimately the Islamic revolution of 1978–79. But once the challenges of these definitive turning points were courageously met, women were forgotten and their issues were sidestepped.

What we are witnessing in Iran today is a natural consequence of years of feminist presence and the active participation of powerful women in the public sphere, which has taught girls that being a woman does not mean just being a mother or a wife and that women must be present and fighting in order to achieve their rights and demands.

These women are putting their lives on the line to save the little that is left of their republic. The majority of them has insisted on nonviolent resistance and protected both the riot police and the common people from being killed or beaten. In return, they have been brutally beaten and even killed by the security forces, as best known in the tragic case of the twenty-six-year-old philosophy student Neda Agha-Soltan, who was shot by a sniper on the streets of Tehran. Her last moments were captured on a cell-phone video camera and have now become the iconic symbol of the Green Movement.

The Green Movement seems to be way ahead of all its leaders and theorists, but if it is ever to succeed, it is imperative for the leaders of the feminist groups to participate in its inner leadership circle and not to back down one iota from women's demands for civil liberties once the dust settles. For that to happen a coalition of various women's rights organizations and positions will have to be part and parcel of defining what exactly this Green Movement is. As the month of June draws to a close, and after two weeks of heavy crackdowns on the protesters, there is no way of knowing what will become of this movement. But whatever its future holds, the leaders of the women's rights movement will have to keep the heroic struggles of women in the forefront of their minds and not allow their blood to have been shed in vain.

A WAVE FOR LIFE AND LIBERTY:
THE GREEN MOVEMENT AND IRAN'S INCOMPLETE REVOLUTION
Asef Bayat

July 7, 2009

How can we make sense of the 2009 post-election crisis in the Islamic Republic of Iran? Why after a decade of seeming silence did a spectacular political movement emerge to pose such a formibable challenge to Islamist rule? Has this been a class struggle or the revenge of secularism against theocracy? Is Iran on the verge of yet another revolution?

The key to answering these questions is understanding how the current situation both reflects and is the outcome of Iran's deep political and social divide between a doctrinal regime which regards people as dutiful subjects and a large segment of the population who see themselves as full citizens of a republic. The root cause of the crisis lies in a historic twist: Iran experienced an "Islamic revolution" without first developing an "Islamist movement," one that could "socialize" and connect the expectations of the people to the visions of the Islamist leadership.

In the absence of such an Islamist movement, "Islamization" was then inaugurated primarily *after* the revolution by the Islamic state from above, and often through coercion and compulsion. As a consequence, from the very first days of the Islamic Republic the process of Islamization provoked dissent. Today's crisis is the legacy of that disjuncture over the very meaning of the revolution.

The layers of "independence"

In the days and weeks leading up to the collapse of the Shah's regime on February 11, 1979, the cry of millions of Iranians echoed through the city streets and filled every public square: *"Estiqlal, Azadi, Jomhuri-ye*

Eslami!" ("Independence, Freedom, Islamic Republic!"). These essential yet broad demands—emblazoned on almost every banner, tract and placard—became the calling card of the Iranian revolution, an aspiration that united the protesters and the emerging revolutionary leadership.

Yet it did not take long before these respective parties began to articulate more precisely what they meant by these terms, and what they wanted from the revolution. This process set the stage for protracted discontent on one side and repression on the other.

For many Iranians in the late 1970s, the revolution was a nationalist, anti-imperialist movement in which *estiqlal* (independence) was a key goal. At the time, most people felt that Iran was a "dependent" nation, dependent above all on the US. The evidence for this belief abounded: the Shah had been reinstalled on the throne in 1953 by the United States after a CIA coup toppled the secular democratic government of Mohammad Mosaddegh, who had nationalized the Iranian Oil Company the previous year. The US put its support behind the Shah, and for a generation he used a notorious secret police agency (Savak) to rule Iran with an iron hand. It was natural, then, that the quest for independence was expressed in the vocabulary of the "third-worldist" and anti-imperialist discourse characteristic of the 1970s. This outlook galvanized millions of Iranians across the political spectrum—secular, religious, nationalist and Marxist alike.

The vast majority who embraced this political outlook believed that Iran could be independent yet still engage with the world at large. For example, there seemed to be many possible parallels with the social and political upheavals in Latin America at the time. Thus, for the protesters, there was no automatic correlation between the fight for independence and supporting national autarky and isolation.

However, the position of the Islamist revolutionary leaders turned out to be very different. For them, national "independence" was a protective shield against external interference and influences, which was a critical tool for securing the regime's social control. The Islamic regime sought to insulate itself from the encroaching ideas and diverse life-styles unleashed by a globalizing world.

What lies behind this attitude is that Iran's is a peculiar doctrinal regime whose legitimacy is grounded on narrow and exclusive "religious values." The hardline Islamists have always feared that these values might not be able to hold firm if the nation opened up to the outside world. In fact, part of the Islamists' critique of globalization is linked to their deep anxiety over losing their self-worth in Iran itself. These rulers could only open up to the world if they possessed a much stronger degree of political and ideological self-confidence at home. Lacking such confidence, Iran's rulers had to transform the rhetoric of "independence" (and, by extension, "authenticity") into a sacred entity, a virtue whose violation would invite punishment. This is the logic that leads them to target oppositional ideas, politics and individuals as "foreign," "Western" or "American" (as in "Western intellectual," "American Islam" or "American freedom"). So, the idea of "independence" has become a pretext for curtailing freedoms at home. Perhaps the millions of revolutionary Iranians who marched against the Shah in the late 1970s had an implicit understanding of the dangers of this rhetoric, which is why they extended their chant beyond *estiqlal* (independence) to include the second key ingredient of the revolution: *azadi* (freedom).

The meanings of "freedom"

What did the Iranian people mean by the term *azadi* at the time of the revolution? In public discourse in the late 1970s, *azadi* was essentially linked to "justice." It implied liberation from repression, from the fear of despotic bosses, bureaucrats, traffic police, the village gendarmerie and, above all, from the fear of Savak (the secret police). Freedom represented a desire for inclusion without fear.

The revolution and the collapse of the Shah's regime in February 1979 brought a good deal of freedom. In the months and weeks after the Revolution a spectacular sense of relief and liberty was palpable. This was expressed in a multitude of ways: from a tremendous increase in public media outlets and the people's presence in the civic arena, to so-cial and political activism in neighbourhoods, schools, offices, factories, farms and even the army.

But this "Spring of Freedom," as it was called at the time, soon came to an end. A series of events punctuated the shift: the ratification of the constitution of the Islamic Republic in the referendum of December 1979; the hostage crisis following the seizure of the US Embassy that soon followed; the invasion of Iran by Saddam Hussein's army in September 1980. A number of hardline vigilante groups, brandishing clubs and guns, began to dominate public spaces, heralding the advent of a new social order. Any "non-conformist" young people, women, and religious minorities underwent harsh social control and moral discipline. Free-dom of expression, organization, and open dissent rapidly diminished.

Amid harsh external (Iran–Iraq war) and internal conditions (re-pression and suppressed conflict), the demand for *azadi* (freedom) was pushed to the sidelines. It only resurfaced after the end of the war in 1988 and in the early years of the presidency of Hashemi Rafsanjani (1989–97); it reached its peak under the reformist presidency of Mo-hammad Khatami (1997–2005), when greater opportunity for political expression became available. But by then, the meaning of "freedom" had undergone a shift of register.

In this new period, *azadi* was articulated not only in terms of po-litical inclusion, but also, and especially, in terms of civil and individual liberties. Perhaps at no time in Iran's history has there been such a pow-erful demand for individual rights and civil liberties, and a longing to be able to choose one's preferred lifestyle. For most young people, the major concern became reclaiming youth itself—the desire to choose what to wear, what to think or watch or listen to, and who to marry. Young women wanted to be free from the constant surveillance of the moral authority of the state, enforced *hijab* and oppressive laws. They struggled to follow their lifestyle, pursue their hobbies, play a role in public life, make decisions in family matters, study, choose their life partners, and be seen and heard.

This quest for individual rights partly reflects a broader process of *individuation* that Iranian society has been undergoing in the thirty years since the 1979 Revolution. A creeping modernity has resulted from expanding urbanization (70 percent), increases in general literacy (80 percent) and college education, mobility, and the inescapable footprints of globalization. This modernity manifests itself in a host of social processes, including the "nuclearization" of the family, the general trend toward smaller, two-child households and apartment living, new trends of possessive individualism, and a more significant presence of meritocracy and implicit ageism in the public sphere.

These changes have not diminished general religious belief *per se*, though there is a strong disdain for clericalism and political Islam. Rather, Iran has moved toward a post-Islamist realm where people wish to combine their Islam with modernity, their religiosity with rights, and their faith with freedom.

This understanding of "freedom" differs from that of the Islamist leaders. From the beginning, in fact, Islamists expressed little interest in the idea of freedom. In the 1980s and 1990s, most of them equated *azadi* (freedom) with hedonism, moral laxity, decadence and westernization; even more so when it became the main outcry of the banished democrats, liberals, middle-class women and urban youngsters.

True, Ayatollah Khomeini had spoken the language of *azadi* when he was in opposition to the Shah, but he said little about it after ascending to power. His successor as Supreme Leader, Ayatollah Ali Khamenei, was among those who realized the appeal of "freedom" among the young and refused to discard the concept altogether; instead he claimed for it a genealogy that was essentially divine and Islamic. The notion of "spiritual freedom," he argued, entailed the "freedom to fulfil one's obligations," to "do grand work and to make grand choices" as a means of self-elevation. The other kinds of freedoms people were demanding stood in violation of Iran's religious rule, the kernel of the Islamic Republic.

The rules of the game

The legitimacy of the Islamic Republic derives from "divinely ordained values," or "Islamic principles." It is an Islamic state based upon the principle of *velayat-e faqih* ("the rule of the supreme jurist," who is currently Ayatollah Khamenei). In effect, he is ultimately in a position to determine what defines those "divinely ordained values."

Yet not all is divine in this political order; there is also room for the people, who can enact laws through their elected deputies in a Western-style parliament and execute them through a presidential office. But the "Islamicness" of both the people's deputies and their laws must first be sanctioned by the Guardian Council, a small group of clerics and lawyers who are effectively blessed by the supreme leader. This closed circuit of power and patronage reproduces the dominance of the Islamist clique which rules Iran today.

Is this what the millions of revolutionaries had in mind when they were uttering, "*Jomhuri-ye Eslami*" (Islamic Republic)? In the late 1970s, the term clearly signified a regime change from monarchy to republicanism, from autocracy to democracy. But the adjective "Islamic" in "Islamic Republic" was unclear for many.

In truth, Iranians had made no prior reference to such a republic. Ayatollah Khomeini's idea of *velayat-e faqih*, which he articulated in his book *Islamic Government* in the early 1970s, was basically a matter of Shi'a jurisprudence rather than a blueprint for governance; it remained almost totally unknown to the public until after the revolution.

During the revolution, people seemed to equate the term "Islamic republic" with the vague idea of a just, pious and accountable or democratic alternative to the dictatorship of the Shah. Ayatollah Khomeini confirmed this perception during a NBC television interview on November 11, 1978, when he acknowledged that "the Islamic Republic will be truly democratic." In fact, the draft constitution of the Islamic Republic (which Ayatollah Khomeini approved while in Paris) was fairly secular and democratic. It was inspired by the French republic's constitution and bore no reference to divine sovereignty or to *velayat-e faqih*, only to a "Council of Guardians" that included six lawyers and five clerics who were to oversee legislation.

However, before its final ratification in a constituent assembly, the hardline Islamists from the Revolutionary Council and the newly formed Islamic Republican Party radically altered the draft, turning it into the document that it is today. They did so by launching a massive populist campaign in support of some classic leftist redistributive demands: land reforms, homes for everyone, nationalization of industry and foreign trade, and land confiscation, all garnished with copious anti-US rhetoric. The Islamists included all of these demands in a radically altered constitutional draft and denounced anyone in opposition to it (whether liberals, secularists, or even moderate Muslims) as pro-capitalist, pro-Western, and counter-revolutionary (in short, very similar to what Ahmadinejad is doing today). In this highly charged mood in which many critics feared to speak out, hardline Islamists succeeded in pushing through the altered, Islamized constitution, which eventually would help secure the power of a new religious oligarchy in the Islamic state.

The revenge of history

The Islamic state has been neither totalitarian (at least not yet) nor stubbornly pre-modern (it utilizes the contemporary institutions of a parliament, a president and modern bureaucracy). But it remains deeply authoritarian, patriarchal and ideological, and it deprives millions of citizens participation in the decisions concerning public life. It continues to violate human rights and impose harsh social control, moral discipline and a misogynous treatment of women. An overwhelming emphasis on people's obligations to the state stands in sharp contrast with the people's pursuit of rights and republicanism.

The reform movement of the 1990s, which fed into the reform government of 1997–2005, came into being precisely to rectify this republican deficit, to democratize the Islamic Republic. The spectacular mood, energy and optimism that followed the election of Mohammad Khatami heralded the coming of Iran's "second revolution," one that was destined to put the finishing touches on the revolution of 1979. People believed that a new way of doing politics was on the horizon, the politics of peace, not the politics of violent revolution. Khatami, a middle-ranking cleric, won a landslide victory (70 percent of all voters in an 80 percent turnout) with a platform of "reforms"—democracy, the rule of law, meritocracy, tolerance and civil society. "Reform," a term which in the 1980s would have invoked a sense of betrayal, now became the catchphrase of the time, a symbol of the politics of hope.

But the reform government did not emerge out of the blue. It represented a broader post-Islamist movement which had been developing since the early 1990s in the course of the post-war reconstruction. This post-Islamism articulated the sentiments of women, young people, students, intellectuals and politically marginalized groups who agitated for social, political and religious openness. It aimed to transcend the Islamist project, to undo the religious state, curb social control of gender and moral discipline, and end the monopoly of religious truth. The movement sought to establish a secular democratic state within a broadly pious society in which the language of rights regained its former prominence.

Khatami's reform project meant to put the political objectives of post-Islamism into practice. The strategy was to empower civil society from below while negotiating legal and institutional change at the top, where conservative Islamists still wielded real power. Civil society gained strength, and social-movement activism, civic life and a fairly free press assumed unprecedented energy. A series of open debates, which focused on religious politics, the rule of law, violence, women and the West, shook the hardliners' moral standing. The conservatives' institutional power had changed little; they still controlled the army, the police, the Basij militia, as well as institutions of propaganda and numerous violent pressure groups. But the reform discourse posed a very serious challenge to the doctrine of the *velayat-e faqih* (the rule of the Islamic jurist) because it came from within.

The vengeful hardliners, wounded by the reformists' social hegemony and political success, embarked on a massive and violent political operation to win back what they had lost throughout these years. Ahmadinejad and his government embody that attempt to roll back history.

They sought a return to the revolutionism of the early 1980s by forging new sources of legitimacy within populism, radicalism and messianic discourse. These hardliners were and are determined to forestall another reform government. They aggressively consolidated the conservative Islamists' power in line with the visions of Ayatollah Mesbah Yazdi—Ahmadinejad's doctrinal mentor—by stripping the Islamic Republic of its republican component, by turning it into an Islamic state, in which elections would serve not as a venue for the free expression of ideas and dissent, but simply as a stage to play out the nation's allegiance to the supreme leader, who embodies the true essence of the "Islamic system."

But how can these "men of religion" justify this pervasive fraud, blatant illegality and astonishing deceit? The truth is that the very "sacred" system of *velayat-e faqih* that the hardliners strive to maintain can be used to justify and indeed sanctify such drastic measures. In their view, the "Islamic rule" (*velayat*) takes precedence over all other obligations (*owjib wajibat*), and the supreme *faqih* (Islamic jurist) holds the absolute power to change or disregard any law, precept and even religious injunction he deems detrimental to the "Islamic rule." If ignoring the constitution or preventing people from attending to their daily prayers are justified for the expediency of the system, why not electoral fraud? In such an ethical framework, lying can become an act of obligation, a virtue.

A class struggle?

It is therefore shortsighted to reduce the crisis to the bickering of the Westernized, urban middle and upper class Iranians against a supposedly pro-working class and anti-imperialist Ahmadinejad who claims to have won the elections. History seems to repeat itself. During the hostage crisis in the early 1980s, there were similar sentiments shared by the international left and its Iranian counterpart, before the latter was liquidated by the very regime they called "anti-imperialist."

The key to the Islamists' "anti-imperialism" is not the emancipation of the subaltern, but self-preservation. Ahmadinejad's "anti-imperialism" has done little for the well-being and the emancipation of ordinary people: the excluded, the poor and women. If anything, hardliners have deprived most citizens of their economic security and human rights, while their extremist rhetoric and exclusionary practices have justified and dignified neoliberal enemies in the West. Their undemocratic precepts have given ammunition to the most intolerant Islamophobes and warmongers in the United States and Europe, enabling them to wage a protracted campaign in which mostly poor and downtrodden Muslims get victimized.

Under the "anti-imperialist" Ahmadinejad, scores of NGOs have been closed down; hundreds of dissident students, university faculty, women and civil society activists have been incarcerated and the mass protests of teachers, bus drivers and other workers have been suppressed. Under Ahmadinejad's government, subsidies were cut, privatization reached new heights (an eighteen-fold increase from 2001–3), and a 25 percent inflation rate brought low-income people to their knees. Ahmadinejad's 2005 electoral campaign focused on fighting corruption, generating jobs and redistributing oil money. But under his government, cronyism and corruption exploded and there was a 13 percent increase in people living below the poverty line. In fact, based on economic policies and support for the public sector, Mir Hossein Mousavi is certainly much farther to the left than Mahmoud Ahmadinejad.

Moreover, the rivalry between Ahmadinejad and Mousavi does not reflect a rural–urban divide. In truth, both candidates seem to have support from both constituencies. In the past three decades, Iran has become an increasingly urban and literate society. Creeping urbanity (through growing education, electrification, a nuclear-family structure, specialization, media expansion and newspaper reading) has brought the countryside into the orbit of an urban pulse in which a vocal public sphere, associational life, respectable journalism, eleven million Internet users and 100,000 bloggers pose a serious challenge to the very Islamic state which originally stimulated these developments.

Ahmadinejad's regime is tied not to the working class as such but to a peculiar "regime class," an ideological community comprised of both the poor and the affluent that is brought together through state handouts (special subsidies, preferential payments, favors, bribes, commissions) and then socialized into a hardline ideological paradigm. Thus, many lower-class war veterans, Basijis and members of the vast religious sector (many mosques, shrines, seminaries, schools, or cultural associations) share the regime's proceeds from oil income with rich cronies, contractors and people from the revolutionary institutions—and are thus encouraged to support a hardline government that has alienated millions of Iranians.

In this light, the nightmare of yet another term for Ahmadinejad caused unprecedented enthusiasm for the reformist candidates. Iranian people, many of whom refused to vote in the previous election in 2005, utilized the election schedule, and a rift within the power elites to turn their quiet discontent into a spectacular open mobilization involving grassroots activism, coalition-building and massive street marches in quasi-carnivalesque fashion; all of which raised great hopes and expectations. The shocking outcome of the elections in Ahmadinejad's favor inspired a profound moral outrage that in turn fed into a broad-based protest movement, the largest and strongest in the history of the Islamic Republic.

This movement is neither a class struggle against a pro-rural government nor a secularist war against religious rule. Instead, it embodies a post-Islamist democracy movement to reclaim citizenship within a ethico-religious order. It articulates the long-standing yearnings for a dignified life free from fear, moral surveillance, corruption and arbitrary rule. Emphatically indigenous and principally nonviolent, it represents a green wave for life and liberty.

The movement started strong, but soon faced a violent crackdown by the regime. The thinking class (strategists, campaigners, writers) was incarcerated, reformist media was almost shut down, and free communication was suspended. The street showdowns were gradually weakened by state violence and intimidation (at least seventy people were killed and four thousand arrested), a neurotic propaganda campaign in state-controlled media, Stalinist-type mass trial of opposition figures, and psychological warfare. But collective dissent has continued.

In the short run, the regime has prevailed. But many things have already changed forever. The ruling circle faces an unprecedented crisis of legitimacy. The Supreme Leader is no longer the neutral arbiter who gets the last word; he has become the target of contention. The very ability of Islamist rule to accommodate the desires of its rights-conscious citizens is now up for debate. And the people have shown that they are quite capable of expressing their collective will once they get a chance.

The crisis is likely to continue. The popular claims for life and liberty, so integral to people's everyday lives, will remain and grow, expressing themselves in daily acts of individual defiance, before bursting collectively into the open once they find a crack in the governing body and an opportunity to do so. In sum, a large number of Iranians are likely to remain ungovernable.

For now, the movement has decidedly been against the idea of a revolution. But revolutions rarely announce their arrival in advance. Rather, the pressure builds up to a point where protesters find themselves capturing barracks or opening prison gates, and adversaries make a mad dash to the border. Whether or not a movement becomes revolutionary depends as much on the character of the conflict as on how the government's adversaries react. Today, most of the protesters clearly want reform, not a revolution. Only the future can tell if the regime itself will turn these reformers into revolutionaries.

IRAN'S TIDE OF HISTORY:
COUNTER-REVOLUTION AND AFTER

Fred Halliday

July 17, 2009

It is already five weeks since the presidential elections on June 12, 2009 in Iran, whose official results and handling by the authorities provoked an immediate and nationwide outbreak of popular demonstrations. It may appear that the authoritarian ruling clique headed by Iran's spiritual and political leaders (Ayatollah Khamenei and Mahmoud Ahmadinejad, respectively) has in this period been able to contain and push back the challenge to its power.

The deployment of police, Basij militiamen and Revolutionary Guards has crushed the mass street protests; at least dozens and perhaps hundreds of the leaders and top advisers of the reformist presidential candidates have been arrested; and a climate of fear has been imposed. The most visible manifestations of the hugely impressive popular movement of the "Persian Spring"—whose eruption took almost all observers by surprise, and which quickly won an amazing breadth of support across Iran's social groups and regions—seem to have been closed down as suddenly as they burst into the open.

Yet even a vigorous clampdown has been unable to extinguish all public displays of dissent. The open defiance by thousands of opposition supporters around Friday prayers at Tehran University on July 17, 2009 is but a surface indication of the heaving anger below. The gathering heard a call by the former president and influential figure Hashemi Rafsanjani for those arrested in the protests to be released. It is a significant intervention in a delicate phase, when factions within the regime as well as millions of disaffected Iranian citizens are positioning for the even more decisive confrontations ahead.

If past performance is anything to go on, the exertion of state violence since the election is only the beginning. In a pattern familiar from earlier phases of the Islamic Republic—as well as during the Shah's regime—opposition members will continue to be brutalized in prison and then forced to engage in televised "confessions": acts of deliberately preposterous humiliation designed not to reveal the truth (about "foreign conspiracies" or whatever), but to terrorize and break the will of the regime's opponents.

More ominous is what may follow this phase of detention, mistreatment and humiliation. Many precedents, in particular the repression of the liberal and left opposition in 1979–81, suggest that once foreign correspondents have been expelled from Iran and international attention has moved on, the actual killing of detained opposition members can proceed. In the past, such killings followed fake trials where executions were justified under the catch-all charge of "waging war on God," or by alleged escape attempts.

The revolution's dialectic

Many who know the modern history of Iran—be they Iranian or someone like myself who followed and witnessed the events of 1978–9 when the Islamic Republic came into being—will be struck by the many parallels, insights, warnings and differences offered by that earlier moment and the post-election upsurge of 2009. The apparel, slogans and precise demands may seem far apart, but the opposing forces are similar at heart.

The contempt and the urge to repress the peacefully and democratically expressed views of others were evident in the first months of the Islamic Republic; they reached a critical point in the mobilizations of summer 1979, when left and liberal forces—seeking to defend the freedom of the press and the rights of women and ethnic minorities—were confronted by gangs of *hezbollahi* thugs, mass pro-Khomeini demonstrations, and the newly established Revolutionary Guardforces, all determined to subdue the yearnings for such freedom and rights.

I recall, in particular, an educational encounter in August 1979 with a Revolutionary Guard who had come with his colleagues to close down the offices of the independent newspaper *Ayandegan*. When I asked this *pasdar* (revolutionary guard) what he was doing, he replied, "We are defending the revolution!" I asked, "Why are you therefore closing the paper?" He declared, "This newspaper is shit." When I mentioned that two million people read the paper, he replied, without reservation, "All right, then these two million people are shit too!" Thus was my induction into the political culture of the Islamic Revolutionary Guards.

But if such incidents from the early period of the Islamic Republic cast some light on the recent popular explosion in Iran, other analogies—above all with challenges to communist rule in east-central Europe after 1945—also suggest themselves. This is true in a deeper, sociological sense as well as in the texture of the protests themselves. For their main rallying cry was and is at once contemporary and full of historical resonance that derives from Iran's formative Constitutional Revolution of 1906. What they demand, and what the opposition presidential candidate Mir Hossein Mousavi has reiterated in his statements since the demonstrations, is a broad range of freedoms: of expression, of social behavior, of media.

In a sense, the Islamic Republic has, like communism, lost its original ideological credibility and has prepared the way for its own demise: above all by educating people. The demonstrators in June 2009 did not, after all, carry posters of Shia imams (Ali or Reza) or chant religious slogans; far fewer brandished pictures of Lenin, Mao Zedong or Che Guevara. These demonstrations, like the mass movements that challenged communism, were part of what Jürgen Habermas called, apropos 1989, a "revolution of catching up"—the demonstrators wanted to be part of the modern world and wanted their country to take its rightful and collaborative place in it.

Just as millions of citizens in east-central Europe began to express their dissatisfaction beyond the terms of reformist communism in the 1980s, so the Iranian demonstrators of June 2009 articulated a program that was larger and more international than that of their predecessors, one born of the increased awareness of the outside world produced by education, the Internet and the very real pluralism of information and opinion that, for all its repression in other spheres, the Islamic Republic has permitted.

The closing option

The analogies between the Iran of 1978–9 and the east-central Europe of 1989 also underline an important if as yet obscure contrast in this Iranian crisis. It may be apposite to quote here an astute observation made by Lenin. He believed that a successful revolution must meet two conditions. The first, often invoked, is that the people cannot go on being ruled in the old way. The second, neglected but equally important, is that the rulers cannot go on ruling in the old way.

Here indeed lies both the originality and the enigma of the ongoing Iranian convulsion of 2009. The success of Mir Hossein Mousavi in inspiring a mass movement in the weeks just prior and subsequent to the presidential election can be explained more or less straightforwardly as the confluence of three factors:

- Long-term buildup of dissatisfaction with the social, economic and political actions of the Islamic Republic
- A particular revulsion with the political direction and economic failures of Iran since Mahmoud Ahmadinejad came to power in June 2005
- A series of significant short-term events and processes in the days leading up to the election (including public reaction to Ahmadinejad's vulgarity during his TV debate with Mousavi and the creative use by the opposition of SMS, Facebook and other communications).

By contrast, the nature of the divisions within the state is much less definable, though divisions do exist. To observe Iran in these weeks is like watching a stage where only some of the actors are in the light:

there is another, equally important, process underway which remains in the shadows. This is the conflict within the clerical and political elite, more broadly, the Islamic nomenklatura—the 5,000 or so clergy, politicians and businesspeople with special access to the rents from oil, gas and trade who have coalesced into Iran's new ruling group.

The fissures within this elite are indicated by the open defiance of former presidents Hashemi Rafsanjani and Mohammad Khatami; they run through the clerical city of Qom and much of the official political networks. Whether they also split the armed forces, the *pasdaran* (Revolutionary Guards) and the intelligence services is unclear: but a working initial premise is that until evidence emerges that these security bodies are indeed divided, the Khamenei–Ahmadinejad camp will retain the initiative. Reports from Qom indicate that the regime is doing all it can—including the use of bribes and intimidation—to keep the majority of the clergy on its side.

It would thus be mistaken, in this context at least, to assume that the post-election protests mark the beginning of the end of the Islamic Republic. It may turn out this way, but the precedent of 1979–81 is sobering. At a time when Ayatollah Khomeini and his associates faced much greater challenges than this one, and when it seemed to many that the regime would fall, it managed to survive by mobilizing all of its supporters and exercising brutal repression of its opponents.

A different outcome in the period of revolution itself carries the same lesson. Few expected the regime of the Shah, which had international support and a modern army of 400,000, to crumble in the face of unarmed demonstrators within a matter of months. It is no easy task to evaluate regime resilience in Iran.

The opening door

But if the character of the intra-regime tensions and the immediate fate of the Islamic Republic are hard to read, the post-election demonstrations have most certainly created a new framework for the understanding of Iran's political world.

The protests have opened the history and legacy of the Islamic revolution itself to a range of different interpretations, and, by extension, to a questioning of established ones. For example, for many years after 1979 the Marxist left cleaved to the belief that it had "made" the revolution, only for its achievement to be stolen by Ayatollah Khomeini and the clergy. This argument always obscured another and greater act of usurpation by the clerical elite, which involved suppressing the role of the much larger nationalist constituency of opposition to the Shah and his alliance with the United States that played a very significant role in the revolution.

The demonstrators of 1978–9 did not want the Shah, but nor did they want a dictatorship of ayatollahs. They wanted, in the signal slogans of the revolution, "independence" and "freedom." Many prominent Iranian figures of the time acted as representatives of this trend, among them the liberal prime minister Shahpur Bakhtiar, who tried to manage a democratic transition after the Shah relinquished power and was assassinated in Paris in August 1991; Ayatollah Hossein Ali Montazeri, Khomeini's chosen successor, who spent the years 1997–2003 under house arrest in the city of Qom for criticizing clerical control of the state; and followers of the former prime minister Mohammad Mossadeq, overthrown in the coup of 1953, who organized the 1979 anti-censorship demonstrations.

In the same way that Lenin and the Bolsheviks pushed aside not only their tsarist opponents, but also Russian liberals, social revolutionaries and Mensheviks, so Khomeini and his associates set out to monopolize the post-revolutionary state and extinguish both their political rivals and the very memory of their historical contribution. It is the great victory of the brave citizens of Iran who took to the streets in June 2009, and affirmed their rights in peaceful and dignified fashion, to have reclaimed this history, which belongs to all Iranians.

Their demonstrations thus have opened a door to Iran's past as well as its future. Another slogan of the epic popular tide of 1978–9, "*Marg bar fascism, marg bar irtija*" (Death to fascism, death to reaction), may yet combine with the *"Marg bar dictator"* of the 2009 marches in a way that heralds the end of the demagogic clique that now rules Iran. The people of Iran, and their friends and admirers the world over, can only hope that this day comes sooner rather than later.

"I AM NOT A SPECK OF DIRT, I AM A RETIRED TEACHER"

Ervand Abrahamian

July 23, 2009

Iran has a healthy respect for crowds—and for good reason. Crowds brought about the Constitutional Revolution of 1906. Crowds prevented the Iranian parliament from submitting to a tsarist ultimatum in 1911. Crowds scuttled the 1919 Anglo-Iranian Agreement, which would have in effect incorporated the country into the British Empire. Crowds prevented General Reza Khan from imitating Atatürk and establishing a republic in 1924; as a compromise, he kept the monarchy but named himself shah. Crowds gave the communist Tudeh Party political clout in the brief period of political pluralism between 1941 and 1953. Crowds in 1951–53 gave Mohammad Mosaddegh, the country's national hero, the power to take over the Anglo-Iranian Oil Company and to challenge the shah's unconstitutional control of the armed forces. Crowds—aided by clerics—provided a backdrop to the 1953 military coup organized by the CIA and MI-5. In 1963, crowds began what soon became known as Khomeini's Islamic Movement. And, of course, crowds played the central role in the drama of the 1979 Islamic Revolution—with the result that the new constitution enshrined the right of citizens to hold peaceful street demonstrations.

It was an awareness of the importance of crowds that prompted the regime to rig the presidential elections last month and thus inadvertently trigger the present crisis. In the months before the elections, Mahmoud Ahmadinejad seemed to be a shoe-in for a second four-year term. He enjoyed easy access to the mass media; his competitors were limited to websites and newspapers that were closed down at any provocation. He had won his first term after running a populist campaign against Ayatollah Akbar Hashemi Rafsanjani, the former president who epitomized the regime's worst features—nepotism, cronyism and financial corruption. He enjoyed the support of Ayatollah Khamenei, the Supreme Leader, who shared his deep distrust of the West and probably his ambition to pursue a nuclear program at all costs.

Ahmadinejad also had the backing of much of the military-clerical-commercial complex running the country: the Revolutionary Guard and the affiliated Basij militia with more than three million members; the clerical "foundations," quasi-state organizations that employ hundreds of thousands of people; and the bazaar merchants with their lucrative contracts with the central government. He had placed so many former colleagues from the Guard in key positions that some claimed he had carried out a quiet coup d'état. He had consolidated his support among the evangelicals, known in Iran as the "principalists," by courting Ayatollah Mesbah Yazdi, an influential right-wing cleric in Qom who sits on Iran's Assembly of Experts; by often referring to the imminent return of the Mahdi (the Messiah); by generously patronizing the Jamkaran shrine where the Mahdi was supposedly last seen; and by claiming he had felt his divine presence when denouncing the US before the UN General Assembly. He had channeled the money from the recent oil bonanza into mosque construction, rural projects, government salaries and even cash handouts. He boasted that he was putting the oil money on people's kitchen tables. Some American presidents win elections by cutting taxes. Ahmadinejad tried to win by handing out potatoes.

What is more, the reform movement seemed divided and disillusioned. In the 2005 elections, faced with a choice between Ahmadinejad and Rafsanjani, many reformers stayed at home. In 2009, Mohammad Khatami, the reform president between 1997 and 2005, was poised to run, but then withdrew, leaving the reform field to Mir Hossein Mousavi and Ayatollah Mehdi Karoubi. The former, an architect turned academic, had not been seen in the political arena since 1989; between 1981 and 1989 he had served as Khomeini's prime minister. In 1997, reformers had privately asked him to run for the presidency, but he had deferred to Khatami. Like many members of the intelligentsia in his generation, Mousavi first entered politics fired up by a mix of Islamic fervor and Fanonist anti-imperialism. But once the revolution had achieved its main goals—the overthrow of the shah and the declaration of independence from the US—many of these militants gradually came around to the view that the Islamic Republic would wither unless it allowed greater democracy, pluralism and individual rights. The reactionary clergy, they realized, now posed the main obstacle to Iranian modernity. Karoubi, a close associate of Khomeini who had served as the speaker of Parliament, head of the Association of Militant Clergy, and director of the Martyrs Foundation, shared many of these sentiments and in one respect was even more liberal, advocating greater privatization of the economy. He had run in the 2005 elections, gaining much support in his home region, and after the elections had lodged an official complaint that the Revolutionary Guard had manipulated the vote in favor of Ahmadinejad. It is generally suspected that the Guardian Council, which has the authority to vet presidential candidates, permitted Karoubi and Mousavi, as well as Mohsen Rezaee, the moderate-conservative former commander of the Revolutionary Guard, to run this time because it was confident that they had little chance.

This confidence was reinforced by a pre-election poll taken by a Washington-based organization called Terror Free Tomorrow: The Center for Public Opinion. The poll found that of 1,001 Iranians interviewed by phone from outside Iran, 34 percent favoured Ahmadinejad; 14 percent Mousavi; 50 percent had not yet made up their minds; 80 percent wanted the constitution to be altered so that the Supreme Leader would be elected directly by the public; 70 percent wanted to give the UN greater access to the country's nuclear facilities; and 77 percent wanted better relations with the US. Apologists for the regime who continue to cite this survey ignore these findings, as well as the significance of the name and location of the polling organization.

Once the actual electoral campaign—by law restricted to just ten days—got started, the race became much tighter. A similarly dramatic shift in public opinion also occurred in 1997. Then the general expectation had been that the well-known conservative candidate would win an easy victory over Khatami, the little-known reformer. Yet the latter's campaign had suddenly caught fire: 80 percent of the electorate came out to vote, and more than 70 percent supported him. Such volatility is understandable in a country which doesn't have any deep-rooted political parties.

This time three major factors converged to produce a shift in public opinion. The first was the series of six prime-time televised debates, which were watched by almost every household in the country. These debates galvanized the whole electorate. Instead of attacking each other, the challengers focused their fire on Ahmadinejad, concentrating on his economic record. They took turns describing reliable statistics—in sharp contrast to those produced by the president—that put inflation at 25 percent, unemployment at 30 percent, and the number of those living in poverty at a record high. Ahmadinejad tried to change the subject, harping on Rafsanjani's wealth and falsely accusing Mousavi's wife of pulling strings to obtain her doctorate. This angered women and reminded viewers that four of Ahmadinejad's own ministers had claimed phony foreign degrees.

Ahmadinejad was also sharply criticized for damaging national "honor"—through, for example, his denial of the Holocaust—and for pursuing adventurist foreign policies that isolated Iran and jeopardized its security. His opponents all favoured better relations with the outside world. Ahmadinejad had won the 2005 election by running not only against Rafsanjani but against Bush. This time he had neither. Instead he had to contend with Obama, who had removed the main stumbling-block to negotiations—the prerequisite that Iran should stop all uranium enrichment. He had accepted the right of Iran to have a nuclear program. He ceased all talk of "regime change." He apologized for the 1953 coup. He ended the irritating practice of differentiating between the Iranian government and the Iranian people, and instead addressed himself to the "Islamic Republic of Iran." And he offered to end economic sanctions if Iran would give verifiable guarantees that it would not build nuclear weapons. For many Iranians, foreign relations were tied to domestic bread-and-butter questions. It was clear that there would not be jobs for the ever increasing number of high school and college graduates unless the country's vast untapped gas and oil reserves were developed. It was equally clear that these reserves would not be developed unless relations with the West—and especially the US—improved. Karoubi made fun of Ahmadinejad for boasting that the Iranian educational system was so good that a high school pupil had achieved nuclear fusion in her basement. At one point Ahmadinejad lost his cool and called Karoubi a "Hitler."

The second factor was Mousavi's ability to challenge Ahmadinejad on his own turf. Once Mousavi had returned to the limelight, he was quick to remind the public that he had been Khomeini's prime minister in the "heroic days" of war and revolution. Besides his reputation as a competent administrator, he nationalized a host of industries, launched a rural construction program, drafted a progressive labor law, advocated land reform, and introduced wartime price controls and rationing, thereby narrowing the income gap between rich and poor for the first and probably only time in Iranian history. He wasn't just a populist talking ecstatically about the good old days; he had been a key figure in those days. His Mir title also helped—"Mir" is the Azeri version of "Seyyed" and signifies descent from the Prophet and the twelve Imams. An impressive number of organizations and personalities prominent in the early days of the revolution threw their weight behind him. They included the labor unions; the Association of Qom Seminary Teachers; the Association of Militant Clerics; the Mujahideen Organization of the Islamic Revolution; Grand Ayatollah Montazeri, at one time the designated Supreme Leader; Ayatollah Taheri, the senior cleric in Isfahan; Hojatoleslam Khoeni, the mentor of the students who took over the US Embassy; Hojatoleslam Mohtashemi, Khomeini's main troubleshooter in Lebanon when the Revolutionary Guard presided over the creation of Lebanese Hezbollah; and relatives of Revolutionary Guards martyred in the Iran–Iraq war. Meanwhile, Ahmadinejad's own populist credentials were tarnished when a member of his inner circle told the press that he had placed many family members and associates in high positions. On the campaign trail, in order to woo secular nationalists and the old left, Mousavi brandished a large portrait of Mossadeq—anathema to the right-wing clerics.

The third factor was the women's movement. Mousavi's wife, Zahra Rahnavard, a scholar, artist and prominent champion of women's rights, entered the fray and campaigned alongside her husband—the first time this had happened in Iranian history. This galvanized the women's movement—especially the One Million Signatures Campaign, which takes in a wide spectrum from Islamic feminists to liberal nationalists to leftist and even Marxist activists. The women's movement had been crucial to Khatami's victories. It was poised to be just as important to Mousavi.

By the last days of the campaign, good-natured crowds were pouring into the cities, threatening to turn the world upside down and, most serious of all, mocking those on high—in one poster, Ahmadinejad was pictured with Pinocchio's nose. The government appeared to be losing control of the streets. The Washington polling agency that had expected an easy Ahmadinejad victory admitted that its predictions were probably out of date. Eyewitnesses reported that the election had turned into a "real race," that the demonstrations were "rattling" the government and that the Revolutionary Guard was fearful of a "velvet revolution." Some polls taken by the opposition predicted a victory for Mousavi. Even if these polls were too optimistic, they did indicate that Ahmadinejad's lead had been drastically cut—perhaps to the point where he would not win the required 50 percent in the first round and would therefore have to compete against his main opponent in a second round, as required by the constitution.

A second round would have posed a serious threat: it would have led to more campaigning and more unruly street demonstrations. It would have accentuated the shift in public opinion. And it would have strengthened Mousavi (Karoubi made it clear that he would endorse him in a second round). It was generally thought that Ahmadinejad wouldn't be able to improve on the number of votes he gained in the first round and so would enter any second round at a clear disadvantage. To pre-empt this, the Interior Ministry, which oversaw elections and was headed by a millionaire friend of Ahmadinejad, acted decisively, giving Ahmadinejad such a resounding majority that it dwarfed the votes gained by his opponents. The minister had purged unreliable civil servants from the electoral commission, and some even claimed that Ayatollah Mesbah Yazdi had issued a fatwa allowing the faithful to miscount votes. He restricted the number of permits issued to poll observers and even prevented some permit-holders from entering the polling stations. He set up more than 14,000 mobile polling trucks, making the vote count easy to fiddle with; printed far more ballots than there were eligible voters; cut off communications to Mousavi and Karoubi's headquarters on the day of the elections (Mousavi's offices in Qom were torched in a mysterious attack); and, as a clincher, broke precedent by not having the ballots tabulated on the spot at the end of election day, but instead rushed to the ministry where they were "counted" by his aides.

Within hours of the polls closing, the interior minister declared Ahmadinejad to be the winner with 66 percent of the vote. Mousavi, he said, had won only 33 percent. The minister also declared that a record number of people had voted—85 percent of the electorate. Congratulating the nation on the victory, Khamenei described the result as "divinely inspired." Three days later, the ministry issued more detailed statistics with provincial breakdowns: Ahmadinejad had won 24.5 million votes, Mousavi 13.2 million, Rezaee 678,240 and Karoubi 333,635. According to Chatham House, these statistics present serious problems. In two provinces, more than 100 percent of eligible voters voted. Karoubi, who received more than five million votes in 2005, got fewer than 340,000 this time, and lost even in his home province. For Ahmadinejad to have won more than 24 million votes, Chatham House found, he would have had to keep all the votes he received in 2005, win over those who had voted for Rafsanjani on that occasion, as well as all of those who had stayed at home and up to 44 percent of the voters who backed reform candidates.

This decisive "victory" was intended to put an end to street demonstrations, but it had the opposite effect, outraging many who felt not only cheated but insulted—especially when Ahmadinejad described those who questioned the results as "specks of dirt." There were vociferous protests in many parts of the country, and Mousavi and Karoubi called for a silent rally to be held at Azadi (Freedom) Square in Tehran on Monday, June 15. Around a million people heeded the call—the conservative mayor of the capital put the number at three million. The scene was reminiscent of the rallies held in the same square during the 1979 Revolution. As in 1979, the security forces were kept away to prevent clashes. The rally drew all kinds of protesters: old and young, professionals and workers, bazaaris and students, women wearing sunglasses and headscarves as well those in full-length chador. Lines of protesters five miles long converged on the square from the better-off northern districts as well as from the working-class southern ones. Volunteers, many of them election workers, gave the procession a semblance of organization. Students marched to Freedom Square from Revolution Square, near the university campus, under a banner reading "From Revolution to Freedom." Others displayed banners saying, "What Happened to My Vote?" or "Ahmadinejad, you could not see our votes but you could see the divine light"—an allusion to the president's supposed experience at the UN. An old man carried a sign that read, "I am not a speck of dirt, I am a retired teacher." Eyewitness accounts agree that the feeling was not so much against the Islamic Republic as against the stifling of the reform movement. It was a mass protest against vote-rigging. Exiled groups, not surprisingly, hailed these scenes as a revolutionary challenge to the Islamic Republic—an interpretation peddled, for different reasons, by the regime itself. However it is interpreted, it was the largest rally held in Tehran since the height of the Islamic Revolution. Similar rallies were also held in many provincial capitals, notably Isfahan and Shiraz.

Government spokesmen tried to control the damage by arguing that the opposition might have some support in the cities but that Ahmadinejad had carried the countryside. This argument was soon picked up by Western policymakers—especially State Department diplomats—who had argued in favor of striking a "grand bargain" with Iran in the fashion of Nixon in China and were worried that a potential rapprochement would be sabotaged by the unrest. But the few reliable public accounts from the countryside dismiss the notion that Ahmadinejad has a strong rural base. Although the Islamic Republic is strongly supported in the countryside, rural inhabitants constitute only 35 percent of the country's population, and, more to the point, many people there strongly dislike Ahmadinejad because of his broken promises and because he funneled state benefits to the Revolutionary Guard, Basijis and employees of the clerical foundations. Eric Hoogland, who has studied rural Iran for many years and cannot be described as an opponent of the Islamic Republic, claimed that in the region he knows well outside Shiraz—a region that should be Ahmadinejad's heartland since it is Shia and Persian-speaking—only 20–25 percent supported him.

Shaken by the June 15 rallies, the regime launched a massive crackdown, the full extent of which remains unknown. It banned all demonstrations, threatened to execute anyone participating in or calling for such protests, and sent out tens of thousands of Revolutionary Guards and Basijis on motorbikes, armed with assault weapons, knives and truncheons. The regime sent vigilantes into university dormitories. At least twenty people were killed in the clashes and more than 4,000 associates of Mousavi and Karoubi were arrested—their main strategists and campaigners, as well as journalists sympathetic to the opposition. It jammed foreign broadcasts, shut down newspapers and websites, disrupted telecommunications and expelled many foreign journalists, while others were confined to their offices and some jailed. The regime's inforcers broke into private homes and arrested those suspected of shouting "God is great" from their rooftops. A state media campaign claimed that the opposition was inspired, financed and organized by a sinister "foreign hand": Britain, and the BBC, tended to be singled out here. (The regime put less blame on the US, perhaps in order to leave the door open for future negotiations.) The regime also tortured prisoners, including prominent public figures, who were made to confess before TV cameras that they had participated in a Western plot to launch a velvet revolution. As a sop to public opinion, Khamenei asked the Guardian Council—twelve conservative judges—to investigate complaints of electoral irregularities. The Guardian Council found a discrepancy of three million votes, but concluded that this would not have made much of a dent in Ahmadinejad's eleven million lead. States that orchestrate 99.5 percent electoral support for their candidate can always claim that 10 or 20 percent here or there will not make much of a difference, but Iran has a tradition of relatively competitive elections. Mousavi and Karoubi, endorsed by many prominent clerics, rejected this verdict, called for new elections, and even declared the presidency of Ahmadinejad illegitimate.

The regime appears to have weathered the storm, at least for the time being. The revolt has not turned into a revolution, even though these events have much in common with those of 1979—similar rallies, similar slogans ("God is great"), similar tactics and similar griping about "foreign interference." But there are major differences: the monarchy had almost no support, but the republic has a solid base—25 percent of the population consider themselves true believers. In 1979, the shah had lost the allegiance of the armed forces, but the republic is fully equipped with three million Revolutionary Guards and Basijis, trained to deal with civil disturbances. The monarchy had been challenged by a mass revolutionary movement. The Islamic Republic faces a mass reform movement that wants to strengthen its democratic features at the expense of its theocratic ones.

The crisis has created two long-term dangers for the regime. First, the presidential office continues to be held by a demagogic politician who does not shy away from confronting the US, and who seems to have little grasp of his limits. He claims Iran is a major power—maybe even a superpower—and dismisses the US as a spent force that "can't do a damn thing." It's not for nothing that the other candidates consider him a dangerous adventurist. Nuclear negotiations are unlikely to go anywhere. On the contrary, they are likely to degenerate into acrimony, leaving the US in a much stronger position and Iran in a much weaker position than ever before. Not surprisingly, the Israeli government cheered Ahmadinejad's victory—a Mousavi victory would have been an obstacle to a possible Israeli strike on Iran's nuclear facilities. Second, the crushing of the reform movement has closed off avenues for change and dampened hopes for peaceful evolution. By denouncing children of the revolution as foreign-paid "counter-revolutionaries," Khamenei, Ahmadinejad and their allies have alienated a considerable portion of the population—maybe even the majority—and could end up transforming reformists into revolutionaries. By moving away from democracy toward theocracy, the regime has removed an important component of its original legitimacy. Some would argue the country has ceased to be a republic and has become a military-backed theocracy—a Shia imamate equivalent to the medieval Sunni caliphates.

BERLUSCONI IN TEHRAN

Slavoj Žižek

July 23, 2009

When an authoritarian regime approaches its final crisis, but before its actual collapse, a mysterious rupture often takes place. All of a sudden, people know the game is up: they simply cease to be afraid. It isn't just that the regime loses its legitimacy: its exercise of power is now perceived as a panic reaction, a gesture of impotence. Ryszard Kapuściński, in *Shah of Shahs,* his account of the Khomeini revolution, located the precise moment of this rupture: at a Tehran crossroad, a single demonstrator refused to budge when a policeman shouted at him to move, and the embarrassed policeman withdrew. Within a couple of hours, all Tehran had heard about the incident, and although the streetfighting carried on for weeks, everyone somehow knew it was all over. Is something similar happening now?

There are many versions of last month's events in Tehran. Some see in the protests the culmination of the pro-Western "reform movement," something along the lines of the color-coded revolutions in Ukraine and Georgia. They support the protests as a secular reaction to the Khomeini revolution, as the first step towards a new liberal-democratic Iran freed from Muslim fundamentalism. They are countered by sceptics who think that Ahmadinejad actually won, that he is the voice of the majority, while Mousavi's support comes from the middle classes and their gilded youth. Let's face facts, they say: in Ahmadinejad, Iran has the president it deserves. Then there are those who dismiss Mousavi as a member of the clerical establishment whose differences from Ahmadinejad are merely cosmetic. He too wants to continue with the atomic energy program, is against recognizing Israel, and when he was prime minister in the repressive years of the war with Iraq enjoyed the full support of Khomeini.

Finally, and saddest of all, are the leftist supporters of Ahmadinejad. What is at stake for them is Iranian freedom from imperialism. Ahmadinejad won because he stood up for the country's independence, exposed corruption among the elite and used Iran's oil wealth to boost the incomes of the poor majority. This, we are told, is the true Ahmadinejad: the Holocaust-denying fanatic is a creation of the Western media. In this view, what's been happening in Iran is a repetition of the 1953 overthrow of Mossadegh—a coup, financed by the West, against the legitimate premier. This not only ignores the facts (the high electoral turnout, up from the usual 55 to 85 percent, can be explained only as a protest vote), it also assumes, patronisingly, that Ahmadinejad is good enough for the backward Iranians: they aren't yet sufficiently mature to be ruled by a secular left.

Opposed to one another though they are, all these versions read the Iranian protests as a conflict between Islamic hardliners and pro-Western liberal reformists. That is why they find it so difficult to locate Mousavi: is he a Western-backed reformer who wants to increase people's freedom and introduce a market economy, or a member of the clerical establishment whose victory wouldn't significantly change the nature of the regime? Either way, the true nature of the protests is being missed.

The green colors adopted by the Mousavi supporters and the cries of "Allahu akbar!" that resonated from the roofs of Tehran in the evening darkness suggested that the protesters saw themselves as returning to the roots of the 1979 Khomeini revolution, and cancelling out the corruption that followed it. This was evident in the way the crowds behaved: the emphatic unity of the people, their creative self-organisation and improvised forms of protest, the unique mixture of spontaneity and discipline. Picture the march: thousands of men and women demonstrating in complete silence. This was a genuine popular uprising on the part of the deceived partisans of the Khomeini revolution. We should contrast the events in Iran with the US intervention in Iraq: an assertion of popular will on the one hand, a foreign imposition of democracy on the other. The events in Iran can also be read as a comment on the platitudes of Obama's Cairo speech, which focused on the dialogue between religions: no, we don't need a dialogue between religions (or civilizations), we need a bond of political solidarity between those who struggle for justice in Muslim countries and those who participate in the same struggle elsewhere.

Two crucial observations follow. First, Ahmadinejad is not the hero of the Islamist poor, but a corrupt Islamofascist populist, a kind of Iranian Berlusconi whose mixture of clownish posturing and ruthless power politics is causing unease even among the ayatollahs. His demagogic distribution of crumbs to the poor shouldn't deceive us: he has the backing not only of the organs of police repression and a very Westernised PR apparatus. He is also supported by a powerful new class of Iranians who have become rich thanks to the regime's corruption—the Revolutionary Guard is not a working-class militia, but a mega-corporation, the most powerful center of wealth in the country.

Second, we have to draw a clear distinction between the two main candidates opposed to Ahmadinejad, Mehdi Karroubi and Mousavi. Karroubi is, effectively, a reformist, a proponent of an Iranian version of identity politics, promising favours to particular groups of every kind. Mousavi is something entirely different: he stands for the resuscitation of the popular dream that sustained the Khomeini revolution. It was a utopian dream, but one can't deny the genuinely utopian aspect of what was so much more than a hardline Islamist takeover. Now is the time to remember the effervescence that followed the revolution, the explosion of political and social creativity, organizational experiments and debates among students and ordinary people. That this explosion had to be stifled demonstrates that the revolution was an authentic political event, an *opening* that unleashed altogether new forces of social transformation: a moment in which "everything seemed possible." What followed was a gradual closing-down of possibilities as the Islamic establishment took political control. To put it in Freudian terms, today's protest movement is the "return of the repressed" of the Khomeini revolution.

What all this means is that there is a genuinely liberatory potential in Islam: we don't have to go back to the tenth century to find a "good" Islam, we have it right here, in front of us. The future is uncertain—the popular explosion has been contained, and the regime will regain ground. However, it will no longer be seen the same way: it will be just one more corrupt authoritarian government. Ayatollah Khamenei will lose whatever remained of his status as a principled spiritual leader elevated above the fray and appear as what he is—one opportunistic politician among many. But whatever the outcome, it is vital to keep in mind that we have witnessed a great emancipatory event which doesn't fit within the frame of a struggle between pro-Western liberals and anti-Western fundamentalists. If we don't see this, if as a consequence of our cynical pragmatism, we have lost the capacity to recognize the promise of emancipation, we in the West will have entered a post-democratic era, ready for our own Ahmadinejads. Italians already know his name: Berlusconi. Others are waiting in line.

Is there a link between Ahmadinejad and Berlusconi? Isn't it preposterous even to compare Ahmadinejad with a democratically elected Western leader? Unfortunately, it isn't: the two are part of the same global process. If there is one person to whom monuments will be built a hundred years from now, Peter Sloterdijk once remarked, it is Lee Kuan Yew, the Singaporean leader who thought up and put into practice a "capitalism with Asian values." The virus of authoritarian capitalism is slowly but surely spreading around the globe. Deng Xiaoping praised Singapore as the model that all of China should follow. Until now, capitalism has always seemed to be inextricably linked with democracy; it's true there were, from time to time, episodes of direct dictatorship, but, after a decade or two, democracy again imposed itself (in South Korea, for example, or Chile). Now, however, the link between democracy and capitalism has been broken.

This doesn't mean, needless to say, that we should renounce democracy in favor of capitalist progress, but that we should confront the limitations of parliamentary representative democracy. The American journalist Walter Lippmann coined the term "manufacturing consent," later made famous by Chomsky, but Lippmann intended it in a positive way. Like Plato, he saw the public as a great beast or a bewildered herd, floundering in the "chaos of local opinions." The herd, he wrote in *Public Opinion* (1922), must be governed by "a specialized class whose personal interests reach beyond the locality": an elite class acting to circumvent the primary defect of democracy, which is its inability to bring about the ideal of the "omni-competent citizen." There is no mystery in what Lippmann was saying, it is manifestly true; the mystery is that, knowing it, we continue to play the game. We act as though we were free, not only accepting but even demanding that an invisible injunction tell us what to do and think.

In this sense, in a democracy, the ordinary citizen is effectively a king, but a king in a constitutional democracy, a king whose decisions are merely formal, whose function is to sign measures proposed by the executive. The problem of democratic legitimacy is homologous to the problem of constitutional democracy: how to protect the dignity of the king? How to make it seem that the king effectively decides, when we all know this is not true? What we call the "crisis of democracy" isn't something that happens when people stop believing in their own power but, on the contrary, when they stop trusting the elites, when they perceive that the throne is empty, that the decision is now theirs. "Free elections" involve a minimal show of politeness when those in power pretend that they do not really hold the power, and ask us to decide freely if we want to grant it to them.

Alain Badiou has proposed a distinction between two types (or rather levels) of corruption in democracy: the first, empirical corruption, is what we usually understand by the term, but the second pertains to the form of democracy per se, and the way it reduces politics to the negotiation of private interests. This distinction becomes visible in the (rare) case of an honest "democratic" politician who, while fighting empirical corruption, nonetheless sustains the formal space of the other

sort. (There is, of course, also the opposite case of the empirically cor-
rupted politician who acts on behalf of the dictatorship of Virtue.)

"If democracy means representation," Badiou writes in *The Meaning
of Sarkozy,* "it is first of all the representation of the general system that
bears its forms. In other words: electoral democracy is only representative in so far as it is first of all the consensual representation of capitalism, or of what today has been renamed the "market economy." This
is its underlying corruption." At the empirical level multi-party liberal
democracy "represents"—mirrors, registers, measures—the quantita-
tive dispersal of people's opinions, what they think about the parties'
proposed programs and about their candidates etc. However, in a more
radical, "transcendental" sense, multi-party liberal democracy "represents"—instantiates—a certain vision of society, politics and the role
of the individuals in it. Multi-party liberal democracy "represents" a
precise vision of social life in which politics is organized so that parties
compete in elections to exert control over the state legislative and executive apparatus. This transcendental frame is never neutral—it privileges
certain values and practices—and this becomes palpable in moments
of crisis or indifference, when we experience the inability of the democratic system to register what people want or think. In the UK elections
of 2005, for example, despite Tony Blair's growing unpopularity, there
was no way for this disaffection to find political expression. Something
was obviously very wrong here: it wasn't that people didn't know what
they wanted, but rather that cynicism, or resignation, prevented them
from acting.

This is not to say that democratic elections should be despised; the
point is only to insist that they are not in themselves an indication of
the true state of affairs; as a rule, they tend to reflect the predominant
doxa. Take an unproblematic example: France in 1940. Even Jacques
Duclos, the number two in the French Communist Party, admitted that
if, at that point in time, free elections had been held in France, Marshal
Pétain would have won with 90 percent of the vote. When De Gaulle
refused to acknowledge France's capitulation and continued to resist,

he claimed that only he, and not the Vichy regime, spoke on behalf of the true France (not, note, on behalf of the "majority of the French"). He was claiming to be speaking the truth even if it had no democratic legitimacy and was clearly opposed to the opinion of the majority of the French people. There *can* be democratic elections which enact a moment of truth: elections in which, against its sceptical-cynical inertia, the majority momentarily "awakens" and votes against the hegemonic opinion; however, that such elections are so exceptional shows that they are not as such a medium of truth.

It is democracy's authentic potential that is losing ground with the rise of authoritarian capitalism, whose tentacles are coming closer and closer to the West. The change always takes place in accordance with a country's values: Putin's capitalism with "Russian values" (the brutal display of power), Berlusconi's capitalism with "Italian values" (comical posturing). Both Putin and Berlusconi rule in democracies which are gradually being reduced to an empty shell, and, in spite of the rapidly worsening economic situation, they both enjoy popular support (more than two-thirds of the electorate). No wonder they are personal friends: each of them has a habit of "spontaneous" outbursts (which, in Putin's case, are prepared in advance in conformity with the Russian "national character"). From time to time, Putin likes to use a dirty word or utter an obscene threat. When, a couple of years ago, a Western journalist asked him an awkward question about Chechnya, Putin snapped back that, if the man wasn't yet circumcised, he was cordially invited to Moscow, where they have excellent surgeons who would cut a little more radically than usual.

Berlusconi is a significant figure, and Italy an experimental laboratory where our future is being worked out. If our political choice is between permissive-liberal technocratism and fundamentalist populism, Berlusconi's great achievement has been to reconcile the two, to embody both at the same time. It is arguably this combination which makes him unbeatable, at least in the near future: the remains of the Italian "left" are now resigned to him as their fate. This is perhaps the saddest aspect of his reign: his democracy is a democracy of those who win by default, who rule through cynical demoralisation.

Berlusconi acts more and more shamelessly: not only ignoring or neutralizing legal investigations into his private business interests, but behaving in such a way as to undermine his dignity as head of state. The dignity of classical politics stems from its elevation above the play of particular interests in civil society: politics is "alienated" from civil society, it presents itself as the ideal sphere of the *citoyen* in contrast to the conflict of selfish interests that characterise the *bourgeois*. Berlusconi has effectively abolished this alienation: in today's Italy, state power is directly exerted by the *bourgeois*, who openly exploits it as a means to protect his own economic interest, and who parades his personal life as if he were taking part in a reality TV show.

The last tragic US president was Richard Nixon: he was a crook, but a crook who fell victim to the gap between his ideals and ambitions on the one hand, and political realities on the other. With Ronald Reagan (and Carlos Menem in Argentina), a different figure entered the stage, a "Teflon" president no longer expected to stick to his electoral program, and therefore impervious to factual criticism (remember how Reagan's popularity went up after every public appearance, as journalists enumerated his mistakes). This new presidential type mixes "spontaneous" outbursts with ruthless manipulation.

The wager behind Berlusconi's vulgarities is that the people will identify with him as embodying the mythic image of the average Italian: I am one of you, a little bit corrupt, in trouble with the law, in trouble with my wife because I'm attracted to other women. Even his grandiose enactment of the role of the noble politician, *il cavaliere,* is more like an operatic poor man's dream of greatness. Yet we shouldn't be fooled: behind the clownish mask there is a state power that functions with ruthless efficiency. Perhaps by laughing at Berlusconi we are already playing his game. A technocratic economic administration combined with a clownish façade does not suffice, however: something more is needed. That something is fear, and here Berlusconi's two-headed dragon enters:

immigrants and "communists" (Berlusconi's generic name for anyone who attacks him, including the *Economist*).

Kung Fu Panda, the 2008 cartoon hit, provides the basic co-ordinates for understanding the ideological situation I have been describing. The fat panda dreams of becoming a kung fu warrior. He is chosen by blind chance (beneath which lurks the hand of destiny, of course), to be the hero to save his city, and succeeds. But the film's pseudo-Oriental spiritualism is constantly undermined by a cynical humor. The surprise is that this continuous making-fun-of-itself makes it no less spiritual: the film ultimately takes the butt of its endless jokes seriously. A well-known anecdote about Niels Bohr illustrates the same idea. Surprised at seeing a horseshoe above the door of Bohr's country house, a visiting scientist said he didn't believe that horseshoes kept evil spirits out of the house, to which Bohr answered: "Neither do I; I have it there because I was told that it works just as well if one doesn't believe in it!" This is how ideology functions today: nobody takes democracy or justice seriously, we are all aware that they are corrupt, but we practise them anyway because we assume they work even if we don't believe in them. Berlusconi is our own Kung Fu Panda. As the Marx Brothers might have put it, "this man may look like a corrupt idiot and act like a corrupt idiot, but don't let that deceive you—he *is* a corrupt idiot."

To get a glimpse of the reality beneath this deception, call to mind the events of July 2008, when the Italian government proclaimed a state of emergency in the whole of Italy as a response to the illegal entry of immigrants from North Africa and Eastern Europe. At the beginning of August, it made a show of deploying 4000 armed soldiers to control sensitive points in big cities (train stations, commercial centres and so on.) A state of emergency was introduced without any great fuss: life was to go on as normal. Is this not the state we are approaching in developed countries all around the world, where this or that form of emergency (against the terrorist threat, against immigrants) is simply accepted as a measure necessary to guarantee the normal run of things?

What is the reality of this state of emergency? On August 7, 2007, a crew of seven Tunisian fishermen dropped anchor 30 miles south of the island of Lampedusa off Sicily. Awakened by screams, they saw a rubber boat crammed with starving people—44 African migrants, as it turned out—on the point of sinking. The captain decided to bring them to the nearest port, at Lampedusa, where his entire crew was arrested. On 20 September, the fishermen went on trial in Sicily for the crime of "aiding and abetting illegal immigration." If convicted, they would get between one and 15 years in jail. Everyone agreed that the real point of this absurd trial was to dissuade other boats from doing the same: no action was taken against other fishermen who, when they found themselves in similar situations, apparently beat the migrants away with sticks, leaving them to drown. What the incident demonstrates is that Agamben's notion of *homo sacer*—the figure excluded from the civil order, who can be killed with impunity—is being realized not only in the US war on terror, but also in Europe, the supposed bastion of human rights and humanitarianism.

The formula of "reasonable anti-semitism" was best formulated in 1938 by Robert Brasillach, who saw himself as a "moderate" anti-semite:

> We grant ourselves permission to applaud Charlie Chaplin, a half Jew, at the movies; to admire Proust, a half Jew; to applaud Yehudi Menuhin, a Jew; and the voice of Hitler is carried over radio waves named after the Jew Hertz ... We don't want to kill anyone, we don't want to organize any pogroms. But we also think that the best way to hinder the always unpredictable actions of instinctual anti-semitism is to organise a reasonable anti-semitism.

Our governments righteously reject populist racism as "unreasonable" by our democratic standards, and instead endorse "reasonably" racist protective measures. "We grant ourselves permission to applaud African and Eastern European sportsmen, Asian doctors, Indian software programmers," today's Brasillachs, some of them social democrats, are telling us. "We don't want to kill anyone, we don't want to organize any pogroms. But we also think that the best way to hinder the always unpredictable, violent actions of the instinctual anti-immigrant is to organize reasonable anti-immigrant protection." A clear passage from direct barbarism to Berlusconian barbarism with a human face.

COUNTER-REVOLUTION AND REVOLT IN IRAN:
AN INTERVIEW WITH IRANIAN POLITICAL SCIENTIST HOSSEIN BASHIRIYEH

Danny Postel

June–August 2009

Hossein Bashiriyeh is one of post-revolutionary Iran's key political thinkers. Known as the father of political sociology in Iran, he has influenced both the study and practive of Iranian politics through his voluminous writings and his extensive teaching career at the University of Tehran (1983–2007). In 2006 President Ahmadinejad challenged Iran's university students to "scream" and ask, "Why are there liberal and secular professors in universities?" The following summer, Bashiriyeh was fired from the University of Tehran.

As the author of a classic study of the Iranian Revolution (The State and Revolution in Iran), *and given your recent comparative work on "transitional situations," what are your impressions of what's been happening in Iran in the aftermath of the June 12 presidential election? Some have argued that we are witnessing "a great emancipatory event" (Slavoj Žižek); "something quite extraordinary, perhaps even a social revolution" (Hamid Dabashi); a "velvet coup" (Anoush Ehteshami); "the final acts of a protracted war for the control of the Iranian economy" (Behzad Yaghmaian); even an attempt to "abolish the people" (Pepe Escobar). How would you characterize the situation?*

I think that the aftermath of the election constituted a catalyst for a potentially revolutionary situation facing a government caught in a number of crises. More specifically, it has signified a fatal crisis of cohesion and unity. Of course, the basically authoritarian electoral theocracy had been more or less experiencing a number of crises that have affected its bases of power. Generally speaking, ideological-authoritarian regimes may develop crises in the sphere of their ideological legitimacy, administrative efficiency, internal elite cohesion and coercive capacity. If all these crises occur at the same time, the situation may be described as revolutionary; out of these crises emerge the necessary ingredients for a political opposition, i.e. mass discontent, ideology, leadership and organization.

For a revolutionary situation to develop at least these eight factors are required: the four regime factors (crises) and the four revolutionary-movement factors. Obviously all these factors are dialectically interrelated and enhance each other. In the case of the Iranian regime before the election, I would say that a considerable degree of the first two crises had already come about, but the crisis of unity and cohesion had been contained since 2004, and there was no crisis of coercion or domination at all. I think that the aftermath of the election signified a quite unprecedented crisis of elite cohesion and unity, further intensifying the crises of legitimacy and efficiency. Never before had an internal rift caused such a large-scale mass mobilization of opposition.

In the specific case of the Iranian regime, a more or less chronic crisis of legitimacy had been caused by a number of factors and developments. Four major causes can be identified: (1) the rise of a more republican interpretation of the dominant Islamist ideology; (2) the contradictory nature of the constitution, in terms of seeking to combine theocratic and democratic principles of legitimacy; (3) an increasingly noticeable gap between ruling-class practice and its legitimizing ideals; and (4) a widening gap between public opinion and official ideology as a result of the increasing secularization of social values and attitudes. In any case, even if the elected offices may be said to be periodically legitimized by popular elections (although elections are controlled), the unelected offices are no doubt subject to an erosion of legitimacy as a result of the four factors I've outlined. As I will explain later, I think the grave crisis of cohesion and unity resulting from the June election has also actualized the underlying crisis of legitimacy.

In terms of a crisis of efficient management, I would argue that the Islamist government has suffered from a chronic crisis of efficiency throughout its rule; the more recent intensification of the crisis since 2005 has resulted from irregular and erratic economic policies and practices, political nepotism and general mismanagement. The adoption of a politically useful discourse of alms-based Islamic welfare policy by the fundamentalist faction in power has, according to expert views, caused economic disruption, inflation, recession and increased unemployment. Irregular redistributive policies, price intervention, and a reduction in interest rates have contributed to the critical situation. Obviously, in the absence of a crisis of cohesion and elite unity, economic problems may have no political outcomes, but as rifts develop within the regime, they may expand the possibility of political mobilization by opposition forces. However, in the actual mass political mobilization that occurred in the aftermath of the election, the motivating force was not the economic conditions, but rather what I consider to be a sense of political frustration and inefficacy, mainly on the part of the urban middle classes, who found that their vote and their political participation to be of no consequence in changing the political situation. The mass mobilization resulted from a gap between rising political expectations and the outcome of the election—a gap which has become very intolerable indeed.

But the real meaning of the aftermath of the June election seems to me to lie in the unprecedented intensification of a crisis of cohesion and unity. Such a crisis had emerged and persisted in the 1980s under Ayatollah Khomeini himself. But, as mentioned, never before 2009 had internal divisions led to such a mass political mobilization and massive repression. From the beginning, the Islamic state witnessed internal divisions over economic policy, the interpretation of Islamic law, emphasis on the Islamic versus republican nature of the constitution, and so on. In the 1980s two parties emerged: the Party of Tradition and the Party of Khomeinists; the former supported non-intervention in economic affairs and a traditionalist jurisprudence; the latter advocated economic intervention and redistribution, as well as a dynamic jurisprudence— but this division was contained as a result of Khomeini's arbitration.

Then in the early 1990s a new division emerged within the Party of Islamic Tradition itself, as the ruling elite under Rafsanjani sought to modernize the Islamic state and readjust it to the requirements of globalization. That internal division did not lead to popular mobilization, as the ruling elite succeeded in containing the rift as an internal affair. The division within the ruling parties and elites was intensified from 1997, when the old Khomeinists came to power and sought to democratize the Islamic state by augmenting its republican aspects. That division led to the political activation and mobilization of new middle classes, the rise of new parties, and violent confrontation. However, from 2004 the core clerical elite, led by the Supreme Leader's office, sought to minimize internal divisions by ousting the supporters of modernization and democratization from power and by creating new political formations and alliances, especially the Party of Fundamentalism (or Party of Principalists). The power bloc since 2004 has been occupied by an alliance of the fundamentalist and traditionalist-conservative parties to the detriment of the reformists. Given the controlled nature of popular elections in the country, the ruling factions have now sought to retain their positions by what the reformists regard as an electoral coup followed by repression. What is meant by an electoral coup is in fact a late "political abortion" or an "abortive coup" preventing the reformist baby from coming into life.

On the whole, I think developments since June 12 can be understood and explained in terms of a grave crisis of elite cohesion and unity, which has not been solved by arbitration as in previous episodes, but has been met with violence and repression. Generally, there is little doubt about the vital importance of internal divisions and opposition for change under ideological regimes such as the Islamic Republic, particularly in the absence of any organized external opposition. However, the issue of disunity has not led to a crisis of coercion and domination; there are no apparent rifts within the armed forces, no rival military force, and the ruling elite's will to power and repression seems to be intact. But crises of cohesion cause other problems for ideological regimes, such as further undermining regime legitimacy, paving the way for the organization of popular discontent, and providing leadership and ideology, the other necessary ingredients of a revolutionary situation.

At any rate, the aftermath of the June election can be understood in terms of the intensification of internal divisions and polarization between ruling factions. But unlike previous episodes, it has led to the mobilization of popular opposition on a very large scale. The highest degree of internal division in the regime's history has now been reached, causing polarization, confrontation and an expanding circle of "counter-revolution."

As you observe, never before in its thirty-year history had the Islamic Republic seen such mass political mobilization. Why is this happening now, in your view?

Obviously, mass mobilization or the mobilization of a large number of people for political purposes—especially in a polarized form and under an authoritarian regime—does not come about easily or frequently; it is only rarely and under exceptional circumstances that political leaders or parties succeed in calling people onto the streets in huge numbers, as happened for a few days following the June 12 election in Iran. Given this, we need to know what those exceptional circumstances and conditions are that make mass mobilization possible.

Since mass mobilization is a rare occurrence in the politics of authoritarian regimes, it follows that its outbreak cannot be explained by reference to "ordinary" situations prevailing under those regimes, such as economic problems and crises, government incapacity, general mass discontent, or political repression. Although these may constitute the eventual ingredients of the mobilization episode, the mobilization itself requires specific mechanisms in order to come about; it is through these mechanisms that those raw elements may be articulated. As the history of mass mobilization shows everywhere, the phenomenon is not a mechanical one, resulting from some "objectively" undesirable socio-economic and political conditions per se; it is the "subjective" channeling of those objective conditions which is the key element.

In general, three rather complementary theories have been advanced in order to explain why and how mass mobilization becomes possible: first, the theory that regards mass mobilization as a rare and exceptional psycho-social or existential condition which results from the development of an intolerable gap between popular expectations and the possibility of meeting them. From this psycho-social perspective, for example, persistent poverty or persistent prosperity do not lead to mass action; rather it is a dramatic shift from prosperity to poverty or from poverty to prosperity that creates the gap between expectations and the possibility of meeting them. According to this theory, the famous Davies' J-Curve, collective action may take place at the point where the gap is widest, or most intolerable. So the theoretical dispute concerning whether it is abject poverty or prosperity that leads to insurrection is thus resolved. Another major theoretical debate has been going on concerning whether mass collective action becomes possible in a mass society or in a society experiencing the development of a civil society; this dispute is similarly resolved in the theory of segmented civil society, according to which there is no possibility for mass political mobilization in a repressed mass society on the one hand, and there is no need for such a mobilization in a fully grown and developed civil society, on the other; so it is under conditions of segmented civil societies that mass mobilization of the type we have witnessed in Iran may come about. A third, political, theory relates the possibility of mass action and mobilization to internal ruling elite disunity. In the specific case of Iran in June 2009, a combination of these three factors made possible the large-scale mobilization of the people.

First, an intolerable gap resulted from rising expectations before the election and violent repression after the election. The result was public indignation and anger on an unprecedented scale. Obviously, the rising expectations were political in nature, not economic (as in the theory mentioned above). For a few weeks, a large, mainly urban, middle-class-based socio-political movement emerged around the two reformist candidates, Mousavi and Karoubi, mobilizing a large segment of the population in the name of the Green Movement for reform and change. The period of the electoral campaign was marked by festivities, public discussions and gatherings, heated debates, hopeful projections for change, intriguing TV debates between presidential candidates, popular excitement, relative freedom of the press, critique of government performance, political publicity and propaganda, and the reactivation of political groupings and parties.

As the unexpected election results were announced, the atmosphere changed completely and a mood of public despair and anger replaced the exuberant mood of hope and expectation. The focus on a single issue—the rigging of the election—polarized the population, leading to mass street demonstrations against the manipulation at the polls. The first week after the election witnessed the height of the gap mentioned above. The leaders of the movement were also successful in concentrating on the single issue of fraudulence. The second week, however, witnessed a rather different situation, as the Supreme Leader in his Friday prayers endorsed the offical election results and vowed to suppress any further street demonstrations. On the whole, the gap resulting from rising political expectations and the anger and disappointment caused by the manipulation of the election inspired the mass mobilizations which have had no precedent during the thirty years of Islamic rule in Iran. In the weeks since, however, the sense of anger has been gradually replaced by a sense of fear, as the security forces have shown no sign of mercy in ruthlessly crushing any public gathering or demonstration.

Regarding the second factor—the civil society versus mass society debate—I would argue that developments during the so-called reconstruction period from 1989 to 1997, as well as the reform period from 1997 to 2005, paved the way, to a certain degree, for a slow transition from mass society to a segmented civil society. The emergence of civil associations, independent student organizations, associations of writers and journalists, a rather independent press and increasing independence of arts and culture from government control were all signs of this transition from mass to civil society, albeit in a circumscribed way. A number of similar (though much more limited) collective actions and mass protests had already occurred during the reconstruction and reform periods (like the uprisings in Islamshahr, Qazvin and Mashad, and the 1999 student uprising known as 18 Tir), but the recent mass mobilization was very different in nature, scope, intensity of government reaction, and particularly in terms of its consequences in disclosing the real character of the political system for the majority of the people. The violent confrontation took place on a mass scale, the lines of division between the government and the public opposition were clearly drawn, and a state of disillusion came about. On the other hand, it seems that the civil-society base of the mass mobilization was not wide or strong enough to sustain the opposition movement—though the role of political repression has been much more decisive in this regard.

Finally, the widening divisions within the ruling elite and the popular awareness thereof were highly effective in generating the public outburst. Internal disunity took place on a number of levels: first, despite sharp differences between the ruling fundamentalists and the contending reformists, the reformist candidates had been approved by the Council of Guardians, and the reformists obviously confirmed their allegiance to the constitution and the theocratic system. All this (apparently) provided a margin of safety for the public to come out on the streets and demonstrate in large numbers. In this way, they were supporting some of the candidates and political figures who had, presumably, been endorsed by the core clerical elite.

At a second level, emerging signs of division between the fundamentalist faction in power and the traditionalist-conservative parties within the power bloc (especially between Rafsanjani and the fundamentalists) generated the expectation (or perhaps the illusion) that the traditionalist-conservative clerics would actively support the Green

Movement; so the perception was that the movement enjoyed the tacit support of some conservative parties who had become disenchanted with the economic and foreign policies of the ruling fundamentalist faction. And finally, on a third level, signs of some emerging divisions *within* the ruling fundamentalist faction, in parliament and outside, and reluctance on the part of many fundamentalist MPs to support the current president's candidacy, might have provided further encouragement for the supporters of the opposition movement. Of course, following the announcement of the election results, and with increasing polarization of attitudes, some of those more secondary rifts would disappear as the conservative and traditionalist parties rushed to support the government and the position of the Supreme Leader at a time of deep crisis that threatened the very existence of the Islamic regime.

On the whole, although such an occasion for mass mobilization had been dreamt of by the external and even internal opposition groups for a long time, it had not been planned in any way; rather, it was the result of a rare political conjuncture—as is the case with almost all revolutionary situations.

At a recent panel discussion, the sociologist Ahmad Sadri argued that we are witnessing the "beginning of the end of the Islamic Republic." Do you agree?

In order to begin to think about any breakdown, we need to know the consequences of the recent crisis and confrontation for the political system; that is, we need to ask what difference the recent developments have made to the regime in terms of the eight various analytical factors I laid out earlier. The consequences of the recent crisis and confrontation are manifold, and we need to assess the durability of the government in terms of these consequences.

My general argument has been that if the political system had previously experienced any sort of crisis, it is now intensified and has gone through a qualitative change. In terms of ideological legitimacy, the preexisting deficit has now become a first-degree crisis of legitimacy. From its inception, the Islamic Republic claimed to be at least partly based in popular support and consent; one could argue that in the conception of the Islamic Republic, the noun "Republic" is more essential than the adjective "Islamic." Elections have been held regularly, and even the Supreme Leaders have considered elections and popular participation a major basis of the political system. Of course, as we know, elections in the Islamic Republic are restricted in the sense that all candidates in all elections have to be declared qualified by the Council of Guardians, which is the legislative arm of the Supreme Leader. In any case, according to the opposition, which enjoys a mass following, even the institutionally restricted elections have not been respected by the regime itself.

During the June election, all four candidates had been endorsed by the Council of Guardians and indirectly by the Supreme Leader, yet popular support for the two reformist candidates has increasingly been regarded by the regime as counter-revolutionary, and as we have seen, peaceful protesters have been beaten and crushed for legally protesting against the official election results. In the eyes of supporters of the mass Green Movement, they had done nothing except legally protest against the election results, but they were treated ruthlessly and violently. The Council of Guardians itself admitted, on the basis of a partial recount, that some three million votes had been manipulated. If a full recount had been allowed, perhaps the allegations of the reformist candidates would have been fully corroborated. The Supreme Leader's endorsement of the official election results—even before the partial recount, which he himself allowed—caused the sense of illegitimacy to spread, in the eyes of the protesters and opposition, from the government to the entire political system.

Furthermore, the Supreme Leader's rather explicit permission for the ruthless suppression of any demonstrations, and their actual violent suppression, further intensified the crisis and deficit of legitimacy. If previously there was a second- or even third-degree crisis of legitimacy, in the sense that the policies of the government had faced popular objection, the recent turn of events have caused a first-degree crisis of legitimacy to come about, throwing into question the legitimacy of the entire system.

Therefore, in terms of legitimacy, the recent confrontation has had several consequences. Firstly, it has somewhat exposed or uncovered the nature of the power structure. The Supreme Leader had long been regarded (at least by the politically uninformed or misinformed) as being neutral in factional rivalries, standing above the various factions like an impartial judge. This illusion was shattered by the Leader himself when he announced that he had personal political preferences and would support the current government at any price. Previously, there was a disagreement concerning the role and position of the Supreme Leader. Some political activists and commentators regarded him as politically weak or impartial. Accordingly, he did not have a base of social support for himself, despite his great institutional powers, and so he had to adjust to the policies of whatever president was in power (Rafsanjani from 1989 to 1997 and Khatami from 1997 to 2005). But, in fact, he had been trying to uphold his own power and position. This had not been possible during the presidencies of Rafsanjani or Khatami, but Khamenei eventually emerged as the architect of a fundamentalist alternative to reform and democratization after 2004 by encouraging the formation of the fundamentalist bloc, which won various elections in 2003, 2004, 2005, 2008 and 2009.

So the Leader's own pronouncements and actions demonstrated that he was the core figure and the real coordinator. In terms of legitimacy, however, this was not in his self-interest, as he removed all the mists of illusion and put himself in direct confrontation with the popular opposition. In a superficial sense, which is very meaningful in the history of modern Iran, he was moving from a constitutional to an absolutist sort of *velayat* (rule). So, on the whole, the recent confrontation has made the power structure of the regime more transparent for the general public.

A second consequence of the recent crisis and confrontation is going to be a growing concern among the ruling cliques about the disruptive nature of elections and high popular participation. Elections will be considered disruptive, and mass participation in elections will not be seen as an advantage for the regime. If this is going to be the case, then the legitimacy of the regime will be further undermined.

Thirdly, and in a parallel way, the people can be expected to lose their belief in the value of voting and political participation, which is yet another factor in the erosion of political legitimacy. In this way the electoral aspect of the theocracy is going to be discredited from both directions, and the regime will have to rely more heavily on the undemocratic or clerical-aristocratic aspect of the system.

A fourth outcome of the recent confrontation, which should be taken into account in any assessment of the future course of events, is the expansion of the circle of "counter-revolution." Some hardliners are already talking about the "new hypocrites," a throwback reference to the Mujahideen-e-Khalq, or MKO, which was ousted from the political arena in the early years of the revolution and which was labeled as the "party of hypocrites." I think the most important impact of the current upheaval and confrontation (which again has to be reckoned with in any projection of the future) is the increasing disappearance of the feeling of fear, which has been the main basis of the political order. The hallmark of current developments is a feeling of courage to express long pent-up grievances. As a rule, both on an individual as well as a social level, anger kills fear. The government did everything it could, in the span of a few weeks, to make the general public angry, frustrated and desperate. The "counting" of the votes, the humiliating arrogance, the intimidation, the brutality, the detentions, the violent repression, and so on, caused widespread anger and indignation. If all the pent-up grievances had been suppressed for years due to fear, now the anger caused by imprudent government action is paving the way for a catharsis.

Authoritarian regimes usually attempt to compensate for the loss of ideological legitimacy either by resorting to more coercive and repressive measures or by turning to more public welfare services. In the case of Iran after June 2009, the coercive dimension or base of the regime has expanded as a compensation for the legitimacy deficit. This in itself denotes a transformation in the character or type of the regime, which is becoming more militaristic; the armed forces now utilize a militaristic language in reference to the opposition movement. This tendency is of vital significance for the future course of developments, if the political system is to remain in place. Given the prevailing economic situation mentioned above, as well as the limited managerial capability of the government, there is little chance of success for any attempt to compensate for the loss of legitimacy through the expansion of the public sector and provision of welfare; indeed, the system had already been suffering from a crisis of efficient management.

Out of the four main bases of regime stability—legitimacy, efficiency, elite unity and coercive capacity—it seems that only the latter has remained functioning, at least for the time being. The unity of the ruling elites of the Islamic Republic has also been somewhat damaged. To be sure, factionalism, as discussed above, had always existed among the ruling elites. Interventionism versus non-interventionism, socio-economic modernization versus adherence to tradition, and Islamization versus democratization have been some of the major points of contention in the life of the Islamic Republic over the last thirty years. But in a sense, all these cleavages and rifts had been non-antagonistic; the significance of the recent confrontation is that it has turned non-antagonistic divisions and rifts into antagonistic ones. Several moderate and reformist parties which had been regarded as members of the family of the Revolution are now being castigated as counter-revolutionary. The unity of the ruling elites is being damaged as antagonistic rifts are emerging, firstly between reformist and fundamentalist parties, secondly within the clerical institutions, and thirdly within the military elite. More indications of increasingly antagonistic rifts are emerging every day.

It seems that the reformist parties are not to be tolerated anymore, as hundreds of party leaders and members are being detained and imprisoned. They are already disqualified as illegitimate and counter-revolutionary parties; in fact, it seems that political party activity will become meaningless in the emerging power structure. So the reformist parties will definitely find themselves in an entirely different situation and consequently will have to adopt new positions, if they can continue to exist at all. The Participation Front has been hit the hardest. There are also some indications of growing division within the clergy associated with the Supreme Leader and the more independent-minded clerics in Qom, who have tacitly or explicitly opposed the crackdown. There are even some signs of division within the Revolutionary Guards. In the early years there were some differences of opinion between the commanders of the western and southern war fronts; following the crackdown, an open letter was written by a number of older commanders to the Supreme Leader, questioning his endorsement of the election results before a full investigation had taken place and the violent repression of the protest demonstrations. Still it seems that the regime's point of strength lies in its coercive capacity and the unity of its coercive forces at a time when the legitimacy of the political system is coming under question. So, in responding to your question, the strengths and weaknesses of the regime should be taken into account.

Likewise, we need to take into account the state of the opposition movement, its strengths and weaknesses. We need to consider the four factors in relation to the opposition movement that has erupted. In analyzing socio-political opposition movements, as already mentioned, we need to examine the state of mass discontent, the organizational network, the ideology and the leadership of the movement. Concerning popular discontent, historical experience shows that potential mass dissatisfaction and discontent in authoritarian regimes becomes effective when made actual through a specific catalyst. Socio-economic and cultural discontent must become politicized to have political effects. What politicized all the pre-existing potential discontents was the issue of election fraud as alleged by the opposition candidates supported by a large popular movement. We have already explained why and how public anger and indignation was produced as a result of government actions. Now all the grievances began finding a political focus or epicenter. The annulment of the election was the first public request, but as the mass demonstrations were followed by intimidation and suppression, a new cause for anger and frustration was added to the initial one, now targeting the leadership of the Islamic Republic. The steam of general public discontent, as it were, was now finding a political engine. Thus public discontent was being organized into a specific public demand. As we have seen, public discontent without organization and mobilization leads to nothing. In terms of organization, a quite adequate organizational network (including the electoral headquarters, student organizations, electronic means of communication, the Internet and so on) has emerged, and it has proved capable of providing the necessary rudimentary functions. Of course, the organizational capability of oppositions has a converse relation to the coercive capacity of regimes. In our case so far, government coercion has almost demolished the organizational capability of the opposition, but things are not going to remain as they are now. For one thing, the organizational capacity of the opposition is a function of its leadership. A number of people have emerged as leaders, but, as usually happens in such situations, moderate leaders will be gradually replaced with more radical ones. So far Mousavi, Karoubi and Khatami have led the movement very cautiously and moderately, while Ayatollah Montazeri has issued a very significant statement justifying public rebellion against the theocratic system, claiming that the regime is essentially already deposed because of its unjust and cruel treatment of the protesters. The gradual replacement of moderate leadership by more radical figures would also mean an escalation in the ideology of the movement, from questioning the election results to questioning the very legitimacy of the whole power structure.

So two factors stand out as decisive in the outcome of the turmoil: the coercive capacity of the government and its ability and readiness to use it; and the leadership of the movement and its ability and readiness to redefine its ideological objectives and enhance its organizational capability.

Speaking of the leadership of the movement, some have questioned whether it really has any. What do you make of this? Is Mousavi the movement's leader, or is he being led by the movement? To the extent that the movement has a horizontal or decentralized structure, do you view this as a weakness or a strength—or neither? And what does this all portend for the movement's prospects?

Usually, leaders of revolutionary or oppositional movements can be classified into three main types: ideologues, mobilizers/orators and managers. Sometimes all the three types may merge into a single leader, but most of the time different leaders represent the various types. Ayatollah Khomeini was both an ideologue and a mobilizer/orator, but the management of the movement was left to local leaders, as he was in exile at the time. Lenin turned out to be a combination of the three types, as was Mao. In the case of today's Green Movement in Iran, the role of leadership is not concentrated in one person, so the three leadership functions are not performed. There is no ideological leader, in the sense of grand ideological schemes; it is more of a democratic than an "ideological" movement. The aspirations of the movement are clear enough, and some of them can even be traced back to the current Islamic Constitution. Statements and pronouncements issued by Mousavi and Karoubi as well as some high-ranking clerics such as Montazeri, Saanei and Kadivar clearly indicate the movement's ideological aims.

Oppositional ideologies can be offensive or defensive in posture. Revolutionary movements usually require an offensive ideology, projecting a completely different or novel socio-political order and structure, whereas defensive ideologies usually present public grievances or complain about the encroachment of the regime upon the rights of the subject population. Defensive ideologies and ideological leaderships are usually characteristics of "revolts" rather than revolutions; peasant revolts, tax revolts, bread riots and aristocratic rebellions are usually based on a defensive ideology. We could call Iran's Green Movement an "electoral fraud revolt." The religious revolt or rebellion of 1963 against the shah's policies, led by Ayatollah Khomeini, was a defensive revolt; it attempted to safeguard the constitution against the modernizing autocratic tendencies of the shah. In a sense, the current Green Movement is rather similar to the 1963 revolt, in that it is similarly a protest against autocratic and militaristic tendencies and repressive policies in the name of the existing constitution (although the repression now is much more brutal than it was then). Ayatollah Khomeini had similarly asked for the proper implementation of the constitution. But a defensive movement or revolt can turn into a revolutionary movement, as was the case with the Puritan Revolution in England and the American Revolution. I think that the Green Movement can resurrect the ideals of the Constitutional Revolution of 1906, as well as the aspirations of the early phase of the revolution of 1979. And this would be good enough, as the most fundamental political conflict and cleavage in Iran since the end of the nineteenth century has been that between autocracy (whether royal or clerical) and democracy/popular sovereignty. To become more offensive, however, the ideology needs to be differentiated from the dominant theocratic tendency in the constitution, and this is what the current oppositional leadership seems to be rather reluctant to propose.

More recently, however, the office of the Supreme Leader has come under attack for engaging in repressive and illegal acts. Two open letters reportedly issued by the Association of Previous Majles (Parliament) Deputies and the Association of Qom Religious Teachers and Clerics have blamed the Supreme Leader for what has transpired since June 12 and have declared him incompetent to continue as the Supreme Leader according to the constitution. They have called on the clerical Assembly of Experts to reconsider the leader's competence for leadership. If the Assembly of Experts could gain some independence from the office of the Supreme Leader and could represent the clergy at large and exert control over that office, the democratic aspect of the theocracy would be greatly enhanced. In that case, the independent members of the clergy could emerge as the main leadership group in a would-be transition from absolutist theocracy to constitutional theocracy, or even to a pure and simple democracy.

With regard to the second function—mobilization—given the state of repression, the current opposition leadership is severely restricted. The existing, rather weak civil society associations have been further repressed and restricted. There is an obvious connection between repression and mobilization: with increasing repression, the chances for mass mobilization decrease, as the cost of political activity rises, while less repression, or more toleration—or at least vacillation—on the part of the regime encourages mass action. In the case of Ayatollah Khomeini and his close associates in the 1978–9 revolution, political mobilization was facilitated by the fact that they were in exile and could easily call on the people to rise against the regime and risk their lives in the face of repression. But the current oppositional leadership does not enjoy the same immunity. They are not ready to go to the extreme in the face of severe repression. Finally, the managerial structure of the leadership is not tightly knit together, again because of repression. As a rule, opposition leaderships in revolutionary movements gain decisive importance and roles under two types of conditions: first, when the state has more or less lost its monopoly on the use of the means of violence (as in the case of the English, Chinese, Cuban and Nicaraguan Revolutions), and second, when the regime is in a state of vacillation and hesitation vis-à-vis the use of violence, and as a result the opposition gets the opportunity to mobilize (as in the case of the 1979 Iranian Revolution). As we have already seen, revolutions do not take place merely because there is mass discontent, a large opposition movement, and a revolutionary ideology and leadership. They still do not take place even if, in addition to all that, the regime suffers from severe crises of legitimacy, efficiency and unity. What usually sounds the death knell for authoritarian regimes is a crisis of coercion and domination. Obviously, a strong and ideologically-dedicated leadership can contribute to such a crisis of domination and coercion by constantly enticing the public in the face of severe repression and by resorting to all forms of political campaign.

Finally, under the current circumstances I think that the rise of a dissident cleric, such as Montazeri, at the head of the movement, could make a great deal of difference in terms of political mobilization and the realignment of political forces and actors.

Several parallels have been drawn between the present events and those of 1978–9, the most obvious being the mass street demonstrations and the echoes of "Allah-u-akbar." In fact, during the revolution of three decades ago it took much longer—many months—for the crowds to grow to the size we saw within a matter of days in June 2009. On the other hand, some argue emphatically that this is not a revolutionary movement or situation, pointing to the fact that the "Green Wave" phenomenon is bound up with the presidential candidacy of a figure (Mousavi) who was operating within the framework of the Islamic Republic. How do you view this? As a scholar of the 1979 Revolution, do you see parallels between the two moments?

It seems to me that the current confrontation may well turn into a thoroughly revolutionary situation, given the intensity of popular anger and frustration and the humiliating way the government has responded to it. But there are, as always, both similarities and differences between the two historical situations. In any case, there is no need for the current confrontation to be an exact replica of 1979 in order to turn into a revolutionary situation; it may do so on its own merits.

Now we can elaborate on the similarities and differences in terms of the several theoretical criteria we have already used to explain the nature of the situation. So first, in terms of a crisis of legitimacy, it seems that the Islamic regime has been depleting its own legitimacy from within by violating its own rules. The reformist candidates were allowed to stand for election, but then peaceful protests on the part of their supporters regarding the disputed results were violently and brutally suppressed. The shah's regime at the time was facing the opposition of an outside contender in Khomeini, one who would normally be repressed by an authoritarian regime. So for such a regime, the shah's repression could seem more "normal" (norms of repression) than the Islamic regime's repression, as it is repressing an opposition which is an insider, or part of the family, as some say. From another perspective, legitimacy also has something to do with longevity and durability; the imperial monarchy had been in place for 2,500 years, whereas Islamic theocracy has been around for only thirty years. Obviously, the institution of Persian monarchy had been in a state of crisis since the late nineteenth century, leading to the Constitutional Revolution (1906–11), which provided a criterion for gauging the legitimacy of the system, i.e. the shah was to reign and not rule, and the breach of the constitution in this regard was a sure sign of the royal government's crisis of legitimacy.

A similar argument has been developed in the case of the Islamic Republic, in the sense that the Sovereign Theologian (or Supreme Leader) should stand above factional conflicts. However, there is a great deal of difference between the constitutions of 1906 and of 1979 in that the latter is evidently not constitutionalist but absolutist: there is no real separation of powers and the Ruling Jurist (or Supreme Leader) has supremacy over the three branches of government. So we cannot speak of a deficit of legitimacy only in this very technical and restricted sense, since the Ruling Theologian both reigns and rules. On the other hand, this in itself is obviously in contradiction to the ideals of a popular revolution, which was supposed to restrict the power of the ruler, and it points to the more general and historical problem of legitimacy as far as the theocracy is concerned. But there is a more mundane sense of a legitimation crisis experienced by the general run of the people, and that is felt when, instead of persuasion, force is used to keep a people in its place. This is exactly the meaning of the crisis of legitimacy as it is unfolding, and the situation has become grave.

A clear difference between the two historical situations is to be found in the rulers' will to repression. The shah's regime, after an initial period of suppression, lost its will to power and gradually shifted to a policy of moderation, toleration and compromise: the shah's hearing of the message of the revolution, the negotiations with the National Front, the Bakhtiar regime, the Paris negotiations, the Shah's flight and so on. Apparently, the Carter human rights policy and US pressure (in the context of differences of interest and opinion between Washington and Tehran following the oil embargo of 1973) had something to do with the loss of the will to repression. But so far the Islamic regime's will to repression has remained firm, though maybe it is still too early to judge, given the circular nature of demonstrations and protests taking place every now and then, in a fashion reminiscent of the events of 1978. In terms of US–Iran relations, it seems that the current administration's approach may have contributed to the will to suppression.

The decline or continuation of the will to suppression is partly a result of the state of unity within the ruling group; in the case of the shah's regime, elite unity was in a sense damaged by the Carter human rights policy, and the shah vacillated between repression and relative toleration. As we have already seen, some major signs of division within the ruling elite of the Islamic Republic are also emerging. Once begun, such divisions and rifts are hard to contain; they tend to escalate and drag all political actors into the abyss. Hence the current confrontation seems increasingly to be creating a revolutionary situation.

Differences also exist in terms of the nature of the opposition. In terms of popular discontent, a similar pattern has occurred, a pattern I have already explained in terms of the J-Curve theory. In the case of the Shah's regime, a long period of economic stability and growth from 1962 to 1976 was followed by a sharp reversal and downturn, creating an intolerable gap between popular expectations and government capabilities. In the case of the Islamic Republic, the same pattern has come about, albeit with a different content, which is not economic but political: a long period of moderation and relative toleration under Rafsanjani and Khatami from 1989 to 2005 (the post-Khomeini period) was followed by a sharp reversal and downturn under the militaristic-fundamentalist regime of Ahmadinejad. The specter of its repetition in June 2009 caused widespread fear, anger and dread, and led to the confrontation.

In terms of ideology, it seems that the current confrontation is more specific in nature than was the case with the slogan of "Islamic Republic" in 1978–9. Indeed, its specificity makes it non-revolutionary, since, at least as far as the top leaders are concerned, its aim is to annul the disputed election. However, as with the early phase of the 1978–9 revolution, the moderate opposition was calling for the implementation of the constitution and a constitutional monarchy. Obviously, it was the leadership of Ayatollah Khomeini which made the difference, calling for a complete revolution—something the reformist leaders have not been willing to take up; the most they have called for so far is a referendum to endorse or annul the election results, which has to be sanctioned by the leaders of the Islamic Republic.

So, on the whole, it seems that some of the ingredients of a revolutionary situation have already come about, but some others have not (yet) materialized.

What do you make of the responses of certain leftists in the Western hemisphere to the events unfolding in Iran? James Petras defended the official election results and dismissed any doubts about their authenticity as an imperialist "hoax." MRZine (the online organ of the venerable socialist magazine Monthly Review*) openly defended Ahmadinejad as an anti-imperialist. Hugo Chávez has embraced Ahmadinejad as a "revolutionary" ally. The Foreign Ministry of Venezuela even denounced the Iranian street demonstrations in the following words:*

> *The Bolivarian Government of Venezuela expresses its firm opposition to the vicious and unfounded campaign to discredit the institutions of the Islamic Republic of Iran, unleashed from outside, designed to roil the political climate of our brother country. From Venezuela, we denounce these acts of interference in the internal affairs of the Islamic Republic of Iran, while demanding an immediate halt to the maneuvers to threaten and destabilize the Islamic Revolution.*

But there also have been strong critical responses from others on the left to such statements—those of Reese Erlich, Hamid Dabashi, Saeed Rahnema, the Campaign for Peace and Democracy, and others. What is your impression of these contending positions?

Such unfavorable reactions to the popular movement in Iran are not hard to explain. I think they result from three factors: first, ignorance of and misinformation about the nature of the political system in Iran since the Revolution, including the various historical phases it has gone through and the widening gap between official ideology and public opinion, particularly the rapid secularization of society under the theocracy; such regimes end up being more popular among some foreigners than among their own people. Secondly, these reactions result from financial and commercial self-interest and the special favorable commercial relations Iran has with some of the countries mentioned; obviously, they think more of their own national interests than the interests of the Iranian people. In my opinion, analyses resulting from such positions and interests are not much worth discussing from an academic point of view. Ideological regimes tend to create their own satellites or close friends, who obviously endorse their policies and actions. Here we can add Islamist parties and organizations in the Arab world and their ideological/commercial ties with the Islamic Republic. Thirdly, such analyses result from the analysts' attachment to and use of obsolete theoretical and conceptual frameworks, divorced from current developments (what Ulrich Beck calls "zombie categories"); as a result, they accept demagogical positions at face value and confuse fascism with socialism.

In the leftist responses you have mentioned, I think that their authors have forgotten all about the democratic dimensions of Marxism and have fallen prey to demagogy in this case. They sometimes forget that the extreme right and the extreme left look deceptively similar. In the case of Venezuela, a combination of pseudo-leftist appraisals and commercial interests have been at work. The Venezuelan government knows nothing about the political situation and public opinion in Iran,

which is increasingly turning against the foreign allies of the Islamic
Republic. Russia's support has already brought about chants of "Death
to Russia" from protesters on the streets of Tehran.

Regarding more theoretical responses, I would say that the type of
long-term class analysis applicable to the case of Iran is very different
from the type of class analysis usually applied in a short-term sense.
From a long-term historical perspective, the main social conflict has
been taking place not among the social classes belonging to one social
formation, but between those belonging to two social formations: pre-
modern and modern. The historical meaning of various political developments in Iran should be understood in terms of this underlying
conflict: the Constitutional Revolution signified the victory of the social
classes of the modern formation over the social forces of the traditional/
pre-modern formation. In its own peculiar way, the absolutist state
structure of the Pahlavi regime further strengthened the modern social
formation (albeit in the framework of modernization from above under
a dictatorship). The traditional social forces made a comeback after the
revolution of 1979 and imposed the traditional political-cultural pattern
of elitism, authoritarianism, patrimonialism and cultural order, discipline and obedience under the rule of a theocracy. With the subsequent
development of the modern formation and its social forces, advocating
the ideas of citizenship, political equality, democracy, popular sovereignty and socio-cultural freedom (as partly seen in the Green Movement), the underlying contradiction between the world of coercively
reconstructed tradition and the democratic path is bound to come to a
head, as we are witnessing now.

PART II

BEYOND "WHERE IS MY VOTE?"— A GREEN VISION TAKES SHAPE

THE KEY FEATURES OF THE GREEN MOVEMENT:
AN INTERVIEW WITH DISSIDENT CLERIC MOHSEN KADIVAR

Rooz Online

August 31, 2009

Mohsen Kadivar is a philosopher, theologian, and dissident. Born in Iran in 1959, he obtained the certificate of *Ijtihad* (the highest level in Islamic Studies) from Grand Ayatollah Hossein Ali Montazeri at the Qom Seminary in 1997 and his Ph.D. in Islamic Philosophy and Theology from Tarbiat Modarres University in Tehran in 1999. Kadivar has authored 13 books (in Persian and Arabic) and over 50 articles in Islamic studies (philosophy, theology, jurisprudence and political thought). Kadivar's writings on the theology of freedom in Islam has been sharply critical of the doctrine of *velayat-e faqih* (rule of the Islamic jurist), which he has argued is an innovation in Shia political thought instituted in Iran by Ayatollah Khomeini in 1979. This controversial theory places temporal and spiritual power in the hands of the most qualified religious scholar. Kadivar, together with an increasing number of religious scholars in Iran, have questioned the religious authenticity of this form of autocratic rule. In 1999, Kadivar was convicted by the Special Court for Clergy for his writings and sentenced to eighteen months in prison on charges of having spread false information about Iran's "sacred system of the Islamic Republic" and of helping enemies of the Islamic revolution. He is currently a Visiting Research Professor in the Department of Religion at Duke University. The following interview was conducted by *Rooz Online* (www.roozonline.com) a popular pro-democracy and reformist website.[1]

Prior to the June 12 elections, there was a debate whether one should vote or not. In retrospect, and in view of what has happened, do you view the current situation we are in to be the result of mass participation in the vote?

What has happened in Iran is both good and bad. But overall, I think any reasonable man will conclude that the benefits outweigh the negatives for the Iranian nation.

And people were not prepared for the negatives.

Yes, people did not think they would be asking, "Where is my vote?" or that the state would shoot at demonstrators.

Let's diverge from the subject of the interview for a moment and look at the nature of the state in dealing with people who have protested in the past. People like the cleric Mesbah Yazdi have said that sexually abusing twelve-year-old boys and girls is not a problem when they have challenged the Islamic state, and there are individuals who not only shoot at the children of this land, but aim for their head and heart. This is pre-meditated murder. What are the roots of such views and violence?

I have not heard Mr. Mesbah say this and doubt he would, because this is against all the foundations of the Sharia, ethics and humanity. In Islam we do not even accept such behavior against infidels. About violence, the fact is that the situation faced by the current despotic system is similar to a spider's web—when one thread is broken, the whole system crumbles. Millions have said that the person who was announced the winner of the election was not the one we voted for. The state engages in violence to protect its position of power. Protests take place all over the world, but the order to shoot people is given only by the highest authority in every country. Such an order is not issued by any police agent, head of a police station or by a paramilitary person. And this is how it used to be prior to 17 Shahrivar ["Black Friday," September 8, 1978].

So one must ask who gave the order to fire to these inexperienced and simple individuals. Regardless of who he is, he bears the biggest responsibility to God and to this nation.

In Iran, the supreme commander is Mr. Khamenei.

When they claim that he has absolute authority, then he certainly has absolute responsibility as well. Legally and from a religious perspective, the supreme authority is accountable.

Let's return to the elections. What would have happened in the elections if people had not voted?

The state's choice would have easily prevailed and things would have continued as they have during the last four years. People participated and disrupted all these plans. The cheaters did not think this would be the outcome. They thought that people would protest for a few days and then calm down. They did not think that the candidates and their supporters would insist on their demands. They did not expect it and so resorted to violence against them.

So of the two choices, you support the people's participation in the election?

Precisely. The majority of Iranians are not happy about the current domestic, foreign, cultural and economic policies being pursued and they want change. People are not after a revolution because that is very costly and its outcome is uncertain. So they have chosen to pursue their demands peacefully, through reforms and other legal methods. They participated in the elections to change the state of affairs. However, the rulers say that people are ignorant and that they do not really understand their interests. They argue that they have been appointed by God and His representative to rule over this mass of people. We know their interests better than they do. The principal fight now is between the people and the state. People say, "We understand," while the leader of the regime says, "No, I know better," and that his choice must become the president.

From the state emerged the coup, and from the people came the Green Movement. What are the features of the movement?

It depends on how you look at it. If you look at what has been said and published in the last two or three months, you will see that every person sees himself as a supporter of the Green Movement. So it has countless guardians, including those who did not vote. Now that this movement is getting somewhere, those who abstained from voting say we have been saying these things for the last thirty years. They too wear the green band.

What is the relationship between the Green Movement inside the country and the outside world?

There are some four million Iranians living abroad, including students who have only recently left Iran for study as well as third generation Iranians who hardly speak Persian. Just like those inside Iran, they are pure, shining and green, and they do not say anything more radical than what the people inside Iran are saying. Their goal is to tell the world exactly what those inside Iran are saying. We have no issues with them and I kiss their hands. If they were inside Iran, they would be no different than the youth who are there now. There is of course another group that is still caught in the views of twenty or thirty years ago. But the Green Movement as a group is critical of what the officials of the Islamic Republic have been doing; they have a foundational criticisms. The Green Movement has a clear difference with the Royalists. And just as the Green Movement abhors religious despotism, it also detests American agents. It has a clear demarcation with the Mujahideen-e Khalq organization. These are the people who in the past held a hand of friendship with

Saddam Hussein, a sworn enemy of the Iranian people, and who along with him launched a war against Iran. They are opportunistically trying to connect themselves to the Green Movement; they want to hijack it. If they really want to do something for the Iranian people, they should be supportive of them. Some of them have come to the conclusion that they must stay with the Iranian people. But one must clearly know that the leadership of the Green Movement is inside Iran and that these people cannot have a decisive role in this.

So what are the main features of the movement?

These are foremost in the statements and positions that have been announced by those who have gained the votes of the people: first of all Mir-Hossein Mousavi and then Mehdi Karoubi. Khatami too continues to enjoy a large public following. Then follows the calls of the people as announced in their peaceful demonstrations. People want to peacefully remove a usurper president and replace him with their own choice. Beyond that, one can identify the following features of their methods and demands:

First of all, this movement is peaceful and against violence. Second, it is democratic and wants to uphold human rights. It is anti-despotic; it is against dictatorship in all forms. Third, it is independent and not planned by any foreign government. It is born from inside the houses of the Iranian people. It was the children of the revolution who took to the streets because they had been humiliated and their votes ignored and because they were told that they did not understand and that others knew better. So it is a purely Iranian and national movement and Iranian interests are its highest aspirations.

Fourth, this movement is not after a revolution. It wants to attain its goals legally through the use of the existing constitution. People say that the constitution is referred to only when the rulers want to impose their will on the people. Only the provisions of the Supreme Leader and the Guardian Council are enforced. It is as if there are no other provisions in the constitution regarding the rights of people. The third chapter of the constitution, in which the most basic rights of the Iranian people are outlined, is completely ignored. These include freedom of belief, protection from torture, prohibition against reading people's mail, the right to the presence of a jury when convening press and political courts, the right to be represented by a defense attorney in criminal court, the right to peaceful demonstration, prohibition against forcing people to make false confessions and depriving people of their freedom in the name of the independence of the state, a ban on despotism and censorship, etc.

Fifth, the leaders of the movement and its supporters have chosen green as its color, which carries meaning for us. Mousavi has repeatedly said that the nature of this movement is Islamic and has asked that all slogans begin with "Allah-u-akbar" and that Islamic institutions should be used as much as possible. And this is what people have done. The movement's motto is "Allah-u-akbar, death to the dictator." Nobody can negate the powerful slogan of "Allah-u-akbar." "Death to the dictator" is also a natural outburst, like the call of "Death to the Shah" from the 1978–9 revolution.

Sixth, this movement is absolutely against using religion as a tool. It is repulsed by religious despotism. It detests the abuse of Islam. It is against the negation of people's rights and the denial of their vote. It is against the view that people are inferior and lack understanding. It advocates and supports rational, merciful and intellectual Islam.

Seventh, it is an ethical movement. It is against lies, cheating and treason. Nothing is higher than the truth; one must rise up against a lying regime which has trampled on ethics and morality.

So this is an anti-despotic and anti-dictatorial movement. Still, you talk about attaining its goals through the constitution. But this constitution also provides for an absolute ruler and an assembly of experts which is supposed to monitor the work of the leader but, in practice, does not. Can one say that a review of the constitution is one of the goals of the movement as well?

Unlike past reform movements, this one believes in small goals but great resistance and hard work. This resistance has experienced martyrdom. Its impact has been great. The first step of the movement is to install the elected president, bring down the usurper president and expose the cheaters. The leaders of the movement have not gone beyond this call. Other calls will automatically be raised subsequently. We do not have the necessities for changing the constitution at this moment.

I did not mean to ask whether we should or should not make such a call. What I meant was that if the people's choice becomes president, will reviewing the constitution be inevitable?

Under those circumstances, yes. But political prudence dictates that we should not be after such a thing now. It would create unnecessary sensitivities. Mousavi has clearly said that when people attain the necessary authority, then changes would need to be made. If the real structure of power changes, you can be confident that changing the legal framework will not be difficult. So we can add an eighth feature to the movement, which is to be realistic and take one step at a time.

It appears that it is because of the need to change the constitution that those in power resort to violence against the public.

Yes. They read minds. Anyone who looks at these events can make such a conclusion. Anyway, it is one of the most important accomplishments of the movement that during the last thirty years the Iranian state has neither been a republic nor Islamic. People's will and determination has not been respected because the rule of a single man has been dominant. It is not Islamic because Islam means respecting the dignity of the human being, respecting justice, respecting ethics, being merciful. Islam means freedom. As a person knowledgeable in Islam, I ask, which Islamic principles have been respected and followed by this regime? Justice or violence?

So the interpretation of Islam offered by Khamenei, Ahmadinejad, Mesbah Yazdi and others is different?

A good deed can always be misused, just as a secular government can turn to fascism or become democratic. When a fascist interpretation of secularism is presented, can we condemn secularism? The same is true for an Islamic government. It could be interpreted in fascist terms with dictatorial elements or democratic ones.

Secular fascist regimes and secular democratic ones have real examples. Can you give an example of a democratic Islamic republic?

Just because there is no record of it does not mean it cannot exist. It did exist during the rule of the Prophet. It existed during Imam Ali's days. In fact, this is what was meant by the Islamic Revolution. Islamic intellectuals claim that Islam and democracy are fully compatible. But one can clearly say that the Iranian regime has shown that democracy and *velayat-e faqih* (rule of the Islamic jurist) are not compatible. Human rights and *velayat-e faqih* are not compatible. Republicanism and *velayat-e faqih* are not compatible. These are the contradictions that have come to light in practice. Just as Marxism-Leninism turned to Stalinism and failed, it does not mean that Trotskyism is necessarily a failure too. Some Islamic propagandists say that *velayat-e faqih* equals Islam and so a failure of the latter means a failure of Islam. Today, the greatest opponents of religious despotism are also against concept of *velayat-e faqih*.

What is the clergy's role in the Green Movement? Is their current position in the interest of traditional religious institutions?

A minority of the grand ayatollahs (i.e. *Marja-e Taqlid*, "sources of emulation") are in tune with the Iranian people. Some such as Grand Ayatollah Montazeri are in the frontline of the Green Movement. His historic announcement on 19 Tir this year [July 10, 2009] is comparable to the statement made by Ayatollah Khorasani during the 1906 constitutional movement against Qajar despotism or Ayatollah Khomeini's historic *fatwa* against Pahlavi despotism during the Islamic Revolution. Montazeri said that an administration that does not enjoy the vote of the people will not rule thoughtfully, its justice is flawed, and its rule is illegitimate. He has expressly said what needs to be said at this historic moment, and he has added that people must act in ways that have the least cost but maximum benefit—i.e. by pushing aside a despotic ruler. Other ayatollahs have made similar remarks at their own level. Ayatollah Sanei, for example, has raised some of the complaints made by people, which is why he has been attacked by the rulers. On the other hand, the reality is that some grand ayatollahs do support the regime, but they are in the minority. In fact, it is just one ayatollah, and he is said to be regretting his support and has stopped it.

Who is this?

Ayatollah Nouri Hamedani. But there is a large group who neither oppose the Green Movement nor support the actions of the regime. Some have shown their sympathy for the people even though they have not issued a formal statement. They may have sent a message, but it has not been public. Unlike past movements, when it was said that the clergy were the leaders, if I compare the actions of the people with the religious leaders and clergy today, this time we can say that people are ahead of the clergy and have passed them by, with the exception of Ayatollah Montazeri. People have passed by most of the grand ayatollahs.

What is the impact of this on the clergy's standing?

Anyone who does not raise an eyebrow when he sees that his nation is being assaulted, its people killed, tortured, forced to make false confessions, etc., will fall, because according to the Prophet he is an accomplice to this evil.

Does this not impact the faith of people?

Fortunately, people can see the difference between the faith and those who claim to defend it. People do not treat equally the Islam of Ayatollah Montazeri and the Islam practiced by the silent clergy. By looking at the clerics that support the Green Movement and those that are silent, people indicate their awareness of the type of Islam that they support. People are not willing to listen to the silent clergy about their faith, let alone those that actually advance despotism.

What are your concerns about the Green Movement and what hopes do you have?

The Green Movement is the hope of the Iranian people now. And just as Mousavi has said, this is the "Green Path of Hope." I hope that our hope will not disappoint us. In any case, in light of the power structure in Iran, this is a difficult job. We must thank Mousavi and Karoubi for the resistance that they have shown up till now. I fear that people will go even faster than our leadership suggests. If this vast public energy could bring a more satisfying leadership into power, then certainly more accomplishments would come about. Still, one must recognize that many of those who do have leadership qualities for this movement are behind bars and under medieval pressures. These prisoners have been carefully selected. We have not had a short list of failed movements. We must learn from them. Our problem during the reform period [Khatami's administration (1997–2005)] was that nobody led this movement. We must plan and have programs. If this movement is to go somewhere it needs deeper planning and greater activism. My deepest concern is that the natural tendency of the youth is to become disappointed and turn to violence. The road to freedom is a long and winding path. It cannot be achieved overnight. Without plans, without consultation, without an organization, this movement can die. I am concerned about the cooling of this zeal. We must strengthen our politcal parties and non-governmental organizations. If the youth do not join these organizations and prefer to act unilaterally, we will fail.

What is Ahmadinejad's problem? Do you think he is concerned about the ethical requirments of his faith?

We cannot read other people's minds but from the available evidence I doubt if his concern is religion. Someone who is concerned with the ethics of his faith will not be the cause of such atrocities; such a person does not lie and he does not commit treason. The first requirement for accepting faith is to respect the rights of the people.

And my final question: do you have a green band?

When I was in New York for prayers, my young friends gave me a green band which I put on my clothes during the prayers and I used it the next day when I gave a talk at Columbia University. I am proud to be a small part of the Green Movement of the Iranian people and, at the very least, I pray for its victory.

I also congratulate you and your colleagues for the thousandth issue of *Rooz Online*. I hope that with the victory of the Green Movement, we will soon witness a paper version of *Rooz Online* in Iran.

THE GREEN PATH OF HOPE

Muhammad Sahimi

September 5, 2009

Mir Hossein Mousavi, the main reformist candidate in Iran's presidential election of June 12, has issued a new statement explaining how he envisions the future and the role that the "Green Path of Hope," the movement that he is founding, can play in it. The strongly-worded statement accuses Ayatollah Khamenei—without naming him—and the hardliners of distorting Islam, violating the constitution, destroying morality in society, and forgetting the ideals of the 1979 Revolution, the most important of which was political freedom for all. His statement begins:

> Dear decent, free, and informed Iranian nation:
>
> Nearly three months ago, when you participated in Iran's tenth presidential election, you went to the ballot boxes with the belief that, based on the repeated statements of officials and the great efforts of civil organizations, your votes would be protected against the goals of a small power-hungry group. But, the repeated violations of the law, the organized fraud and the bitter events that took place after the election created tremendous regret from an event that could have been a great foundation for the future of the country.
>
> Due to the unwise acts of the officials, a propaganda campaign by the state-controlled media [radio and television] and the attacks of the official and unofficial security forces on the peaceful gatherings of the people, the problem that could have been addressed fairly and without taking sides [by the officials] was turned into something totally unclear that created deep and broad social fissures [between the people and the government], the outcome of which is nothing but the loss of trust that people had in the political establishment.

A very large number of responsible people in the social, cultural and political domains, the exalted sources of emulation [the grand ayatollahs] and the informed groups in the religious schools and academe reacted to the lies propagated by the state-controlled media, the show trials that have no basis in law or religion, the revelation of a long list of the victims, the inhumane treatment of those arrested, and the existence of illegal detention centers, and demand investigating them. In addition, all those who support the Islamic Republic, which is the fruit of the century-old struggle of the people for achieving freedom, independence [from foreign powers] and social justice and advancement under the guide of their religion, are worried [about the future of the country].

Preserving the territorial integrity and the national independence, protecting the country against the greed of foreign powers, and defending the principles of the Islamic Republic in the accelerated events that are happening one after another, has necessitated, more than ever, finding a way out of the present [dire] situation; although we are all well aware that there are those in the governmental and quasi-governmental organizations who believe that the only way they can stay in power is through creating repeated crises and avoiding addressing the problems and difficulties they have created themselves.

They [the hardliners] are still trying to cover up and hide the present crises with even more severe crises and broadening their unwise behavior to dangerous limits, so much so that after creating so much complexity in the country, they have begun dangerous whispers, talking about expelling a large number of our responsible academics from the universities, without thinking about its dangerous consequences.

It is due to the present circumstances that creating a social movement (and not a governmental one) for addressing the problem has become unavoidable. [This movement] should draw from all the popular potentials of the Islamic Republic [meaning the rights specified in the constitution]. The basis for the movement is accepting the reality of the existence of a wide variety of beliefs and thinking in the great, ancient, and God-believing nation of

Iran. This is, in fact, the path of God's prophets and their successors... History shows that whenever governments have tried to destroy the variations existing in the thoughts and beliefs of a society, they have had to resort to dictatorship. The result has never been a unified society but the emergence of hypocrisy in people's lives...

Over the past few months a powerful [social] force of our nation has been liberated, which must be employed for the long-term future of the nation. Our people are well aware of what they want, and saw what they can achieve through what took place over the past few months. They know that they have the power and capabilities to achieve what they want and that the intellectual elite and the experts are also with them in this endeavor. Therefore, the question that we are all asking each other is what should be done with this renewed hope and the powerful capabilities [that exist]?

To answer the question, we must first be aware of what we should want in order to obtain the best results. If we fail to find the right answer, at least a part of this powerful [social] force will be wasted...

Unlike the propaganda by the government, it is we who want the return of tranquility and trust [in the political system], and it is we who avoid violence. We have very clear and rational demands: we want to preserve the Islamic Republic. Strengthening national unity, the revival of moral identity of the political establishment and rebuilding the popular trust as the most important component of power in the political structure of the country will not be possible except by accepting people's rights; gaining their ultimate satisfaction for the results of what the political establishment has done and having complete transparency in whatever is done. In the Green Movement that has started we do not demand something unusual and untimely. What we want is the restoration of people's rights that have been lost.

Restoration of which rights? First and foremost are the rights that the constitution has recognized for the people, and the demand for carrying them [articles of the constitution that recognize the rights] out without taking anything away from them. Yes, the constitution contains ways of managing some aspects of the country [meaning the distribution of power among the elected and unelected organs of the political system] that perhaps are not appropriate for the present state of our society and the world but the same constitution has also suggested ways of reforming them. In our national consensus the legitimacy of all the pillars of the political system is based on the vote and trust of the people to the extent that even an institution like the Guardian Council [a constitutional body that vets candidates for most elections and interprets the constitution], which appears that it cannot be monitored by the people, can in fact be monitored by them.

Without being explicit, Mousavi is clearly referring to the institution of the *velayat-e faqih* (the rule of the Islamic jurist) represented by the Supreme Leader, who controls most levels of power, when he mentions those aspects of the constitution that "are not appropriate for the present state of society and the world." Again, without being explicit, he is also clearly referring to the article of the constitution which allows holding referendum on important issues that the nation faces, when he says that the constitution has put in place ways of reforming those aspects. He also criticizes the Guardian Council, whose members are ordinary people and who like everyone else may commit errors and be seduced by power.

He then continues:

Yes, there is so much potential in the constitution that has not been turned into practical reality. The officials react to this reality as if [turning the potentials of the constitution into reality is] *mostahab* [a religious term meaning something that if done would be good, but if not done, it would not be a sin or violation of laws]. No! It has never been that way! The officials must turn the potentials of the constitution into reality. The constitution is a document in one whole piece. One cannot emphasise those aspects that provide for the interests of certain people and groups, but ignore, or carry out incompletely those aspects that recognize people's rights.

After thirty years [since the 1979 Revolution] we still have some principles of the national pact [the constitution] whose mention about putting to practice angers officials, as if the person who speaks about them has opposed the Islamic Republic. Providing people with social and political freedom; elimination of discrimination; judicial security and equality for all with respect to the law; inseparability of freedom, independence and territorial integrity of the country from one another, protection of people's credibility, belongings, and lives; banning inquisitions; freedom of the press; banning inspection of [people's] letters, eavesdropping and any type of surveillance; freedom for [founding] political parties and social groups; freedom for peaceful gatherings; depositing all of the government's earnings [meaning tax, oil income, etc.] in the national treasury; defining what constitutes political offense and having a jury [when one is put on trial for the offense]; freedom of expression and [having the opportunity to] speak about it on the Voice and Vision [the state-controlled national network of radio and television]... all the above have very clear articles [devoted to them] in the constitution. These are the articles that are easily violated, or are put into practice incompletely and through interpretations that are the opposite of the true spirit of the national pact [the constitution], to the extent that even teaching ethnic minorities in their own language has encountered difficulties.

The ideals of the Islamic Revolution have been treated the same way [by the hardliners]. We demand the revival of the forgotten goals that started this tremendous movement [the 1979 Revolution], the great slogans of the Revolution that [even] speaking about them today makes some people angry, as if these were the slogans of the counter-revolutionaries. One of them is freedom: freedom of opinion, freedom of expression, freedom after the expression, freedom of electing and being elected, freedom with the meaning that our people had in mind as one of the most important goals of the Bahman 1357 [February 1979] revolution, so much so that the victory of the Revolution was called the spring of freedom. This [type of] freedom, meaning political freedom and the right to fearless criticism, has always frightened to rulers.

What is violated more today than the ideas of Islamic

Revolution, the Islamic Republic and the constitution is Islam itself, a religion that is mentioned often but practiced very little [by the hardliners]. They filter religion so that whatever does not suit their interests is forgotten, while their own views and expediency are introduced as the true Islam. This is done to the extent that indisputable lies are expressed on the Voice and Vision. Some of the worst offenses are introduced as a commitment to the Prophet's religion, torture and murder of imprisoned people [are justified] and other offenses are committed that even embarrasses the pen from writing them down.

If there is one mission for a religious ruler, it is to lay a better ground on which people can base their lives on their religious beliefs. [If this is true] why then has the gap between our society and an ethical life been widening? This gap is not our revolutionary inheritance. In the hot summer of 1358 [the first summer after the Revolution in 1979] many people fasted for the first time in their lives [during the fasting month of Ramadan] and enjoyed the [moral] experience. This was our revolutionary inheritance. Our Revolution's inheritance was morality in society during the holy defense [the period of war with Iraq from 1980 to 1988].

So without naming him, Mousavi criticizes the Supreme Leader and his reign. He accuses him and the hardliners of distorting Islam, violating the constitution and ignoring the true ideals of the 1979 Revolution, including and most importantly, freedom of expression and freedom to fearlessly criticize the government without persecution. He accuses Ayatollah Khamenei of destroying morality in society, instead of strengthening it as the religious ruler.

The statement continues,

Sacrificing people of Iran! There is a pact for the children of the Islamic Revolution that in order to return it [the Revolution] to its original ideals, they must make every effort. And there is also a commitment on the part of your comrades and those who want to help you not to commit any treason in the struggle against liars and cheaters against the trust that had been created [between the people and the government]. At the same time it is a duty of ours not to be afraid of blame and to be as courageous as we can when there is something that can be done in the interest of the country and the people.

Here Mousavi is saying that it is his duty to continue to aid the struggle of the people:

Therefore, it is based on such commitments that I suggest we continue the green path of the last several months in order to achieve our ideals. It is the Green Path of Hope, the path that you began before the election and are still continuing along with firm steps, a path full of prayers and *takbir* [shouting "Allah-u-akbar," God is great] with small and large gatherings, personal efforts, discussions, and questions and answers.

Mousavi makes it clear that the Green Path of Hope is not a political group or party but rather a social movement that builds from the bottom up. He says:

We call the movement a "path" because we do not wish to think of any success that we will have as an end [to the movement] by itself, rather we wish to always look forward to more advancements and achievements.

In the statement, Mousavi explains that he selected the color green for its Islamic connotation. (The color had actually been suggested to Mousavi by one of his young supporters on a trip during his presidential campaign.)

Mousavi also makes it clear that the Green Path of Hope, as a movement for reviving and strengthening the national identity of Iran and Iranians will emphasize the minimal common points and goals between all the political groups and parties in order to make it as broad as possible. He recognizes that the Iran of before and after the election are vastly different:

Compared with what existed before, our nation has undergone fundamental changes. A self-organized and vast social network that has taken roots in society is protesting the violation of its rights. The network has unique characteristics that must be considered when making decisions about the solutions [to our problems]. Thus, I suggest that the answer to the question of "what should be done" is strengthening this social network. Our historical experience also indicates that people have achieved their [national] goals only when such networks have been strong and active. Thus, it is our present duty to be active in broadening the network.

Mousavi then explains how the task should be pursued.

We Iranians, wherever we are, must first strengthen the social nuclei among us. We should recognize the importance of such nuclei and try to strengthen them... In family gatherings, with our neighbors and friends, in gatherings for reading the holy Quran, in religious, cultural, and literary societies, associations, political parties, labor unions, professional organizations, in groups of people who play sports together, or show up in artistic events, with our classmates, graduates who get together, colleagues that are friends... They all represent such social nuclei.

We will be successful if we get together around the same slogans [goals], deep slogans that can yield our demands. An important part of the capabilities of the movement that has emerged is due to the common slogan and ideals that we all share. A golden balance is an important characteristic of such slogans and ideals: If we add to them, some people will no longer adhere to them, and if we make them narrower, many people may not find any hope for themselves in it. If we wanted to participate only in an election, the maximum support would have been enough. But, in a great social movement, the majority can be victorious only when it achieves consensus, because then it will have irrefutable legitimacy.

Mousavi then criticizes the fact that despite huge oil income over the past four years, a significant part of society is still struggling with the basic necessities of life and has to rely on handouts and donations by the government, distributed by Mahmoud Ahmadinejad in order to attract votes. He then says:

> We believe that freedom will be lasting only if it is accompanied by social justice. Just as the present limitations for the freedom of expression and gathering are of great concern, so also is poverty, corruption, and discrimination on a vast scale...

Mousavi then outlines what the hardliners can do to get the country out of the present crisis. The minimum, in his view, includes the following:

1. Forming a truth commission, one whose findings and verdicts are likely to be accepted by all sides, to investigate the violations of law, fraud during and after the election, and punishing those who were responsible.
2. Revising the election law in such a way that free and fair elections can be held.
3. Identifying and punishing those who were responsible for the crimes committed by all organs of the government, including military, police, and the media.
4. Helping those who have been hurt and injured after the elections, especially those who have lost loved ones; releasing from prison all the campaign workers and political activists; dismissing the bogus charges against them; restoring their credibility, and ending all the threats against them.
5. Putting into practice Article 168 of the constitution by defining precisely what constitutes a political offense, and using a jury when the offenders are put on trial.
6. Guaranteeing freedom of the press, and changing the biased behavior of the Voice and Vision in order to eliminate all the limitations on its programs so that the political parties can use the Voice and Vision to express their positions regarding various issues. Furthermore, revising the law that governs the Voice and Vision to make it responsive to people's demands.
7. Putting to practice Article 44 of the constitution regarding

privatization so that private radio and television stations can also be created.

8. Guaranteeing the right of the people to gather and demonstrate by putting into effect Article 27 of the constitution.

9. Passing legislation forbidding the military from intervening in political as well as economic affairs.

The statement ends by saying:

> We have entered a path that made the old young and the young experienced. I ask God to help both you [the people] and myself.

THE PEOPLE RELOADED

Morad Farhadpour and Omid Mehrgan

September 14, 2009

In the weeks following the disputed presidential election in Iran, the majority of people in Tehran and other cities (including Shiraz, Ahwaz, Tabriz and Isfahan) were on the streets, protesting against the theft of the election by a handful of the state's agents at the top level. It was not a rigged election in the usual Western sense. There were no added votes or replaced ballot boxes. The election was conducted properly, the votes were taken and probably even counted, the figures transmitted to the Ministry of Interior and it was there that they were totally disregarded and replaced by fictitious results. That is why all the opposition forces, together with the people, called it a coup d'état. The violent reaction of the state, the expulsion of the international media, the casualties in the streets, the shutdown of local newspapers, and the arrest of more than 500 dissidents must be sufficient to persuade international community that the annulment of the election is a legitimate demand.

It is worth emphasizing the correct political essence of this movement and its potential for self-transcendence, moving beyond its present demands. This politicization of large masses may be difficult to observe from the outside, particularly after thirty years of isolation and media misrepresentation of Iran (including the tendency to dwell on "security" matters critical to the western states, such as the nuclear issue, terrorism and so on). That is why any examination of the current situation needs to be set in the context of the recent history of radical politics in Iran.

Many Iranians are recalling the 1979 Revolution and the 1997 reform movement. Many of the protesters' slogans are new versions of those adopted in 1979. The routes of demonstrations are the same as those taken against the Shah. But this does not mean that people are imitating the 1979 Revolution; there are many new possibilities and creativities, many formal and thematic inventions.

Calling the regime's bluff

The expression "people reloaded" tries to capture this sense of repetition without mere imitation. For thirty years, the regime has claimed that freedom and, more recently, justice have been realized, praising the Iranian people for their political commitment and courage. Now people are taking these claims literally, calling the regime's bluff. People are trying to redeem the lost hopes and aspirations of the revolution, as they did once before by electing Khatami in 1997. But this time, we are much more resolute and creative.

The affinities became even more explicit when compared with the 1997 reform movement and its aftermath, including the crushing of the student protest in 1999. It is as if people are trying to redeem the 2nd of Khordad [May 23, 1997], to revive the unfinished hopes and dreams of those days. But this time, the protest is by no means limited to students and intellectuals. Although in 1997 Khatami was elected with twenty million votes from the most varied sections of the nation, the movement then was characterized by the political and cultural demands of the middle class, of students and educated people. But, apart from this, what is the true significance of the 2nd of Khordad Front, the pro-Khatami reform movement, for politics in Iran?

On the 2nd of Khordad [May 23, 1997], for the first time since the revolution, we encountered a dichotomy between the republican state and the totalitarian system of the Islamic Republic of Iran. This is known as the *nezam* (system), which is based on the principle of *velayat-e-faqih*, the supreme divine authority of senior mullahs. This duality was intensified as a result of the fact that the leader of the opposition, Khatami, was at the same time the head of the state. It was the only occasion when this duality—which is, in a sense, one between the development of productive forces and cultural backwardness, between secular democracy and religious fanaticism—became explicit. Before and after that period, the state and the *nezam* have been basically in accordance, although the system used the state as a tool for bureaucratic management of its internal and external affairs, and this on many occasions led to a disruption of day-to-day functioning of the state as the chief organ of socio-economic development.

One of the reasons, if not the main reason, why elections in Iran are of such importance for democratic movements, despite attempts at boycotting them, lies precisely in the significance of this duality. In other words, elections have been the only occasions when it has been possible for the people to challenge this archaic and theocratic system, particularly as regards their social life and economic welfare. Since World War II, the Iranian state has acted simultaneously as an instrument of plundering at the service of the power elite and as the main agent of development. This explains why the state has been the main object of popular movements. But the state has always somehow managed to escape popular control, thanks to its economic independence based on oil revenue.

Since the revolution, the process of building a modern bourgeois state has always been sacrificed to the requirements of the n*ezam*. At times, this has led to a conflict between capital (both the Iranian private sector and international capital) and the state. As long as the state remains dependent on the *nezam*, the advocate of regression and anti-modernism, the state/capital cannot function as the means of socio-economic development—a process that has its own discontents, aptly and righteously exposed by the Marxist tradition.

Fighting on two fronts

For this reason, the progressive and socialist opposition in Iran is faced with the difficult and unprecedented task of fighting on two fronts: against religious fanaticism and the authoritarian factions of a semi-democratic government, as well as against Iran's integration into global capitalism (as a backward, raw-material-producing country). In this sense, the Iranian intelligentsia is very similar to that of nineteenth century Russia and Germany. We are a handful of schizophrenics who are both for and against progress, development, capitalism, state management and so on. In other words, for us, the Faustian problematic is formulated in a typically Hamletian way.

However, we should not forget that despite all these complexities, the key fruit of the 1979 Revolution was politics itself—that is, the process of politicization of people as distinct from both the n*ezam* and any form of state-capital-nation building. For all these reasons, any radical politics in Iran must entail a dialectical relationship with the state. Due to the aforementioned dualities, our politics cannot bypass the state in an anarchistic way. This is due to both the state's role in socio-economic development and the political necessity of strengthening civil society. We are neither dealing with a pure politics à la radical French philosopher Alain Badiou, nor with a classical Marxist politics, limited to class struggles. Nor are we dealing with the liberal-democratic politics of human rights—which was, by the way, the dominant discourse of opposition in Iran before Mousavi. Our radical politics includes all these elements, but it is not reducible to any one of them. To use Italian theorist Giorgio Agamben's terminology, it is a politics of "people against People" —that is, voiceless, suppressed people against "People" as officially constructed by the state. The current movement materializes, in many respects, this very politics.

Ahmadinejad and the left

The question that has confused the Western (left) intelligentsia and caused the most misunderstandings regarding Iran is whether Ahmadinejad is a leftist, anti-imperialist, anti-privatization, anti-globalization figure. A common answer is "yes." That is why certain misguided Western leftists tend to regard the current mass movement in support of Mousavi and against Ahmadinejad as the struggle of neoliberalism against anti-imperialism and of privatization and liberal democracy against the enemies of US global hegemony.

The other confused camp is the Western (more or less) Islamophobic liberals, who are inclined to identify Ahmadinejad with Al-Qaeda and refer to Mousavi as another example of Islamic, anti-democratic ideology because of his Islamic Republican career in the 1980s. One could say that this camp is also caught up in an illusion based on simplistic Eurocentrist generalizations about Islam/Muslims and a lack of familiarity with the Iranian historical context. We should thus answer the simple question: What is actually at stake?

Apart from the French revolutionary triad of liberty, equality, fraternity, which is common to all modern emancipatory politics, one could say that the main bone of contention in this struggle is precisely politics itself, its life and survival. Our government is called the Islamic Republic of Iran. Today the republican movement, which has always been downgraded by the conservatives, is being annihilated. It is precisely through this very outlet that any popular politics, from social movements of dissent and class politics to the defense of human rights, might survive.

Another common analysis, heard from both supporters and opponents of the mass protests in Iran, is that this is a youth movement, at its best similar to the 1968 student protests in the West. The young generation in Iran, the analysis goes, armed with the Internet, socialized by social networking sites, tired of Islamic ideology, has awakened, claiming the right to live its own way of life, and so on. According to this approach, which is evoked by a number of journalists, it is only middle-class intellectuals, students, feminists and other educated people in large cities who are rallying on the streets, communicating with each other thanks to the Internet and mobile phones.

The people versus the People

What is striking is that the state discourse in Iran widely promotes this very analysis. The ruling elite, using a populist rhetoric, tends to single out a certain section of the nation and call it the People. The state television, known as *Seda-va-Sima*, is the main place where this People is represented, indeed constructed, mostly through the usual populist tactic of one nation versus the evil external enemy as the alleged cause of all trouble. It presents a unified, pure, integrated image of the People, all devoting themselves to the *nezam*, all law-abiding, religious and so on. This image of the People is daily imposed on the masses and inscribed onto the body politic.

Against this formally constructed People, with the state as its formal face, another people has emerged, a subaltern, muted people, claiming its own place, its own part in the political scene. The June 2009 election was a decisive opportunity for this people to assert itself through the figure of Mousavi, who insisted on people's dignity as a key political right from the very beginning.

But why him? Why not, say, Karoubi, the other reformist candidate? Has Mousavi, the present leader of the mass movement, appeared on the scene in a purely contingent way? Is it by mere chance, by force of circumstances, as it were, that he has turned into the leading figure of reform-freedom-democracy incarnate? The answer is no.

To elucidate this, we have to draw attention to the tradition from which he has emerged and to which he has repeatedly referred to during his electoral campaign. As noted previously, this tradition is rooted in the 1979 Revolution and has been revived in the Second of Khordad [May 23, 1997 reform] movement. In contrast, Karoubi's "politics" was based on a subjectless process in which different identity groups would present their demands to the almighty state and act as their passive, divided, depoliticized supporters.

In fact, Karoubi's campaign, with its appeal to the Western media by using the word "change" in English and its use of celebrity figures, was the one that could be called a Western, liberal, human rights-loving, even a pro-capitalist movement. The fact that millions transcended their immediate interests and risked their lives to join a typically universal militant politics in defense of Mousavi and their own dignity should be enough to cast aside all doubts or misguided pseudo-leftist dogmas.

The most striking consequence of the revival of politics in Iran is a reconfiguration of everything and everyone. Under the midday sun of politics, a minimal shadow separates everyone from him/herself, from his/her cultural, economic and social identity. Persons and factions that were hitherto classified according to their lifestyles and economic statuses, and who were considered politically indifferent or even hostile to politics per se, came together freely to join the movement led by Mousavi.

From their point of view, everything has become crystal clear and the border separating true and false is no longer a matter of scrutiny. In this political high noon in Iran, their choices are for them as certain as two plus two equals four. On one side of this political divide belong the universal values of liberty, equality and dignity of citizenship, while all the personal and factional idiosyncrasies remain on the other side.

THE HINGE OF HISTORY

Roger Cohen

November 3, 2009

Ever since June 15 in Tehran I've been asking the most alluring and treacherous of historical questions: "What if?"

What if the vast protesting crowd of perhaps three million people had turned from Azadi (Freedom) Square toward the presidential complex? What if Mir Hossein Mousavi, the opposition leader, had stood before the throng and said, "Here I stand with you and here I will fall?" What, in short, if Azadi had been Prague's Wenceslas Square of 20 years ago and Mousavi had been Vaclav Havel?

In history, of course, the hypothetical has little value even if at any one moment—like that one in the Iranian capital three days after the disputed election—any number of outcomes was as plausible as what came to pass.

Retrospective determinism (Henri Bergson's phrase) now makes it hard to imagine anything other than the brutal clampdown that has pushed Iranian anger beneath the surface. Yet of course things might have ended differently.

In 1989, the revolutionary year, the Tiananmen Square massacre happened in Beijing and, five months later, the division of Europe ended with the fall of the Wall in Berlin. Could it have been otherwise? Might China have opened to greater democracy while European uprisings were shot down?

We cannot know any more than we know what lies on the road not taken or what a pregnant glance exchanged but never explored might have yielded.

All we know, as Timothy Garton Ash observes in *The New York Review of Books,* is, "The fact that Tiananmen happened in China is one of the reasons it did not happen in Europe."

And now those events of twenty years ago—Europe's 11/9—are pored over by historians in search of definitive answers to how that world-changing moment transpired, and pored over by twenty-first-century repressive governments to ascertain wherein exactly lay the weakness (as they see it) of Mikhail Gorbachev, the man who would not open fire.

The history of 1989 is still being written—a plethora of new books testify to that. The history of Iran in 2009 will also be written many times over. Truth is elusive, but it's worth recalling that beyond the inexorable historical forces at work in moments of crisis, there often lies one person's decision in a particular confused moment.

The hinge of history hangs on a heartbeat.

Harald Jaeger is a good reminder of that. I first met him in Berlin a decade ago. He's the former officer in the East German border guards who, on the night of Nov. 9, 1989, opened the gate at Berlin's Bornholmer Strasse, ending the Cold War.

Now 66, Jaeger recently retired to a small town near Berlin where he cultivates his garden. When I saw him a few weeks ago, he was wearing a blue T-shirt and gold-rimmed spectacles: an ordinary-looking gray-haired guy with a frank gaze. He's not been invited to the elaborate twentieth-anniversary celebrations but bears no rancor. "To put it in a nutshell," he told me, "It was a lucky moment."

I tried to imagine him at his post twenty years ago, facing a growing crowd, defending the border that had been his life, knowing that a senior official (Günter Schabowski) had just said East Germans could travel "without meeting special provisions," unable to get clear orders from his superior, wavering, alone.

Just after eleven p.m., he gave the order to open the gate. How did he feel? "Sweat was pouring down my neck and my legs were trembling. I knew what I had done. I knew immediately. That's it, I thought, East Germany is finished."

Jaeger had not set out to terminate a country. Behind him lay great forces: Pope John Paul II; Lech Walesa and the heroic Poles of Solidarity; Soviet economic collapse; Ronald Reagan's "tear down this wall;" Gorbachev's refusal to go the Tiananmen route; the irrepressible stirring of the myriad European souls imprisoned at Yalta.

Yet, despite all this (history's long arc), the event itself—the unimaginable event—still needed a single beleaguered officer to open a gate rather than open fire. A decade ago, Jaeger told me: "I did not free Europe. It was the crowd in front of me, and the hopeless confusion of my leadership, that opened those gates."

Having been in that Tehran crowd, I know the force was with it. I felt myself how fear evaporates with such numbers. Nobody, not in 2009, can slay millions. Behind those Iranians, too, lay greater forces, all Iran's centennial and unquenchable quest for some stable balance between representative government and religious faith.

The millions didn't want to overthrow the Islamic Republic; they just wanted the second word in that revolutionary name to mean something—enough, anyway, for their votes to count.

What if they had wheeled and borne down on the fissured heart of power in the instant of its disarray? What if this had been Iran's "lucky moment?"

I have no answer to my "what if?" but 1989 suggests this: One day the dam must break when a repressive regime and the society it rules march in opposite directions.

"MULTIPLIED, NOT HUMILIATED":
BROKEN TABOOS IN POST-ELECTION IRAN

Ziba Mir-Hosseini

December 17, 2009

The on-camera martyrdom of Neda Agha-Soltan, the twenty-six-year-old philosophy student shot dead during the protests after the fraudulent presidential election in Iran in June, caught the imagination of the world. But the post-election crackdown has claimed two other victims whose fates better capture the radical shift in the country's political culture. One victim was the protester Taraneh Mousavi, detained, reportedly raped and murdered in prison, and her body burned and discarded. The other is Majid Tavakoli, the student leader arrested on December 8, after a fiery speech denouncing dictatorship during the demonstrations on National Student Day.

Following his arrest, pro-government news agencies claimed Tavakoli had been caught trying to escape dressed as a woman and published a series of photographs showing him wearing a headscarf and chador—a common version of the "modest" garb (hejab) mandated for women by the Islamic Republic. Escape attempts in such gender-bending disguises are a classic trope in Iranian political history. The best-known instance was when the first president of the Islamic Republic, Abol-Hasan Bani-Sadr, after his deposition in 1981, allegedly fled the country in women's dress—the Fars News Agency put a photo of him in a scarf next to that of Tavakoli. But pre-revolutionary Iran clerics, too, such as Ayatollah Bayat, are said to have evaded the shah's authorities by concealing themselves beneath chadors, which pro-government media outlets now choose to ignore.

To be nabbed in this act is portrayed by the state as doubly shameful—a prisoner so afraid of punishment that he literally denies his manhood. In this case, the shame was pictured not only draped over Tavakoli's head and shoulders but also etched on his face, unshaven, his eyes downcast. The exposure of Tavakoli's "cowardice" was intended to humiliate a hero of the student movement, but it backfired when an Iranian photographer invited men to post pictures of themselves wearing hejab on Facebook. Men responded en masse, inside and outside Iran, asserting, "We are all Majid."

There are many ways, indeed, in which the June presidential election, and the Green Movement that emerged in its aftermath, herald the coming of an egalitarian shift in the politics of gender and sexuality in Iran.

Rights and honor

In 1995, I listened to a recording of a lecture given by the leading religious intellectual Abdolkarim Soroush to *Daftar-e Tahkim-e Vahdat*, the main student organization in Iran, on the theme of the emergence of rights-based as opposed to duty-based approaches to religion. In response to a question about the disregard for human rights in Iranian society, Soroush said something that stayed with me, to the effect that, "Until we recognize rights [*haqq*] as being just as important as sexual honor [*namus*], we cannot speak of respect for human rights."

The analogy between the defense of rights and honor is intriguing. It captures the Islamic Republic's obsession with sexuality and the control of women, as well as the intimate link between democracy and sexuality that energizes the Green Movement.

In Iran, as in many neighboring countries, sexual honor is a core value, so deeply ingrained in the dominant culture that it is rarely questioned or even discussed except when it is attacked or infringed. Girls are brought up to understand that their honor resides in their bodies; boys are taught that one of their prime duties is to protect the honor of their sisters. These practices mean that a woman's sexual morality is always the concern of some man: her father, brothers, husband, sons.

Before the 1979 Revolution, these notions were strong throughout Iran, but the spread of education and liberal ideas had weakened them in certain sectors of society, mainly among the educated middle class in the larger cities, and particularly in affluent north Tehran. Notions of women's right to control their own bodies were germinating and certain liberal laws were passed that improved the gender imbalance. The 1967 Family Protection Law restricted polygamy and gave women more or less the same rights as men to divorce and receive child custody.

After the revolution, one of the first acts of the revolutionary council was to dismantle the Family Protection Law. The victorious Islamist "brothers" took upon themselves the duty of "protecting"—in other words, controlling—the honor of all their "sisters." Honor became collective and the state took charge of it. The authority of the regime, in fact, came to hinge on its success in policing sexual morality. Women's "rights" were only those granted them by the rulings of Islamic jurists, and relations between the sexes—in private as well as in public—were strictly confined by red lines set in old jurisprudential texts. An official gender policy and culture were instituted, epitomized by compulsory head-covering for women, which high-ranking clerics such as Ayatollah Ahmad Azari-Qomi called the "culture of hejab." The Islamic government instituted gender segregation in public space, criminalized sexual contact outside marriage and reduced women to sexual objects, depriving them of many legal rights they had acquired before.

This effort to turn back the clock was frustrated by the fact that after the revolution women retained the right to vote and participated in education at a much higher rate than men. Not surprisingly, perhaps, over the decades since the revolution, the state's assumption of the role of protector of women's honor has led many men and women, particularly the young, to challenge the rhetoric and values of honor as a way of challenging the state's denial of their individual rights. By the time of the 2009 election, many of the Islamic Republic's sexual and moral red lines had been crossed in much of Iranian society—and not just in prosperous, educated north Tehran.

The election and its aftermath suggest that rights—especially the right to vote and to have one's vote counted—have indeed now become as important in Iranian culture as honor. Violation of this right created such fury, such a gut reaction, that huge crowds came out in the streets of many cities, with women at the forefront of the demonstrations, in open defiance of the regime's rule of public gender segregation. Popular anger was at first focused into a single slogan: "Where is my vote?" As the protests have developed, however, they have seen a transformation in which a close link between rights and sexual honor is increasingly played upon in both the regime's repressive actions and the Green Movement's responses.

The personal is political

Iranians of today, from both genders, all classes and all parts of the country, have rejected or at least questioned many of the gender codes and sexual taboos firmly enforced by the Islamic Republic over the past thirty years. So, at least, the current government appears to believe; hence the countrywide Social Morality Plan (*tarh-e amniyat ejtema'i*) instated by President Ahmadinejad in 2006 in an attempt to reimpose the rigid codes of dress and comportment that prevailed in the earliest days of the revolution. Further evidence is provided by several novel elements in the 2009 election campaign and its aftermath.

The first element was the nature of women's political participation. For a long time, a division, if not an antipathy, between "secular" and "religious" women has marked the politics of gender. The distinction refers to political attitudes, not personal piety. "Religious" women, in the main, believed that the country's laws and social norms should be based upon Islam, while "secular" women might be anti-clerical or supportive of complete separation of mosque and state. Many women of all persuasions backed the reformist President Mohammad Khatami (1997–2005) because he promised concrete improvements in women's lives, but the divide lingered nonetheless. On the eve of the 2005 presidential election, at the end of Khatami's second term, when secular women's groups organized a rally in front of Tehran University to ask for equality, framing their demands in constitutional terms, women from the official reformist parties did not join them. They did not want to break all ties with the establishment and be seen as siding with the newly emerging secular feminists, who for their part were keen to keep their distance from religious reformists.

But in April 2009, forty-two women's groups and 700 individuals, including both secular feminists and religious women from the reformist parties, came together to form a coalition called the Women's Convergence. Without supporting any individual candidate, the coalition posed pointed questions to the field. They raised two specific demands: first, the ratification of the UN Convention on the Elimination of Discrimination Against Women and second, the revision of Articles 19, 20, 21 and 115 of the Iranian Constitution, which enshrine gender discrimination. Using the press and new media, they put the candidates on the spot to respond.[1] Women's demand for legal equality became a central issue in the campaign season. Distinguished filmmaker Rakhshan Bani-Etemad made a documentary, available on the Internet, which registers the voices and demands of these women and the replies of the candidates.[2] Ahmadinejad was, of course, the only candidate not to appear.

The second novelty was the appearance of Zahra Rahnavard at the side of—and even holding hands with—her husband, the candidate Mir Hossein Mousavi. Though many women politicians have served in the Islamic Republic's legislature, they had been absent from high-level politics, and the 2009 campaign was the first time that a woman appeared as an equal partner and intellectual match for her man. Rahnavard, in fact, was the more charismatic and articulate of the couple. Her open support for women's rights and human rights changed the tone of the campaign. She was also blunt in many of her remarks, which inspired the youth of the country. For instance, in Mousavi's second campaign film, Rahnavard is shown in conversation with the renowned actress Fatemeh Motamed-Arya. At one point, she observes, "A woman does not even own her own body. If you go to the hospital for an operation, you need the permission of a man."

The third novelty, in the election aftermath, is the availability on

the Internet of letters to male political prisoners—key reformist figures and people active in Mousavi's campaign—from their wives. What
makes these often very affecting love letters especially significant is that
many of the writers are women from religious backgrounds who now
have no qualms about speaking of their physical longing for their men
and who question the very justice system that has imprisoned them.
They are breaking another taboo, challenging the confinement of expressions of sexual desire and love to the private sphere. So the policies
of the regime have generated a paradox: having politicized the sexuality and honor of all Iranian women, previously a private matter for the
family and the local community, the regime now finds its own adherents
taking the policies' spirit to an uncomfortable extreme—by making the
personal political, in true feminist fashion.

The fourth, and perhaps the most important, novelty is that the
regime has been caught breaking its own taboos, with the revelations
of the extensive sexual abuse and rape of detainees of both sexes. Those
who are demanding political rights, the government seems to be saying,
have no sexual honor. The fate of Taraneh Mousavi is just one of the
more egregious examples. These atrocities and the allegations of more
have horrified the public—and many leading clerics. The role played by
defeated reformist candidate Mehdi Karoubi in the disclosure of these
sexual abuses, his support for the victims, and the authorities' refusal
to allow proper investigations have added further to the rumors and
led gradually to other victims breaking their silence. One of Karoubi's
witnesses, a male rape victim, refers to his decision to disclose what
happened to him as "committing social suicide," which speaks to the
power of the taboo—but then, once a taboo is broken, it loses its power.
On December 16, Britain's Channel 4 TV broadcast an interview with a
refugee member of the Basij, the paramilitary force charged with carrying out the arbitrary detention and abuse of protesters, movingly detail-
ing his horror at what occurred. "I have lost my world," he says, choking
back tears. "I have lost my religion." The clip has rapidly spread through
Iranian cyberspace.[3]

The political prisoners include a number of women, ranging from Azar Mansouri, deputy head of the reformist Mosharekat Front, to human rights activists, journalists and students.[4] Some have been released, but none were among the victims of the show trials held in September, when well-known reformist personalities "confessed" on camera that there could be no cheating in the Islamic Republic and that the opposition was mistaken and misled. This government strategy had worked well in the 1980s, when "confessions" and shows of remorse by opposition leaders were regular features. But this time, far from convincing people of the integrity of the election, the show trials displayed the brutality of a regime prepared to go to any lengths to destroy former revolutionary allies who had now become reformists and leaders of the Green Movement. And this tactic, too, backfired, as messages of understanding, eulogies to the pragmatism of the political prisoners and voluntary "confessions" started to appear on the opposition-friendly websites.

Together with the Tavakoli episode, these aspects of the election aftermath have discredited the regime's "culture of hejab" and shaken the very foundation of the government's Social Morality Plan.

"Multiplied, not humiliated"

The Green Movement is not dead. In fact, it is still in its infancy, not yet fully formed. Pluralist, organic, colorful, fluid, it has moved beyond the stage of "Where is my vote?" to tackle a range of issues that animate the population, not just the restive middle-class urban youth of a thousand Western newspaper headlines, but many strata of society. The protests on National Student Day and the creative response to Tavakoli's staged escape attempt are further evidence of the movement's vibrancy and grassroots nature.

The campaign in support of Tavakoli has became an occasion for both solidarity and spirited debate among different elements in the Iranian opposition, as well as for condemnation of state-imposed hejab and gender discrimination, and a celebration of women's equality and their involvement in the Green Movement.[5] "Majid Tavakoli was multiplied,

not humiliated," read one poster. The students issued a statement referring to Tavakoli as the "honor of the students' movement" (though the
word for "honor" here, *eftekhar*, is neither sexual nor gendered). They
stress that what matters is resistance to injustice and the struggle for
freedom in Iran, a struggle that will undoubtedly continue, whether in
male or female clothing. On December 15, the attorney and Nobel Peace
Prize winner Shirin Ebadi welcomed the response of the "veiled men"
as a blow for human rights against discriminatory laws, a move that
honors both men and women, and touches upon the true meaning of
feminism.[6]

The popular response to the fraudulent June elections shows, above
all, that the hardliners now in control of all centers of power in the Islamic Republic have not realized that the early revolutionary rhetoric
and political chicanery that worked well enough in the 1980s have gone
hopelessly stale. The more they deploy the same old tricks, the less remains of the legitimacy of the regime. The "culture of hejab" and the
regime's ability to manipulate the discourse of sexual honor have passed
their sell-by date, and a "culture of rights" has taken over the popular
imagination.

AYATOLLAH MONTAZERI'S BRAVE STRUGGLE FOR JUSTICE

Payam Akhavan

December 22, 2009

In the post–9/11 world, the image of an Islamic cleric as a human rights champion doesn't readily come to the Western mind. Yet that is exactly the legacy of Grand Ayatollah Montazeri, who passed away on December 20 at the age of 87. He is being mourned by millions—both secular and religious—in Iran and beyond. The White House praised him as a figure "internationally respected for his unwavering commitment to universal rights," and the Shia faithful declared him a "legend of endeavour, jurisprudence and spirituality." In life, as in death, he symbolizes the disillusionment of devout Muslims with an authoritarian theocracy that has cynically exploited religion as an instrument of self-preservation for the past thirty years. His struggle for justice explodes the myth that totalitarian ideologies that serve profane political interests are somehow authentic expressions of sublime Islamic beliefs.

Ayatollah Montazeri was one of the founders of the 1979 Revolution that established the Islamic Republic of Iran. Such was his prominence that in 1985 he was selected as heir to the Supreme Leader, Ayatollah Khomeini. Just a few months before Khomeini's death in June 1989, however, Montazeri's fortunes took a dramatic turn when he became an outspoken critic of human rights violations. When an estimated 4,000 leftist political prisoners were executed at the end of the Iran–Iraq war in 1988, he condemned the abuses and was unceremoniously removed from the regime's inner circle. Had he stayed silent, he would have assuredly become the next Supreme Leader. He chose justice over the temptations of power.

This was the beginning of two decades of defiance that came to represent the failed promises of the 1979 Revolution. In 1997, Montazeri was placed under house arrest after he brazenly questioned the dictatorial powers of the current Supreme Leader Ayatollah Khamenei, whom he outranked in the Shia religious hierarchy. Despite his old age and frail health, after the disputed elections on June 12 that gave rise to unprecedented protests in Iran, Montazeri backed the opposition's claims of electoral fraud and issued a fatwa declaring the Ahmadinejad government illegitimate. Just as it was said of the Holy Roman Empire that it was neither Holy nor Roman, Montazeri famously remarked that the Islamic Republic is neither "Islamic" nor a "Republic."

The life of Montazeri is a rebuke to certain Western commentators who appear oblivious to the complexities of religion and politics in the Islamic world. Those on the political left tend to be apologists for human rights abuses in the name of "cultural relativism," arguing that we in the West should not impose our liberal values on those with different beliefs. Those on the political right tend to perceive Islam as the haven of fanatics and terrorists, and they argue in favor of Western hegemony in order to liberate people from backwardness and tyranny. Both views fail to grasp that the Islamic world is not a fossil in a museum; rather, it consists of a diverse range of dynamic and complex societies. The interrelationship between Islam, culture and politics in a transition from tradition to modernity is not fundamentally different from what European civilization experienced through centuries of revolution and war. Authoritarianism that invokes Islam as the basis of legitimacy is less a reflection of an authentic Islamic tradition and more an instrument of absolute power in modern states.

Since it was adopted as Iran's official religion in 1501, the tradition of Shia Islam under successive monarchic dynasties was the separation of state and religion. The merger of the two in the 1979 Revolution was justified as a "return" to an imaginary tradition that never really existed, but the nativist narrative and mythical claims of authenticity were appealing to a society in revolt against Western domination. The intellectuals that pioneered political Islam, however, were inspired as much by

Marxism in the academies of Paris as they were by the study of Quranic scripture in the seminaries of Qom and other holy cities.

When I served with the United Nations in Cambodia, a member of the royal family explained that he had sent his son to study at Moscow University in the Soviet Union rather than the Sorbonne in Paris, to ensure he would never become a communist! Romantic ideologies are more appealing at a distance, which is perhaps why Ahmadinejad's anti-Western polemics are popular in the Arab street where people suffer under pro-Western despots but not in the Iranian street where people have experienced the reality of the Islamic Republic's tyranny for thirty years. The anti-utopian ethos of liberalism was fully embraced in Europe in recent history only after the devastating impact of utopian ideologies disillusioned the masses. The contemporary grassroots democratic movement in Iran is similar in that it arises in opposition to the excesses of an absolutist ideology.

Amidst the misconceptions between the Western and Islamic worlds that threaten to transform the myth of a clash of civilizations into a catastrophic reality, unconventional human rights champions like Ayatollah Montazeri forcefully demonstrate that the transcendent human rights values that unite peoples' aspirations are far more important than their differences.

DELEGITIMIZING THE ISLAMIC REPUBLIC OF IRAN WITH A *FATWA*:
THE SIGNIFICANCE OF AYATOLLAH MONTAZERI'S POST-ELECTION LEGAL RULING OF JULY 2009

Ahmad Sadri and Mahmoud Sadri

July 5, 2010

The historical consequences of the Green Movement of 2009 remain uncertain. But our cognitive frames of reference have undergone a paradigm shift during the thirty-first year of the Islamic Republic. The flawed constitution of revolutionary Iran, with its awkward combination of democracy and theocracy, finally disgorged its commitment to democracy with the violence of expelling poison. People protested in the streets and were suppressed with the typical means of an autocratic tyranny: street thugs, filthy dungeons and show trails. The cadre of the regime that generated the reform movement of the last decade (and that had ruled Iran for the two terms of Mohammad Khatami's presidency, from 1997 until 2005) was unceremoniously purged as parvenu revolutionaries of the fascistic right and the military, industrial and economic octopus of the Revolutionary Guards (IRGC) squeezed the life out of what remained of Iran's civil society.

The sing-song rigmarole of Friday prayer leaders' speeches accuse the Green Movement of sedition or *fitneh*. The Green response came from the top of the hierarchy of Shia jurisprudence, the Grand Ayatollah Hossein Ali Montazeri (1922–2009), in the form of a formal religious ruling. Iran has a long history of issuing politically significant legal rulings (fatwas) to undermine oppressive governments and legitimize popular social movements. The first of such rulings dates back to the dramatic "Tobacco Protests" that followed on the heels of the 1890 fatwa of the Grand Ayatollah Seyyed Hassan Shirazi against the "Tobacco

Concession" granted by Naser al-Din Shah to the British Imperial Tobacco Company. It started a series of challenges to the absolutist government that culminated in Iran's 1906 Constitutional Revolution.

By the turn of the twentieth century, subversive fatwas had become
integral to Iran's progressive social movements. The Constitutional Revolution was supported by fatwas issued by a new generation of Grand
Ayatollahs, including Akhound Molla Mohammad Kazem Khorasani.
Ayatollah Khomeini's fatwas of 1964 and 1977 against the capitulation
treaties and other excesses of the Shah's government played a crucial
role in the anti-Pahlavi riots and civil disobedience activities that comprised the 1978–9 revolution.

The significance of the July 2009 fatwa issued by Grand Ayatollah
Montazeri must be understood in this context. This fatwa spells out the
conditions of voiding the social contract that lies at the basis of the legitimacy of the Islamic Republic. Ayatollah Montazeri wrote these legal
rulings in response to a traditionally ornate and legally well-crafted que-
ries of the exiled dissident cleric Mohsen Kadivar (currently a Visiting
Professor at Duke University). Ayatollah Montazeri was one of the architects of Iran's theocratic system. He was the closest disciple and later the
heir apparent of Ayatollah Khomeini, the Islamic Republic's charismatic
founder. After publicly denouncing some of the harsh practices of the
state in the 1980s (including the summary execution of thousands of political prisoners), Montazeri was publicly rebuked and dismissed from
his position by Ayatollah Khomeini. Montazeri was then confined to his
house and a small circle of his graduate seminarians in the city of Qom.
In 1997, shortly after the election of the reformist president Mohammad
Khatami, Ayatollah Montazeri issued a statement against the practices
of the reigning Supreme Leader, Ali Khamenei, triggering fresh restrictions that made the aging grand ayatollah a virtual prisoner in his own
house until his death in 2009. The government unsuccessfully tried to
prevent crowds from flocking to his funeral. Even after his death, thug-
gish pro-government bands attacked and ransacked his offices.

It is noteworthy that it was in the final year of his life (poetically coinciding with the Green uprising) that Ayatollah Montazeri issued the most radical fatwa of his entire life. The man who helped construct the theory of "rule of the Islamic jurist" (*velayat-e faqih*) that became the legal skeleton of the constitution of the Islamic Republic lived to forge a legal instrument for a revolution against that same system. It was the late Ayatollah Khomeini who transformed the quietist tradition of Shia jurisprudence into an Islamist ideology. Montazeri, his closest disciple, helped "establish" Shia Islam in Iran by means of this legal theory. Three decades later, Montazeri crafted a new fatwa for dismantling it, based on another legal theory that he crafted.

At the heart of Ayatollah Montazeri's 2009 rulings is the theory of automatic annulment of a political system if and when its leaders lose the trust of the people. The relationship between the people and their leader, according Montazeri's final fatwa, is analogous to that between a client and his/her appointed agent. Once the agent loses the trust of his/her client, the legal relationship is, by definition, dissolved. In such a situation, the clients (i.e. the people) are not obliged to produce proof for the incompetence and malfeasance of their political leaders. They do not even need to formally dismiss their leaders. According to Ayatollah Montazeri, an agent (government) that has lost the trust of his client (the people) is no longer entitled to his position. In other words, in absence of the fiduciary relationship, the legal contract between client and agent is automatically dissolved. Here the legal principles of "presumption of innocence" and charity or "assuming good faith unless the contrary is proven" are also suspended. Without the trust of the client, the agent cannot presume to represent him/her. Once the leaders lose the confidence of the people, the burden of proof is on them to demonstrate that they are worthy of popular confidence and trust. In other words, Montazeri's fatwa relieves the people, who are powerless in confronting the immense bureaucratic and security machine of the state, from legally proving the misconduct of the leaders. Rather, it falls upon the leaders to demonstrate their innocence.

The salience of this argument is evident in the context of skeptical response to the Green Movement in the West. American critics such as Eric A. Brill, Flynt Leverett and Hillary Mann Leverett have been calling on the Greens of Iran to produce positive proof of misconduct by the government of Mahmoud Ahmadinejad in the June 2009 election. They expect Mousavi, who is routinely accused of treason and subversion, whose friends and allies are imprisoned and coerced in show trials, to incriminate himself by launching a one-man investigation of the election. Mousavi (and indeed the entire opposition) did ask for the formation of an impartial body to conduct an investigation, but this was rejected by the Supreme Leader and the Ahmadinejad government. The formation of such an independent body was necessary because the normal bodies that would adjudicate election irregularities were tainted with flagrant expressions of support for the incumbent and with participating in the election fraud. The fox is, after all, not usually put in charge of counting how many chickens it has killed.

In his now-famous 2009 fatwa, Ayatollah Montazeri ruled that an impartial body must adjudicate disputes under conditions in which the trust between the people and the government has broken down. In the context of the Islamic Republic, this means that available legal authorities (the Guardian Council, the Expediency Council, the Council of Experts) are not qualified to settle the disputes concerning the legitimacy of the government because they were suborned by the Ahmadinejad government and the office of the Supreme Leader.

Ayatollah Montazeri ruled that the struggle against the usurping authorities is religiously incumbent on all believers. No one, he contends, has leave to shirk the responsibility of ousting illegitimate political leaders. Political struggle for freedom, in other words, is not optional. Hence Montazeri, who once helped design and implement Iran's Islamic polity, came to formulate a theory for its dissolution. The Thomas Hobbes of the Iranian Commonwealth emerged as its John Locke.

Legal rulings of Grand Ayatollah Montazeri on the political legitimacy of the Islamic Republic of Iran

Letter from Mohsen Kadivar to Grand Ayatollah Montazeri, July 6, 2009

In the Name of God the Most Merciful,

To the auspicious audience of theologian and jurist, our most erudite and courageous master, the Grand Ayatollah Montazeri, may his presence endure.

Peace be upon you,

I congratulate and offer my good wishes on the occasion of the birthday of Imam Ali (Peace be upon him), commander of the devout, guide of the oppressed, and the superlative leader of those who seek justice and freedom. We celebrate this holiday at a time when dozens of your eminence's followers have perished, hundreds are wounded and thousands more have been imprisoned for daring to peacefully protest the trampling of their rights by the Iranian government. It is cause for sorrow that this assault on people's rights has been waged in the name of Islam and Shia beliefs. Grievously have the wicked flown the green banner of Ali [the First Imam of the Shia—Sunni Muslims know him as the fourth Rightly Guided Caliph] while treading on the black path of Muawiah.[1]

I have been instructed by your eminence that transmitting the wisdom of the Quran and the teachings of our Prophet and his household is the surest way of fighting injustice and oppression at all times. Now, this modest student of yours is constrained by the necessities of the times to seek your guidance in keeping the dim flame of hope alive in the innocent hearts of a young generation. This generation has been treated with utmost cruelty in the name of Islam. It has been offered superstition in the name of Shia beliefs, and it has been wounded and weakened by lies, dishonesty and betrayal. Now this generation is at your door and you are a beacon of hope for the oppressed people of Iran. This generation shall never forget your courageous defense of the plundered rights of the people in 1997 that culminated in more than five years of house arrest for your eminence. Now, I hope that your eminence honors this humble student by offering your legal rulings on the following questions and thus pierce the darkness of this dungeon. These are indeed questions that the long suffering but proud people of Iran ask their religious leaders.

I take this opportunity to express my gratitude that you will spend your precious time to prevent the "justice-oriented" Shiite jurisprudence (*fegh'h*) from sliding into the depths of the "security-oriented" apologetics of oppression that has been the hallmark of the "Ash'ari" school [followers of the early tenth-century anti-rationalist jurist Abu al-Hasan al-Ash'ari]. This is a favor you extend to the pious believers who thirst for truth. I thank you from the bottom of my heart and hope that you will remember this humble and cast away student in your prayers.

May your exulted honor be everlasting,
Mohsen Kadivar

Ayatollah Montazeri's Response
In the Name of God, the Most Merciful
"And soon will the unjust assailants know what
vicissitudes their affairs will take!"
—Quran, Chapter 26, Verse 227

Prominent Sir, Hojatoleslam wal-muslemin, Dr. Mohsen Kadivar, may his effusions be everlasting,

I greet you and reciprocate your good wishes. Noting that a detailed answer to your questions requires a more expansive occasion I nevertheless briefly touch upon some answers.

First question:
Since, according to binding law—namely, conditions implicit in the contract of employment of public servants—occupying certain positions are contingent upon such necessary qualities as justice, honesty, competence

and popular electoral support, what is the ruling on those who continue to occupy such public offices after they have repeatedly failed to uphold the conditions of their employment and obtained qualities contrary [to those necessary for their office] leading to conviction approaching certainty [that they have forfeited the right to occupy those public offices]?

Response to the first question:
Voiding any of the said conditions [for the occupation of public office] mentioned in the above question, [conditions that] according to both reason and religious law are of the essence of the aptness and legitimacy of the principle of management and administration of public affairs, shall necessarily constitute the automatic dismissal [of the occupying individual] without the need to take further action [by the people] for such dismissal. Under such conditions the directives of such [holders of public office] will not be authoritative.

But voiding conditions that according to reason and religious law are not of the essence of discharging managerial and administrative duties, but which nevertheless have been agreed upon by the parties, will give the choice to the people to dismiss their managers and administrators. In this case, people can, if they so wish, dismiss the occupant from public office as a result on his violations of agreed upon conditions.

However, voiding conditions of justice, honesty or obtaining and maintaining the popular electoral support are among the [former] conditions that are of the essence of management and administration of public affairs. Voiding of these [essential] conditions therefore will lead to the suspension of the principles of "assuming the best" (*al-haml-u 'ala al-sehhah*) and "innocent until proven guilty" (*asalat-ol bara'ah*) in cases related to the discharging of public duties.

The burden of presenting reliable and reasonable proof that religious or civil law have not been violated in discharging public duties, that rights of people have not been violated and that the occupier still deserves the public trust rests on the occupier. [People need not prove his misdeeds, rather] it is his duty to persuade the people [that he has not violated the conditions of his employment.] If there is a disagreement in such a case, the occupier ought to defend himself in front of a free, fair and impartial judge. According to reason and religious law, the adjudication of an organization that is dependent on him will not be authoritative.

Second question:
What is the religious obligation of people vis-à-vis such occupiers [of public office] who despite repeated "enjoining to righteousness and dissuading from evil" (one of the principle religious obligations of every Muslim) administered to them by people of good faith, nevertheless persist on their actions in violation of religious law?

Response to the second question:
As stated above the occupiers [of public office] who have, based on reason and religious law, forfeited their managerial and administrative positions are automatically released of their duties. Their continued occupation of their jobs has no legitimacy whatsoever. If they persist on remaining at their positions by force or by deception, people must ascertain their lack of legitimacy and demand their dismissal in the least costly and most expedient way while observing the axiom of "the easiest and most beneficial path." It is self evident that this is a general duty that applies to everyone regardless of social position. No excuses may be adduced to shirk this responsibility.

Of course, elites who are more familiar with civil and religious law, are capable and possess an authoritative voice bear more responsibility. They must unite and cooperate to spread the information and devise solutions by founding parties, organizations and private as well as public gatherings. Imam Ali, our leader, stated in his last will and testament: "Do not abandon the principle of 'enjoining to righteousness and dissuading from evil' for then the worst among you will dominate you and your prayers will not be heard." The domination and control of the wicked is the natural result of abandoning the principle of "enjoining to righteousness and dissuading from evil" because the wicked abuse all opportunities [to consolidate their dominion].

Third question:

Do perpetrating and persisting on cardinal sins, detailed below, void the principle of "disposition to justice" [necessary for those in positions of political authority] and engender the [opposite] principle of "disposition to injustice"?

a. Ordering and causing the murder of innocent individuals.

b. Causing (with greater liability than the perpetrating) armed intimidation and harassment, as well as striking and injuring of innocent people in public venues.

c. Forceful prevention of the exercise of the religious obligation of "enjoining to righteousness and dissuading from evil" and the duty to "exhort the leaders of the Muslim community," through blocking of all the rational and legitimate channels of peaceful protest.

d. Abolition of liberty, incarceration of the "enjoiners to righteousness and dissuaders from evil," and exertion of pressure on those individuals in order to extract false confessions from them.

e. Prevention of the circulation of information and censorship of the news that is the required prerequisite of the exercise of the two religious obligations of "enjoining to righteousness and dissuading from evil" and "exhorting the leaders of the Muslim community."

f. Defamation of dissidents and justice-seekers on the grounds that "he whoever disagrees with the government is a mercenary of the foreigners and a spy of the alien powers."

g. Fraudulence, bearing of false witness, and untruthful reporting in matters related to the public's rights.

h. Betraying the nation's trust.

i. Tyranny of opinion and ignoring of exhortations of the exhorters and admonitions of the knowledgeable.

j. Prevention of the exercise of the religiously sanctioned right of the collective to determine the national destiny.

k. Demeaning Islam and debasing the [Shiite] religion through presentation of a violent, unreasonable, aggressive, superstitious and tyrannical portrait of Islam and the Shiite religion to the world.

Response to the third question:

Perpetrating all the above mentioned sins or persisting on some of them constitute the most telling and salient evidence of the lack of "the disposition to justice." [Such actions] are the embodiment of open inequality and injustice. Truly, if such sins would not constitute the corruption and clear violation of justice in public eye, then what sins would constitute such a violation!?

It is evident that if any kind of sin, particularly any of those listed above, is perpetrated within the framework and in the name of religion, justice and law, it will have ramifications beyond the sin itself as it involves the additional sins of deception and tainting the countenance of religion, justice and law.

In cases where certain affairs seem to be just and legitimate from the point of view of the rulers, yet illegitimate, corrupt and tantamount to the injustice and loss of rights from the point of view of the people, then an appeal to the judgment of just, neutral and mutually agreeable arbiters must be the operative principle.

Fourth question:

Can the appeal to phrases such as "protection of the regime is among the most incumbent of the necessities" justify the violation of people's legitimate rights and trampling of numerous moral and religious standards such as sincerity and honesty? Can one, under the pretext of "the expedient interest of the regime" lay aside the authentic principle of "justice" that has been the distinguishing attribute of the political jurisprudence of Shiite Islam throughout history? What is the religious duty of the faithful if some government officials would have mistakenly replaced their own personal interests for those of the regime and continue to persist in their error?

Response to the fourth question:

Protection of the regime, in itself, is neither essential nor, per se, obligatory; particularly when the regime is equated with a person. When one speaks of a regime whose protection is among "the most incumbent of the necessities," only a regime that is preparatory and instrumental to the upholding of justice and discharging of religious obligations and rational premises can be intended. The necessity of the protection of such a regime is of the "contingent" variety [that is, the necessity is contingent on its discharging of its proper functions]. With this in mind, resorting to the phrase, "protection of the regime is among the most incumbent of the necessities" when it is made with the intention to justify and conceal the operations of the administrators and their functionaries who pretend to render justice on behalf of others is fallacious because it emphasizes the general principle while what is in doubt is its instantiation [al-tamassok bel-'amm fe-shobhat el-mesdaghiyah]; it prejudges the case and reaches a self-serving conclusion without exposing the premises to examination. If offering such an argument is the result of ignorance, then it should be corrected by "enjoining to righteousness and dissuading from evil."

But it must be self-evident that one cannot protect or fortify the Islamic Regime with unjust and un-Islamic acts, as the very need for [an Islamic] regime is based on the necessity of rendering justice and protecting rights or, to put it more succinctly, the implementation of Islamic commandments. How is it imaginable that through injustice and un-Islamic acts, a just and Islamic regime would be secured and strengthened?

A regime that is based on club-wielding, injustice, violation of rights, usurpation and adulteration of votes, murder, subjugation, incarceration, medieval and Stalinist tortures, repression, censorship of newspapers and means of communication, imprisonment of the thinkers and elites of the society on trumped-up charges and extraction of false confessions—especially when these are extracted under duress—is condemned and unworthy before [the tribunal of] religion, reason and the world's wise observers.

Based on the authentic traditions that have reached us from the infallible household of the Prophet (peace be upon them), admission and confession in prison do not have one iota of legal or religious value and cannot become a basis for a verdict [*Wasa'el al-Shiieh*, the chapter on admissions, section 4; also, the sections on the punishment for theft, section 7].

The discerning people of Iran, too, are fully aware of the nature of such confessions, whose earlier examples are recorded in the histories of the Fascist and Communist regimes. The nation of Iran realizes that such confessions and false, show-trial interviews are extracted from their captive sons through force, torture and threats, in order to conceal the regime's own wrongdoings, and with the intention of besmirching and degrading the people's peaceful and legal protests.

Those involved in such plots must realize that the managers, operators and agents of the extraction and transmission of such false confessions and interviews are religiously errant and legally liable. The country belongs to the people, not to you and me. The decision belongs to the people. [Political] administrators and managers are people's servants. People must be free to assemble to defend their rights through oral and written means.

The shah of Iran heard the voice of the revolution when it was too late. It is hoped that those in charge of Iran's affairs will not wait that long, that they will show flexibility in the face of the demands of the nation. It is advisable to stop the regression as soon as possible.

Fifth question:
What are the religious clues for ascertaining that the condition for "tyrannical mandate" has been obtained; and what is the duty of the learned clergy (may God exult their word) and [what are] the obligations of the public upon its [tyrannical mandate's] advent?

Response to the fifth question:
Tyranny means deliberate opposition to the commandments of religion, the principles of reason, and the covenants of the people, as embodied in laws. He who is in charge of the affairs of the people and opposes

these principles would be a tyrant and his mandate would be, likewise, tyrannical.

The obligation to determine such a condition lies, in the first place, with the educated elites of the society, those who are knowledgeable in religion and independent from the rulers. Similarly, it is incumbent upon the society's thinkers, legal scholars and experts who are familiar both with the principles of reason and law and the procedures of establishing the deliberate opposition [of the above mentioned government officials to the will of the people] to adduce solid and ascertainable evidence [of such misdeeds]. The said elites will be able to perform this duty only if they are free and independent of all government influence and political and factional considerations.

Secondly, it is incumbent upon the public within the radius of their own awareness of the commandments and laws, and with the help of their religious and rational resources, to remain in direct contact with the religious, cultural, economic and political realities, and be aware of the deliberate opposition of the rulers to religion and law.

Finally, to summarize, justice or injustice of the rulers is a palpable reality in the society and its ramifications are evident. This face is not covered behind a mask. Everyone, within his or her capacity to understand and act, has a responsibility to resist instances of injustice and corrosion of people's rights, and must alert others as well. [The spreading of awareness shall be done] so they too can engage in "enjoining to righteousness and dissuading from evil", and strive toward offering a solution.

Indeed it is not conceivable that a justice-seeking person would be unwilling to walk on the path of justice or that he would be fearful, or occupy him/herself or others with delusions and procrastinations under the pretext that s/he is powerless to effect change. Fearing those created by God is tantamount to taking partners with the God, and engaging in self delusions and procrastination is embracing darkness and casting others unto it.

It has been the tradition of the infallible Imams (peace be upon them) to struggle on the path of social justice. If they only occupied themselves with private religious matters, then why would they be subject to so much oppression, violations, incarceration, surveillance and, ultimately, martyrdom?

God has taken a solid oath from the knowledgeable, particularly the knowledgeable in religion, not to remain silent in the face of injustice: "Allah has taken a pledge with the learned that they should not acquiesce in the gluttony of the oppressor and the hunger of the oppressed" [*Nahjul Balagha*, third sermon].

Obviously, upholding this covenant has great rewards just as it has great costs: "Do people reckon that they will be left to say 'We believe,' and [that they] will not be tried? We certainly tried those that were before them, and assuredly God knows those who speak truly, and assuredly, He knows the liars" [the Quran, Chapter of Spider (29), verses 2, 3].

"It won't straighten by a whim; it won't materialize by a wish,
   This is a path of long and grave suffering"

May God grant you success.
17th of the month of Rajab, 1430, 19th of the month of Tir, 1388 [July 10, 2009]
The holy city of Qom
Hossein Ali Montazeri

THE DECADE'S FIRST REVOLUTION?
THE PHENOMENON OF THE GREEN GANGLION
Gary Sick

January 2, 2010

We may be witnessing in Iran the first example of a post-modern rebellion. On the surface, there appear to be many similarities between today's events and the Iranian revolution of 1978–9. However, the differences may be even more important.

Thirty-one years ago, the opposition had a single leader, Ayatollah Ruhollah Khomeini, who inspired his followers from his exile abroad by sermons delivered on cassette tapes. In today's Iran, the rulers have tried to eliminate anyone who might be able to lead the opposition. Top aides and relatives of Mir Hossein Mousavi and Mehdi Karoubi, the ostensible leaders of the Green Movement, have been arrested, subjected to show trials, and in a few cases killed. Mousavi's nephew was reportedly assassinated by agents of the regime during the turbulent weekend of Ashura, a national holiday of mourning.

However, attempts to lop off the head of the opposition—a predictable tactic for a regime composed of men who made the revolution in the 1970s and who know what a potent symbol a leader can be—have failed to achieve the desired effect. Instead, the opposition has gone viral.

Rather than a hierarchy flowing down from one or more individuals at the top, or even the classic cell structure of a clandestine organization, the Iranian opposition most resembles a ganglion, a tangled bundle of nerve cells in which each part of the system is constantly and instantly in touch with all other parts. We may see the real leadership of the opposition emerge from this Twitter, Facebook, YouTube, cell-phone, digital-camera, email, Internet collective.

In the meantime, Mousavi and Karoubi serve as the symbols of the

Green Movement. But they are actually relics of the past, and they seem to be following their younger compatriots rather than leading in any meaningful way. This is not the Iran of thirty-one years ago, the Iran of Khomeini.

This post-modern syndrome raises a host of problems for those who would like to get a better idea about what is going on and where it may go from here. Old prescriptions may turn out to be entirely wrong, and there is no experience to provide even the outline of a new model. Of course, this is equally true for the Iranian regime, which seems to be baffled and bewildered at the lack of success of its shock-and-awe campaign. Perhaps things are just as unpredictable for the opposition. One suspects that a lot of improvising is going on. Is there a grand strategist at work somewhere, devising a new ideology or government structure or action plan? If so, he is remaining very quiet for the moment.

For a rebellion to become a revolution and eventually succeed in overthrowing the old regime, it must persuade a wide swath of the population that it is going to win. It was intriguing to look at the array of candid photos posted on the Internet during and after the Ashura weekend, in which you catch occasional glimpses of middle-aged women and men in the predominantly younger crowd. But this was very different from the Ashura demonstrations of December 1978, when millions of people flooded into the streets and marched in unity. They were confident at that point, nearly twelve months into the revolt, that the secular shah would not dare attack them on such a holy day. Iran's clerical leadership, it seems, has no such qualms.

There is no clear script for what lies ahead. Those who jumped to the conclusion in July and August that the opposition was unsustainable in the face of determined repression simply misunderstood what was going on beneath the surface. Resistance is not merely marching. But now that the opposition has shown an increased willingness to confront and even clash openly with the police, some are concluding that the regime is about to collapse. That is probably also premature. I continue to believe that this rebellion is less a sprint than a marathon, with each side attempting to wear out its opponent in a contest of endurance.

After the Ashura weekend, Iran's rulers must know that their legitimacy is in shreds. Their attempts to claim that all the violence and killing was the work of foreign hands or that the opposition chose to kill its own supporters—even its own relatives—in order to denigrate the government are not likely to persuade many people. Mustering crowds of regime supporters and stage-managing counter-demonstrations will work only if the regime's supporters have the same conviction, spontaneity and determination as the Greens.

But the regime still has all the instruments of coercion and repression under its control, despite occasional instances of police or even individual Basijis changing sides in the face of determined opposition. The Revolutionary Guards have not yet been tested. In the revolutionary year of 1978, scores of military conscripts deserted and returned to family and village. But that had no appreciable effect on military performance until the top leadership itself began to waver and retreat. Mostly, soldiers follow orders, even when they don't necessarily like what they are doing.

One often forgotten development in the 1978 revolution is that the revolutionaries themselves were prepared to conduct secret negotiations behind the scenes. William Sullivan, the US ambassador in Tehran in 1978, initiated indirect talks with some of the top revolutionary leaders in the country and even reached an understanding of sorts. Sullivan's talks were so secret that he failed even to mention them to his own government in Washington, thereby dooming them to failure. But the fact that Khomeini's representatives were prepared to participate in such talks was significant, and it suggests that the possibility of an attempted accommodation should not be entirely excluded.

Despite all the uncertainties, two facts are clear at this point: (1) The regime has handled the problem in such a way as to amplify its failings and to undercut its religious and revolutionary credentials; and (2) the opposition is not intimidated and is simply waiting for the next opportunity to demonstrate its growing strength. That opportunity may not be long in coming.

AN OPPOSITION MANIFESTO EMERGES:
STATEMENT BY FIVE RELIGIOUS INTELLECTUALS
Muhammad Sahimi

January 4, 2010

The hardliners' plan to exploit the events of Ashura to arrest the leaders of the Green Movement—Mir Hossein Mousavi, Mehdi Karoubi and Mohammad Khatami—appear to have been defeated, at least for now.

After counter-demonstrations by the supporters of the hardliners on Wednesday, December 30, the nation was in a state of suspense. People were worried about what was coming next. But Mir Hossein Mousavi issued his Statement No. 17 on Friday, January 1, in which he said he was ready to die for the cause of the Green Movement and listed a minimum number of demands that must be met in order to deliver the country to a calmer state. The statement has already caused considerable squabbling among the hardliners and deepened fissures in their camp. As the outspoken reformist journalist Abbas Abdi said, "Mousavi has thrown the ball into the hardliners' court."

On Sunday, January 3, five important religious intellectuals issued a joint statement in which they declared their full support for the leaders of the Green Movement and listed ten demands that they believe must be met in order to get the country out of deep crisis. The ten demands include the five that Mousavi had already listed and are, in fact, practically identical to what he had listed in his Statement No. 13.

The five signatories are Dr. Abdolkarim Soroush, the distinguished Islamic scholar; Dr. Mohsen Kadivar, a student of Grand Ayatollah Montazeri and a progressive cleric and outspoken critic of Ayatollah Ali Khamenei; Akbar Ganji, an investigative journalist and a leading dissident intellectual who was imprisoned for six years; Ataollah Mohajerani, former paliamentary deputy and Minister of Culture and Islamic

Guidance in the first Khatami administration (a short period during which Iran enjoyed a relatively free press); and Abdolali Bazargan, son of former Prime Minister Mehdi Bazargan, a well-known Islamic thinker.

The statement begins by declaring that

> Six months ago millions of Iranians demonstrated [peacefully] in the streets, in order to regain their rights that, through the treacherous elections, had been taken away from them, and to protest against all the insults and belittling by the government. The security and military establishment responded to the peaceful demands of the people violently and ruthlessly, and tried to prevent people from being present in the public domain and in public debate and they attempted to link the Green Movement with foreign powers and their policies.
>
> The hardliners thought that they could, by a bloody crackdown on a legal uprising, put an end to the people's protests, as they had done in the past. But, despite all of their efforts, the flames of awareness burned higher and the sounds [crying for] reforms [grew] louder; the Movement became stronger by the day.
>
> Grand Ayatollah Montazeri, who passed away at a critical moment in our country's history has, over the past five decades and particularly the last six months, defended the fundamental rights of the citizens of the nation and shone as the spiritual leader of the Movement. His death gave new life to the Movement and revealed all the injustice that had been done to him, which angered the nation even more as the month of Muharram was coming, a month that is synonymous with demanding [people's] fundamental rights and rising up against dictatorship and oppression. The people's protests, following the long historical tradition in Shia culture, were at their height on Ashura, and the informed nation [of Iran] that has learned from the life of Hossein [the 3rd Shia Imam and a most revered figure in Iran, who was killed in October 680 in his war against the dictator of his time] targeted the oppressor of our era [meaning the hardliners and Ayatollah Khamenei].

The statement continued:

It is clear that the extremists in the ruling elite resort to violence because they know that they lack a broad social base of support and a secure future. They want to accelerate the occurrence of the "final confrontation" and "the day of reckoning" [the day that they finally put down the uprising], in order to force the ambivalent forces within the political establishment to accept the *fait accompli*, and reduce the great forces of democracy to violent rioters.

But what this regime has done has angered and hurt deeply across a wide social strata, from young people, women, and religious and ethnic groups, to intellectuals, clerics, academics, workers and political activists. The talk of "the enemy's conspiracy" by the unjust Supreme Leader [Ayatollah Khamenei] over the past twenty years and its [mis]use for inventing [imaginary] enemies and creating fissures among the people (such as [saying]: the press is the enemy's base; the intellectuals work for the enemy; the Green Movement is a colored conspiracy of the enemy for overthrowing [the regime]) have transformed [in the regime's view] a great part of the nation to the enemy's front which must be oppressed by the organs of repression.

This is a reference to what Ayatollah Khamenei has been preaching since he was appointed the Supreme Leader in 1989. Anyone or any group that has criticized him and his policies has been accused by him of being linked to an imaginary enemy that he has never described or identified. The statement then continued:

We believe, as a small part of the nationwide Green Movement, that at this point in time, the demands of the movement can be summarized as follows, which can be used as the basis for the future mobilization of the movement and its relationship with the ruling elite. A part of these demands has already been mentioned by Mr. Mir Hossein Mousavi in his Statement No. 17 that, in view of the difficult political conditions of the country, these represent the minimum demands. We fully support the positions of the leaders of the Green Movement in Iran (Mousavi, Karoubi and Khatami), and believe that the optimal demands of the Green Movement of the Iranian people at this point are as follows.

1. Remove Mr. Mahmoud Ahmadinejad [as the president] and hold a new presidential election under the supervision of neutral organs; abolish the vetting process of candidates [by the Guardian Council] and form an independent election commission that includes the representatives of the opposition and protesters, in order to draft the rules and regulations for holding free and fair elections.

2. Release all the political prisoners, and investigate the torture and murder of the protesters over the past several months in open courts in the presence of a jury and the attorneys of [the victims'] own choice, and compensate those who have been hurt and their families.

3. [Provide] free means of mass communication, including the press, the Internet, radio and television; abolish censorship and allow banned publications to resume; expand non-governmental TV and satellite channels; end the filtering of the Internet and make it easily accessible to the public, and purge liars and provocateurs from [national] radio and television.

4. Recognize the rights of all the lawful political groups, university student and women movements, the NGOs and civil organizations, and labor unions for lawful activities and the right to peaceful protest according to Article 27 of the constitution.

5. Independence of the universities [from political meddling and intervention]; run the universities democratically by the academics themselves; expel the military and quasi-military forces from the universities and abolish the illegal Supreme Council for Cultural Revolution [that interferes in the affairs of the universities].

6. Put on trial all those that have tortured and murdered [people] and those who ordered the past crimes, particularly those over the past several months.

7. Independence of the judiciary through the election [rather than appointment] of its head; abolish illegal and special courts [such as the Special Court for the Clergy]; purge the judiciary of biased judges and ban judiciary officials from giving political

speeches and carrying out the orders of senior officials [the president and the Supreme Leader] instead of implementing the laws fairly and neutrally.

8. Ban the military, police and security forces from intervening in politics, the economy and culture and order them to act professionally.

9. Economic and political independence of the seminaries; and prevent politicizing the clerics to support the government and ban the use of Friday prayers sermons for issuing illegal and anti-religious orders [by the clerics].

10. Elect all the officials who must become respond to criticisms and limit the number of terms that they can be elected.

The statement ends by declaring that:

Not meeting these [legitimate] demands of the Green Movement and increasing the [violent] crackdown and oppression will not only not help us to pass the [present] crisis but will also deepen the crisis with painful consequences, for which only the Supreme Leader will be responsible.

FROM BIRMINGHAM TO TEHRAN:
MARTIN LUTHER KING, JR. AND THE GREEN MOVEMENT

Sohrab Ahmari

January 19, 2010

"The aftermath of nonviolence is the creation of the beloved community. The aftermath of nonviolence is redemption. The aftermath of nonviolence is reconciliation. The aftermath of violence is emptiness and bitterness."
—Dr. Martin Luther King

As the United States celebrates Martin Luther King, Jr. Day, it's worth wondering whether the great civil rights leader would equate the American present with his "beloved community" where children "will not be judged by the color of their skin but by the content of their character." The US has certainly made tremendous strides—including the election of an African-American president—toward realizing Dr. King's dream. Nevertheless, deep racial inequality in the form of de facto—if not de jure—segregation persists in many areas of American life, particularly housing and education. Dr. King's struggle, then, should retain its resonance for generations of Americans to come.

But Dr. King's legacy is also an international one. His bequest to the world is a comprehensive methodology for effecting social change that has inspired people of conscience everywhere seeking to assert their universal rights. The nonviolent strategies pioneered by Dr. King and his associates in their fight against American Apartheid have been put to good use by activists across the planet who seek to challenge autocratic governments, reduce gang-related violence, and achieve post-colonial reconciliation.

Iran today is arguably the most vital proving ground for Dr. King's ideas. The Iranian Green Movement has consciously transposed to its setting the techniques once used by African-Americans to face down vicious white deputies and their attack dogs. In Iran, the role of the southern deputies is taken up by the baton-wielding Basijis, who mercilessly veer their motorcycles into crowds and indiscriminately beat protester and bystander alike. As numerous YouTube videos attest, the Iranian protesters more often than not retain the moral high ground by refusing to use violence against the Basijis they capture; rather, the people offer water and tend to their brutalizers' wounds.

Dr. King's historic march on Washington too has been matched by the solemn and awe-inspiring silent march of hundreds of thousands of Tehranis toward *Meydan-e Azadi* (Freedom Square) on June 15, 2009. And the Alabama bus boycott has found its Iranian version in the form of throngs of Tehrani commuters spontaneously erupting into "Ya Hossein, Mir Hossein!" and other opposition chants as they wait for the subway.

The faith-based dimension of Dr. King's activism has been paralleled by the Green Movement's reappropriation of Islam as a liberatory faith. As Abbas Milani has explained, "Thinkers and theologians identified with the democratic movement have been offering a new reading of Shiism that makes the faith more amenable to democracy and secularism." Just as Dr. King's struggle against American Apartheid was rooted in his conviction that "all of God's children" deserve full civil rights, so the Iranian democrats have sought to discover a Shiism which condemns suppression of dissent, discrimination against women and minorities, and state-sanctioned brutality.

As the regime ominously vows to unleash even more violence against dissidents, it is important to note that Dr. King did not just leave behind a tactical toolkit for civil disobedience and nonviolent protest. He also offered a holistic vision of social transformation and transition that can provide powerful moral and practical guideposts for the Green Movement today. Reconciliation and forgiveness are critical components of this vision.

Some Iranians rightly fear that the potential fall of the Islamic Republic, like that of the shah, might give way to yet another tyranny or worse. If and when the Islamic Republic does collapse under the weight of ever-growing popular discontent, the new generation of Iranian change-agents can avoid the tragic mistakes of the 1979 generation by hewing closely to King's guideposts.

This might mean, for example, that even the very worst human rights offenders in the previous regime be afforded the right to fair trials and procedural safeguards—despite the fact that many such offenders have denied these same rights and safeguards to the Iranian people for some three decades. It may also involve the recognition that Islam is likely to remain a part of Iran's political culture, even under a post–Islamic Republic democracy. This recognition should in turn lead to an understanding that attempts to forcefully banish religious parties from the polity are likely to backfire and lead to future instability.

Finally, Dr. King's warning that "injustice anywhere is a threat to justice everywhere" should be a clarion call for people and governments of conscience around the world to continue to stand in solidarity with the Iranian pro-democracy movement.

A MOVEMENT CENTURIES IN THE MAKING
Hamid Dabashi

January 2, 2010

The paramount question these days, six months into the making of the Green Movement, is will the Islamic Republic fall? Is this another revolution in the making, like the one we saw in 1979? Or will the military apparatus of the Islamic Republic crash through the streets of Tehran and other cities like a fully-charged armadillo and turn Iran into a theocratic dictatorship, ruled by a military junta like Pakistan, clad in an ideological fanaticism borrowed and expanded from Mullah Omar and the Afghan Taliban?

For the last six months, since day one of this uprising, lovingly codenamed the Green Movement (*Jonbesh-e Sabz*), I have consistently called and continue to call it a civil rights movement. This does not mean I am blind to its revolutionary potential, violent dimensions, or destructive forces. It does not mean that the Islamic Republic may not, or should not, fall. I keep calling it a civil rights movement because I believe that the underlying social changes that have caused and continue to condition this movement are hidden behind a political smoke screen. As our attention is diverted by the politics of the moment, I have kept my ear to the ground listening to the subterranean sounds and tremors of an earth holding some 200 years of anti-colonial modernity in its sinuous, silent core.

Beyond the pale and patience of politics, and the attention span of a Twitter phrase, I have called this a civil rights movement because I see something in that polyclonal green that defies augury. That color green signals many things to many people, meanings that no one can entirely legislate or regulate or incarcerate.

For thirty years—not just over the last six months—the Islamic Republic has systematically distorted a cosmopolitan and multifaceted political culture and, by hook or by crook, shoved it down the narrow and suffocating chimney of a militant Islamism that is, of course, integral to that culture but has never been definitive to it. From anti-colonial nationalism to Third World socialism (all with an enduring feminist underpinning) many issues have been equally, if not more, definitive to that political culture. The Islamic Republic, as we know it today, is not a state apparatus—it is the ultimate result of successive crises of political mismanagement in the Middle East: the American hostage crisis of 1979–81, the Iran–Iraq war of 1980–88, the mass executions of dissidents in 1988, the Salman Rushdie fatwa affair of 1989, the Gulf Wars, the Israeli–Palestinian conflict, and then, in the aftermath of the 9/11 attacks, the Afghanistan and Iraq debacles. The Islamic Republic has managed to keep itself afloat over a sea of troubles, but it has never, in the last three decades, been in a position of permanence or uncontested legitimacy, so it could not suddenly lose it in just the last six months.

As the Islamic Republic managed its successive crises, a belligerent generation of oppositional figures and forces—now famously exemplified by the Pahlavi monarchists and mujahideen militarists—followed suit. This generation was not careful about choosing its enemies, and it effectively transmuted into them: undemocratic, dogmatic, cultic, frozen in time. The Green Movement emerged from beyond the border of banality and boredom that separate the Islamic Republic and its opposition, hovering in a third space that gives life, liberty and hope to millions of people who live outside the ideological reach of the closed society and its enemies.

This new generation breaks all the rules. If you want to understand what is happening in the Green Movement, listen to the thunderous and defiant lyrics of the great Iranian rapper Shahin Najafi. If Iranian cinema of the 1990s was the vision and vista of Khatami's reform movement, Shahin Najafi's lyrics and music are the elegiac voice and loving fury of the Green Movement.

Left with the contorted character of the Islamic Republic's Constitution, and particularly the undemocratic obscenity of its office of the

Supreme Leader, the older revolutionary generation of Iranians hit a wall. We had nowhere to go. The new generation of Iranians poured into the streets not with our habitual chants of "Where is my gun?" but with their strange but beautiful incantation, "Where is my vote?" You may hear this generation chant, "I will kill, I will kill, he who killed my brother," but watch carefully for the instant a Basiji militiaman drops his helmet and finds himself in the middle of a chaotic embrace of protesters. Men and women rush to bring him to safety, pour water over his head to cool him off, kiss and cuddle him as the brother that he is, then they put a green scarf around his neck to make him one of their own. The color green: it means you are a descendent of the Prophet of Islam; and it means the poetry of Forough Farrokhzad, the poet laureate of our most cherished moments of solace and solitude:

> I plant my hands in the small garden—
> I will grow green—
> I know
> I know
> I know
> And sparrows will nest and egg
> In the grooves
> In between my inky fingers.

These children you see roaming the streets of Iran with song and dance, they have all been hatched in those inky eggs that our sister Forough planted in between her fingers inside that little garden. That's why they are all so green and beautiful.

This uprising has seen phases of civil disobedience and shades of civil unrest—but its skeletal vertebrae is a nonviolent drive toward democratic institutions. The current republic will either accommodate their demands and survive, or else resist and be washed away. The similarities between what we are witnessing now and what we did some thirty years ago should be carefully assayed—there are similarities, but not everything round is a walnut, as we say in Persian.

The collapse of the Islamic Republic is almost irrelevant to the persistence of this civil rights movement. Clearly, the regime is disintegrating under the pressure of its own feeble constitution—a massive military-industrial complex on one side and a simulacrum of republicanism on the other—but the course of the civil rights movement is almost independent of that state apparatus. There is no possible scenario that will divert it from its main objective—the attainment of liberty, the rule of law, democratic republicanism, civil liberties, civil rights, women's rights, and rights of the religious and ethnic minorities.

One of three potential actions will allow the Islamic Republic to adapt to this movement and its unfolding demands, depending on how desperate the current leaders become: (1) dismantle the office of the Supreme Leader (*velayat-e faqih*) altogether but keep the rest of the constitution intact; (2) reconvene a constitutional assembly to create a whole new constitution ratified by a national vote; or (3) discard the very idea of an Islamic republic altogether and determine the next form of the government by plebiscite.

Against the inevitability of change, a number of scenarios might also attempt to impose themselves. The most immediate possibility is an open military coup by the Pasdaran [Revolutionary Guard]; the second is a US/Israel-instigated economic embargo and/or military attack; the third is internal implosion or takeover of the uprising by such militant opposition forces as the mujahideen or the monarchists (with the help of the US and Israel), or a combination of both. All these scenarios have only one factor in common. They will categorically fail if they refuse to recognize the nature of this movement as an inherently nonviolent civil rights movement that will demand and exact civil liberties—freedom of expression, freedom of peaceful assembly, freedom to form political parties, and freedom to choose a democratic government.

The color green will remain the uncertain solace of this movement—no one will ever know exactly what it means—and that is a good thing. For it always means something contrary to what the people in a position of power think it means.

TURNING POINT:
WHERE IS THE GREEN MOVEMENT HEADED?

Muhammad Sahimi

January 2, 2010

The funeral of Grand Ayatollah Hossein Ali Montazeri on December 21, and the Ashura demonstrations on December 27, marked a turning point for Iran's democratic movement. The demonstrations showed that even after a violent six-month crackdown on peaceful protesters, political figures, journalists and human right advocates, the Green Movement has not been weakened, but has instead strengthened and expanded to many cities and towns around the country. This is already a significant victory for the Green Movement. The question is: where is it going to go from here?

First off, let's be realistic. Many Iranians would like to believe that the hardline regime is in its death throes. But such optimism must be tempered. The hardliners' ability to maintain power through force has not been diminished and is likely to outlast the Islamic Republic's crisis of legitimacy. The struggle for democracy in Iran is a marathon, not a sprint. There is still a long way to go.

Reports indicate that the Islamic Revolution Guards Corps (IRGC) has moved anti-riot armored vehicles into Tehran and other large cities. This means that although the Green Movement is much stronger than at its inception, the near future may not bring an all-out victory or defeat, but cycles of unrest and repression, unless the movement takes its next steps carefully and realistically. What are those steps?

First and foremost, the Green Movement must continue to act in a nonviolent manner. The call for nonviolence has angered some. Perhaps they don't realize that the nonviolent nature of the Green Movement has been the most important reason for its success so far.

It should also be noted that there is a vast difference between self-defense—which is legitimate—and adopting violence as a tactic, which can only hurt the Green Movement. The former scenario means that the Movement defends itself—physically, if necessary—when attacked; the latter implies that the Movement goes on the offensive and employs force and violence. The two are not identical.

But how would violence hurt the Green Movement?

First, if violence is imposed on the hardliners, they will fight to the end, simply because they have no place to go. When Mohammad Reza Shah Pahlavi came under attack thirty years ago, his core supporters could move to Europe or the United States—and many did. There are no such options for the hardliners. I doubt that even the people of Syria or Shia-controlled areas of Lebanon or Iraq will be hospitable toward them. Add to this the mentality of many of the top IRGC commanders who believe that they should have been killed more than two decades ago in the Iran–Iraq war and who look upon their survival as a sort of "bonus." Many have no fear of losing their lives, which makes them even more dangerous. They will not don women's clothing to escape Iran the way Abolhassan Banisadr, the Islamic Republic's first president, did after he was sacked in June 1981. I believe most, if not all of them would refuse exile, even if they had such an option (which they do not).

In September 2007 Ayatollah Ali Khamenei took the unusual step of abruptly firing the top IRGC commander Major General Yahya Rahim Safavi and replacing him with Major General Mohammad Ali (Aziz) Jafari. Why? Because General Jafari firmly believes that the West wants to create a "velvet revolution" in Iran to overthrow the Islamic Republic. As one of his first acts, General Jafari decentralized the decision-making process for the IRGC commanders by creating local command centers in each of the thirty-one provincial capitals around the country. He made it clear that he was taking that step to be better prepared to confront the "internal enemy." He said he viewed the "internal threat" to be more dangerous than the external one, another indication that the IRGC was prepared for battle.

Second, if the Green Movement turns to violence, we may see Tehran's equivalent of the 1989 Tiananmen Square massacre in China, when thousands were slaughtered by the Chinese army. Indeed, China has supplied the IRGC with the same anti-riot armored vehicles that it used on the students. We should keep in mind that the Chinese democratic movement was also very strong at the time (although provocations by foreign countries were also influential in those events); after the slaughter, however, the movement was essentially destroyed. In short, the IRGC is ready to fight to the end, should the Green Movement resort to force.

Third, the fact that a Tiananmen-style event has not yet occurred may indicate that even within the higher IRGC echelons there is a split on how to deal with the crisis. If the IRGC high command had been unified, we would have probably seen the use of violence on a much larger scale.

At the same time, we have not yet witnessed the arrest of some key figures of the movement. After former president Ali Akbar Hashemi Rafsanjani was supposedly defeated by Mahmoud Ahmadinejad in the second round of the 2005 presidential election, Ayatollah Khamenei reportedly told him, "If you had won the election, the IRGC would have assassinated you." So the fact that Rafsanjani and the people around him, who are deeply despised by many of the hardliners, have still not been arrested may be yet another indication that the IRGC high command is not unified. It should be kept in mind that after Banisadr's ouster in 1981, Ayatollah Ruhollah Khomeini appointed Rafsanjani commander-in-chief of the armed forces until the end of the war, which enabled him to foster close relations with many of the young IRGC commanders who are now in high positions.

Similarly, despite much rhetoric against Mir Hossein Mousavi, Mehdi Karoubi and former president Mohammad Khatami, none of them have been arrested yet, even though the hardliners at the top of the IRGC command, such as Brigadier General Yadollah Javani (head of the political directorate of the IRGC), General Jafari and Brigadier General

Seyyed Masoud Jazayeri (deputy chief-of-staff of Iran's armed forces), have repeatedly called for their arrest, as well as the arrest of Ayatollah Mohammad Mousavi Khoeiniha, the leftist cleric who is viewed by the hardliners as a key figure behind the scenes.

In addition, the regular army has been totally silent. The only notable figure who has spoken out is the chief-of-staff of the armed forces, Major General Hassan Firouzabadi, a close friend of Ayatollah Ali Khamenei. During the Iran–Iraq war, Ayatollah Khamenei, who was the president at the time, frequently visited the war front and forged a friendship with some of the commanders, including General Firouz-abadi (who is also a physician).

Fourth, a violent confrontation with the IRGC and the Basij militia might lead to a civil war, pitting the people and possibly a large part of the regular army against the IRGC and Basij. Given that ethnic minorities make up a significant portion of the population, and have been suffering for decades (before and after the 1979 Revolution) as a result of cultural and economic discrimination at the hands of the central government, a large-scale confrontation between the people and the armed forces may stoke separatist tendencies among them. It is certainly true that the vast majority of the people consider themselves first and foremost Iranian, and only then a Turk, Kurd, Lor or another ethnicity, but there are also extremists among ethnic minorities who harbor separatist tendencies and are supported by foreign powers, in particular Israel.

A group based in Baku, Republic of Azerbaijan refers to Iran's Azerbaijan provinces as "southern Azerbaijan" and advocates a merger with the Republic of Azerbaijan—never mind that this Republic was actually part of Iran until 1828. The group was treated with political significance by the George W. Bush administration. Another group, the Ahwaz Liberation Organization, says it wants to liberate "Arab Khuzestan" from Iran and is reportedly supported by British agents. Then there is the Jundallah group that claims to fight on behalf of the Baluchi people. Though the group claims not to harbor any separatist claims, one can never be sure what may happen if Iran is thrown into total chaos, particularly given the support that the United States is believed to provide to it.

We must keep in mind that more than three decades ago, when the 1979 Revolution was gathering steam, the Cold War was at its height, and Iran was in the Western camp and shared a long border with the Soviet Union. Therefore, its territorial integrity was guaranteed. In the event of a conflict now, I am not sure that would be the case. Such a potential danger might only be assuaged if the Green Movement remains nonviolent.

It is often claimed by those who support economic sanctions against Iran that this policy can eventually lead to the downfall of the Islamic Republic. The example often cited to bolster their argument is South Africa. Aside from the fact that there have been many cases in which sanctions had no effect—Iraq, Cuba and North Korea, to name just a few—the apartheid regime gave up power in South Africa because the white minority came to realize that resisting the black majority was futile and would lead to a loss of political and economic power anyway. At the same time, the African National Congress, led by Nelson Mandela and his comrades, assured the white leaders that there would be no campaign of revenge against them. Sanctions actually played only a small part in bringing down the apartheid regime.

Similarly, the split in the IRGC high command, and the silence of the regular army, must be used to advantage. The rank and file of the armed forces and the Basij militia must come to the realization that the rule of the hardliners is no longer tenable, and that if the confrontation continues, they will eventually lose everything and be faced with nowhere to go. This will not be possible if the Green Movement becomes violent. Only a nonviolent confrontation will be able to attract a great number of the armed forces.

Next, the Green Movement needs a national leadership team. It is true that the movement has so far been a horizontal one, meaning every supporter has acted as a sort of local leader, but a national movement also needs national leaders. It is one thing to send e-mails and Tweets inviting people to take part in demonstrations, but what is really needed is to form a leadership team and prepare it for transition to a new stage of the struggle, or even for a new government.

Some say that the leaders will emerge from the ranks of the youth, particularly those in the universities. This is both idealistic and naive. Iran is a complex country in one of the most turbulent regions of the world. It faces significant problems with the international community over such important issues as its nuclear program. These facts alone illustrate that Iran and the Green Movement need experienced leadership.

As always, there are the pretenders. The monarchists, for example, advocate Reza Pahlavi for this role. But he has lived his entire adult life outside Iran, and monarchy has no significant support base in Iran. The Mujahideen-e Khalq Organization (MKO) also likes to make claims to leadership. But in addition to its numerous acts of treason against Iran and Iranians, its structure is strikingly similar to the Islamic Republic: it has a Supreme Leader (Masoud Rajavi) and an Ahmadinejad-style "president" (Maryam Rajavi).

There are also pretenders to the leadership like Mohsen Sazegara and Mohsen Makhmalbaf, who send messages "to the people of Iran" as if they were the true leaders of the Green Movement; they are in fact only trying to position themselves to become leaders. Sazegara opposed voting in the June 12 election and had close relations with arch-hawks such as Michael Rubin (an advocate of harsh sanctions against and war with Iran) at the American Enterprise Institute, a think tank that has been no friend to the Iranian people. He also had close ties with the Washington Institute for Near East Policy, an offshoot of the US pro-Israel lobby group AIPAC, before gravitating toward the Green Movement out of pure opportunism.

This leaves us with the reformist leaders. Grand Ayatollah Montazeri was the true spiritual leader of the Movement before his untimely death, but there is no question, at least in my mind, that Mousavi, Karoubi and Khatami currently symbolize the Green Movement. Among the three, Karoubi has been the most outspoken, Khatami the most cautious, and Mousavi the most prudent.

All three have grown with the movement. Khatami no longer just alludes to the excesses of the regime but has taken increasingly firmer positions against it. Mousavi no longer uses the language of the 1979 Revolution (except occasional tactical references) and has taken increasingly tougher positions as well. For him, and for many Iranians, this is no longer about the rigged election, but the future of Iran. And Karoubi, though always frank, has made statements that are entirely unprecedented in the history of the Islamic Republic. Just recently, he said that the crimes committed on the day of Ashura were worse than the Shah's brutality.

Until recently, the jury was still out on whether this trio truly led the Green Movement. It was particularly unclear whether Mousavi was truly interested in fundamental changes or even possessed the character to take firmmoral stands. Two important points about Mousavi must be considered.

One, by all indications, he is recognized by most of the supporters of the Green Movement inside Iran, as well as the hardliners, as the symbol and the leader of the opposition. Some Iranians in the diaspora—particularly the monarchists—claim that "he is just an excuse." That is absurd. True, he was an excuse for many Iranians in the diaspora, but I do not believe he was or is for those living in Iran. The manner by which he has handled the assassination of his nephew on Ashura, refusing to issue a statement about it, saying there was no difference between his nephew and other martyrs of the movement, has only added to the respect that most people in Iran have for him.

Second, Mousavi's role in the political killings of the 1980s is exaggerated. He was not in charge of the judiciary, nor did he control the Intelligence Ministry and the IRGC, which carried out the executions. He does bear a tremendous moral responsibility and at some point he must clarify his own thinking about the killings and his silence throughout the years. But, without meaning to take away any significance from those historical and catastrophic events, I believe that at this historic moment this issue is not the most urgent.

In my view, Mousavi's most recent statement, No. 17, issued on January 1, 2010, has truly demonstrated his political skill and has elevated him to the true national leader of the opposition. Some say that by implicitly recognizing Ahmadinejad's government he has in effect retreated. This is simplistic thinking and absurd for at least three reasons.

One, accepting the reality of a government is not the same as accepting its legitimacy as a product of a free and fair election. The hardliners control all levers of power—money, military, executive decision-making, the judiciary and the Voice and Vision of the Islamic Republic (the national radio and TV networks). The only real power that the Green Movement has is its infectious popularity.

Second, it is naive to believe that the hardliners do not have any social base. They are probably supported by up to 20 percent of the population—and they are armed to the teeth. If we are to believe the various leaks out of the Interior Ministry right after the rigged June 12 presidential election, Ahmadinejad received about eleven million votes, representing 25 percent of eligible voters, which is also consistent with what the internal polls of the reformists had indicated.

Third, immediately after seemingly accepting the reality of Ahmadinejad's government and declaring that he was not afraid to die for the cause of the people and the Green Movement, Mousavi mentioned the "uncommon support" that Ahmadinejad received, meaning support by the IRGC and Ayatollah Khamenei himself. In other words, Mousavi was saying that without that support, the government will be immediately revealed to be shaky at best. In addition, Mousavi mocked Ahmadinejad's performance and sarcastically pointed out that, although he and his comrades are accused of having links with foreign governments, it is Ahmadinejad who sent congratulatory letters to the leaders of the same nations. He also pointedly affirmed,

> Suppose that through arrests and violence, silencing people and shutting down the [reformist] newspapers and [other] means of mass communication, calm and silence return to society. What

are you [the hardliners] going to do about [the fact that] people's judgment about [the legitimacy of the] political establishment has changed? What are you going to do about the destruction of the legitimacy [of the political system]? What are you going to do about the world's rebuke and astonishment at [your] government's use of so much violence against your own people? What are you going to do about all the unsolved economic problems that due to the utter incompetence of the government continue to proliferate? On what basis of competence, national resolve [for supporting the government] and effective foreign policy are you going to remove the shadow of foreign powers that demand more concessions and [approve more] resolutions [at the United Nations Security Council]?

Thus, it is clear that Mousavi has only nodded to the fact that there is a government, however illegitimate, with much power behind it. Besides, this nod to the (illegitimate) government creates more divisions in the conservative camp. Many in that camp are not happy about what is happening; they truly believe that the nation is in a deep crisis and want to do something drastic about it.

Mousavi waited to issue his statement until after Wednesday's pro-government counter-demonstrations, in which he, his comrades and the entire Green Movement were threatened with physical annihilation. This was very clever and prudent. Mousavi's goal, as I have also emphasized in my analyses, is to keep the Movement peaceful, hopeful and upbeat.

Once the issue of the leadership has been settled—and it seems to have been—the next important issue is organization at the national level. The Green Movement delivered the message on Ashura that it was willing to pay any price to resist the military-clerical dictatorship and to advance democracy. Such an expression of readiness by the people must be reciprocated by the leadership by presenting them with ideas and solutions for the crisis that reflect a national consensus. It is clear that the hardliners have been trying their best to prevent the emergence of such a consensus, but it is the task of a true national leadership to come up with a solution, regardless of the difficulties.

The first step toward developing such a consensus is, in my opinion, for Mousavi to place less emphasis on the religious aspects of his thinking; I say this as a practicing Muslim myself. No one can expect Mousavi to set aside his religious thinking and system of belief, but it is not unreasonable to expect him not to emphasize a "true religious government," even if he thinks that it can be democratic. Instead, he must emphasize those aspects of his thinking that foster national unity. Mousavi is a true patriot, and therefore, there is nothing wrong with emphasizing Iranian patriotism. At the same time, the strength of the Green Movement should be its acceptance of different schools of thought. People from all walks of life with all shades of thinking support the movement. On Ashura, people demonstrated their national unity, regardless of their different ideologies. I have no doubt that some may still believe that a "true" Islamic Republic (however it might be defined) can be democratic, but there are others, who probably outnumber the first group, who do not believe this can be done. To understand where this position comes from, all Mousavi needs to do is think back to the 1979 Revolution. At that time too there was a national movement. Many practicing Muslims, such as the author, supported the Revolution precisely because we thought that it would lead to the establishment of a democratic government.

I perfectly understand Mousavi's caution. Religion still influences a significant segment of the population, particularly in small towns and villages. Why else would hardliners use violence on Ashura to force people to defend themselves, and then use their own violence as an excuse to stage counter-demonstrations (under the pretext that the religious sentiments of Iranians have been insulted) and call for physical elimination of the opposition? In sum then, Mousavi should de-emphasize a religious political program, not reject religion all together.

If these principles are recognized, Mousavi's nine demands, as laid out in his Statement No. 13, can be used as the basis for continuing to advance the Green Movement. These nine demands are:

1. Form a truth commission, such that its findings and verdicts are accepted by all sides, to investigate the violations of law and fraud during and after the election, and punish those who were responsible.

2. Revise the election law in such a way that free and fair elections can be held.

3. Identify and punish those who were responsible for the crimes that have been committed in all organs of the government, including the military, police and the media.

4. Provide support and assistance to the victims of the post-election crackdown, especially the families of those who lost loved ones; release from prison all the campaign workers and political activists, dismiss the bogus charges against them, restore their credibility and put an end to all the threats being made against them.

5. Put into practice Article 168 of the constitution by defining precisely what constitutes a political offense, and use a jury when the alleged offenders are put on trial.

6. Guarantee freedom of the press, and change the one-sided behavior of the Voice and Vision [the official state radio and television network] in order to eliminate all the limitations on its programs, so that the political parties can use the Voice and Vision to express their positions regarding various issues, and revise the law that governs the Voice and Vision to make it responsive to people's demands.

7. Put in practice Article 44 of the constitution regarding privatization, so that private radio and television can also be created.

8. Pass legislation to forbid the military from intervening in political as well as economic affairs.

9. Release all the political prisoners.

Note that in his latest statement, Mousavi mentioned five of the nine demands as the starting point, but also said that other demands can be added.

By acting in such a prudent manner, Mousavi has put the onus on the hardliners and elevated himself to the level of a true national leader of the Green Movement. He has also made it clear that he wishes for the Green Movement to remain nonviolent. By advancing national unity and democratic principles, as well as de-emphasizing religious aspects of his thinking, Mousavi can be the best person to lead Iran's march toward democracy.

THE GOALS OF IRAN'S GREEN MOVEMENT:
AN INTERVIEW WITH ABDOLKARIM SOROUSH
Robin Wright

January 6, 2010

Five major figures in Iran's reform movement issued a manifesto on Sunday, January 3, calling for the resignation of President Mahmoud Ahmadinejad and the abolition of clerical control of the voting system and candidate selection. Journalist Robin Wright interviewed one of the signatories, reform-movement founder and scholar Abdolkarim Soroush, about the manifesto, which also calls for the recognition of law-abiding political, student, non-governmental and women's groups; labor unions; freedom for all means of mass communication; and an independent judiciary, including popular election of the judicial chief. The signatories, all Iranians living outside the country, also include dissident cleric Mohsen Kadivar; former parliamentarian and Islamic Guidance Minister Ataollah Mohajerani; investigative journalist Akbar Ganji; and Abdolali Bazargan, an Islamic thinker and son of a former prime minister. Robin Wright, a former diplomatic correspondent for the *Washington Post* and author of four books on Iran since 1973, is now a senior fellow at the US Institute for Peace in Washington, DC.

Why did you decide to issue a manifesto now?

The Green Movement is in its seventh month now, and I and my friends have been following events very closely and have been in touch with some of our friends in Iran. After [the protests on] Ashura on December 27, we came to realize that it was a real turning point. It was at that time that the regime decided to crack down on the Green Movement. In one instance, the regime rolled over a protester and killed him. It was a very severe message to all the protesters and defenders and supporters of the Green Movement that it intends to crush the movement harshly.

On the other hand, we have also individually been frequently asked by our friends: What are the real demands of the Green Movement? because the Green Movement was something that jumped on the scene. There was no planning for it. The election was the beginning, and it just evolved and evolved. As it evolved, some demands had emerged, but there was nothing that showed what was in the minds of the leaders of the movement.

The five of us thought that because we are close enough to the leaders of the movement—Mir Hossein Mousavi, Mehdi Karoubi and Mohammad Khatami—and know their demands, we should start drafting a manifesto or statement about the Green Movement. So we started drafting, and then Mousavi's statement [that he would die for the movement if necessary] was issued [on January 1]. Since we are living outside the country, don't have to fear [the government], and know what is in the mind of the people, we decided to publish our own statement to make clear what Mousavi's intentions and goals of the Green Movement are.

Whose views does this manifesto reflect—just the leadership or the wider range of followers?

This is a pluralistic movement, including believers and non-believers, socialists and liberals. There are all walks of life in the Green Movement. We tried to come up with the common points for all. We know there are many more demands, many more than these.

Maybe in the next stage, they may demand redrafting the constitution. But for now, they would like to work within the framework of the constitution, and we were careful not to trespass those limits.

One of the suggestions we made was on the border [of going beyond the basic demands], which was the suggestion that the head of the judiciary should be elected rather than appointed by the Supreme

Leader. I suggested that point—if we have changes in the constitution, we have to make the head of the judiciary elected. But the majority of the points reflect the mind of the leadership.

What difference will this manifesto make?

It will make the goals and objectives clearer and better defined and articulated. At this stage, we need it. I've said for years that the Revolution was theory-less. It was a revolt against the shah—a negative rather than a positive theory. I insisted that if there is going to be another movement, it has to have a theory. People should know what they want, not just what they don't want. So we are trying—in a modest way—to put forward a theory for this movement.

Goals and objectives are based on theories and foundations. And we do have theories about liberty. We have not brought those theories into these points, but they underlie the points. They are invisible to the armed eyes, meaning the regime.

What's next for the Green Movement?

Nobody knows. There are all sorts of cries that the leaders of the Green Movement should submit themselves to the Supreme Leader, but that won't take place. Both sides have to be prepared for a serious negotiation. That could be the next stage. [Former President] Akbar Hashemi Rafsanjani might step in to start a negotiation for national reconciliation.

Can the regime crack down to the point of eliminating the Green Movement?

I don't think so. It is a product of the reform movement, which was suppressed. Ahmadinejad did his best to remove all sort of reform movements and to start a new era. But the regime could not put out the fire. And now we have the Green Movement, which is a culmination of the reform movement, a new stage.

I hope the government recognizes it has to have negotiations with the Green Movement and will have to sacrifice something for them to be productive. Heaven forbid that it turns into violence, which would be bad for the Green Movement and the country.

Will compromise satisfy the new generation of reformers?

Compromise has a negative connotation. But if even one of these demands is fulfilled—such as freedom of press—that will be enough to change drastically the political scene and atmosphere of the country. If they accept one of these ten demands—and not the rest—it will revolutionize the whole country. Maybe release the prisoners; so many competent people are in prison. Any one of these would revolutionize the atmosphere.

AGAINST THE STATUS QUO:
AN INTERVIEW WITH IRANIAN TRADE UNIONIST HOMAYOUN POURZAD

Ian Morrison

January 8, 2010

Before we speak about the current situation, could you explain the organization of which you are a part, the Network of Iranian Labor Unions (NILU)?

The idea for the NILU first arose about three years ago. Some of us already had union experience dating from before the 1979 Revolution. It upset us that, with millions of workers, there were no Iranian unions independent of the state, but only the semi-official Islamic Workers' Councils. What gave NILU its initial impetus was the Tehran bus drivers' actions led by Mansour Osanloo and his friends.

There was a nucleus of independent labor organizations in various trades, but the government always moved quickly to stifle that independence. Iran's Labor Ministry and the Ministry of Intelligence have standing directives to crush independent workers' activities, regardless of which faction is running the country. The government is very brutal in its attempts to destroy the nascent labor movement.

On the surface it looks like not much is happening with union labor activity in Iran, but even in the face of government oppression, many workers are secretly engaged in organizing underground unions. These efforts have not yet peaked. Also, organizers have to walk a fine line, since once you get too big you are more easily detected. So labor organizers have to be careful how they recruit, and how many workers meet together at once. But the nucleus of the movement is in place, and once the situation allows for it, there will be a huge mushrooming of independent labor unions. The NILU operates in two different trade associations. We are also doing our best to start publication of a national labor press. The task is to make labor news available and to begin to provide some political analysis.

Could you explain the political crisis in Iran that has unfolded since the election and how it is affecting your efforts to organize labor?

First of all, anybody who tells you that they have a full picture is lying, because the situation is very crazy.

There are at least five dozen semi-autonomous power centers, factions and groups vying for influence. Not even [Supreme Leader Ayatollah Sayyid Ali] Khamenei knows for certain what will happen tomorrow. But this does not mean there is complete anarchy. Speaking generally, there are at present four major centers of power, or rather, three plus one. The first three are Supreme Leader Khamenei, President Mahmoud Ahmadinejad and the Revolutionary Guards, while the fourth, the nascent popular movement, is of an altogether different character, though it still remains somewhat amorphous. It is still finding its own voice, needs and strengths—but it continues to evolve. For the foreseeable future, the first three powers will more or less effectively determine how things will turn out. This said, Khamenei is already weakened. This is for two reasons: he apparently has health problems, and more importantly, he has had made huge political blunders. In another country, people would probably say, "He's only human." But, in Iran, he is not only human. He is somewhere between human and saint, at least for his supporters and propagandists. But saints are not supposed to make blunders, at least not so many in so short a time!

What is the relationship between the NILU and the nascent popular movement?

There is no organic relationship between them, just as there are no organic relationships to speak of between the different elements of this movement. Mousavi does not even have an organic relationship with his own followers because of the pervasive power of repression. So, the nascent labor movement's relationship with the popular movement is tenuous both by necessity and because of the way things have evolved. That said, we fully support their goals and will participate in all demonstrations. We even support Mousavi himself because he has remained steadfast, at least up until now, in defending the people. So long as he continues to do this, he deserves our support. Of course, if he changes tack, that is a different story. We think this is a truly democratic movement such as we have not seen in Iran before, including during the Revolution. Every group involved with the Iranian Revolution, without exception, believed only in monopolizing power; democracy was nobody's concern. But now there is a very mature movement in that sense, particularly among the young people, and the fact that it has withstood so much violence in the last few months shows that it is deeply rooted. Many people were worried at first that the protests would fizzle out, but the continuation of the actions up to this day vindicate our support. The Iranian government has really gone overboard with stopping the protesters—it has been very bloody and violent—and still they have been unable to squash the protests entirely.

But do you think Mousavi stands for workers' rights at all? He seems to have a checkered political history.

We do not know what his stance is. He seems generally favorable to workers' rights, but, at any rate, our platform is not identical to his. The movement supporting Mousavi is a broad national-democratic front; we are all working with a sort of minimum program. The movement has formulated no long-term plans, and it is now in danger of being decimated. We do not have any illusions that anyone in the leadership of the Green Movement is 100 percent on board with workers' rights, but this is not the time to discuss that. Right now, we are fighting a dangerously reactionary dictatorship. Things will become clearer as time goes on, but right now we do not seek to magnify the differences among those opposing the dictatorship.

There are some who see Ahmadinejad, because he is so anti-American, as anti-imperialist, and thus as leftist. What is your response to such characterizations?

Well, the problem with this argument is that it assumes everyone in the world who rants and raves against the US or Israel is somehow progressive. Osama bin Laden, Mullah Omar, Saddam Hussein and Mahmoud Ahmadinejad—these men are all more truly anti-American than any leftist. But the rhetoric of Ahmadinejad and his ilk is all demagoguery, as far as we are concerned. Either it is in the service of power politics, or else it is just a fig leaf to hide the disgrace of their own politics, which in all these cases is profoundly anti-Left and anti-working class.

Still, in the peace movement here some people are uncomfortable taking a stand against Ahmadinejad or policies in Iran because they think that this is tantamount to supporting American policy.

Well, I can tell you how every democratically-minded person in Iran would reply: Ahmadinejad is essentially creating the ideal situation for foreign intervention. He is deliberately provocative. For instance, there is no need to use the kind of language he uses against Israel; it is genuinely odious, his frequent comments about the Holocaust and the like. But he speaks like this for a reason: he is a right-wing extremist seeking to rally his people through fear and hatred. That is what he is doing. To us it is actually incomprehensible how anyone could support Ahmadinejad just because he rants and raves about America. It really makes no sense to us. When I tell people in Iran that there are some progressive groups in America that support Ahmadinejad, they think I am pulling their leg. It makes no sense to them. But I know that this goes on and, to the extent it does, it gives the Left a bad name.

What is your take on Venezuelan President Hugo Chavez, who is very popular on the Left in America? He is frequently interviewed in progressive organs such as The Nation, *among others. He appears on the mass media as leading a front against America together with Ahmadinejad.*

We really do not know. We are really confused as to why Chavez is Ahmadinejad's buddy. It makes no sense to us. It has made it almost impossible in Iran to defend his Bolívarian Revolution. When you have people being beaten or tortured, and so on, and then tell them, "Well, there is this government that supports your government, but these guys are good guys," it is difficult to fathom, really. We hope that Chavez changes his policy, because when there is a change of government in Iran it will be accompanied by a total rupture with everyone who supported Ahmadinejad.

In your view, what is fueling the current crisis?

Well, let me go back to a point I was making earlier. Ayatollah Khamenei, because of his errors, has seen his status diminished. He no longer has about him the mystique that once so terrified and intimidated people. Then you have Ahmadinejad, who has turned out to be a rogue element for the regime, one that is perhaps doing more damage than good for them right now. Then there are the Revolutionary Guards, who have the bulk of the real power in Iran. They have made a power grab all over the country, so that now they control the economy, the political situation and the parliament. Still, Khamenei, Ahmedinejad and the Revolutionary Guards are in an ongoing struggle for power. They unite only in the face of common enemies, whether internal or foreign, and not always even then.

The current crisis in Iran is best understood as a set of concurrent crises. First, there is the legitimacy crisis, which I discussed just now with reference to Khamenei; second, there is the political crisis in which the various factions within Iranian "politics" cannot agree on anything; third, there is the economic crisis which the ruling class is utterly incapable of addressing. The country was in recession even before the election. What will bring the economic crisis to a head is Ahmadinejad's plan to cut all the subsidies, which are quite big—between 15 to 20 percent of the GDP (though no one really knows for sure the exact amount, due to the lack of transparency in the administration). The supposed populist Ahmadinejad intends to cut the subsidies for transportation, utilities, energy and even for staples such as rice and wheat. After this happens, there will be spiraling inflation, of course. The cut in subsidies for energy and utilities will force factories currently operating at a loss and/or below capacity to engage in massive layoffs. That is when we will see a number of labor actions. There may also be short-lived and violent urban uprisings. But rather than these riot-like urban uprisings, we are focusing on organizing labor to bring the country to a halt if need be.

Iranian labor is in a really awful situation, arguably the worst since its inception a century or so ago. With millions of workers in the formal sector, we still lack official, legal, independent unions. On the other hand, the situation is ideal for organizing. The labor force is ready for independent assertion, though they need the kind of support that only comes from dedicated organizers.

Iran's spiraling political and economic crisis coincides with another crisis that is only just beginning, the international crisis regarding the nuclear problem. Diplomatic talks are failing, as was inevitable. We feel that the regime is trying to build a bomb, but probably not testing it for a while. There is a clear danger that this might lead to an air attack or to some other form of major military intervention, which would divert attention from the internal situation. Indeed, as I said above, this is what this regime is hoping for. It would be a monumental mistake if there were to be an attack against Iran, since the nuclear program can only truly be stopped if the popular movement becomes more substantial and is able to change the government, or at least force changes in its policies.

*So your sense is that, with the nuclear program, Ahmadinejad is actually
trying to provoke aggression?*

Indeed. We condemn any kind of foreign intervention, but we also
condemn Ahmadinejad's provocative policies, in part because they are
geared toward provoking just such an intervention. Anyway, we do not
think the military route is the way to go with this, because it is not likely
to succeed even in halting the nuclear program. We think the labor
movement in Iran is poised to play a strategic role, even on the international stage, because once the working class organizes itself, it really can
cripple the regime, especially given the current economic crisis. And, as
I say, a major strike wave is looming in Iran.

The situation for Iranian workers right now is dismal. For the last
four or five years the demand for labor has dropped. There is also the ma-
nia for imports that Ahmadinejad has encouraged for the last five years.
The result is that across the country factories are facing shutdowns and
bankruptcy. There is also an immigrant Afghan labor force of roughly
seven hundred thousand, with whom we sympathize, and whose expulsion from the country we oppose just as we oppose the many forms of
coercion and discrimination this government levels against them, but it
is a fact that their acceptance of as little as 50 to 60 percent of normal
salary exerts downward pressure on everyone's wages. So, if you look at
all these factors, you see that things are really awful for Iranian workers;
their bargaining position is weak. In the current environment, once you
go on strike or you have some sort of shutdown, they can easily fire you
and find someone else.

The labor status quo has also changed. Few people are aware of
this, but Iran once had very progressive labor laws. In the aftermath
of the Revolution, it was very hard to legally fire workers. But now, 65
or 70 percent of the labor force consists in temporary contract workers
who lack most basic rights. They can now get fired and be deprived of
their benefits quite easily. This is what makes the situation so very ripe
for organizing, and makes organization necessary, despite the regime's

brutal repression. They do not allow for any labor organizations independent of the state, and they are ruthless. The least that could happen to an exposed labor organizer is that he gets fired and thrown in solitary confinement for several months.

This year is critical for the Iranian labor movement in many ways, and we need support of all kinds. Iran is in great danger. The government acts like an occupying army. It treats the country's ethnic minorities—Kurds, Baluchis and Arabs—as though they were foreign nationals. The resulting national disintegration grows worse day by day. At the same time, extremist groups are finding it increasingly easy to operate. Among the Sunni minority, fundamentalism is growing.

After the election, there is nothing to be said in favor of this regime. Before the election, there were perhaps some disparate elements within the government working toward reform, but this has ceased to be the case. All that remains is extremely retrograde: the government is ruining the country's culture and economy, while sowing discord among the people. They are turning minorities against each other and against the rest of the country—Shia against Sunni, not to mention men against women—all because the Islamic Republic state wants to retain and expand power. When these methods fail, they turn to brutal and undisguised repression.

I am wondering about the comparison of what is happening today to the 1979 Revolution. There were mass mobilizations then, with various leftist groups and parties involved, but when the shah fell, it left a power vacuum that was filled by reactionaries. First, is the comparison salient? Second, is there the possibility of a power vacuum emerging, and what can the labor organizers do in this situation?

You are wondering if, because there is not a clearly formulated platform for the movement, it may go awry, and extremist groups come to power? Of course, this is a possibility. But I think there are reasons to be optimistic. Thirty years of this sort of psychotic, pseudo-radical extremism has really taught everybody a lesson. You have to be either extremely naive or a direct beneficiary of the system not to see that the country has been harmed. In general, the young people are more mature than their parents' generation. The youth do not have the same romanticization of revolutionary violence, which was one of the reasons things got out of hand in 1979. It was not only the clerics that were extremists—practically every group endorsed revolutionary violence of one kind or another; it is just that in their mind their violence was justified, whereas everyone else's violence was "reactionary." The new generation does not hold those beliefs. Iranian society has a strong extremist strand, but I believe that is changing now. There is a belief in tolerance, in wanting to avoid force, and in trying to understand one's political opponents rather than just crushing them. This is something extremely important and not altogether common in much of today's Middle East.

Let me also say, along these lines, that Islam has never really undergone a reformation. But we are seeing signs of this happening in the Iran today. It is happening very quietly in the seminaries. It could only happen where Islamists have actually come to power and shown beyond all doubt the inadequacy or even the bankruptcy of their ideas and their ideologies. This forces healthy elements within the clergy—not those who are out there to enrich themselves, but those who are religious because they are utopian-minded—to go back to their books, to the Quran, and to revise the old ideas. Such clerics are not in the majority, yet they are sizable and they are spread throughout the clerical hierarchy from grand ayatollahs to the lowest clergy. Earlier, the idea of reforming the medieval interpretations of the Quran and Islam came mainly from Muslim intellectuals, but now a considerable part of the religious hierarchy is coming to the same conclusion. Some are operating in very dangerous circumstances. There is a Special Court of the Clergy, similar to the Inquisition courts, that want to silence them. But such ideas cannot be silenced so easily.

If there is a military attack on Iran, it will set back the progress of many years. This is exactly what the regime wants, at this point, which is why Ahmadinejad is so provocative. He wants the Israelis to launch an air strike. The West cannot simply bomb a few installations and think that it will all be done. The current regime would strive to escalate that fight. Even if Obama verbally condemns an intervention in Iran by another nation, Iran will use it as a pretext to expand the fight, and things will rapidly get out of hand. It would provide him with a new recruitment pool, which is drying up because the best and brightest of Iran do not now go into the Revolutionary Guards. Their recruits today are opportunists or those who simply need the money. The people are turning against the regime. What could change all this is if we came under attack, if, as they would claim, "Islam is threatened." The regime might then successfully stir up nationalistic sentiments, though perhaps not so much in Tehran, but that is only fourteen million or so. Most of the country lives in smaller towns, and the only news they get comes from state broadcasts. These people could become recruits, leading to all sorts of awful things. In the meantime, at the very least we will continue to see street fighting, riots and so on. The youth will only endure torture and being kicked out of schools up to a point. As it is, the regime opens fire on peaceful street demonstrations—I have seen it myself. The government's hope is that some of the young people will arm themselves and fight back. That is one of the dangers here.

You are here for the US Labor Against the War Conference. What sort of relationships do you hope to build with other labor unions in America and around the world?

First, I want to communicate to them what is happening in my country, that there is a labor movement and that it needs support. More specifically, even though there is no guarantee that this will change what this government is doing, we hope with the help of our American friends to put together an international committee of labor unions in defense of Iranian labor rights. The Iranian state does not even pretend to care what the international community or the general public thinks of them.

Still, they are weaker now than ever before, and the regime is concerned about what might come after a military action or major sanctions. So, for the first time it looks like they are going to be sensitive to what trade unions, especially those against intervention, have to say, or what they will do. In fact, Ahmadinejad's government has been sending envoys to the International Labor Organization (ILO) and courting it assiduously. They go out of their way to placate them, whereas ten years ago they did not give a damn what the ILO thought. So there may now be some scope to pressure the regime to release imprisoned labor organizers. In addition to that, we would like to inform the American labor movement and the public at large of the dangers of any kind of military intervention.

Do you think there are any possibilities for a labor party in Iran? That is a problem all over the world. Different labor organizations meet up, and there are groups that believe in various trade union rights, and they release statements to that effect. But there is no political body that consistently stands up for working people.

I may have sounded like too much of an alarmist, for I emphasized the dangers. But the opportunities are also great. Like I said, you have almost eight million workers in need of organizing. They will even be able to organize themselves, if the situation changes. The Green Movement holds promise, I think. It came totally out of the blue; no one expected it, from the Ministry of Intelligence to the opposition and the foreign governments. This means there are elements that could coalesce into a progressive and democratic labor party. It should not be forgotten that Iran not only has a huge working class, but also a tradition of left-wing activity going back some 100 years. The working class in Iran, moreover, is no longer semi-proletarian as it was during the Iranian Revolution. This generation of workers has advanced political skills and a mature political worldview. You are no longer dealing with peasants just come to the city. Iran is fairly industrialized in many ways, and these workers have their own subcultures. We have a good situation in that sense. So yes, there is a good possibility that we will have a strong labor party. The conditions are there, but none of this will materialize without a strong, deeply rooted labor movement.

So what needs to be done? We must put across to other sectors of society what the working class stands for. The protest movement is now primarily middle class. That is its primary weakness. But once labor strikes get underway in the next few months, we hope they will change how the Green Movement sees the workers, themselves and their moment. It is our job as labor activists to put across a genuine working-class platform and to familiarize the country with working-class demands.

We cannot, as some Left groups do, start condemning the Green Movement just because it lacks a strong Left component. It is the Left's job to influence the movement and to see that its demands and wishes are incorporated—not just with respect to Mousavi, but to the movement as a whole.

We cannot start condemning the movement even if and when it starts lurching to the right, because, again, it is the Left's job to be there side by side with it. By being there, I mean, for example, our press must also reflect their concerns and their needs. We should not be supercilious, but rather have a healthy dialogue with all the different contingents within it. Above all, we should not speak from above in a condescending manner. Only when we are side by side with the people who are fighting on the streets will they listen to us. In the last six or seven months, there has been an incredible growth of interest in the Left among young people. This has been very spontaneous. If anything, the old generation mishandled their political situation and turned young people off by looking down on them.

If the labor movement gets its act together, it could really help the present popular movement, which, on its own, lacks the muscle to stand up to the regime. With the workers on board there can be economic strikes. In 1979, there were people yelling and clamoring in the streets for months, but it was only when the oil workers entered the picture that the Western governments told the shah to leave.

Because of all this and because of the fact that the labor movement, by its nature, tries to avoid extremism or revolutionary romanticism, there is reason to hope. The labor movement's pragmatism allows it to stave off the dangers of extremism from both Left and right. The two main labor unions, the sugar cane workers and bus drivers, are resolute in protesting against the status quo and advancing their political and social agenda. They are supported by over 90 percent of the work force. If you talk to bus drivers in Tehran they are all upset about what has happened recently, but you never hear anything disparaging about the union leadership and what they have done. This shows the kind of work organizers have done. This was not a spur-of-the-moment thing. They organized over several years and held many sessions with intellectuals who taught them constitutional rights, economics and so on. But, of course, there have been mistakes, as is to be expected. But those mistakes were necessary in some ways, so that the rest of the labor unions will not repeat them.

THIS MAGIC GREEN BRACELET

Nasrin Alavi

January 20, 2010

The picture above shows Hassan and Yasser Khomeini (centre and right, respectively), grandsons of the former Ayatollah, offering their condolences to the family of the deceased.

Following the contested presidential election in June 2009, Iran saw the largest street protests in the thirty years of the Islamic Republic. The hashtag "#iranelection" dominated the micro-blogging site Twitter and even inspired a worldwide solidarity campaign, as the voice of a nation's resistance was heard in real-time YouTube footage of protests and in a deluge of tweets and blog posts. The Huffington Post hailed the micro-blogger persiankiwi—with over 35,000 followers—as "one of the most reliable and prolific Iranians on Twitter." Most of his readers could understand his nonviolent fight for democratic rights, but perhaps many failed to notice that his posts were threaded with verses from the Quran.

Paradoxically, the opponents of the Islamic state have chosen "Allah-u-akbar" or "God is great" as their battle cry. This is a new generation that has largely responded to tyrannical violence with democratic non-violence, yet they refer to slain protesters as *Shahids* (Islamic martyrs), much to the annoyance of religious and secular elders. This new generation has revived the moral legitimacy of the Iranian "cause" through very modern cyber-methods.

Protesters often chanted the names of Iran's war heroes, adding that "They were the real Basij"—a taunt directed toward the Basij militia that have brutally regained control of the streets on behalf of the regime. One of the "Great Shahids" or heroes of the Iran–Iraq war was Mohammad Ali Jahanara, who, at the age of twenty-six, commanded the ordinary townsfolk of Khorramshahr who fought the Iraqi invasion of their town inch-by-inch for forty-five days before it fell to the enemy. A common tweet in the post-election period read, "Tell Jahanara the Baathists are in Tehran, they are firing on our girls." In fact many of those who have openly endorsed the Green Movement (the resistance movement that coalesced around defeated presidential candidate Mir Hossein Mousavi) are the actual children of war heroes such as Jahanara, Zeinadin, Bakeri and the Hemat brothers, all of whom have countless roads, hospitals and schools named after them. This phenomenon led cleric Mohammad Reyshahri to state last week that there is "no art in making a member of a Martyr's family into an insurgent."

Children of the revolution

Students have continued to take a stand, despite the deaths, the Stalinist show trials and mass arrests. The authorities have haphazardly swung between conciliation and vicious oppression. In December, in a seemingly conciliatory move, Mohammad Mohammadian—Ayatollah Ali Khamenei's emissary in the Office of University Affairs—told an academic gathering that "according to the polls available, 70 percent of students voted for someone who does not head the nation's administration [in other words, not for President Ahmadinejad]. This in a way causes disappointment... but those who have voted for others have our respect." Thirty years after the Revolution, the state is grappling with its own demographic "success" and does not seem to know how to come to terms with one of the youngest and most educated populations in the region.

A simple glance at the background of Iran's prominent student leaders tells you that, by and large, they are not the children of affluent citizens of north Tehran, but instead come from provincial working-class families or are the children of rural schoolteachers and clerks. The Western media cliché of an opposition limited to the urban upper class belies the current realities. These future leaders of Iran commonly hail from the very heartland of Ahmadinejad's purported support base.

On December 21, as hundreds of thousands attended the funeral for Ayatollah Hossein Ali Montazeri, the opposition demonstrated that it can make its presence felt in Iran's Vatican, the holy city of Qom. Montazeri, once a powerful establishment figure, was sidelined for his criticism of the mass execution of thousands of young political prisoners in the 1980s. He even condemned Khomeini's fatwa urging the assassination of author Salman Rushdie, saying, "People in the world are getting the idea that our business in Iran is just murdering people." In 2004 he protested that the Iranian people did not go through a revolution in order to "substitute absolutist rule by the crown with one under the turban."

A really cool mullah

I followed the funeral via the blogs of young writers based in Qom and others making there way there. Many of those who came from Tehran reported that, to their surprise, not only were the vast majority of the protesters either from Qom or the provinces, but they were also angrier and more daring; as one writer put it, they "had the balls to chant slogans, the sort we would never dare chant in Tehran." A well-known blogger wrote about a group of villagers generously sharing their rustic lunch with protesters. A "really cool mullah" who had offered to host a "busload" of mourners for the day told her, "Iran needs a Renaissance!!!!!!!!!!" The ten exclamation marks are the writer's, not mine. Elsewhere, an overwhelming outpouring of online grief followed, ranging from the self-described Marxist and labor activist who wrote of his "deep mourning" for the Ayatollah as a democratic defender of human rights, to Iran's Nobel laureate Shirin Ebadi, who described Montazeri as the "father" who had inspired her to end her silence and "defend political prisoners."

Masih Alinejad is a female journalist whom Ebadi defended after she became one of many casualties of Ahmadinejad's ferocious campaign against the press. Alinejad described in her blog how a nation without a free media had conducted a magnificent state funeral online: "I want to tell you of the mourning of a generation of 'non-believers' for an Ayatollah" and how respectfully the "lifeless, honorable body of religious guide was carried on the shoulders of a cyber community."

This generation's true leader

I must also tell you about the vast and sometimes startling support that exists both online and in the streets for Mir Hossein Mousavi. Many have described Iran's protest movement as lacking "leadership." I don't know how loud the protesters have to shout "Yah Hossein, Mir Hossein,"—as they seem to have done at each and every rally to date (and immediately posted it on YouTube)—before the outside world will hear them.

As one blogger puts it: "Our fanatics have a lot in common with our exiled commentators. They both call us 'duped and naive' and Mousavi a 'temporary vehicle' or an 'accidental leader' of an opposition. Yet no-one has ever been able to connect and unite us as Mousavi has. As a university lecturer for the last twenty years, Mousavi also grew up with the children of this revolution and he understands us like no-one else... my generation's truly elected prime minister is Mir Hossein."

In the pro-Mousavi cry of "Yah Hossein," protesters invoke Seyyed Al-Shohada, the highest Shahid or martyr [Imam Hossein, the third Shia Imam, grandson of the Prophet Muhammad and a holy figure in Shia Islam], which to the vast majority of Iranians immediately conveys a stand against tyranny. This generation's Islamic martyrs include the philosophy student whose fatal shooting was captured by camera phone and has been viewed millions of times online—"Shahid Neda" Soltan, as she is often called. Or twenty-six-year-old doctor Ramin Pourandarjani, who died of poisoning after his refusal to sign falsified death certificates at the Kahrizak prison. Or nineteen-year-old Mohsen Ruholamini, a member of the conservative student Basij who died in the very same detention center after protesting against election fraud.

Khomeini's grandchildren

Such Islamic deification of the young casualties of this pro-democracy movement is met with revulsion by the regime and occasionally by the secular opposition as well. But for many observers, an even more surreal development in this shifting religious and political landscape is that family members of the founder of the Iranian revolution, Ayatollah Khomeini, are by and large reformists who support the Green Movement. For example, after clashes between police and demonstrators in Tehran on December 26, hundreds were arrested and at least eight people killed, including the nephew of the opposition leader Mir Hossein Mousavi, who was shot in the heart. The picture above shows Hassan and Yasser Khomeini (centre and right, respectively), grandsons of the former Ayatollah, offering their condolences to the family of the deceased. In past months they have visited many of the families of prominent political prisoners. Hassan Khomeini is widely respected for having volunteered and fought on the front line during the war with Iraq, unlike most offspring of the clerical elite.

In December, pro-government Basij attacked and broke up a gathering at the Khomeini family mosque at Jamaran that was hosted by Hassan Khomeini. In the same month, Mohammad Reza Khatami, who is married to Zahra Eshraghi, another of Khomeini's grandchildren, was arrested. The revolution can perhaps eat its children and get away with it. But eating the children of its founder may well prove to be taking it a step too far. This election has pushed revolutionary Iran into uncharted waters, exposing cracks in the leadership and leaving them entirely open to the elements.

Confessions of a political hooligan

Lady Plum began keeping a blog about six years ago. Her many readers have followed her daily thoughts through her pregnancy and life as a young mother. She generally steers clear of politics. Yet after attending a protest rally with her child and her mother, she wrote a post titled "Confessions of a Political Hooligan"—a term commonly used by state media to describe opposition protesters:

> There is a bitter sentence about our society that has always been difficult to reject. "We don't deserve democracy..." They had divided us by appearance. Devout, western, downtown [working-class] intellectual, pauper and hooligan... Being together has shattered this. This magic green bracelet has worked wonders with our culture, our feelings and our hearts. These gathering in my town, without censorship, exaggeration, trickery and lies... We stand as our true selves.
>
> I am moving in silence with a child in my arms and hand in hand with a woman who is the meaning of my life and they call me a hooligan. The madman, who hollers dishonourable insults, throws stones and shows me a knife, is called the people. But I have learnt that in this game he has to come with me and then we shall be called the people. I can see in his eyes that he has lessened, become smaller, even though he shows no shame as he looks at me. He cannot help but feel ashamed in front of my child who holds up his fingers in victory in the face of his strange barbarity.

Iran's coming of age

This is not just a fleeting brawl about an election result. During Iran's Constitutional Revolution of 1906, hopes of democracy were dashed and authoritarian rule was implemented with the help of foreign powers. A generation later, the democratically-elected government of Mossadegh was finished off in a coup backed by Britain and the US. For many, the past haunts the present and has sowed the seeds of Iran's current dilemmas.

Throughout Iran's recent history, each generation has endeavored to bring about political change. In the last 150 years, Iran's absolutist monarchs were either ousted by the people or forced to flee into exile—with the one exception of Mozafaredin Shah, who gave in to pro-democracy activists and agreed to create a parliament and hold elections.

Today, the establishment has exposed its totalitarian ambitions in the way it handled the election results, in the the brutal crackdowns and the mass arrests. "They," to use the word Iranians commonly direct at the powerful, are today revealed as the architects of their own misfortune. "They" have made this a fight to the end.

This is not an uprising that can be suppressed. Some have argued that just as the Chinese rose up after the Tiananmen Square protests of 1989 and were crushed, this will be crushshed too. But here there is neither the unity of an ideological hierarchy nor recourse to a growth economy that might pacify the masses. Ultimately, this story is not going away because it is not merely about an election result, but about the coming of age of a generation whose nonviolent fight for civil rights must prevail.

As the blogger Opium writes, "This election—whatever it was, whatever it did—it made us big and it made you small."

THE STRUGGLE FOR IRAN'S SOUL

Christopher de Bellaigue

January 27, 2010

Iran's electoral controversy of last June is starting to seem like a quaint irrelevance next to the conflict that the two sides are now waging for possession of the country—not simply its institutions and resources, but also its identity and culture. The end of the struggle will almost certainly mean defeat for one party, and not, as once seemed possible, co-existence. There will not only be political winners and losers, but moral ones too. Iranian tradition holds that fortune favors the righteous, and all the characters in this latest epic lay claim to that mantle.

The crisis is part of a struggle between Iranians who want their country to join the community of nations that is roughly in agreement on both the challenges facing the human race and the mechanisms for tackling them, and those who don't. The supporters of President Mahmoud Ahmadinejad's main challenger in the June election, Mir Hossein Mousavi, present themselves as modern, plugged-in internationalists. Since the crisis began, they have adeptly used the Internet to circumvent the state and publicize their cause to foreign media outlets. The state, on the other hand, has sought solace in principled isolation. Like Kipling's cat, Iran walks on its own.

Iran withdrew into itself after the revolution of 1979. The Islamic Republic's semi-democratic, semi-theocratic system of government, topped by an institution known as the rule of the Islamic jurist, is unique. Its participation in the world economy is largely restricted to trade: Iran sells oil and buys capital and consumer goods. Its role in world diplomacy is mostly confined to pursuing its own, anti-Western agenda. Ideas and information must get around walls of censorship and official indifference, and sometimes never do. Few Iranians, for instance, seem to know about global warming.

Living in Tehran, as I do, one of a very small number of Westerners to remain, it is possible to feel incubated from many of the issues that concern other countries. Iran's solitude has fostered a sense of exceptionalism, at once hubristic and defensive. Yes, Iran's opposition movement shares characteristics with Europe's 1989 revolutions—its reliance on "people power," for instance, to press a broad (and, as yet, ill-defined) agenda of peaceful change. At the same time, watching events from behind a curtain of culture and history, it's hard to ignore the intimate, coded nature of the struggle.

Since the crisis began and the authorities banned anti-government rallies, the opposition has developed a highly idiosyncratic modus operandi. Prevented by the security forces from staging protests, activists exploit the opportunities furnished by official days of commemoration or mourning, when the authorities encourage people to take to the streets in support for the Islamic Republic. Protesters duly comply, but instead shout subversive slogans.

Some call not only for democratic reforms but also for ending the Islamic Republic. An increasing number show their willingness to fight the security forces, hurling rocks and bricks at the better-armed riot police and Basij militiamen.

There were plenty of such battles on December 27, the great Shia day of mourning, Ashura. Ashura is the anniversary of the martyrdom of the Imam Hossein, the Prophet Mohammad's grandson and a pretender to the caliphate of Islam. In 680, Hossein and his men were wiped out by the army of Shemr, under the command of the rival Omayyids in Damascus. In time the rift gave rise to two rival sects within Islam, the Sunnis and the Shias, with Shias recognizing the descendents of the Prophet as leaders. These days, Ashura is commemorated by Shias everywhere, notably in Iraq and Pakistan. But only in Iran, the largest Shia state, does it have an encompassing, national character.

Hossein's martyrdom has long been a shorthand for sacrifice,

Islamic militancy and the pursuit of justice. Ashura in Iran is marked each year with solemn fanfare. The streets fill with processions of flagellants, prayer halls teem with sobbing mourners beating their chests, and street corners grow misty from cauldrons filled with pullulating stews of meat and pulses donated by local philanthropists.

This time was different. From early in the morning of December 27, the streets of central Tehran were full not of mourners but of members of the security forces: police, volunteer militia, and riot police in body armor. This did not prevent many thousands of opposition demonstrators from taking to the streets, as they have done intermittently since June, chanting anti-government slogans and, when attacked, entering into battles with the forces of law and order. At least eight people were killed that day, including a nephew of Mir Hossein Mousavi, and hundreds more were injured and arrested as Tehran descended into chaos and violence.

Three days after Ashura, the authorities staged their own rally. I watched as the streets of central Tehran thronged with hundreds of thousands of chador-clad women and grim-faced men. They held aloft flags adorned with devotional verses and shouted slogans denouncing acts of desecration that the opposition had committed, they said, on December 27.

According to participants in the pro-government rally, the opposition had turned the most solemn day in the Shia calendar into a grotesque exhibition. They had attacked mourners and the security forces, setting fire to vehicles and buildings, whistling and clapping. "What they did," one man said, "was more Shemr than Shemr himself." He and the other members of the crowd shouted, "Death to Mousavi!" and "Death to opponents of the Guardianship of the Jurist!" Then, prompted through loudspeakers, they started chanting encomia to Ayatollah Ali Khamenei, the country's Supreme Leader.

Further state-organized responses to the events of Ashura followed. Marches and demonstrations were staged across the country and were covered exhaustively by state television. Ashen-faced news presenters introduced footage of rioters celebrating in front of burning buildings, and pro-government clerics duly lambasted the godless demonstrators.

• • •

Standing among government supporters at the epicenter of the rally I attended on December 30—and not without discomfort, particularly when the crowd shouted, "Death to Britain!"—I cast my mind back to the eve of Ashura several days earlier, which I had spent in Zavareh, a small provincial town at the edge of Iran's inhospitable Kavir desert. I had gone there not as a reporter but in search of a famous Ta'zieh, or Shia passion play, which is performed on that day in the town's elegant Hosseinieh, an arcaded congregational space of some antiquity that was recently restored with the help of pious locals.

Together with my six-year-old son Jahan, I watched a seemingly endless procession of flagellants dressed in black, each group from a different part of the town, move through the Hosseinieh, striking their backs gently with chains on short handles, taking small, crab-like steps in time to the rhythmic lamentation of a man singing into a microphone, accompanied by pounding drums and crashing cymbals.

Eventually, at one a.m., the Ta'zieh started. Jahan had been blinking hard with the effort of staying awake. Now he came to life as the scarlet, plumed figure of Shemr prowled the stage proclaiming his evil intent, and Hossein's brother, the heroic, handsome Abol Fazl, prepared to make a suicidal sally to the river Euphrates to bring water for the Imam's followers. Hossein's sister, Zeyneb, was played by a man who concealed his moustache with a black veil, a picture of demure, if rather broad-shouldered, feminine virtue. Peering over a cloth partition which divided the male from the female spectators, watching the chador-clad women shower Abol Fazl with donations in return for cups of sanctified water, and the young men kiss the Imam's green flag, I could imagine myself being back in the provincial Iran of half a century or more ago.

During a break in the play, as a master of ceremonies praised those who financed the building of the corridor that allowed women to enter the Hosseinieh without encountering men, I started talking to a young man sitting next to us. He turned out to have been Ahmadinejad's election campaign manager. In June, he said, Zavareh had been overwhelmingly pro-Ahmadinejad. Now, he went on, alluding to the growth of a dangerous opposition movement in faraway Tehran, it was even more so. Looking around me, I believed him.

We left at three a.m., after Abol Fazl lost his arms, and ultimately his life, trying to draw water from the Euphrates. (Hossein himself would only be martyred the following day.)

Many people had predicted violence on Ashura, and I wanted to get Jahan back to Tehran, a five-hour drive away. I heard on the radio that hardliners had broken up a speech about Ashura and the Imam Hossein by Mohammad Khatami, a former reformist president and a Mousavi supporter.

The Imam Hossein's martyrdom was a symbol for the 1979 revolutionaries and inspired millions to volunteer during the Iran–Iraq war in the 1980s. Iranians have other heroes, some from pre-Islamic history and mythology, but none rivals this lord of martyrs as an embodiment of chivalry, piety and self-sacrifice. Iranians write poems and pop songs for him; children are taught that the revolutionaries of 1979 vindicated his memory.

The question is, which revolutionaries? Many members of today's opposition invoke the same symbols and memories as the hardliners. The text of Khatami's interrupted speech about Ashura contained an allusion to the "highest and strongest right in the social sphere," namely "the right of the individual to determine his destiny." This is not an extrapolation that any hardliner would make from the tragedy of Ashura. In their eyes, it is a dangerous, Western-inspired innovation.

The opposition have also described the violence of December 27 in religious terms, using the terms of reference set by their adversaries. According to them, it is the security forces who behaved like Shemr. In a statement on January 2, Mousavi declared that he was ready for martyr-dom, placing himself in a tradition that extends from the Imam Hossein to the Iranians who lost their lives in the Iran–Iraq war.

. . .

When Khatami's reform movement emerged in the 1990s, it claimed to be the heir of the founder of the revolution, Ayatollah Ruhollah Khomeini. Today's opposition, being a mutation of the same reform movement, does the same, and the conservatives reply with the same accusations: that the reformists' pledges to improve the Islamic Republic are a smokescreen hiding their real intention, which is to abolish it.

Undoubtedly, many opposition supporters still adhere to the idea of reform as the solution to the current crisis. But others have disengaged themselves from the old terms of reference. They are stirred by ideas about Western-style democracy and do not rationalize their pursuit of freedom of the individual with recourse to the Imam Hossein's mar-tyrdom. For the moment, the opposition is united, but in the future, a fracture along these lines may take place. Mousavi's calls for reform within the framework of the Islamic Republic have the support not only of Mehdi Karoubi, another defeated presidential candidate, but also of several influential intellectuals. Outside the country, however, where Iranian exiles—many of them hopelessly out of touch—observe events with fascination, there is support for a more radical transformation.

Iran's conservatives have seized on these tensions to depict their adversaries as opportunists who aim to destroy Islam. The religion's history includes examples of enemies who coat their evil intentions in pieties. Mousavi and his friends have been added to the list.

If the current dispute were solely a political one, the conservatives would have declared it won long ago. Since 2005, when Khatami stepped down from the presidency, the conservatives have held all the levers of the state, including the supreme leadership, government, parliament and armed forces. Rather, what we are seeing now is the denouement of a more opaque conflict, centering around issues of culture and identity.

The Persian word for culture is *farhang*. A Westernized, middle-class Iranian may use it to refer to the nation's creative output—films, books and art—or perhaps mores. But the word is most often heard from official mouths. It is elastic, taking in almost every facet of an Iranian's life. Before 1979, the shah's government steered citizens toward a *farhang* that was, on the surface at least, Western; since then, the authorities have tried, through *farhangsazi*, or "culture-making," to create a nation of pious Shias in a state of perpetual ferment, enamored of the Islamic Republic and the rule of the Islamic jurist, and inspired by their "Islamic-Iranian" identity. At its most extreme, farhang has a solely negative connotation, meaning rejecting all that is Western.

Farhangsazi is an elite activity, in which senior politicians and academics tell people how to think and behave. Recently, I heard an official on the radio say that Iran needed "cultural engineering." More than a century after Western fashions first appeared in Tehran, scandalizing traditionalists, government support is being offered for the development of a "national dress." The supreme leader has inveighed against the teaching of humanities—"whose foundations are materialism and disbelief in divine and Islamic teachings." A proposal to ban co-ed universities comes under *farhang*'s rubric, for it would counter the *farhang* of fraternizing between the sexes, which harmed the *farhang* of arranged marriages between virgins.

Hostility to the West is as old as Iran's modern engagement with Europe, which began in earnest in the second half of the nineteenth century. Then European ideas, goods, travelers and investors entered the country under the watchful eye of a suspicious, but impecunious shah and a generally hostile clerical establishment. Educated Iranians experienced a rise in national consciousness, although they were divided over how to reconcile their pre-Islamic heritage and the Persian language—which distinguished them from their Arab neighbors—with their supranational, Islamic identity. Finally, while there was consensus over the greed and unscrupulousness of the Europeans, attitudes toward the European commodities of knowledge and modernity were less uniform.

In the middle part of the last century, Mohammad Mossadegh was Iran's most inspirational nationalist. Mossadegh was a European-educated secularist who regarded Britain's constitutional monarchy as a model, but he colored his message as much with Islam and traditional notions of justice as he did with national sovereignty. In 1951, Mossadegh oversaw the nationalization of the Anglo-Iranian Oil Company, which most Iranians regarded as an agent of British imperialism, and became prime minister immediately afterward. Two years later, after failing to agree to a compromise with the British, the Americans and his internal enemies, Mossadegh refused to use violence to save his premiership from a CIA coup. For his readiness to face martyrdom rather than compromise his beliefs, some of his supporters compared him to the Imam Hossein.

Over the past decade, benefiting from record oil prices, urban Iranians have become noticeably more materialistic, and more liberal in their approach to mores and culture. This has prompted charges of vacuous hedonism, but it is noticeable that many of the women who have pushed the dress codes to the limit are now engaged in a more deadly struggle— on the streets of the capital, in combat with the Basijis.

• • •

If the reform movement is to be captured by any ideology, it is likely to be nationalism. There is little evidence that the opposition would be less uncompromising than the government in defending the country's nuclear program. And many opposition members argue that the country's rulers have shunned Iran's pre-Islamic heritage in favour of Arab-imported Islam; they shout, "Neither east, nor west, but an Iranian Republic!" In place of the US, Britain and Israel, the traditional bogeymen, demonstrators shout slogans against Russia and China, whose diplomatic and economic support have partly mitigated the effects of Western pressure. Many Iranians believe allegations that Russia has been giving lessons to Iran's security forces, and they regret the decline of local manufacturing at the hands of Chinese imports.

A newspaper recently reported that China produces the chains that flagellants use during Ashura, the helmets worn by actors in the Ta'zieh, and the belts to which mourners attach heavy metal standards for the Ashura processions. Even the pro-government newspaper Iran expressed dismay that China has captured the lion's share of the country's stationery sector. For a nation so concerned about cultural imperialism, it is ironic that exercise books and pencils emblazoned with a British bear repackaged in Hollywood should enter the country thanks to Chinese mass production.

The nationalism of the opposition is anathema to supporters of Iran's rulers, who fear the country may be separated from its Islamic core. "What does an 'Iranian Republic' mean?" Ayatollah Abdullah Javadi Amoli demanded in December. "If the country could achieve independence through an Iranian Republic, it would have done so in the time of Mossadegh. The only thing that made Iran proud and victorious was Islam and Hossein." The dichotomy is simplistic, but the words point to a truth about a seemingly modern struggle. Iran's present agony stems from old debates: about virtue, gallantry and justice.

IRAN'S REVOLUTIONARY ECHOES AND THE FORWARD MARCH OF HISTORY

Said Arjomand

February 2, 2010

Iran's continued unrest, now extending through the thirtieth anniversary of the revolution that toppled the shah, raises the question of whether the Islamic Republic is about to fall. As in 1979, millions of Iranians have taken to the streets, this time to protest electoral fraud in the presidential vote last June.

The cheated presidential candidates, both veterans of the revolution, instinctively thought they were witnessing a replay of history. Mir Hossein Mousavi saw the green symbols of the demonstrators as representing the color of the House of the Prophet and urged his supporters to continue their nightly rooftop chants of "God is Great!" Thus, the first slogan of the opposition invoked the religious credo of the 1979 revolutionaries. More recently, protesters chanted it during the funeral demonstrations for Grand Ayatollah Montazeri in the closing days of 2009.

Yet we risk being led astray by memories of 1979. It is far too soon to predict another revolution. But the divide between Iran's society and its government is much greater today than it was under the shah thirty years ago. Change seems just as inevitable.

Technological advances greatly favor the protesters of today. Text messages, Twitter and the Internet are infinitely superior to the smuggled cassettes of Ayatollah Khomeini's speeches that fueled the opposition in 1979. What's missing this time, however, is a charismatic leader comparable to Khomeini. Indeed, the striking feature of the Iranian opposition movement is the lack of effective leadership, despite the astonishing persistence of protests. As Mousavi has readily acknowledged, neither he nor the other presidential candidate, Mehdi Karoubi, feels like they are in charge.

The greatest difference between 2009 and 1979 was created by the revolution itself. Revolutions give birth to a new political class, and Iran's Islamic revolution was no exception. The Iranian leadership formed after the revolution consisted of a narrow ruling stratum and a much broader supporting group that was given charge of administration and political mobilization. In the twenty years since Khomeini's death, the composition of this political class has changed drastically. The clerical elite has gradually lost power to the military-security groups, from whose ranks President Ahmadinejad emerged. Bureaucratic and security services dominated by the Revolutionary Guards and its militia, the Basij, are now firmly in command.

The leader of the Islamic Republic, Ayatollah Ali Khamenei, blessed the Revolutionary Guards' decision to steal the presidential election. By siding squarely with the military-security apparatus headed by Ahmadinejad, Khamenei has alienated an important segment of the ruling clerical elite. He has also reduced his own status as the ultimate arbiter in Iranian society, a role that was central to Khomeini's dominance of the system. As a result, he has produced a rupture between the two pillars of the revolutionary regime: the clerical elite and military-security structure.

The growth of Khamenei's personal, extra-constitutional power introduces a strong element of uncertainty into Iran's future. Political regimes that rely on personal power, commonly known as dictatorships, prove to be fragile in crisis. This was the weakness of the shah's regime, which collapsed as he became paralyzed in his decision-making. There was nothing behind him supporting the system.

Khamenei's backing of the June 2009 putsch now appears to be a costly mistake. With this single error, he has undermined what had appeared to be a robust post-revolutionary course for the first and only theocracy in modern history. The cries of "God is Great!" have now been overtaken by chants of "Death to the dictator!" in recent demonstrations in Tehran, Tabriz, Shiraz and other Iranian cities.

The Iranian regime is now critically dependent on decisions made by one man, the Supreme Leader. For that reason, it is demonstrating a degree of fragility that is comparable to that of the shah's regime in the latter part of the 1970s.

Most spokespeople of the Green Movement advocate civil disobedience instead of revolution. Earlier this month, Ezzattolah Sahabi, who was a member of the revolutionary provisional government in 1979, issued a statement in Tehran stating categorically that "a revolution in today's Iran is neither possible nor desirable." At roughly the same time, five prominent opposition intellectuals living in exile released a reformist, not revolutionary, manifesto directed against the "despotic guardians."

But there is little chance that these children of the Islamic revolution—now graying reformists—will remain in control of the Green Movement, which now reflects the aspirations of a post-revolutionary generation of young women and men.

The ayatollah-dictator and the Revolutionary Guards have tried their best to discredit their opponents by concocting, through forced confessions at show trials, a conspiracy of regime change based on a "velvet revolution" produced by "Western social sciences." Deep down, they know there is no conspiracy. Their fear is grounded in what they see in front of them: the forward march of history.

PART III

CONFRONTING SETBACKS, RETHINKING STRATEGY

THE REGIME'S PYRRHIC VICTORY

Mr. Verde

February 12, 2010

Pyrrhic victory (noun): A victory achieved at too great a cost (after Pyrrhus, king of Epirus, who suffered staggering losses in defeating the Romans)

This year's 22 Bahman [February 11] anniversary may have been the most widely discussed since the 1979 Revolution, but with continued disruption of communications in Iran, the flow of information about the events was always going to be slow. So, reserving comment about the actual events for a later date when more information is available, here's a look at the "big picture" for the Islamic Republic.

The regime has demonstrated that, as on other occasions, it can bus in people, or entice them with free food or fear of their government jobs, for the setpiece event. It has also once again demonstrated that its security forces are very capable of beating peaceful protesters in order to disperse them.

And here comes the problem: this year's events were less like celebrating a revolution that freed the country from tyranny and dictatorship and more like a tyrannical dictatorship celebrating its continued survival.

The more one pays attention to the words and actions of the officials of the Islamic Republic, the more it becomes apparent that there is something wrong. From the start of the post-election protests, the regime has been adamant that the protesters were few in number and did not have a real agenda except causing chaos and mayhem. (There were exceptions when officials, desperate to explain specific situations, talked about millions being on the streets in June, but these were single officials trying to explain away other difficult facts.) If the protesters are so few in number and so insignificant, there is no reason for such heavy security presence. How to resolve this contradiction? Either the regime knows that opposition is widespread or we are witnessing a totalitarian regime in action.

The protests have been ongoing for eight months. This period, from June to February, has covered almost all of the Islamic Republic's official occasions during which it has traditionally encouraged the population to take part in public events, events which are usually used as proof of the regime's popularity and stability. But since June 12, the regime has resorted to naked violence on each of these occaions in order to keep people off the streets. There are only two such days left in this year's calendar that have not been tarnished yet by clashes on the streets: the anniversaries of Khomeini's death (June 4) and the 15 Khordaad uprising (June 5).[1]

The Islamic Republic is a regime built upon ideological symbols, and it relies heavily upon them; the calendar is filled with events that recall to Iranians their history and religious culture. Friday prayers are weekly affirmations of the public's support for the regime, both in a religious and political context. Quds Day in September celebrates the Islamic Republic's support for the Palestinian people. 13 Aban (November 4) commemorates the killing of schoolchildren by the shah's security forces and, perhaps more importantly, the start of the US Embassy hostage crisis, referred to by Khomeini as the second revolution and the Islamic Republic's proof that it stood up to superpowers. 16 Azar (December 7) commemorates the student movements that stood up to the Shah's regime after the 1953 CIA coup. Ashura (December 27) commemorates the uprising by Imam Hossein (the third Shia Imam) against tyranny. 22 Bahman (February 11) marks the victory of the 1979 Revolution that brought about the Islamic Republic. But all of these events are now remembered not for their original symbolic importance, but for the fact that in 2009 and 2010 the security forces of the Islamic Republic have on every one of these occasions beaten and killed peaceful Iranian demonstrators.

The regime has also managed to discredit many of its own nota-ble officials and personalities. Many of the Islamic Republic's former leading figures are in prison on charges of sedition or acting against national security. These days, some very senior politicians and activists are treated as enemies of the state. On the eve of Ashura, government thugs disrupted a speech by former President Mohammad Khatami, in no less a place than the home of the Islamic Republic's founder, Aya-tollah Khomeini. Mir Hossein Mousavi, prime minister during most of the eight-year war with Iraq, and Mehdi Karoubi—revolutionary cleric during the shah's regime, former head of the Martyrs' Foundation, for-mer Speaker of Parliament—are insulted by regime officials on a daily basis, prevented from taking part in official commemorations, and at times shot at with tear gas and beaten. Only eight months ago, both men passed through the formidable filter of the Council of Guardians in order to become presidential candidates. The regime is now calling them leaders of sedition.

The question for the regime is: have these people, who have impec-cable revolutionary credentials, always been leading an insurrection? If so, how is it that for thirty years this fact was missed by the Islamic Republic's many intelligence organizations and intelligence officials? Or could it be that the state of affairs of the Islamic Republic is such that even loyal servants are forced to protest? No enemy would have been able to undermine the ideological symbols and tarnish the reputation of the Islamic Republic with such efficiency.

The regime is fast losing any claim of being Islamic, popular, just or merciful. And its showpiece events have become occasions on which its forces are mobilized to attack its own citizens, even as it pours resources into making a show for TV cameras so that some foreign media with a superficial view of the events can call it a "victory" for the regime. So a Pyrrhic hypothesis: for any regime, especially one that claims to be a popular republic based on Islam, pointing TV cameras at the right-look-ing crowd while beating the "wrong crowd" with all its might, especially on the anniversary of the republic's formation, is not a victory.

THE POLITICAL EVOLUTION OF MOUSAVI

Muhammad Sahimi

February 16, 2010

One of the most significant results of Iran's rigged presidential election of June 12, 2009, has been the political evolution of Mir Hossein Mousavi, recognized by many as the most important leader of the Green Movement. His actions, reactions to new developments and positions regarding various issues, together with his calm, thoughtful and shrewd tactics, represent a new model of leadership that is vastly different from most of what Iran has been subjected to over the past three decades. In my view, Mousavi understands better than anyone else the deep crisis faced by the country.

But this is only half the story. The other half—perhaps the more important aspect of his leadership—is the fact that he does not try to move ahead of the Green Movement, nor does he lose his sense of realism and understanding of what is and is not possible, given the existing power structure. He gauges what people want, what their aspirations are, and how those desires are dynamically evolving. He also constantly evaluates the opposing camp, the hardliners, and the state of their affairs, and then adjusts his tactics with enormous courage and deep conviction, while remaining loyal to the pillars of his beliefs and the principles that he has adhered to in his career as a political leader.

Even a cursory glance at the events of the last ten months demonstrates the astonishingly swift political evolution of Mousavi as a national leader. Though much of the country, particularly the young generation, is only just discovering him, those old enough to vividly recall the Iran of the 1970s and 1980s know that this evolution rests upon a significant record.

The Islamic Leftist of the 1970s

Mir Hossein Mousavi was born on September 29, 1941, in Khameneh in Eastern Azerbaijan province, the main home to Iran's Azeri population. His father, Mir Esmail Mousavi, was a businessman and tea trader in Tabriz, the provincial capital of East Azerbaijan. Mousavi's hometown is also the ancestral home of Iran's Supreme Leader, Ayatollah Ali Khamenei, whose last name means "from Khameneh." In fact, the two men are said to be second cousins.

The young Mousavi moved to Tehran after graduating from high school in Khameneh. He obtained his master's degree in architecture from the National University of Iran, now Shahid Beheshti University, in 1969. He became a lecturer there in 1974 and was then an assistant professor between 1975 and 1977. In addition to Persian, he is fluent in English, Arabic and Turkish.

After graduation, Mousavi founded the Samarghand Company, an architectural design and construction firm. He used the name Hossein Rahjou in his art and design work. The Samarghand Company was also a venue for secret gatherings of Islamic opponents of Mohammad Reza Shah Pahlavi and his dictatorial rule. Participants in the secret meetings at Samarghand included such notable figures as Abdolali Bazargan, Mehdi Bazargan's son and a noted Islamic scholar, and Hasan Aladpoush and his wife, Mahboobeh Mottahedin. The latter two, originally part of the Islamic movement against the shah, later changed their ideology, became ardent Marxists, and were killed by the shah's security forces.

In the late 1960s and early 1970s, Mousavi was closely associated with religious-nationalist groups, such as the Freedom Movement of Iran led by Mehdi Bazargan (1907–95). He participated actively in the sermons and lectures given by Dr. Ali Shariati (1933–77), the sociologist and distinguished Islamic leftist scholar, at Hosseinieh Ershad in Tehran.

Mousavi also worked with Dr. Habibollah Payman. Before the Revolution, Payman, a dentist, published political books and analyses under the pseudonym Habibollah Paydar. When the Mujahideen-e Khalq Organization (MKO) was taken over in 1975 by members who had switched from Islam to Marxism, Payman, together with younger members of the Freedom Movement and some members of Iran's Medical Association, formed the Movement of Militant Muslims (MMM), a leftist Islamic group that is now part of the Nationalist-Religious Coalition headed by Ezzatollah Sahabi. Mousavi was one of the founding members of the MMM. Payman describes him as an "Islamic leftist of the 1970s."

In 1976, the Movement for Islamic Culture was founded by Mousavi, Payman, Tahereh Saffarzadeh (1936–2008), the distinguished poet, writer, translator and university professor, and Dr. Mohammad Javad Bahonar (1933–81), later Iran's second prime minister after the revolution. After the revolution, however, Mousavi distanced himself from the movement.

In the 1970s, Mousavi worked on the architectural design for the Towhid Center, a locus of Islamic opposition to both the shah and currently the Islamic Republic. It was at the Center that Ayatollah Morteza Motahhari (1920–79), a leading Islamic scholar and theoretician of political Islam who was assassinated shortly after the revolution, lectured in the 1960s and 1970s.

Mousavi married Zahra Rahnavard Boroujerdi (b. 1945) in 1969. A student of sculpture design at the University of Tehran when the couple met, she was born Zohreh Kazemi. After becoming familiar with the Islamic struggle against the shah, she changed her first name from Zohreh to the Islamic name Zahra and her last name to Rahnavard, meaning someone who takes the (Islamic) path. She has a bachelor's degree from the University of Tehran in sculpture design, an M.A. from the University of Tehran in Islamic studies, and an M.A. and a PhD from the Islamic Azad University of Tehran in political science. She was the president of Al-Zahra University, a woman's university in Tehran, but resigned after the election of Mahmoud Ahmadinejad to the presidency in 2005. In 2009, *Foreign Policy* magazine ranked her number three among the top 100 global thinkers, describing her as "the brains behind Iran's Green Revolution and the campaign of her husband, opposition leader Mir Hossein Mousavi."

Dr. Rahnavard is from a political family. Her father was a professor in the military college of Tehran and was forced into retirement after a confrontation with an American military adviser. Her mother, Ehtera-mossadat Navvab Safavi, is a close relative of Navvab Safavi (1924–55), a leading figure in the Islamic fundamentalist organization *Fadayan-e Islam*, who was executed by the Shah's government. Rahnavard and Mousavi have three daughters together, Kokab, Zahra and Narges.

Rahnavard was also an admirer of Ali Shariati and active in the opposition to the shah. It is well known that before a speech at Ershad in the early 1970s, Shariati invited the audience to visit the painting exhibition of a "young couple who will have a bright future." They were the paintings of Hossein Rahjou and Zahra Rahnavard. In fact, in addition to their political activities, art has always been a part of the couple's lives. Rahnavard is the first female full professor in the Faculty of Arts at the University of Tehran, a distinction that she was awarded in 2008, and she has received numerous awards for her research work.

Due to their political activities, Mousavi sent his wife and their first two daughters to the United States in 1976, where Rahnavard was active in the old Confederation of Iranian Students. Shortly before the revolution, she and her two daughters returned to Iran.

Imam's premier of the 1980s

Soon after the Shah's regime was toppled, Dr. Bahonar; Ayatollahs Mohammad Hosseini Beheshti (1928–81) and Seyyed Abdolkarim Mousavi Ardabili, a moderate cleric close to the reformists; and mid-ranking clerics such as Ali Akbar Hashemi Rafsanjani and Ali Khamenei founded the Islamic Republican Party (IRP), Iran's dominant political organization until May 1987, when it was dissolved. Mousavi was the IRP's first political director, holding the position from 1979 to 1981, and a member of its central committee until 1982. In 1979, when Ayatollah Khamenei founded *Jomhouri-e Eslami*, the mouthpiece of the IRP, Mousavi became its editor-in-chief as well as its director.

As the editor of *Jomhouri-e Eslami*, Mousavi wrote articles in defense of Dr. Mohammad Mosaddegh, who was disliked by many IRP members, in particular by Dr. Hassan Ayat, a right-wing member who had been a protégé of Dr. Mozaffar Baghai, a supporter of the shah during the 1950s. Strangely, after the revolution, Ayat, who was assassinated by the MKO in July 1981, became an important figure in the IRP. He played a leading role in adding the doctrine of *velayat-e faqih*—political guardianship of the Iranian people by an Islamic jurist, specifically the Supreme Leader—to the Islamic Republic's constitution.

On January 25, 1980, Abolhassan Banisadr was elected Iran's first president in a highly competitive election against nine other candidates. The eleven million votes he received represented 79 percent of the total cast. The inaugural ceremony was held on February 4, in a hospital where Ayatollah Ruhollah Khomeini was recovering from heart illness. Banisadr appointed Mohammad Ali Rajaei (1933–81) as prime minister, but opposed three of the names on Rajaei's list of cabinet nominees: Mousavi as foreign minister, Dr. Mohsen Nourbakhsh (1948–2003) as economic minister, and Behzad Nabavi as minister for executive affairs. Mousavi was rejected because he was "stubborn" and Nabavi because he was a leftist and member of the Islamic Revolution Mujahideen Organization (IRMO), today a leading reformist group. After much negotiation, Nabavi was finally accepted, and Nourbakhsh was appointed as deputy economic minister.

Banisadr was impeached by the Majles, Iran's parliament, on June 21, 1981 and sacked. Mohammad Ali Rajaei was elected as the next president, Bahonar was appointed the new prime minister, and Mousavi the new foreign minister. Both Rajaei and Bahonar were assassinated on August 30, 1981, by the MKO. Ayatollah Mohammad Reza Mahdavi Kani was appointed interim prime minister, while Mousavi remained in his post.

In October 1981, Ayatollah Ali Khamenei, who then held the lower clerical rank of hojatoleslam, was elected the republic's third president. For the office of prime minister, he proposed Ali Akbar Velayati, a pediatrician close to the conservative Islamic Coalition Party (ICP) and currently the Supreme Leader's senior adviser on foreign affairs. But Velayati failed to attain a vote of confidence from the Majles.

Reluctantly, the president proposed Mousavi, who was supported by Ayatollah Khomeini. Khamenei was opposed to Mousavi's appointment because he was an Islamic populist and supported a "leftist" economic program. The Majles quickly gave Mousavi its vote of confidence as all the deputies were aware that he was "Khomeini's prime minister." He was Iran's seventy-ninth prime minister and, as it would turn out, its last.

To placate the right wing, Mousavi appointed several ICP members to ministerial positions: Velayati as foreign minister; Ali Akbar Parvaresh, who has been accused of involvement in the bombing of the Jewish center in Buenos Aires, as minister of education; Morteza Nabavi, currently editor of the right-wing daily *Resalat*, as minister of telecommunications; Habibollah Asgar Oladi Mosalman, one-time leader of the ICP, as minister of commerce; Ahmad Ṭavakkoli, currently representing Tehran in the Majles and a cousin of the Larijani brothers, as minister of labor; Hassan Ghafouri Fard, currently another Tehran Majles representative, as well as a professor at Amir Kabir University, as minister of energy; and Mohsen Rafighdoost as minister of the Islamic Revolutionary Guard Corps (IRGC).

Mousavi also appointed to his cabinet such leading Islamic leftists as Behzad Nabavi (no relation to Morteza Nabavi) and Mohammad Salamati, currently the leader of the IRMO. It is widely believed that Mousavi wished to resign several times during his premiership but each time was ordered to stay on by Ayatollah Khomeini.

Immediately after the revolution, the conservatives had tried to abolish the Organization for Budget and Planning (OBP) due to its socialist underpinnings. According to a long-time friend who worked for the OBP and wished to remain anonymous, the conservatives professed shock at the discovery that the "views of American experts had been found among the documents of the OBP." The right wing wanted to transform the large building of the OBP into a hospital. But in his first speech to the Majles in 1981, Mousavi made it clear that he believed in centralized planning and wanted a strong OBP. He appointed Dr. Mohammad Banki as the institution's head.

Banki tried to bring back the pre-revolution experts of the OBP, and he developed the first five-year development plan in 1982. However, he was soon forced out. Some conservatives thought that planning was interference in God's work. Others, including many ICP members, considered planning to be tantamount to socialism. Banki was replaced by Masoud Roghani Zanjani, who stayed in the post for several years. After Ahmadinejad was elected president in 2005, he effectively eliminated the OBP by transferring its control to the office of the president.

After Ali Khamenei was re-elected president in 1985, he again opposed the appointment of Mousavi as prime minister. At one point, Khamenei nearly decided to quit politics because Ayatollah Khomeini was so strongly supportive of Mousavi. Ninety-nine right-wing deputies drafted a letter to Khomeini, expressing their disapproval of Mousavi as prime minister and then voted against his appointment. When Khamenei heard about the letter, he reportedly said, "Why ninety-nine? Make it a hundred! Add my name." But Khomeini prevailed, and Mousavi ultimately won the confidence vote.

One of the leaders of this "Gang of 99" was Ayatollah Mohammad Yazdi, currently deputy head of the Assembly of Experts, a constitutional body that appoints the Supreme Leader and supposedly monitors his performance. He is one of the most ardent supporters of Khamenei and Ahmadinejad, and an archenemy of Rafsanjani. In the mid–1980s, Yazdi and other right-wingers were in the minority, outnumbered by the Islamic leftists, known at that time as the followers of Khomeini's line, who today make up the bulk of the reformist camp. As Khomeini was seemingly allied with the left, the right-wingers concluded that they did not have to obey the Supreme Leader, as his views were only "advisory." Now that the same right-wingers control the power hierarchy in Iran, they view the issue differently. They now believe that the Supreme Leader is even above the constitution; that his legitimacy is bestowed upon him by God, not by the people; that the task of the Assembly of Experts is not to appoint the Supreme Leader, but to "discover" him, as he is actually appointed by God; and that disobeying him is the equivalent of disobeying God. Obviously, this shift in interpretation has nothing to do with God, Islam and Shiism, but rather with the acquisition of power, wealth and prestige.

Over the next four years, Ali Khamenei repeatedly asked Ayatollah Khomeini to either withdraw his support for Mousavi or issue a *hokm-e hokoumati*, an official, infallible order of the Supreme Leader, as the basis for Mousavi's position. Khomeini refused to do so. He reportedly said, "I do not issue such orders, but as a citizen I have the right to express my opinion." As Supreme Leader, Khamenei, by contrast, has repeatedly intervened in national affairs with such *hokm-e hokoumati*.

Mousavi's success in beating back Khamenei's challenge and staying on as the prime minister also increased the power of the Islamic leftists and relative moderates in his cabinet. He appointed a then obscure leftist cleric, Mohammad Khatami, a future president, as minister of culture and Islamic guidance; Abdullah Nouri, a progressive cleric and highly popular reformist, as minister of the interior; Behzad Nabavi as minister of heavy industry; Hassan Habibi, later Khatami's first vice president, as minister of justice; Bijan Namdar Zanganeh, later Khatami's oil minister, as minister of reconstruction; and Abolghasem Sarhaddi Zadeh, repeatedly jailed as an anti-shah activist, as minister of labor. These appointments helped the Islamic leftists crush the conservatives in the elections for the third Majles in 1988, when Mehdi Karoubi was elected as the parliament's speaker.

It is widely believed that Mousavi was opposed to continuation of the Iran–Iraq war after 1982, when Iran's armed forces pushed Iraq out of most of the territory that it had occupied in the first two years. It has been widely reported that he told Ayatollah Khomeini and others on several occasions that the government was at a breaking point due to the high cost of the war. But the decision to continue the war was Khomeini's alone.

A letter, written in 1988 from Khomeini to Mohsen Rezaee, then the top commander of the Revolutionary Guard and now secretary-general of the Expediency Council, sheds considerable light on the issue. The document was publicly revealed by Rafsanjani, who at the time was commander-in-chief of the armed forces. It was temporarily posted on his website in 2006 and it stirred much debate both within Iran and internationally. In this letter, Rezaee is quoted as telling the Ayatollah, "No victories are in sight for the next five years. If we can organize 350 infantry brigades, purchase 2,500 tanks, 3,000 cannons, 300 war planes, and manufacture laser and nuclear weapons that are nowadays among the necessities of modern warfare, then, God willing, we can think of offensive war activities." The Ayatollah responded that Mousavi's government has told him that it is impossible to continue the war and therefore, he has no choice but to accept UN Security Council Resolution 598, which called for a ceasefire. The war ended in July 1988. That September, Mousavi tried to resign, but Khomeini angrily rejected his resignation.

In July 1989, a month after Khomeini's death, the conservative clerics succeeded in revising the constitution and eliminating the post of prime minister. Mousavi thus stepped down and was appointed by Ayatollah Khamenei to the Expediency Council. He is still a member of the Council, although he no longer attends its meetings.

Mousavi has been widely praised for his management of Iran's economy during the war with Iraq. Despite meager annual revenues of only $6 billion from oil exports, the immense expenditures for the war, a rapidly growing population, a brain drain and sanctions by the United States, there were neither shortages of essentials nor high inflation.

But it was also during Mousavi's premiership that thousands of political prisoners were executed. In fact, the 1980s are perhaps the darkest and bloodiest decade in Iran's modern history. Mousavi has been accused by many, notably the monarchists, the MKO, and some secular leftists, as being responsible for the killings. There is no question that Iran's entire political leadership of that era shares the responsibility; some of them are accountable in their executive functions, while all of them are morally culpable. But one must keep in mind that Mousavi did not control the Ministry of Intelligence, nor the Revolutionary Courts, nor the Revolutionary Guard, nor the entire judiciary that acted as the instruments of the arrest, jailing and execution of all political prisoners. In fact, since the revolution, every minister of intelligence—including Mousavi's, the cleric Mohammad Mohammadi Reyshahri—has been picked by the Supreme Leader.

One can certainly argue that Mousavi should have protested the executions, if he were truly opposed to them and knew about them ahead of time. Mousavi has said that he did not know about the executions of the summer of 1988 before they occurred. In his memoir about those executions, which are an authoratative reference for this event, Grand Ayatollah Montazeri never mentions Mousavi either; in fact, after the rigged June election, he threw his full support behind him, which may strengthen Mousavi's statement. It must also be noted that, as detailed above, it is known that Mousavi wanted to resign several times and that opposition to the excesses of that period was conceivably the motivation. In addition, he was prime minister under the most difficult conditions, during the period when Iran was involved in its long, bloody war with Iraq. Therefore, it is conceivable that Mousavi may have thought that running the country efficiently was his highest patriotic duty. At some point, of course, if he was aware of the executions, he must explain to the nation his true thoughts about them.

Back to arts

After stepping down as Iran's last prime minister, Mousavi returned to art and cultural work. He began teaching at Tarbiyat Modarres University in Tehran. In 1999, Khatami appointed him head of the Iranian Academy of the Arts, a post he kept until two months ago, when Ahmadinejad removed him. During part of his time at the Academy, he was managing editor of its quarterly journal, *Khiyal* (Imagination).

Though no longer active in politics, he was never far removed from it. He was a political adviser to Rafsanjani during the eight years of his presidency from 1989 to 1997. In 1997, Mousavi was the leading choice of the reformists to run in the presidential elections, but he refused. His wife Dr. Rahnavard explained that the reason he demurred from running was the "discouraging messages that he received from higher officials," which many assumed to come from Ali Khamenei, now the Supreme Leader. He was nonetheless so popular that the reformists made huge posters with images of him and Khatami together for the 1997 election campaign. After Khatami won the election in a landslide, he appointed Mousavi as his senior adviser.

In April 2000, after the reformists swept the elections for the sixth parliament, the hardliners began cracking down on the reformist newspapers. Over a two-day period, they banned sixteen newspapers and other publications. Mousavi famously referred to the crackdown as *bastan-e fa'lei matboua't*, which roughly translates as "blind mass closure of the press." The term *failei* stuck and is now part of Iran's political lexicon.

As Khatami's second term was coming to end in 2005, the reformists, in particular Khatami, Karoubi and Ayatollah Seyyed Mohammad Mousavi Khoeiniha, a leading figure among the leftist clerics, asked him to run in the presidential elections, but he refused again. He had witnessed what happened to the Khatami presidency, during which, in Khatami's description, the hardliners tried to create a crisis for the country every nine days. He wanted guarantees that he would be given enough power to carry out his political program, an assurance that Ayatollah Khamenei and the hardliners were not willing to provide.

The candidate of the 2009 election

As the 2009 presidential election approached, the great question loomed as to who would represent the reformists. All eyes were on Khatami, the popular reformist and seemingly the most viable candidate. After much behind-the-scenes discussion, Khatami announced his presidential bid on February 8. He then traveled to the south of Iran, where he was greeted by huge crowds.

But Khatami's candidacy angered the hardliners; it is believed that his announcement enraged Ayatollah Khamenei in particular. During the marches on the anniversary of the revolution, Khatami was reportedly attacked by a group of Ahmadinejad supporters, who tried to beat him with a stick. Two days later, on February 12, Hossein Shariatmadari, editor-in-chief of the hardline newspaper *Kayhan*, threatened Khatami with assassination, "similar to what had happened to Benazir Bhutto in Pakistan."

Before announcing his candidacy, Khatami had consistently stated that either he or Mousavi would run. Although Mousavi had shown little inclination to join the campaign, he announced his candicacy on March 13. Three days later, Khatami withdrew and threw his full support behind Mousavi.

Given the realities of Iran's power structure, Khatami always believed that Mousavi was a better candidate than him; he always considered himself a cultural rather than a political leader. When he withdrew from the election, he said, "I know that I would get the vote if I ran, but the election is not just the voting on Friday. One also needs a candidate who on Saturday is strong enough to push his agenda. Mir Hossein is the man of Saturday." Khatami has proven to be prophetically correct.

Mousavi was endorsed by all the reformist groups and political parties except the National Trust Party of Karoubi, who was a candidate himself. The fundamentalist faction known as the Principlists, which was critical of Ahmadinejad, also quietly put their support behind him. Mousavi was feared most by the conservatives because of his uncorrupted and simple life, his wife (who accompanied him on many of his campaign appearances) and his forthright style of speaking.

Mousavi declared that he had no interest in power and was running only because he thought that the country was in grave danger. During the campaign, he harshly criticized the policies of Ahmadinejad, terming them "harmful to the revolution, the country and its good name." Khatami fully supported Mousavi, making several campaign appearances with him and urging people to turn out in large numbers in order to defeat Ahmadinejad. After the nationally televised debate between Mousavi and Ahmadinejad, Mousavi's support dramatically increased.

The election that took place on Friday, June 12, 2009, in the opinion of a large majority of the people (including this author), was rigged.

Ahmadinejad was immediately declared the winner by a landslide, sending the stunned nation into a spiral of demonstrations and protests. The hardliners responded with violence, killing at least 110 people—including two formal executions and two assassinations; arresting thousands, including reformist leaders, journalists, university students and human rights advocates; torturing, raping and sodomizing an unknown number and closing newspapers. They have even taken hostage children, grandchildren and relatives of the reformist leaders in order to keep them quiet and under control. The assault on fundamental human rights continues unabated.

Mousavi and Rahnavard have also paid dearly for their courageous stands. Mousavi's nephew, Ali Mousavi, was assassinated. Rahnavard's brother, Shapour Kazemi, a distinguished inventor and engineer, was arrested, prosecuted in a Stalinist-style show trial, and given a one-year sentence on trumped up charges. Her nephew, Saleh Noghrehkar, who was an adviser to Mousavi's presidential campaign, was summoned to the notorious Evin prison to answer some questions and temporarily arrested. Rahnavard herself has been physically assaulted.

The election's aftermath

It is in the aftermath of the election that Mousavi has established himself as a true national leader. All we need to do is look at his recent interviews and the seventeen statements he issued after the election to see that his work will have a lasting effect on Iran's history. In Statement 5, Mousavi explained his decision to seek the presidency:

> I decided to run because I wanted to show that the path to a life full of enlightenment is not too long.... To show that it is possible to live a moral life, even during this immoral era.... To declare that lawlessness leads to dictatorship; to remind everyone that respect for human rights does not weaken the system, but strengthens it. I decided to run to declare that people expect honesty and truthfulness from their servants in government and that many of our problems have been created by their lies. I decided to run to declare that backwardness, poverty, corruption and injustice are not our fate.

After the Friday prayers of July 17, during which Rafsanjani described some of the demands of the protesters in his sermon, Ayatollah Khamenei threatened the leaders of the Green Movement. Mousavi responded strongly and immediately, making it clear that he would not retreat from his positions. When he met with the families of some of the imprisoned political leaders on *Mab'as*, the anniversary of the beginning of Prophet Muhammad's prophecy, Mousavi said, "You are not alone. The entire nation represents the families of the political prisoners because they have been imprisoned for defending the ideals and principles of the nation. This imprisonment is a national problem and will remain so."

Responding to the hardliners' charge that the reformists are working with foreign governments, Mousavi replied in the same statement,

> Many of the prisoners are well known and have served the political system and the country for years. Who is going to believe that they collude with foreigners and sell out the country's national interests? Is this not an insult against the nation? Is this not an insult against the forty million voters? Is this not an insult against university students, professors, [government] elite and the hard-working leaders and managers of the nation?

He then warned the hardliners that the protests would continue and that the use of violence against them would prove ineffective: "Thirty years after the Revolution our nation has matured to the extent that it cannot be silenced using the pre-Revolutionary methods. People must be able to express their opinion and protest freely. A free society in the country can protect it much better than any military force."

His prediction has turned out to be true. He refused to issue a special statement after Ali Mousavi was assassinated, declaring that his nephew was "no different from other martyrs."

In reaction to the Stalinist show trials, Mousavi issued Statement 10, which included this passage concerning the hardliners and the death of a young member of a prominent conservative family who was tortured and killed while under arrest at Kahrizak prison:

They say that in the trials that began yesterday, the Revolution's children confessed to having links with foreigners and planning to overthrow the Islamic Republic. I carefully examined what they said and could not find any truth to this but what I did hear was the deep moaning of the arrested who were telling us about their painful fate over the past fifty days. I saw tortured, broken, humiliated people who would have confessed to anything at all. What else could they have said other than the story of their pains? The accused say that Mohsen Ruholamini was martyred because he was righteous. They say that if they had not resisted, these show trials would have happened weeks ago. They say that they repeated what they were told to say by their captors.... The torturers' and interrogators' teeth have reached people's bone, to the extent that their victims are now those who have greatly served the country and the political system; the torturers and interrogators are threatening those who had the most fundamental role in the establishment of this republic and its growth and development.

In his historic Statement 13, Mousavi described for the first time his vision for the Green Movement, and demonstrated that he had come a long way since the beginning of his electoral campaign. First, he discussed the newfound strength of Iran's citizens:

Over the past few months a powerful force has been liberated, which must be employed for the long-term good of the nation. Our people are well aware of what they want, and saw what they can achieve through what happened over the past few months. They know that they have the power and capabilities to achieve what they want, and that the [government] elites and the experts are also with them in this endeavor. Therefore, the question that we are all asking each other is, what should be done with this renewed hope and power?

He talked for the first time about the need to revise the constitution, a theme he has since revisited on numerous occasions: "Yes, the constitution contains ways of managing some aspects of the country that perhaps are not appropriate for the present state of our society and the world but the same constitution also indicates ways of reforming them." He responded to the hardliners' claims about the present government's source of legitimacy by addressing the nature of the group that vets the candidates for elections and interprets the constitution: "In our national consensus, the legitimacy of all the pillars of the political system is based on the vote and trust of the people, to the extent that even an organ like the Guardian Council that apparently cannot be monitored by the people can, in fact, be monitored by them." He then took on the hardliners more directly:

> More oppressed than the ideals of Islamic Revolution, the Islamic Republic, and its constitution is Islam itself, a religion they mention often but practice very little. They filter the religion so that whatever does not suit their interests is forgotten and their own views and expediency are introduced as the true Islam

Reflecting on the first summer after the Revolution and then the war with Iraq, he added,

> If there is one goal for a religious ruler, it is providing a better foundation for people's lives based on their religious beliefs. Why then has the gap between a moral life and our society been widening? This gap is not our revolutionary inheritance. In the hot summer of 1358 [1979] many people fasted during Ramadan for the first time in their lives and enjoyed the moral experience. This was our revolutionary inheritance. Our Revolution's inheritance was the ethics that flowed in the society during the holy defense [the Iran–Iraq war].

Recognizing the diversity of opinion among the supporters of the Green Movement, Mousavi then outlined a list of nine demands as the "minimum that everybody can agree on," including the unconditional release of all the political prisoners, a free press, a ban on the meddling of the Revolutionary Guard in politics and the economy and recognition of the people's fundamental right to peaceful assembly.

Mousavi's made perhaps his shrewdest statement on January 1, 2010, two days after a series of pro-government demonstrations, when the nation was deeply worried that the hardliners would soon initiate a bloodbath. Statement 17 widened the already significant fissures among conservatives, calmed the nation, and—building on the precepts outlined in Statement 13—proposed a way out of Iran's deep crisis. The statement was instrumental in thwarting those hardliners who sought to intensify retaliations against the Green Movement.

In the latest interview posted on his website, *Kalameh*, Mousavi states: "In the first years of the Revolution, people were convinced that it had completely destroyed all of the structures through which despotism and dictatorship could be reinforced. And I was one of the people who believed this. But today I no longer do." He continues:

> Today we can identify those very structures that have led to despotism in the past. We can also identify the resistance people have shown against a return to dictatorship. This is the invaluable inheritance of the Islamic Revolution, clearly demonstrated today with the people's intolerance for deception, lies and corruption. Similarly, the tight control of newspapers and media, the overflowing prisons and the brutal killing of innocent people who are peacefully requesting their rights all reveal the lingering roots of despotism.

Criticizing the right-wing leaders of the Friday prayer, particularly Ayatollah Ahmad Jannati, the ultra-conservative, pro-Ahmadinejad cleric, he observed,

> The people are after justice and freedom. Moreover, they are aware that the arrests and executions are politically motivated and unconstitutional. They despise the monarchy but are also aware that people may be condemned to death based on frivolous accusations and without even being subject to a legal trial. The people know that these executions are carried out only so that a brutal, ruthless

leader of the Friday prayers, one who has constantly defended corruption, violence and deception, can applaud them. It matters not
to him that there are abundant forced confessions and he doesn't
care that those executed have had nothing to do with the election's
aftermath. For him, what matters is the power of the executions to
generate fear. He is ignorant of the power of innocent blood. He
does not know that it was the blood of martyrs that caused the
Pahlavi regime to collapse.

Mousavi then praised the Green Movement, while also making it clear
that the ideals of the Revolution had been abandoned:

And now, in the courageous, defiant and Green rows of people who
demand their rights, we see a continuum of the very resistance we
saw during the war with Iraq and the Revolution. However, we can
conclude that we were too optimistic at the beginning of the Revolution. We can see today that the government, its newspapers, and
its national broadcasting network lie easily. Our people can see
that, in reality, the security and military forces control cases in the
judiciary and that the judiciary itself has become an instrument of
the security forces.

He went on to reflect upon the arrest of Dr. Alireza Hosseini Beheshti,
son of Ayatollah Seyyed Mohammad Hosseini Beheshti, the republic's
first judiciary chief, who was assassinated in June 1981:

We have lost all hope in the judiciary. A system that imprisons an
intellectual, freedom-loving and religious son of the Martyr Beheshti, as well as others like him, sitting him under his father's
photo in the hallways of the courtroom, has moved far away from
the ideals defined during the Revolution....Today, the prison cells
are occupied with the most sincere and devoted sons of this nation:
students, professors and others. They are prosecuted on charges
of espionage or on charges related to financial or sexual misconduct...while the real criminals and thieves who steal public money
are free. Instead of looking for the real spies, they accuse decent
religious people.

When asked to give some examples of despotic mentality that are evident in the behavior of officials, Mousavi responded:

> Perhaps the best example we can observe is the distortion of logical and legal relations between branches of the system. It is very obvious now that the parliament does not have enough sway over the government in matters that fall under its jurisdiction. This is not an argument made solely by those who oppose the government. Moderate conservatives who are aware also complain about these issues. Not responding to issues raised by the National Organization for Auditing, lack of transparency in oil sales and revenue spending, disregard for the fourth development program, destruction of the budget office to avoid audits and reviews, and so on; all are clear examples of a return to the Pahlavi time. There is no need to look any further.

He then criticized the parliament's lack of independence and recalled the deaths of four young demonstrators last summer while under detention at Kahrizak:

> While the Majles has discussed the unprecedented atrocities committed in Kahrizak, one official says that the issue has been blown out of proportion unnecessarily. Another example given these days is the relationship between the judiciary and its enforcemenforces. It is a question of whether the judges make the decisions or the security forces. To what extent can the judiciary exercise its privileges when, in the constitution, a great emphasis has been placed on its independence? In my opinion, one of the obvious cases that demonstrates the persistence of a despotic mentality is the injustice done to constitutional roles of the judiciary and the Majles. The similarities between today's elections and those held immediately before the Revolution are another sign. Compare the voting process for parliamentary elections during the early years of the Revolution with that of today to see if we have moved forward or backward.

Acknowledging that the Green Movement has not paid enough attention to the poor and those in the lower social classes, he noted:

> Before the Revolution, it was a principle that the revolutionary forces and the academic class defended the lower class. It was their honor to be the poor people's friend. In my opinion, the point that all of us should have in mind is that of supporting the hard-working classes. Of course, this must not be for the purpose of using them as instruments but with the intention that the Green Movement's destiny will be tied to the destiny of all the people and particularly with the classes who are productive in economy and science: the workers, teachers and academics. I regret that the intense political problems resulted in less attention to the lower class of society, their problems and their rights. When people's standard of living improves, the roots of freedom grow deeper in society and unity and growth flourish. . . .The underprivileged classes of the society who care for Islamic values potentially have the same demands as the Green Movement. Those who are after a national consensus for change should become more integrated with these classes and pursue their concerns and demands.

Mousavi emphasized that he is open to revising the constitution. In response to the question that reliance on the present constitution would restrict future options, he remarked,

> I have said before that the constitution is not something that cannot be changed. It has changed before in 1988 and it can change again. By considering what people think and demand and what their collective experience as a nation dictates, we can take steps to improve the constitution. Nevertheless, we must be aware that a good constitution by itself is not the solution. We must move toward a structure that imposes a high cost on those who attempt to disobey or ignore the laws.

He also discussed the importance of nonviolence and diversity of opinion in the Green Movement:

My advice to the Basij and security forces is to be calm and kind in their treatment of the people. My advice to followers of the Green Movement is to reduce their self-identifying features, whether they are used to help them stand out a little or a lot. This movement has grown out of the people and it belongs to them. Everyone should be extremely mindful of the diversity of beliefs, values and traditions. But we should never forget our final goal—to create a developed, independent, free and united Iran.

Whatever one thinks of Mousavi and his past, one thing should be clear: he has emerged as the leader of the Green Movement. Though he has humbly and consistently emphasized that it is he who is following the people, not the other way around, he has led the movement shrewdly, strongly and with deep conviction.

IRAN'S COMING OF AGE

Nasrin Alavi

February 18, 2010

On February 16, 2010—the week of the anniversary of the revolution of 1979, marked by a huge official demonstration in Tehran—the anonymous video of the death of Neda Agha-Soltan on June 20, 2009, received the prestigious Polk Award. John Darnton, curator of the Polk Awards, described this record of the shooting of an innocent young student as the "iconic image of the Iranian resistance." He added, "This award celebrates the fact that, in today's world, a brave bystander with a cell-phone camera can use video-sharing and social-networking sites to deliver news."

A few days earlier, the award for the World Press Photo of 2009 was given to an intimate photograph taken by Pietro Masturzo on one of the heated nights that following the election, when residents of Tehran climbed to their rooftops and voiced their dissent in cries of "*Allah-u-akbar.*" The Iranian authorities have tried to control all modes of communication, but such momentary glimpses into a closed society have the power to change perceptions en masse. Palestinian writer Remi Kanazi has noted that the Islamic battle cry of Iranian pro-democracy protesters would once have unsettled many in the West; the fact that the chant of "*Allah-u-akbar*" is now a worldwide inspiration is a revolution all by itself.

Ayperi Karabuda Ecer, the chair of the jury that chose the photo, said that the photo had touched her "both visually and emotionally." Indeed, Iran's pro-democracy movement has been the source of many such poignant images. Another such image, unforgettable for many people inside Iran, is one of a young man called Sohrab Arabi, and it was taken on the day that he was to disappear.

The photo shows the nineteen-year-old Sohrab sitting beside his mother, exhibiting the sort of comfortably safe demeanor that boys from age four to forty adopt around their mothers. She is holding a poster of Mir Hossein Mousavi, the reformist candidate who millions of Iranians believe was the true winner of the presidential elections. Her furrowed brow still shows a gleam of hope; the overall expression of her face is one of determination. The mother, Parvin Fahimi, later wrote, "I lost my son on Monday, June 15, during a peaceful rally held to protest the election results. The crowds were estimated at a minimum of three million. We wanted nothing but peace, tranquility and a freedom of thought."

Sohrab, like Neda, has become a symbol of something larger than himself: of Iran's young people, of the resistance to oppression and deception, even of Iran itself. In his case, his very name reinforces an almost mystic sense of potency and goodness. It would be hard to find an Iranian over the age of five who doesn't know the story of Rostam and Sohrab, from Ferdowsi's renowned tenth-century work *Shahnameh* (Epic of Kings). The ruler Rostam kills the valiant challenger Sohrab, only to find out that the boy was his long-lost son. What makes the event more bitter is that Rostam himself narrowly escaped death thanks to Sohrab's virtue. The "laws of honor" must prevail, according to the *Shahnameh*, such that "he who brings down a valiant man for the first time should not destroy him, but preserve him for a second battle."

Many Sohrabs have been slain in the history of patriarchal Iran. Yet to this day Iranians are taught to treasure the honorable rules of combat to which the ancient Sohrab adhered, and to despise those who flout them. In 1989, near Beijing's Tiananmen Square, a column of tanks ceded to a lone protester; in Iran in 2009 footage taken on a cell phone shows a police truck drive back and forth over a young protester. Today, China is one of Iran's best "friends," though Tehran has neither the ideological unity among the elite nor the growth economy for the masses that could offer equivalent protection.

Since Sohrab was lost to his mother on June 15, 2009, many more Iranians have been attacked, imprisoned and killed; many homes similar to the one in Pietro Masturzo's photo have been invaded and its inhabitants detained for committing the sin of chanting "Allah-u-akbar" in the Islamic Republic of Iran. Yet, astonishingly, many persist in using all available means to defend their Iran and show it to the world. Even during the events of February 11, 2010, overwhelming official censorship was unable to prevent videos of the protests being circulated on YouTube within minutes.

It is hard to explain to anyone who hasn't been to one of these official gatherings—loved by authoritarian rulers from Harare to Kathmandu—the parallel goings on. You could go with busload of school friends and all you remember is a great day out when you made up parodies of the official chants and ate too many freebie sweets. Not this year.

What comes across most forcibly is the enormous security at this "celebration," with endless rows of military personnel, anti-riot police and their vehicles; such a display would prove menacing for government supporters and the opposition alike. Another videophone film highlights the scale of the military presence, in menacing scenes that were never replicated even during eight years of war against an invading enemy. The rulers of revolutionary Iran have never feared their own people as such, and all they can do is to clumsily swing between conciliation and vicious oppression. They are certainly aware of the mounting government hatred and how far they have breached the "laws of honor" by killing every Sohrab and Neda.

The films, images, tweets and blogs that are cast out like messages-in-bottles across the cyber-waves are a central part of people's struggle to narrate their own stories and present the case for justice. Much of the Western media views the issue at stake in terms of a test of strength and sees the "successful" security crackdown of February 11, 2010, as a decisive defeat of the opposition. But this struggle is not about street combat and toppling dictators. It is about the coming of age of a generation whose rightful nonviolent fight for civil rights is both as ancient and as new as Sohrab.

A WINNING STRATEGY:
PRINCIPLES FOR EFFECTIVE CIVIL DISOBEDIENCE IN IRAN

Hamid Farokhnia

March 4, 2010

In the nine remarkable months since the fraudulent June 12 election, more and more people in Iran have come to appreciate the preeminent role that civil disobedience plays, and must play, in their struggle. In the process, millions are turning into seasoned activists simply by coming face to face with the dictatorship in all its malevolence. For every person who has been thrown in jail and tortured, dozens more have become politicized. This has largely been a spontaneous process—and while spontaneity has on occasion helped foil the government's tactics of suppression, it also has its drawbacks. Among these, it increases the odds of being outmaneuvered by a regime that is very powerful and cunning when it is able to set the rules of the game, as happened on February 11. If the Green Movement is to succeed in its quest for democracy and human rights in Iran, it is thus crucial to understand the techniques of nonviolent civil disobedience and how they may be applied most effectively in the current circumstances.

Some in Iran's sprawling Green Movement have adopted the tactics of nonviolent civil disobedience on moral and philosophical grounds, while others have done so out of purely practical considerations. In the interest of maintaining unity, the movement is well advised to adopt the most common factor as the point of reference, namely the utility and efficacy of peaceful civil disobedience as the only viable political tactic in today's Iran. (This is not meant to suggest that philosophical discussion of the merits and demerits of civil disobedience is useless, simply that it is not today's burning question.)

The first point that must be understood is that civil disobedience is not tantamount to pacifism. Under certain circumstances, someone committed to civil disobedience can engage in acts of self-defense against aggressors. But this is the exception rather than the rule, and such responses must never be dictated by a predilection for violence or a hunger for vengeance, as practiced by the other side.

Next on the agenda is the issue of general goals. In an insurrectionary model, the opposition prepares for the day that, through the careful planning of a coup or revolution, its forces will "rise up," depose the enemy's leadership, and then proceed to purge the polity of the adversary's cadres and supporters on a massive scale. This is in contradistinction to a struggle based in civil disobedience where no such dramatic single event is planned for and where much of the regime and its base receive clemency after victory (as happened, for example, in South Africa). So the question is, what is the ultimate goal?

The goal is to erode the pillars of support for the regime until loyalties shift, practical power begins to drain away, and the regime starts crumbling from within. Civil disobedience is thus not primarily aimed at demonstrating the moral superiority of the opposition movement—though that is admittedly one objective—but rather to disrupt the "normal" flow of commerce, politics and everyday life. Clearly, a violent struggle against a much stronger foe has little chance of disrupting "normal" conditions except for fleeting moments, since violence gives the state license to stamp out its opponents with the full range of instruments at its disposal. This is why the Mujahideen's infantile tactics led to the further consolidation of the regime and why, in contrast, the country's rulers have failed to roll back the Green Movement and have been constrained from arresting Mousavi and Karoubi and doing what they do best—engaging in revenge killings and mass executions. Indeed, the regime openly admits that it is facing the worst crisis in its thirty-one years of existence. As is clear by now, the mighty Islamic Republic of Iran is most terrified of the specter not of an insurrection, but of a peaceful "revolution."

In addition, talk of violent insurrection and punitive measures for regime henchmen and supporters robs the movement of its ability to co-opt and effectively neutralize them. Those who support the existing power structure will hardly abandon their position if any incentive to do so is eliminated. This is particularly true in a country like Iran, where the heady mix of politics and religion has spawned vast reservoirs of support for the regime. Who could overlook the fact that more than 40,000 people have nominally signed up for "suicide missions"? Even conservatively estimating true believers at 5 percent, we are still left with nearly 2,000 volunteers. Let's not forget that the mighty US military was almost brought to its knees in Iraq during 2005–6 by the suicide-bombing missions of a cadre of fewer than 900 militants. Besides, the Green Movement cannot afford to cede the religious "center" to the hardliners. This includes the vast majority of clerics, plus millions of the faithful who have been led to believe that the current Islamic Republic is the incarnation of the Holy Writ on Earth and their best hope for the future.

It may appear that stating the movement's position against violence just once or twice would be sufficient. It is not. We must constantly foreground this position and make it a central plank of the platform. This is necessary both for the reasons outlined above as well as to prepare for those moments when violence, whether committed by the regime's forces or others, does erupt. We will be in position then to rightly claim that we have publicly and repeatedly disavowed the use of violence.

Is engagement in peaceful struggle alone sufficient for victory? The answer is, emphatically, no. We also need, concurrently, to put into practice a set of additional strategic principles:

1. *Maximum unity.* Contrary to what many people think, the strength of the Green Movement resides in its plurality and the astonishingly wide spectrum of people engaged in it. We do have our differences, of course. But anything that creates unproductive tension inside our ranks must

be avoided at all costs. It will hardly matter what any differences are today, if there is no movement to speak of tomorrow. As we all know, the hardliners are busy hatching plans for squashing the movement as we speak. They are intent on re-establishing their unchallenged rule one more time after killing and imprisoning thousands.

I have spoken of "unproductive" tension. If a difference of opinion on ideology or tactics leads to division and splintering, its airing is by definition unproductive. If it does not, it may be alright to debate the matter, so long as this is done in a spirit of amicability and solidarity. If we are serious about our demands for a free election, we must maintain a collaborative attitude. We can get at each other's throats in the next parliament that follows a free election. For now, though, differences should not be allowed to divide us. Any force that wants to join the movement, no matter how hesitant, provisional and transient, must be welcomed with open arms.

One caveat is in order here: The movement must be careful not to be associated with those who have blood on their hands or are deeply unpopular, such as the Mujahideen-e Khalq. They should be kept at arms' length, while making sure that they are not turned into implacable foes.

2. *Co-optation.* One of the most important goals must always be to co-opt elements of the regime's forces to the movement's side. We will not win unless this happens. The strategy of co-optation requires maximum attentiveness to the nature of our message and the language we employ. Any gestures that reduce the ability of those not currently part of the movement to shift their loyalties must be avoided. For example, "Death to the Islamic Republic" chants, openly atheistic acts, and threats of violence are all deeply counterproductive.

3. *Neutralization.* Clearly, not all, and perhaps not even most, of the regime's supporters can be won over. But that doesn't mean they should all be counted as perennial enemies. We must convince some of them that this regime has no future, that they are much better off disassociating

themselves from it, and that they may continue to work and live as normal citizens as long as they do not try to dominate the rest of society again.

4. *Persistence.* Civil disobedience is a drawn-out process. The movement should prepare for the long haul and not expect the regime's sudden, precipitous collapse. Of course, if such an event did occur, we would all be very happy, but we cannot build our strategy on such a model. To do so would be to court disaster. We should prepare for a drawn-out fight. Whichever side—the Green Movement or the regime—designs a strategy better adapted to a prolonged struggle will win in the end. The wave of demoralization that followed the events of February 11 would not have occurred had there been a more sober assessment of the situation and a clearer understanding of the nature of the struggle.

5. *Adaptability.* Mistakes are inevitable. This is a constantly evolving situation. The movement needs to learn to adapt quickly to ongoing shifts. The regime is now doing exactly that and so should the Greens. It is alright to make mistakes—they are inevitable in a struggle such as this. What is unpardonable is to continue making the same mistake, like employing the Trojan horse tactic, over and over again.

"IF A NATION WANTS TO CHANGE ITS DESTINY...": ZAHRA RAHNAVARD ON WOMEN'S RIGHTS AND THE GREEN MOVEMENT

March 11, 2010

Awhile ago women's rights activists released a statement claiming that there has been no attention given to their demands since after the election. They wrote that they believe the issue of women is a big part of the current crisis, and without attempting to solve these issues, no broader political solutions would be sustainable. What do you think about this? Do you believe that from the day after the election, the candidates were oblivious to women and their issues?

Truly, why do we women have to sit around and wait for someone to tend to us? We have to be the ones who step forward. We can learn much from the stories of great women in history. We have thousands of years of history to draw on. From the time when, according to the Quran, humanity was one unified nation, or the time when, according to some theorists, women were the prime decision makers, or when, according to archeological findings, the gods who ruled the world were female. The history of civilization tells us that women were the first industrialists, cloth weavers, potters and farmers. Of course, in those times, there were unwritten agreements in which, according to the physical, economic, religious and traditional beliefs, men and women divided tasks. And though it has not been historically proven that there was ever a society ruled solely by women, at least we know that there was a time when they played a huge role in the laws and governance of their society.

What is stopping us now from learning from them? During the

263

recent election, women were treated as first-class citizens, but right after the election that status was taken away from them in a flash. Despite what happened, we must still pursue our demands of freedom, ending discrimination against women and violence, and stopping polygamy.

Are the Green Movement and women's rights movement related? If yes, can you tell us about their link?

On the more general issues, there is considerable overlap between the two movements. On more specific issues, there is a need for the women's rights movement to branch out and push its own agenda above and beyond the support that it gleans from the Green Movement. When it comes to basic rights—such as gender equality, democracy and rule of law—the two movements are in complete agreement. But I would like to firmly assert that in history, general political reform movements and revolutions have shown that women's fight for equality needs to be distinguished from the general political movement for democracy.

In Iran, it is impossible to expect that the general political movement—in this case, the Green Movement—will be able to successfully eliminate inequality and violence against women without help from an established and independent women's movement. The legal push for gender equality with regards to double standards in reparation money, court rulings, legally sanctioned polygamy, and divorce and citizenship laws should be fiercely pursued by advocates of the women's movement.

The general political movements of the past two centuries—the Industrial Revolution, the French Revolution, the pursuit of American democracy, the Bolshevik Revolution, the fall of the Russian communist regime—did not do much to propagate the advancement of women's rights. It was only much later, when women put up a separate fight of their own, that they began to advance their legal rights.

What is the responsibility of the Green Movement toward gender equality?

The Green Movement must understand that today, women are at the forefront; they take initiatives and make sacrifices in an awe-inspiring way, much like they did during the Islamic Revolution. Hence, the movement's platform needs to be mindful of women's rights issues and must incorporate gender equality into its platform. As Mousavi said in a previous interview, the Green Movement is friends of the women's movement, and this friendship means camaraderie.

However, the reality is that the Green Movement is like an umbrella to several other significant social movements—the women's movement, the labor movement, the students' movement and the teachers' movement, among others. The general slogans of the Green Movement are freedom, equality, rule of law and democracy. Leaning too much toward any of the sub-movements can make the Green Movement appear biased. Like I said before, the women's movement, while being supported by the Green Movement, still needs to be active and push forward its agenda independent of the Green Movement as well.

At the same time, in its statements and views the Green Movement should acknowledge the importance of each of these sub-movements, demand the amelioration of the political environment, and push for a government that would ultimately grant the wishes of each sub-movement without appearing biased.

In this situation, what is the role of the current government?

I have repeatedly declared that this government is illegitimate. But, since it has been established as the official one and it recognizes itself officially, it should fulfill its responsibilities accordingly. Right now, they destroy families and condemn women and children to misery by neglecting their demands, repressing them and proposing anti-women legislation in the name of supporting families while, in reality, simply satisfying hedonists. If it claims to be a legitimate government, it should withdraw anti-women legislation immediately, designate committees to restore women's rights, and, inspired by the ideals of the women's movement, interact with the parliament and the judiciary to achieve these ideals. However, this government is incapable of carrying out such deeds.

In the aftermath of tenth presidential election, a group of MPs have decided to pass the so-called family support legislation. This is happening while the slightest protest by students, teachers, workers and journalists against civil rights violations is responded to with threats, arrests and unjust trials. Why are they in such a hurry to pass this legislation, which would legalize polygamy and is more backward than the one passed thirty-five years ago?

This is puzzling for me as well. On one hand they are trying to take advantage of the situation to advance their agenda against the will of the freedom-loving women of this country. They think that the Green Movement does not pay attention to women's issues, and therefore they can use the opportunity to realize their backward agenda. This explains the opportunity for them, but not the reason. So what is the reason? I believe that this government has a retrogressive mindset that seeks violence. They are involved with repressive pressure groups that have imposed their influence on certain layers of the Islamic society, and they have committed many murders, accused and threatened citizens, and physically assaulted their opponents in public gatherings so that they can create a closed society. Today, these groups are in power and have the authority to impose and enforce their views. But even if they succeed temporarily they will be defeated in the long term. They should know that they cannot present their backward views in the name of Islam forever. Islam is a progressive religion. It has the potential to interact with the modern world and new ideas, and its dynamic *Ijtihad* has provided an opportunity for innovation in a contemporary context.[1] Overall, I think the parliament is under pressure by the government to pass these anti-women legislations.

In an interview, you declared that you do not recognize this government and that you will not compromise with it. That interview was greatly publicized and was the focus of the day. What reasons do you see behind such attention to your words?

There were rumors going around back then that leaders of the Green Movement were compromising with the government. Of course, this was the wrong interpretation. Such rumors were further promoted by the conservative right-wing—they do not deserve the word Principlist—newspapers. They were making a big deal out of baseless rumors in order to deflate the spirit of the people, but they were not successful. They said that the Green Movement was frightened, that they had lost and regretted the course of action they had taken. As a member of the Green Movement, side by side with the people, I declared what they thought of such rumors. I did not say anything new. It was the words of the people who have refused to retreat. It is these people that guide the leaders of the Green Movement toward the natural demands of freedom and democracy.

How do you see the future of the Green Movement?

If a nation wants to change its destiny, it will definitely be successful. This is the message of hope from the great Quran. If you help God, God will help you back. It is the promise of the Almighty. If our steps are fixed in this path, we will be victorious and we will breathe a new life into the body of our thoughts and lives.

Some people are very concerned about the outbreaks of violence during the celebrations of the last Wednesday of the [Persian calendar] year [in March 2010]. What is your solution to stop the violence?

Those celebrations are among the ancient national rites of Iranians. Nowruz is a day of joy, a day when people wear smiles and wipe the misery off of their faces. It is when nature blooms in a spring-like fashion, in colorful colors and flowers. Thanks to Nowruz celebrations of the first day of spring, and the kind spirit of this day and its gift of freedom, the Green Movement would definitely be happy and proud. The Green Movement is defined by compassion, resistance and calm. We would commemorate the memories of people like Neda, Sohrab and other martyrs. We would not commit any violence; we would love all people, whether they are Green or any other color. We say to the military members that we love you too. Be our brothers, and give people flowers instead of batons and bullets. If there is a violence, it is violence of the government.

During the last nine months, you have been attacked many times. You were physically attacked on University Students Day [December 7] and on the day of anniversary of the revolution [February11]. You have also been attacked in the form of slanders and accusations from the media attached to the government. One of the leading opponents of the Green Movement went so far as to say that you are a Zionist, that you support the Baha'i minorities and that you have hidden your real views from the people. What is the reason behind all this violence against you?

They know about my dedication to the Green Movement and my role in it. At the moment, putting me in jail won't do them any good, so they have decided to torment me in the streets and the media instead. What illusions! Our good people have not yet forgotten about the thirty books I have written that clearly demonstrate my beliefs and principles. What I can do is given to me by God. Following the saying of the Quran, I'll just tell them not to fight against what is given by God, as it is his will.

They will not be able to suffocate me with the curse of their lies and libel, as the Green Movement provides me with all the fresh oxygen I need to cheerfully and briskly go on.

In one of the media attacks, the opponents of the Green Movement had said that if Mousavi led the government, he would have nominated you as his chief of staff. Is this an attack on you or is it a form of praise to a woman?

The gentlemen who have spread these rumors, who are also aligned with the political right, have not experienced the joy of being an intellectual and an artist in pursuit of his or her nation's freedom. Otherwise, they would know that if they gave us intellectuals and artists everything on the surface of this earth, including all the power in the country, we would throw it all back at them swiftly, as we are completely happy to work with our intellect and art or teaching our lovely students. Nevertheless, I decided to become active during the election campaign to support our ignored constitution, freedoms and democracy, and I will continue to do so in the future. Perhaps, as you mention, these comical statements by the Green Movement's opponents praise the women more so than they realize. I will tell them from here that I'm only one of many women in the Green Movement, all of whom are more capable than I am. What will you do with them?

Ms. Rahnavard, you are well known as an visual artist. One of your most famous pieces is the "Mother's Sculpture" that was placed in Mother Square in Tehran and has become one of the most famous sculptures in Iran during the first two decades of the Islamic Republic. Some of your antagonists have put ropes around the sculpture's neck. How do you feel about that?

For artists, their work is as close to them as their body. It comes from the heart. The artist puts all of his or her love into art, and it becomes the tale of all the untold stories, cries, secrets, morals and dreams that the artist has. But when the extremist forces are taking people's lives just because they seek freedom, whether it is through executions, brutal beatings or other means, what can we expect them to do with a bronze statue? How can they understand what this statue stands for? How can they understand motherhood and art? You saw the reaction of our wonderful people who said, "If you take down the statue, we will bring Rahnavard herself and put her on the stand." I now worry about all of my art. The paintings and sculptures can easily become the objects of such brutality. I hope God will save us all from their illusions.

What are the biggest problems for the Green Movement these days and what are your expectations for the future?

The Islamic Revolution, despite its greatness and glory, was an incomplete project whose goals and ideals should have been realized in the context of the Islamic Republic, but this did not happen. So the Green Movement continues to pursue issues like freedom, democracy, women's rights and the rule of law.

With regard to your question about the Green Movement's afflictions, don't ask me to list all the grievances and sufferings that the movement has endured, as it will take oceans of ink to write them. I don't want to compare, but in the history of dictatorships, imprisoning intellectuals, cutting hands, making minarets of heads and heaps out of bodies has been documented many times before. I hope that those currently in power learn from these notorious examples and spare our beloved republic from such an awful and bitter fate.

So what should they do? What do we expect? What will it take to satisfy us? It is important that the right thing be done; it is not important by whom. So we expect the regime to free the press and media, the reporters, women, men, the young and old. We want them to provide the military forces with flowers, so they can present them to people in compensation for their actions. We want them to free the prisoners. The jails holding freedom-seekers will be planted with flowers and will be turned into gardens. They should be turned into cultural centers and scientific research labs, all efforts should be made to develop our industries and agriculture so our youth will have fewer problems with employment, marriage and education. On the international level, we want carefully crafted and friendly policies that are in line with our national interests. We want the demands of the women, workers, teachers and artists to be met. We want them to guarantee the freedom of expression and thought. These and much more can be fulfilled by any decent establishment. Among civil movements, the Green Movement has a particular sympathy for the women's movement. The Green Movement demands the freedom of all prisoners, particularly the women, whose spouses, mothers and children are impatiently awaiting their release.

"THE REAL REVOLUTION IS THAT PEOPLE ARE ENTERING THE SOCIETY AS AGENTS":
AN INTERVIEW WITH IRANIAN DISSIDENT AKBAR GANJI

Hamid Dabashi

April 2, 2010

The following interview was conducted for the program *The Week in Green with Hamid Dabashi: A Window into the Iranian Civil Rights Movement* (www.weekingreen.org).

When you look at the Islamic Republic of Iran in the past thirty years, do you see the emergence of the Green Movement as an inevitable event?

In my opinion, if we look at the history of the recent events, we might be able to shed light on your difficult question.

The Green Movement didn't happen overnight; it wasn't a work of magic. This movement gradually developed over thirty years. A few people gathered here and there, brought in others, and created journals and newspapers. These people became rivers of thought, and these rivers came together in the May 1997 presidential elections and created the reform movement.

The reform movement knocked Mr. Khamenei and the regime into a coma. Unfortunately, people didn't take advantage of this period and the regime came out of the coma and reacted by trying to close down all possible outlets of free expression. Mr. Khamenei claimed that the newspapers were the enemies' base. As a result, in a very short time, more than 100 newspapers were confiscated, and many journalists were imprisoned.

In the lead up to the seventh parliamentary elections in 2004, the regime disqualified the reformist candidtes, including many sitting members of parliament and thus created an oligarchic parliament. Then the 2005 elections took place, and Mr. Khamenei and the aristocratic regime overcame their divisions and together took over the seventh parliament, the city councils and the presidential election of 2005.

However, all didn't turn out as the regime expected. After four years, the regime had no other solution but to violate the election of June 12, 2009. They announced the election results in less than twenty-four hours because they saw no point in counting the votes, as it would only create problems for the regime. People were shocked. Social movements require a trigger to mobilize the people. People were triggered and they protested in the streets. This trigger came from the election results, but the widespread frustration and dissatisfaction already existed in the society. The elections of June 12, 2009, were only a shock; they were just a trigger, not a cause.

There were myriad other reasons for peoples' frustrations, including many social reasons. You might ask, "What happened?" The reform movement never approved of a social movement or street protests. If you look at the period after the reform era [1997–2005], you see that the reformists always criticized protests. They were scared that a series of events would happen in which things would get out of control, with unknown outcomes. If you look at their writings and statements of the time, you can see their disapproval.

Reformists like Said Hajjarian, who believed that people should pressure the government to agree to negotiate, were exceptions. Hajarian said that social mobilization is a necessity; this was indeed a correct statement. When I issued my *Republican Manifesto* [2002] in which I said that the only solution is social mobilization and civil disobedience, all the reformists disagreed.

What has happened since the elections is that people came to the streets, and it was the people who pushed Mousavi and Karoubi to the streets. Mousavi said that it wasn't the reformists who forced people to the streets, it was the other way around, and he was absolutely right. Such a statement wasn't made because Mousavi wanted to legally take the responsibility off his shoulders. No, he is taking a real stand, as is Karoubi.

The truth was that people came out to the streets and created this social movement. You can see this uprising as foundational and transformative; the society's frustrations with the government already existed, but this frustration was exacerbated in recent years. The real revolution is that we are witnessing people entering the society as political agents. Social mobilization and a real social movement has emerged; this didn't exist before, and it is very important.

What are the issues, problems and obstacles facing the movement?

One of the issues with the Green Movement is that it continues using the same tactic, which is street protests. This makes things complicated. After the June 12 election, the Islamic Republic wasn't ready for such an uprising. However, when protests continued on occasions celebrated by the regime, like November 4 [anniversary of the seizure of the US Embassy], Jerusalem Day, February 11 [anniversary of Islamic Revolution], the regime saw that these are all occasions approved and controlled by the regime itself. So they began to plan things in advance to prevent any protests.

The opposition should think of unpredictable acts; protesting in the streets is predictable and tactics that are repeated over and over can be overcome by the regime. The movement should think of other tactics; there are thousands of other tactics available.

The leaders of the Green Movement who are at the heart of the movement should decide what tactics to use, but I'll give you examples from the 1979 Revolution. One thing that people can do with minimum consequence is to not pay their utility bills. They could also organize workers strikes. The leaders of the Green Movement could ask people to withdraw their money from the banks—the banks are already in crisis because, upon Ahmadinejad's request, they have loaned a huge amount of money to a selected group of people which hasn't been paid back.

The other problem is rushing things, wanting things to be over soon and wanting the regime to fall quickly. This will make things more complicated and will only deceive people. It will create vain disputes, which have already occurred, especially outside Iran.

When this happens, people outside Iran think that the regime is falling, so they rush to grab a piece of this cake. Things get hectic and ideological clashes start over something that doesn't exist. Even if it exists, this is not the solution. We should understand that democracy will occur when we all unite and achieve a pluralist unity.

In your opinion, what is the most important achievement of the Green Movement?

We must look at the Green Movement as a long-term movement. You've asked me about the outcomes of the Green Movement and the first outcome is its social mobilization; the second is that it is turning into a movement. What do I mean by that? A movement has specific characteristics. A movement requires an ideology. Depending on the ideology, people demand civil rights, freedom, democracy, different lifestyle options and pluralism; these are the demands of the Green Movement. The leadership of this movement is developing. At this point, people like Mousavi and Karoubi have become well-known faces of this movement, and they have resisted very well. Mr. Karoubi released a special New Year video message in which he directly addressed Mr. Khamenei's so-called "savior ship" metaphor and called it a life boat that is sinking and is filled with conservatives whom no one accepts.

This is real resistance, while my opposition here in New York is not as consequential. The importance of his message is that it took place in the heart of Tehran. So this movement has an ideology, it has prominent faces and it has mobilized the society. It has been able to attract the sympathy of the international community; today this movement is known all around the world.

I visited Sweden recently and the leader of the socialist party in

Sweden wore the green bracelet on his wrist and announced that he will continue wearing the bracelet until the victory of the Green Movement. You don't see this only in Sweden; you see it in movie festivals and from singers and politicians all around the world. This movement has established itself around the world and this is an astonishing outcome.

We are at the beginning of the Iranian New Year. What do you see for the future of the Green Movement in the new year?

The Iranian regime is dealing with several crises, and it is going to have a hard time overcoming these crises, but people are wrong to assume that the battle is over.

The first is the crisis of legitimacy. Ever since the June 12 election, the regime has struggled with this issue. You can't solve this problem through miracles, and it is impossible to solve this problem logically because the regime has no ideological legitimacy. It is looking for supernatural solutions that don't exist.

Another crisis is exacerbating the first crisis, and that is the regime's crisis of pragmatism. The regime is dealing with severe economic inflation, and this year, with the removal of government subsidies, the inflation rates will increase even more; the parliament has suggested a figure of 20–40 percent. Additionally, the regime hasn't solved the problems of unemployment, housing issues and poor economic growth. Thus, it is clear that the government is dysfunctional, which only aggravates the legitimacy crisis.

In addition, all the masks have been torn away and everything has been revealed. Everyone now knows that the king is naked. Mr. Khamenei showed his true face after the election and you see the slogan in the street, "Death to the dictator."

This movement will continue to grow, but not necessarily in the streets. The battlefields are not limited to one area. The battle should continue in different territories; wherever the regime is present, the opponents should also be present. When the opposition is present everywhere, the regime can no longer defeat them.

This movement is in a very good position. Every single day, a new democratic power is being developed. We need time so that this movement can progress step by step, and a new, independent, democratic opposition can develop. The opportunities are not limited to street protests. The law removing government subsidies will create hundreds more opportunities for us. In a society where there is a deep political discontent, in a society with fifteen million people below the poverty line, the removal of government subsidies will only create a wealthy minority group amongst the government officials. The young generation will use these opportunities.

LAYING LOW BUT NOT GONE:
IRAN'S GREEN MOVEMENT AND THE
GRAY STRATEGY OF PATIENCE

Mohammad Ayatollahi Tabaar

April 30, 2010

Iran's Green Movement has been laying low for the past few months after massive coercive measures carried out by government-sponsored forces, but many believe that the embers of the movement continue to burn. The "people are just waiting for a spark," Mehdi Karoubi, a presidential contender and opposition leader, recently told *Der Spiegel*. Former reformist president Mohammad Khatami has warned that the new Persian Year, which started on March 20, will be the "year of social crises" if the Ahmadinejad administration's "mismanagement" and "strategy of lies" continue. But many analysts wonder whether the Green Movement has a strategy to capitalize on such opportunities, or even to survive in the face of government repression.

While it may be an exaggeration to say that the decentralized Green Movement has a single "strategy," the approach of its top leaders suggests that their hopes lie in exploiting the "gray zones" in Iranian society through a strategy of patience and endurance. The Green Movement already enjoys the support of millions of restless young Iranians, many of whom hope for radical change. But Mir Hossein Mousavi and other top leaders are fixated on what they call the "gray area," made up of religious associations and traditional factions that do not quite support the Green Movement, but are also quietly unhappy with the rise of Mahmoud Ahmadinejad. By pledging unconditional loyalty to the foundations of the Islamic Republic, the leaders of the Green Movement hope to attract or at least neutralize these "moderate conservatives" and influential figures in various religious and political circles.

This strategy rests on the ability of the Green Movement to broaden its appeal into those conservative "gray zones." It has already created an unprecedented gap within the conservative establishment. Capitalizing on their impeccable revolutionary resumés that date back to the consolidating years of the Islamic Republic, the leaders of the Green Movement have striven to push the fault-line as deep as possible into the conservative camp, so that when the next crisis hits they can draw deeper for support.

If it was an election that brought millions of people to the streets last year, the next round of protests could be triggered by social and economic problems and the skyrocketing inflation rate that is predicted to occur if President Ahmadinejad succeeds in removing subsidies on basic commodities. The failure of Ahmadinejad's social and economic policies may create dissatisfaction among the lower social strata that are reportedly his main constituency. Khatami has argued that only the "return to the law" and a more inclusive political process in which all factions are "hand in hand" could weather this looming storm.

Many reformists believe that the record-high oil cash flush of the past few years, Iran's perceived foreign policy successes in Iraq, Afghanistan, Lebanon and Gaza, and the continued expansion of Iran's nuclear program have made Iran's leaders over-confident. If things go worse for them, would the establishment be willing to compromise with an opposition that does not miss an opportunity to emphasize its loyalty to the constitution of the Islamic Republic? So far there is no sign to suggest that the conservatives are eager to negotiate with the internal opposition. But, perhaps a sharper crisis would compel Ayatollah Khamenei to shift his support from ultra-conservative elements to more centrist factions.

Iran's political evolution offers some support for this hope. In the 1980s, Ayatollah Khomeini, the founding father of the Islamic Republic, consistently ensured a balance between two political factions: the Right (conservatives) and the Left (radicals). After his death, the former managed to remove the latter from the political scene. But this did not last long, as the Left reinvented itself and came back as reformists in a land-slide election in 1997. It took Ayatollah Khamenei eight years to remove the Left/reformists from the political arena once more and replace them, not just with the conservatives, but this time with an ultra-conservative faction consisting of a younger generation of revolutionary figures such as the current president. If Ayatollah Khomeini expunged the liberals, Marxists and other political groups after the revolution and then struck a balance between the two wings of his Islamist faction, his successor, Ayatollah Khamenei, has removed the reformists, the "new liberals," in order to strike a balance within his own faction between the "traditional right" and the "new right."

A brief look at Iranian newspapers from the 1980s can give us a sense of how lonely the Supreme Leader is these days. These papers were often covered with pictures and statements of the then top five leaders of the country: 1) the late Ayatollah Khomeini, whose family now supports the opposition; 2) Ayatollah Montazeri, an architect of the Islamic Republic and later long-time dissident cleric whose death back in December on the holy day of Ashura gave a major boost to the Green Movement; 3) Ali Akbar Hashemi Rafsanjani, the powerful head of the Majles and de facto number two politician in the 1980s, now the head of two important bodies: the Expediency Council and the Assembly of Experts. Rafsanjani facilitated Ayatollah Khamenei's ascendance to leadership in 1989, however he now backs Mousavi; 4) then Prime Minister Mousavi, who enjoyed the unequivocal approval of Ayatollah Khomeini for eight years even in the face of numerous unsuccessful attempts to be removed by then President Khamenei; and 5) Ayatollah Khamenei, who in the 1980s was only a ceremonial president with limited authority but is now by far the most powerful man in the country.

Today there is no question that Ayatollah Khamenei is in full control of Iran and its much-dreaded military and security forces that can make life difficult for the US and its regional allies. But it is no secret that his domestic challengers are the children of the revolution, and they cannot be devoured so easily. Currently, President Ahmadinejad and his far-right allies control Iran's executive branch, while the Larijani brothers, who are seen as more "moderate" elements closer to the traditional right, dominate the judiciary and legislative branches. The ever-existing tension between these two sub-factions, primarily evident in fiery debates in the Majles (parliament), demonstrate that there is little mutual respect between the two camps. Nevertheless, this new balance between the "new right" and the "traditional right" cannot easily replace the old political equilibrium. The permanent removal of the Left/reformists is seen as simply too big a pill for Ayatollah Khamenei to swallow.

Equally afraid of massive bloodshed or a sudden collapse of the entire system, the opposition leaders are today pushing for a shift to "moderation," where the old balance is re-established. But this time, it would be based on more "rational" social, economic and foreign policies. Many supporters of the Green Movement may wish for more radical change to bring about a secular political system. But for now they seem to continue to back the current opposition leaders in the hope that guaranteeing the implementation of the current constitution, despite its shortcomings, could pave the way for other, more fundamental changes. And it is precisely the fear of a slippery slope that has prevented Ayatollah Khamenei from making any shift to the center. But the opposition believes time is on its side and that its "gray" strategy of patience, combined with the vital role of the new media in spreading its message, will eventually force Ayatollah Khamenei to make a stark choice between existential crises and a "return to moderation." In the meantime, the opposition will need to ensure that the Green Movement does not itself lose momentum and become gray.

STEPS AHEAD ON MAY DAY:
SIGNS OF PROMISE AS GREEN-LABOR UNITY BUILDS

Hamid Farokhnia

May 2, 2010

Thousands of security officers and special anti-riot policemen were deployed throughout Tehran from morning into late evening in anticipation of May Day protests and gatherings. In a major departure from past practice, the Green Movement last week sent strong overtures to the labor movement by calling on Green supporters to commemorate May 1, International Workers' Day. Some pro-Green websites and blogs urged their supporters to congregate in the late afternoon near the Labor Ministry on Azadi Avenue, one of the spots across which a crowd of two million marched during last year's historic June 25 protests. On that day, thousands had spontaneously chanted, "Ministry of Labor, and no work for labor."

The special police units, with their familiar riot gear and deafening motorcycle formations, were out in full force from around eleven a.m., joined in some areas by Ministry of Intelligence agents. At noon, near the intersection of Valiasr and Enghelab, pedestrians' bags were searched, presumably for offending leaflets. The heavy-handed tactics were clearly intended to intimidate the workers and their supporters. In fact, the effect of the overwhelming police presence was nothing but ironic. By early afternoon, millions of Tehranis had learned firsthand that it was International Workers' Day and that protests might break out against government policies.

At the appointed time—between four and six p.m.—a crowd estimated at 4,000 congregated around the Labor Ministry building. They strode down the sidewalks, sat on the steps of storefronts, stood nearby or drove their cars back and forth. Although a few diehard Greens were disappointed at the modest turnout, it wasn't bad at all, considering that the event was not publicized in a big way and Green leaders had not officially endorsed it.

Elsewhere in Tehran, in front of the parliament building, a planned ceremony organized by the quasi-governmental Workers' House was marred when workers shouted out slogans demanding higher pay and better working conditions. Minor skirmishes with the police led to injuries among a dozen of the workers.

At Tehran University, where President Mahmoud Ahmadinejad turned up for a surprise visit, a spontaneous student rally broke out, featuring chants of "Students, workers, unity, unity."

In the industrial city of Qazvin, where factory closures are taking a heavy toll on workers, the pro-Green Jaras website reported that a few thousand gathered at a local stadium to voice their grievances. Police presence was heavy throughout the city.

On the eve of May Day, Minster of Labor Abdolreza Sheikholeslami attended a meeting in the city of Mashhad to make a speech in which he utterly avoided addressing the labor situation. After the speech, workers protested. One, quoted on the website Kalameh, said, "We were expecting to hear better words from the minister on improving the workers' conditions, but in his speech he did not even say one single word about the workers." In support of striking workers, students at nearby Ferdowsi University reportedly refrained from attending classes for two hours and initiated a hunger strike.

Protests and gatherings by workers and their supporters were also reported by an Iran Human Rights website in Shiraz, Isfahan, Ahvaz, Dastgerd, Sanandaj and even the holy city of Qom.

Despite the absence of large rallies and marches, this can be seen as a successful day for labor and Green activists alike. As far as the labor movement is concerned, thanks to the regime's draconian measures, millions of Iranians are now aware of International Workers' Day and the grievances of workers around the country. The very fact that the Green Movement has expressed support for the workers' cause goes a long way in cementing ties between these two key constituencies. No major political transformation is possible in Iran without Green–labor unity. And obviously, the overwhelming, menacing police presence belies the propaganda that declares the regime a friend to the working class.

A final word, concerning the pessimistic tone of some recent reports. The present political dynamic in Iran does not follow an insurrectionary model or other familiar forms of violent political struggle. We should not expect sudden, abrupt shifts and ruptures. Instead, the ongoing progress toward a true democracy involves slow, incremental change with lots of back and forth between the two sides. The aim is to capture state power not through the repeated application of a particular strategem—large street gatherings and protests—but through a combination of flexible maneuvers, tactics and countertactics. Whichever side in this very serious game is more patient and more adaptable will win. What the movement needs right now, if it is to succeed, is not admonishment for having failed so far to knock out the Islamic Republic Goliath, but encouragement in its pursuit of a process that the Romans referred to as festina lente, "make haste slowly."

IRAN'S GREENS AND THE AMERICAN CIVIL RIGHTS MOVEMENT:
AN INTERVIEW WITH CORNEL WEST

May 6, 2010

The following interview was conducted for the program *The Week in Green with Hamid Dabashi: A Window into the Iranian Civil Rights Movement* (www.weekingreen.org).

Our guest today is Dr. Cornel West, a prominent philosopher, social activist and member of the Democratic Socialists of America. He teaches philosophy at Princeton University. Dr. West, thanks for joining us.

As you know, we are considering the Green Movement in Iran as something very similar to the American civil rights movement. What do you think was the secret of the success of the American civil rights movement that sustained its course and extended it all the way from the middle of the twentieth century to the first decade of the twenty-first century, when we finally had the first African American elected as the president of the United States?

I think the fundamental secret of the civil rights movement was that it was a long revolution with a fundamental commitment to unarmed truth and unconditional love. And by unarmed truth, I mean the condition of truth is to allow suffering to speak, so it could be in American apartheid in the south, it could be in Iran that you actually have courageous, visionary, determined brothers and sisters, be they black or be they Iranian, who are willing to allow suffering to speak, willing to lift their voices, and to do it rooted in a profound love for their people.

Martin Luther King, Jr. had a love affair with poor people and black people. The Iranians have a love affair with the Iranian people, and that love takes the form of justice. We understand justice as what love looks like in public, so when you really love people, you hate the fact that they're being treated unjustly. You loathe the fact that they're being treated unfairly, and you must do something, you must bear witness, and that's in coming together, in organizing and mobilizing.

But sometimes its three steps forward, two steps back. Sometimes there's defeat and then breakthrough. Sometimes there's progress, sometimes there's regress. The history of the civil rights movement in America, the history of the Green Revolution... let me say this, that the Green Revolution is the most significant and exemplary movement for justice in the world today because it is in a part of the world where both reform and transformation are necessary, but rooted in a nonviolent movement tied to love and justice. It cannot but send tremendous effects and consequences for those of us in the American empire.

How can a nonviolent civil rights movement sustain its course against a violent regime that does not hesitate to use cruelty? What are the enduring lessons of Martin Luther King, Jr. and the American civil rights movement in this respect?

First, I just want to say to my dear Iranian brothers and sisters that Martin Luther King, Jr. is smiling from the grave. Gandhi is smiling from the grave. Why? Because any nonviolent movement rooted in spiritual discipline, moral courage and political vision attempts to break the vicious cycle that goes back to the very beginning of the homo sapiens, which is violence, domination, subjugation, revenge, bigotry and hatred. And in the place of it is justice, not revenge—deep love, even if you're willing to sacrifice and die for that love, not hatred and bigotry.

But each attempt to break the cycle can solicit brutality, can solicit barbaric response from the powers that be. We saw that in the south when Bull Connor himself, who was a Sunday school teacher, was willing to actually crush precious young black people as well as older black people. The regime in Iran today is willing to crush precious Iranians who attempt to bear witness to love and justice and truth.

So I think that one can be discouraged, but one should never in any way be paralyzed by despair. Each time Martin Luther King, Jr. led the youth section, he would begin with one sentence. He would say, "Do you have your cemetery uniform on?" which means do you love the people enough to live and die for them? That's a deep question. And I think the Green Movement has shown us that this rich legacy of a nonviolent resistance movement in the face of a brutal and barbaric regime, you have enough people who are willing to actually bear witness and live and die. There's nothing more moving than that. As a Christian, of course, I speak of Jesus, who says, "No greater love does a man or woman have than the willingness to lay down their life."

Now, I'd like you to imagine yourself in Iran, advising the leaders of the Green Movement. How would you chart its course over the next year given the brutal repression of the regime?

I think I would want to highlight three different fronts. The first front would be the Iranian people themselves, to be proud of this group of citizens who are willing to risk their all, life and limb, in order to make Iran free and democratic. One can never downplay the weight, the gravity of that kind of service and sacrifice for the future of Iran. You want to be able to keep them motivated.

The second front would be to try to make some connection with those on the inside of the system, to convince a small slice that they need to have a receptivity. They need to be able to respond to this organized movement, this sacrifice and service, so that it creates some wiggle room on the inside of the system. I think Martin Luther King, Jr. understood this as well. You have to have some folk on the inside who are so touched by the willingness of Iranian brothers and sisters to sacrifice themselves that they put some energy into creating some space on the inside.

My third front would be the international front. Now here we are in the United States. We have a very precious American democratic experiment in the United States, but we also have an imperial system, so there's tension between the two. We need more voices to speak publicly, passionately about the Green Movement in the United States so that the media begins to cast a limelight on it. A limelight on it in such a way not that it reinforces the demonizing of Iran, because it's easy for the mass media and the corporate media in the United States to cast it as just either/or.

No, the Green Movement actually is a new way, a new wave, a new way of engaging in political movement in Iran and in many ways in the Muslim world, and it's magnificent. I teach Mahmoud Mohamed Taha, who I consider a Muslim Gandhi since he was killed in Sudan in 1984; he had the same kind of vision. How do you create a new wave of freedom and democracy, not by imitating the West but by being indigenous to the Middle East, and also learning from the West because, believe me, just as the Green Movement has much to teach us in the United States, it can certainly learn from the legacy of Martin Luther King, Jr. But I think this international front in America, Europe, Latin America and other parts of Asia and the Middle East, and the West Bank, the Gaza Strip—[we would all be better off] if we could see King's legacy taking root against Israeli occupation, so it doesn't lose sight of the humanity of Israeli brothers and sisters and Jewish brothers and sisters, but lets them know that nonviolent resistance can, in fact, create a fundamental transformation of even an occupied people into a free people.

As you know, economic justice is at the heart of any civil rights movement. Iranian workers have just celebrated May 1, or May Day, despite severe state repression. How do you think the relationship between a civil rights movement and a labor movement can be combined in the future?

I think there are two elements to it. One is that there is this fundamental commitment to poor people. As a Christian, I would call it a commitment to loving poor people. I would want the Iranian people to love poor Iranians and love working-class Iranians as much as they love their

TV stars, because we tend to have love affairs with our celebrities. Now what does that mean? That means that when you look at Iranian society, you want to look at it through the lens of poor, working people because there is class struggle going on in every society.

If we're actually going to embrace everyone, that goes with the 25th chapter of Matthew, "What you have done to the least of these, you have done to me,"—the president, the orphan, the widow, the fatherless, the motherless, the oppressed, the poor, the working people—then your social analysis comes in and says, well, let's look at how elites actually behave in Iranian society. Who is this Revolutionary Guard? What kind of bureaucratic status do they have? What kind of privileges do they have? How does that relate to the precious, priceless, poor Iranian brothers and sisters, working-class Iranian brothers and sisters? How do they come together in such a way that, following the Green Movement commitment to nonviolence, they can slowly move from being intimidated and sleep-walking to being courageous and awakened and willing to serve and sacrifice for justice? But the Iranian brothers and sisters need to know that at this particular historical moment, the Green Movement is a fundamental source of inspiration, and any support that we can provide, we are willing to do so.

You've already done it. We're very, very grateful.

Thank you so much, indeed, indeed.

THE HARSHER THE REPRESSION, THE STRONGER THE MOVEMENT GROWS

Shirin Ebadi

June 8, 2010

This weekend will mark the passage of an entire year since the Iranian people took to the streets in droves to protest the fraudulent elections that returned Mahmoud Ahmadinejad to the presidency. These peaceful demonstrations were met with extreme violence by the Iranian regime. Since that day, the people have not backed down and continue to fight peacefully for basic human rights. Meanwhile, the government continues its crackdown on any opposition or dissent with ever increasing brutality.

Just a few weeks ago, on May 9, the lengths to which the regime will go in order to crush its opponents truly came to light. Five political prisoners were executed in secret. Not even their families or their lawyers were notified.

Shirin Alam Holi, a twenty-eight-year-old Kurdish woman, was executed along with four men. In letters from Evin prison, Shirin wrote of being tortured to confess to charges of terrorism. She refused to confess, and this sealed her fate. At least twenty-five other men and women await the same fate on death row.

However, as we see time and time again, the harsher the repression, the stronger the movement grows. And as the story of Shirin Alam Holi demonstrates, women are at the forefront of the struggle for human rights in Iran.

But it is interesting to observe that this powerful feminist movement was not born out of the elections. It has been gaining strength and momentum since the Islamic revolution of 1979—when the regime began imposing laws that were discriminatory against women—and even predates the revolution. Women in Iran have enjoyed the right to vote for nearly fifty years, since 1963. Today, under an even more repressive regime, they are flooding the ranks of doctors, professors and chief executives. Women now constitute more than 63 percent of university students. Is it any wonder that they refuse to stand idly by and accept that their lives are not worth as much as that of a man?

With no leader or central office, the women's movement has resided for the past thirty-one years in every Iranian household that cares about human rights. In the past year, the Green Movement has emerged and modeled itself on this seemingly unstoppable force. With women's rights activists at the helm, the Green network is consistent in its demands for democracy and human rights.

Take the Mourning Mothers, for instance. Every week since June 2009, mothers whose children are in prison, missing or have lost their lives to state-sanctioned violence, gather in Laleh Park in Tehran. Dressed all in black, they carry photos of their loved ones and are surrounded by other women to support and protect them.

Every Saturday they gather peacefully, and every Saturday the police attack, beat and arrest them. This excessive violence and repression by the government has sadly become routine in Iran, but has not deterred the Mourning Mothers. Courageously, they are defending their human rights and, ultimately, those of women everywhere.

In December, peaceful protests on the Shia Muslim holy day of Ashura were followed by a wave of arrests and violence. Dozens of women journalists and human rights activists were targeted, and I was no exception. In an attempt to stop me from doing my work from abroad, the government arrested my sister, Dr. Noushin Ebadi. She has never been politically active or participated in any rallies or demonstrations, but she was arrested and detained for three weeks solely because of my work fighting for human rights.

But these brave women will not stop. They prove that there is no end to the creative ways that Iranian women will fight back. The One Million Signatures campaign has been working since before last year's election to collect signatures from Iranian men and women who oppose discriminatory laws and practices. On March 11, the Change for Equality website, which promotes the campaign, was awarded the first ever Netizen Prize by Reporters Without Borders. The next day—ironically, the World Day Against Cyber-Censorship—Iranian authorities shut down the website for the twenty-third time since it was launched in 2006. It was up and running again just hours later.

The struggle for human rights and gender equality continues in Iran as we mark the anniversary of the disputed elections. This global day of action has united activists, students, NGOs and concerned citizens worldwide to spotlight the horrific human rights abuses that have become all too common.

Women will be at the forefront of this weekend's peaceful activities, as they were today and will be tomorrow. Mark my words, it will be women who will bring democracy to Iran.

PART IV

A LUTA CONTINUA: THE GREEN MOVEMENT'S SECOND YEAR AND THE STRUGGLE FOR IRAN'S FUTURE

A RAGING FIRE UNDER A HEAP OF ASH:
THE GREEN MOVEMENT AT ONE YEAR

Muhammad Sahimi

June 8, 2010

June 12 marks the first anniversary of Iran's tenth presidential election. The people of Iran participated in the voting en masse, not just inside the country, but all over the world in the diaspora: 85 percent of eligible voters participated. There was great hope that the election would close a sad chapter in Iran's recent history—the presidency of Mahmoud Ahmadinejad—and usher in a new era with a more open and tolerant society, representing the first concrete steps toward a democratic political system.

But the people's hopes were dashed after the hardliners rigged the election and committed fraud on a large scale in order to declare Ahmadinejad the "victor." Protests broke out, beginning with a massive demonstration on June 15, 2009 in Tehran. According to Mayor Mohammad Bagher Ghalibaf, three million people took part. Alireza Zakani, a hardline Majles (parliament) deputy, quoted former President Ali Akbar Hashemi Rafsanjani to the effect that at least 3.5 million people had participated. Whatever the precise figure, it was one of the largest demonstrations in Iran's history. The protests strengthened the Green Movement that had emerged just before the election and plunged the country into a deep crisis that has yet to end. The protests began with a simple question, "Where is my vote?" But the people's demands quickly broadened until the very foundations of the Islamic Republic were brought into question.

A well-known reporter for the *New York Times*, who has spent years in the Middle East, asked me the other day where I believe Iran and the Green Movement stand one year after the rigged election and what changes, if any, the movement has brought. In my view, the changes have been deep and lasting, both for the large majority of Iranians who aspire to live in a democracy and for the hardline fundamentalist leadership and its supporters. After years in which the world's view of Iranian society had been deeply distorted, the Green Movement succeeded in drawing a much clearer picture of the country's people, a young, educated, highly dynamic population that wants a democratic political system, the rule of law and respect for fundamental human rights, regardless of anyone's political leanings, gender and ethnicity.

At the same time, the Green Movement has also revealed the true face of the hardline fundamentalists, a narrow segment of the population that is willing to do whatever it takes to retain power, including jailing a large number of people; holding Stalinist show trials that have resulted in long jail sentences for Reformist leaders, university students, human rights advocates and ordinary citizens; torturing, sodomizing and murdering protesters; assassinating innocent victims in order to send a "message" to the people and the movement's leadership; and even refusing to return the bodies of executed young political activists to their families.

With few exceptions, elections in Iran have never been democratic or fair. The regime often bars opposition figures from running. The ruling elite utilizes the vast resources of the nation in order to promote its own candidates and at the same time prohibits the opposition from speaking to the public through its own dailies, weeklies and other publications, and from operating its own TV and radio stations. The opposition is not given any time—let alone equal time—on the national TV and radio network to address the public.

On the other hand, since the 1979 Revolution, elections have been held regularly. With few exceptions, they have been competitive in the sense that there have always been contrasting views about the important issues facing the nation; at least some candidates have supported some of the people's aspirations and the outcome was not known in advance. In short, the elections were not of the type that are held in some parts of the Middle East, such as Egypt, which are foregone conclusions. Moreover, the ruling establishment usually went along with the results, even when they were not to its liking.

But last year's election showed that the ruling establishment is no longer willing to accept displeasing outcomes because it recognizes that it cannot win competitive elections, let alone democratic and fair ones. It thus resorted to fraud.

As a result, the hardline leadership lost any residual legitimacy that it might have had, not only in Iran, but around the world. It can no longer boast to the people of the Middle East and the Islamic world about its "religious democracy." The process of voting was turned into an exercise in futility. There is no point in participating in the electoral process when there is no guarantee that the opposition can run and that the people's votes will be respected. In my view, this is the first important fruit of the Green Movement: it forced the hardliners, in order to retain power, to transform the elections from a dynamic process to a meaningless event, thereby annulling any legitimate claim to that power.

The second important change in Iran's political scene is that Ayatollah Ali Khamenei became a public target of people's anger. His role in creating the crisis that the nation faces, his decision to take sides with a small coterie against a very large majority, his implicit support for violence—as in his Friday Prayer sermon June 19, 2009—have transformed him into a despicable figure in the eyes of many Iranians. An important psychological barrier has been broken: Khamenei is now explicitly held responsible for the ills of the nation.

The country is ruled under a system that Khamenei has upheld since he was appointed Supreme Leader in 1989. The constitution bestows upon him absolute power. With this power, which he has not hesitated to use, comes responsibility for the present state of affairs. A small group of reactionaries led by Ahmadinejad and his supporters in the Islamic Revolutionary Guard Corps (IRGC) have squandered the nation's resources through unprecedented levels of corruption, nepotism and outright theft while the oppression of the people continues unabated and the jails grow overcrowded with political prisoners.

Mostafa Pour-Mohammadi, the head of the National Auditing Organization, recently reported to Khamenei that Ahmadinejad's administration is the most corrupt since the 1979 Revolution. Pour-Mohammadi was Ahmadinejad's first minister of the interior and is a notorious hardliner. His report thus represents a very important development, as the hardliners, and even a substantial part of the population, have long considered the Rafsanjani administration as the benchmark of corruption. Although the report was not publicized—Khamenei ordered it suppressed—it does indicate that even leading hardliners now recognize the depth of the problems with Ahmadinejad and his government.

The protests against the election fraud quickly turned into protests against all that has gone wrong in Iran over the last thirty years and, in particular, since the end of the Iraq war in 1989 when Khamenei came to power. People finally expressed their demands loud and clear showing that they are no longer willing to passively accept what the hardliners do to them. They were, and still are, willing to make great sacrifices. At least 110 people have been confirmed dead. Several of these people have been assassinated outright, from Mir Hossein Mousavi's nephew to Professor Masoud Ali Mohammadi and others.

Mousavi, Mehdi Karoubi, Zahra Rahnavard—Mousavi's wife—and former President Mohammad Khatami have not allowed the blood of the innocent to be forgotten. They have resisted tremendous pressures, they have continued speaking against the crimes of the state, and as the people's demands have broadened, so also have the steps these leaders taken to reinforce the movement. It is difficult for some, especially in the diaspora, to believe it, but the fact is that these four individuals have courageously spoken against the very political system in whose creation they played important roles.

Another important change is that the Revolutionary Guards were finally forced to admit publicly that they held considerable power in Iran. It was already known that major figures in Ahmadinejad's cabinet, as well as many provincial governors, mayors and parliamentary deputies are former Guard officers, and that Ahmadinejad could not have been elected in 2005 without the massive support of the Guards and the Basij militia. Last year's electoral fraud was orchestrated by a one-time Guard officer and former Interior Minister Sadegh Mahsouli; in its aftermath the corps' high command was forced to set aside any pretense. Major General Mohammad Ali (Aziz) Jafari, the Revolutionary Guards' top commander, said last week, "Before being a military organization, the IRGC is a security-political organization." Other Guard commanders have publicly admitted how their forces played the lead role in the violent crackdown when the police and Ministry of Intelligence operatives could not control the protests.

Moreover, the Green Movement has also brought to the surface the deep fissures among the clerics. Except for a small reactionary minority that benefits from the present state of affairs and hides behind the Supreme Leader, most are not happy about what is going on. They recognize that Khamenei's blind support of Ahmadinejad is hurting both the nation and Islam. Some ayatollahs, such as Yousef Sanei, Asadollah Bayat and Ali Mohammad Dastgheib, have spoken publicly and courageously against the crimes of the state. Many other ayatollahs, including Abdollah Javadi Amoli (the Larijanis' maternal uncle), Ebrahim Amini, Musa Shobeiri Zanjani and Hossein Vahid Khorasani, have refused to meet with Ahmadinejad or congratulate him on his "re-election." Still others, such as Ayatollah Naser Makarem Shirazi and, especially, Ayatollah Seyyed Abdolkarim Mousavi Ardabili, have tried to resolve the crisis behind the scenes. Perhaps most importantly, the hardliners can no longer deny their desire to remove Rafsanjani from the political scene and the resulting power struggle is now being played out openly.

The hardliners are keenly aware of the gaping fissures and they are extremely sensitive about their public expression. When Abdolkarim Soroush, the distinguished Islamic scholar, recently urged the clerics in Qom to move to Najaf, Iraq, to demonstrate their displeasure, Ayatollah Mohammad Yazdi—a corrupt reactionary cleric who, together with his son, has been accused of stealing national assets—declared him an apostate. *Kayhan*, the daily mouthpiece of the hardliners, prominently displayed the declaration.

Another fruit of the Green Movement has been the emergence of Mousavi, Karoubi and Rahnavard—and, to a lesser extent, Khatami—as its leaders and symbols, even though they humbly make no claim to such status. By imposing Ahmadinejad on Iran, and in particular transforming Mousavi into the symbol of resistance, the hardliners have committed a strategic blunder that has cost them dearly. If Mousavi had been elected, he would have begun making meaningful, but incremental, changes in the system.

Some say that a President Mousavi would have been the second coming of Khatami who, despite being genuinely good and uncorrupted, often acted indecisively. I disagree. I believe that, had he been elected, Mousavi would have resisted Khamenei's interference in the state's affairs—a view supported by the events of the past year. Khatami put it best when he told his young, angry supporters after he withdrew from the presidential race, "I am the man of Friday, but Mir Hossein is the man of Saturday." Iranian elections are held on Fridays—the "man of Friday" can win the votes. "The man of Saturday," the day after the elections, is the man capable of resisting the hardliners once in office.

Mousavi's transformation has been manifested not only in his rejection of what the hardliners do in the name of the Islamic Republic and Islam. It has also been demonstrated by his gradual move, which began before last year's election, toward genuinely democratic positions. He has supported the rights of ethnic and religious minorities, pluralism within the Green Movement and respect for the ideas of others. At the same time, he has condemned all the crimes perpetrated by the regime. In this regard, both Mousavi and Karoubi have already moved far beyond Khatami's positions at the height of the Reform movement of 1997–2000.

Mousavi has also made it clear that he draws no distinction between himself and any other supporter of the Green Movement. For example, when his own nephew was assassinated, his wife Zahra Rahnavard assaulted, his brother-in-law Shapour Kazemi (a completely apolitical engineer scientist) arrested on bogus charges, and his aides thrown in jail, he restrained his outrage and declared that he was no different from the rest of the Iranian people—he was also a victim of the hardliners' crimes.

In a political masterstroke, Mousavi declared on January 1, 2010, that Ahmadinejad's government is illegitimate and illegal, yet still responsible for the nation. He made it clear that because the hardliners control all levers of power and resources in Iran, they are also responsible for whatever may happen to the country, both domestically and internationally. He issued two warnings. First, he counseled against making radical demands that are not quickly achievable and may only push the nation toward large-scale bloodshed and a resulting loss of support for the movement. On this point, he has stated emphatically, "We should agree on a minimum set of demands so that we can attract the maximum support." Second, he predicted that the hardliners might make concessions to foreign powers that would hurt Iran's long-term national interests just to lower the external pressure on themselves—the recent concessions on Iran's nuclear program and the nuclear fuel swap are examples of precisely what he was talking about.

Mousavi has made such statements while still professing loyalty to what he calls "the ideals of the Imam," Ayatollah Khomeini. Some have attacked him for doing so. In my opinion, talk of loyalty to Khomeini's "ideals" is a mistake and most likely will not bring the movement any new support, but to attack Mousavi, Karoubi and Khatami for talking about Khomeini is also wrong. Mousavi, in particular, has always said that he defends pluralism and respects other people's opinion. He has always said he is a supporter, not a leader, of the movement, precisely because he wants to freely express his opinion without any constraints. At the same time, the hardliners will use anything to attack the trio—so imagine what they would make of a public renunciation of Khomeini. The most important issue for the supporters of Iran's democratic movement is what the trio and other leaders do, rather than what they say.

I must also pay tribute to Karoubi, who has courageously and with utmost honesty spoken against the crimes that have taken place. He has declared repeatedly that he is prepared for the consequences and is not afraid of the threats against him and his family, including the physical assaults on him and his sons. His courage is truly admirable, especially in a country where the Revolutionary Guards and Ministry of Intelligence agents murder people with impunity.

Another important fruit of the Green Movement is the death of Khomeini-ism. Although Rafsanjani proclaimed the end of the Khomeini era back in the mid-1990s, events since 2005, when Ahmadinejad was elected, have demonstrated that Khomeini has become something like Mao Zedong of China. His nominal supporters still mention his name with respect and see to it that huge posters of him hang everywhere, even as they act against many things that he stood for. I should clarify that I am completely opposed to *velayat-e faqih* (rule of the Islamic jurist, the backbone of Iran's political system, as represented by Ayatollah Khamenei), which is the most important inheritance that Khomeini left for Iran. He is also responsible for the execution of thousands of political prisoners in the 1980s. But the point here is to draw a comparison between the broader nature of his leadership and what the hardliners and Ayatollah Khamenei do in his name.

Although he was the Supreme Leader, with unparalleled authority as the icon of the 1979 Revolution, Khomeini rarely interfered in the daily affairs of the nation—a sharp contrast to the behavior of his successor. In addition, he was fiercely opposed to military intervention in politics and the economy, whereas the nation is now essentially run by the Revolutionary Guards. Khomeini always emphasized that "*Majles dar ra's omoor ast*" (the Majles is the most important organ), whereas it has now become little more than an obedient arm of the hardliners. The most important consequence of the death of Khomeini-ism is that it has been amply demonstrated that a nation cannot have a Supreme Leader and be democratic.

All changes outlined above have contributed to the greatest fruit of the Green Movement: the lines have been drawn. There is no longer any pretense. On one side are the Revolutionary Guards, the security/intelligence apparatus, a small faction of reactionary and ultra-conservative clerics, and a narrow social base, probably about 15–20 percent of the population. On the other side is everyone else. Those in the majority have different demands, some economic, others social or political. Some are willing to do anything to bring about meaningful change, some are more cautious. But, they all agree on one thing: the present situation is no longer acceptable or tenable.

A year after its birth, the Green Movement should be recognized for what it does and does not represent:

The Green Movement is not about secularism versus religion but about citizens' rights regardless of their individual beliefs. Some, particularly in the diaspora, have tried to define the movement as secular, but this denies both its origins and the source of much of its internal support. Some demand that the movement's leaders declare that they support a secular system. But that demonstrates a misunderstanding of the movement's current goals.

The goal of the Green Movement at this stage is not the takeover of the government, although it will hopefully be able to achieve that at some point. Rather, in order to grant Iranian citizens their proper rights, it aims to critique the ruling elite and demonstrate with utmost clarity and honesty the regime's many shortcomings.

The Green Movement is not yet strong enough to issue an ultimatum to the ruling establishment. The reasons are at least fourfold. First, the movement has not yet spread to every strata of society. Significant work remains to achieve this. Second, the hardliners still control all of the nation's vast resources; the Greens have none, aside from the people. Third, the hardliners are armed to the teeth and they have demonstrated time and again that they will not hesitate to resort to bloodshed in order to retain power. Fourth, unlike Mohammad Reza Shah Pahlavi, the hardliners do have a significant, albeit narrow, social base. Unlike the shah, the hardliners and their supporters have no place else to go. They have little choice but to stay in Iran and fight. That is why the Green Movement must diligently avoid violence, except in self-defense.

The Green Movement represents, at this stage, a social network, both horizontal and vertical. It is not a true political organization, because as soon as it ever became one, it would be savagely suppressed.

The Green Movement does have a leadership, because no movement can succeed without one. Those who, in the name of democracy, oppose the Green Movement or its present leadership, or even refute its existence, are in denial. The most important aspect of the leadership is that it is not based on individual charisma—as was the case in the 1979 Revolution—but on what it has actually done over the past year. I am aware of the row among some in the diaspora over the movement's leadership. But those who deny its existence are mostly either ambitious opportunists who want to ride the Green waves to power, supporters of the Mujahideen-e Khalq Organization, or members of extremist monarchist factions. At least in Iran, the question of the leadership is a non-issue. But as Mousavi has always emphasized, everyone is equal to everyone else within the movement.

The Green Movement belongs to all the people who share its goals, regardless of who they are. However, note the words of Taghi Rahmani, the distinguished nationalist-religious thinker who has spent fourteen years in the prisons of the Islamic Republic. As he put it, "Those who demand radical actions by the movement should explain what it is that *they* have done for the movement. Are those who have means of mass communications willing to put that to use for the movement, without mentioning their own group or affiliation?" In addition, the critics of the Green Movement should ask themselves whether they can demonstrate their own righteousness and the superiority of their strategy to a large segment of the population. Many take idealistic positions without any regard for the facts on the ground in Iran. From the comfort of our homes abroad, they can take any radical position and present themselves as "super" progressives. But at some point they must come back to earth and deal with the real problems.

Despite the skepticism of some, the Green Movement is alive and well. The strongest evidence is the fact that the arrests of university students, political figures, human rights advocates, feminist leaders, journalists and intellectuals have continued without pause, as have the show trials. Long sentences are still being handed out. Seven people have been executed and another sixteen are on death row. Torture and beatings of political prisoners continue and the threats against the leaders of the movement grow ever louder. Just last week, tens of thousands Basij and Guard forces were moved to Tehran and other large cities. Mousavi, Karoubi, Rahnavard and Khatami have not been arrested, simply because that would ignite a huge explosion.

Finally, let us take a look at the state of media and journalism in Iran since the election. Over the past year, 170 journalists, including thirty-two women, were arrested. Twenty-two journalists have been given a total of 135 years in prison. Eighty-five journalists are awaiting their show trials or their jail sentences. Thirty-seven journalists are in jail, making Iran the second largest prison for journalists in the world after China. One hundred journalists have left Iran. One journalist, Dr. Ahmad Zaydabadi, has been banned from writing for life. Another, Jila Baniya'ghoub, has been banned for thirty years. In a country where a typical journalist makes less than $1,500 per month, $520 million in bail has been paid by journalists to the judiciary. Twenty-three newspapers have been closed or forced to close "voluntarily." One journalist, Alireza Eftekhari, who had worked with the daily *Abrar-e Eghtesaadi*, was murdered on June 15, 2009 [the day on which the first huge demonstrations took place], as a result of repeated blows to the head. His body was returned to his family on July 13, 2009.

The Green Movement, as a Persian proverb goes, "is a raging fire under a heap of ash," with the potential to come to the surface again at any moment. Its strengths must be recognized and built upon, and its weaknesses addressed, in order to make it an all-encompassing movement for every Iranian.

A MARATHON, NOT A SPRINT:
THE POWER OF THE "GRADUAL"

Scott Lucas

June 8, 2010

On June 12, 2009, I was enjoying a night out in London. My wife, who patiently puts up with the daily demands of my website on international affairs, had asked if I could risk trading an evening with Iran's presidential election for dinner and the theatre. I assured her that it was clear that President Mahmoud Ahmadinejad and his leading challenger Mir Hossein Mousavi would move to a second round of voting.

At 7:30 the next morning, the BBC rang to ask for an urgent comment: Ahmadinejad had won in the initial ballot with 63 percent of the vote. After I gave them a remark based more on surprise than insight, I realised two things: 1) I would be covering this story every day until there was a resolution; 2) to do so, I would have to become a student, seeking a variety of teachers to give me a crash course on the dynamics of Iranian politics, economics, religion and society.

It is a year later. There is no resolution, and I am still learning.

I had the good fortune to be introduced to Iran in the years before the 2009 election. I worked with Iranian colleagues and students abroad, and eventually—despite my US passport—I was able to visit the country to teach, participate in seminars, and give interviews to the Iranian media. I even worked as an adjunct professor at a leading Iranian university.

Those opportunities had given me a glimpse of an Iran which was one of the most politicized environments I had ever encountered. There was constant discussion—even as there were limits on that discussion—of what the country was and what it might become. There was consideration, beyond the simplicities of the US versus Iran, of Tehran's role in the region and in the world, there were concerns about an economy facing both internal challenges and external restrictions, and there were glimpses of debates on social and cultural issues. Inevitably, given that I was working with students, there was much attention paid to the "Third Generation" that had grown up after the Iran–Iraq war of the 1980s. I was told often—by both critics and defenders of the government—that thirty years after the 1979 induction of the Islamic Republic, the country was now witnessing a "gradual revolution."

In the weeks before and after the 2009 election, however, change did not seem "gradual." Even watching from a distance, I was swept up in the excitement that surrounded a campaign which, with its televised debates and well-attended speeches, appeared to offer a much louder political voice to Iran's people. That fervor continued after the election, when President Ahmadinejad's victory speech—with its description of opponents as "dust and tumbleweeds"—was met by millions of protesters on the streets of Tehran. The Supreme Leader's Friday prayer in which he vindicated the vote encountered even more demonstrations of anger, dismay and hope. The protests would surge up again after every public encounter: in mid-July after former President Hashemi Rafsanjani's Friday prayer, on Quds Day in September, from 13 Aban (November 4) to 16 Azar (December 7), from the funeral of Grand Ayatollah Montazeri to the commemoration of Ashura on December 27.

These were dramatic, still vivid events, yet I wonder if they misled us into forgetting about the "gradual." Many observers anticipated a knockout blow to be landed either by the Green Movement or by the defenders of President Ahmadinejad. Predictions were uttered about the imminent fall or unshakeable permanence of the Islamic Republic. Each public occasion was proclaimed the crucial episode that would finally determine the inconclusive outcome of June 12, 2009.

Prize fights are settled within fifteen rounds of three minutes each; the quest for civil rights is not. The election, after all, was just the public apex of a larger, ongoing quest for political, economic and social recognition, respect and justice. The Green Movement, as significant as it has become, did not displace the movements for women's rights, student rights, labor rights, legal rights, economic rights, religious rights and the rights of Iran's many ethnic groups. (Indeed, one of the ongoing, "deeper" issues of this past year has been how the Green Movement—if it is more than a symbolic entity—interacts with the activism of these other movements.)

This post-election contest, which rested upon years of discussion and challenge within the Islamic Republic, was always destined to be a marathon, not a sprint.

But marathons are hard to cover in the media. And, in the immediate aftermath of June 12, that coverage—at least by "mainstream" elements—was complicated by a crackdown on domestic and foreign correspondents. The "mainstream," non-Iranian press was effectively blinded within weeks, as reporters were expelled or fled because of intimidation and threats of detention. Camera crews were restricted to their offices and hotel rooms, and bureau headquarters were closed. Iranian journalists persisted, but many of them—eventually more than 100—wound up in jail. By September, even the most prominent reformist newspapers and websites were being shut down, their offices raided and ransacked, their editors put behind bars.

Unsurprisingly, some non-Iranian outlets—deprived of their "normal" capacity for effective reporting—would thus look for the big event rather than the gradual shifts. There would be weeks of silence or muted coverage of internal events, while often headlines were devoted to Iran's nuclear program, and then a sudden burst of attention to a gathering such as the Ashura demonstration or the rallies on February 11, the anniversary of the Islamic Revolution. Then, when that high-profile event did not produce a clean, final "victory," the mainstream media might retreat into somnolence, sometimes after a benediction that the Green Movement had been vanquished.

Well, here's the paradox: amid and even beyond these big events, the "gradual" has triumphed in media as well as politics.

Ultimately, it is not the speed of technology that has ensured that Iran's post-election story is still ongoing in June 2010. Rather, it is the "gradual" efforts of those who, each day, often at risk to themselves, have persisted in telling their tales or passing on information from others.

They are not the international correspondents with news programs named after them. They are not the anchormen and anchorwomen with weekly talk shows meant to define the news. They do not even have by-lines. Sometimes their names are not even their own, but instead are pseudonyms and usernames adopted to ensure that they can report again.

These anonymous messengers remove our blinders by giving us a glimpse of the day-to-day life in Iran. They break up the deafening noise of state propaganda with the sounds of what is happening in their own neighborhoods. They give form to the true meaning of "rights" and "justice."

Ironically and somewhat sadly, I write this just four days before the anniversary of the election as yet another set of articles by analysts tries to define all that we have experienced. One headline blares, "The Green Movement was a historic success. Too bad no one was watching." (No. We are still watching, still writing, still learning.) A commentator proclaims, "Getting the real story out of Iran today is virtually impossible." (Difficult, yes. Impossible, no—thanks to those whom the commentator, focused on mainstream media, never notices.) A journalist declares, "There was no Twitter Revolution inside Iran." (No, but that was never the issue. Twitter is a tool, a powerful tool that allows us to ensure that the "gradual" does not disappear as those in power try to shut down information into and out of Iran.)

(An important caveat: in the mix there is also a redemptive piece by Nazila Fathi which avoids the dismissive generalizations and assesses, "Despite all the obstacles put in its way, the media has done a remarkable job in properly identifying the enormity of the past year's events. The Green Movement has, indeed, shaken the very core of the Islamic Republic. The country is polarized and the regime's legitimacy has been compromised. All of this, the Western media—at least, those of us who had any real experience covering Iran—got largely right."

My one suggestion is that Fathi's "media" includes not only "Western media" but many Iranian journalists and Iranians who report even without official press credentials.)

But, as I write this, irony rebounds and sadness turns back to hope. For I read these edicts from analysts and journalists who try to define, once and for all, what has happened and what may still happen. The victory is in the process, in the pursuit of the "gradual." As long as the search for rights persists in these words of sorrow or hope, then rights cannot be denied. As long as the vision of fairness is offered in these reflections, then others have not succeeded in making us—inside or outside Iran—blind.

The power of the vote may have been taken away on June 12, 2009. Therefore, some may try to pronounce that the Iranians—repressed by their government, bedazzled by false hopes of Twitter—have been reduced to powerlessness. But as long as the power to express is described in the simple but effective phrases of these local authors, then the power of expression remains.

A marathon, not a sprint.

THE GREEN MOVEMENT IS ALIVE AND WELL

Reza Aslan

June 9, 2010

Reports of the demise of Iran's "Green Movement," to paraphrase Mark Twain, have been greatly exaggerated.

In fact, the broad coalition of young people, merchants, intellectuals and religious leaders that took to the streets to protest the re-election of Iran's president Mahmoud Ahmadinejad a year ago this week has been spectacularly successful in achieving the one goal that they all had common: the delegitimization of the Iranian regime. Put simply, the Green Movement, through its blood and sacrifice, has convinced almost all Iranians, regardless of their piety or their politics, that the Islamic Republic in its current iteration is neither Islamic nor a republic.

The Iranian regime bases its legitimacy on two fundamental pillars. The first is its self-ascribed role as the locus of Islamic morality around which the state is founded. This has long been a persuasive argument for its supreme authority, particularly among the so-called "pious masses," the mostly rural, working-class Iranians who look to the state to provide moral guidance in the form of religious laws, charitable trusts (*bonyads*) and government subsidies. It is this pillar of legitimacy that has been most severely damaged as a result of the post-election demonstrations.

The brutality with which the regime cracked down on protesters, the beatings and murder of unarmed children on the streets, the widely reported cases of rape and torture in Iran's sadistic prisons, the public attacks against some of the most senior religious figures in the country— these are certainly not new events in Iran. However, unlike in previous uprisings over the last decade (and there have been many), these actions were broadcast all across the country. Through satellite television, the Internet and sheer word of mouth, almost every Iranian was able to keep up with the daily deluge of images and events that poured out of the country.

But perhaps the biggest crack in the regime's façade of Islamic morality came not from any actions by the Green Movement but through the consolidation of power in the hands of Iran's Revolutionary Guard Corps (IRGC) and the militarization of Iranian politics. For years Iran analysts have been warning about the country's slow drift toward military dictatorship. But the chaotic aftermath of the elections, and the resulting usurpation of the nation's police force by the IRGC (something Iranian law expressly forbids) have formalized the transfer of power in Iran from the clerics to the military-intelligence-security apparatus of the IRGC. Today, the Revolutionary Guard controls almost all levers of Iran's government and, through its subsidiaries in the oil, natural gas and telecommunications industries, nearly a third of Iran's annual budget.

What's more, Ahmadinejad, himself a former member of the IRGC, has been steadily distancing himself from the mullahs who used to run the country. His cabinet has ceased attending meetings of the Expediency Council, whose members represent the interests of the clerical elite. Earlier this year Ahmadinejad told a Persian-language newspaper that, in his opinion, "administering the country should not be left to the [supreme] leader, the religious scholars and other [clerics]." His chief of staff went further, claiming that, "an Islamic government is not capable of running a vast and populous country like Iran."

The regime's religious credentials are now being questioned or openly rejected by some of the most senior religious figures and institutions in Iran. The Grand Ayatollah Hossein Ali Montazeri, who before his death earlier this year was Iran's highest religious authority (the Supreme Leader, the Ayatollah Ali Khamenei, is the country's highest political, not religious, authority) issued a fatwa calling the government illegitimate. The Grand Ayatollah Yusuf Sanei has repeatedly lambasted the regime for, as he put it, using "the religion [of Islam] for their own benefit instead of serving their religion." Even the hardline conservative

Ayatollah Ahmad Jannati, who in addition to being the head of the Guardian Council has been one of Ahmadinejad's most vocal supporters, has made a number of recent public comments critical of the government. Ahmadinejad's relationship with the religious establishment has been so strained that some of the most prominent members of the powerful Assembly of Experts, the generally conservative religious body that chooses the Supreme Leader, boycotted his swearing-in ceremony, as did every single family member of Ayatollah Ruhollah Khomeini, the Islamic Republic's founder.

From top to bottom, the patina of religious legitimacy that the state has thus far enjoyed has been scraped away, most significantly by a new crop of seminary students in Qom (Iran's religious capital) who are increasingly tempering their disappointment in the Islamic Republic with their excitement at the growing influence of the Najaf school led by Iraq's Grand Ayatollah Ali al-Sistani. Sistani, who represents a more traditional, apolitical interpretation of Shia Islam, has been flooding Qom's seminaries with his disciples, while Najaf itself has been admitting a steady stream of Qom students eager to study a version of Shia theology untinged by the political theology of Khomeini. I can think of no greater symbol for the deterioration of the *velayat-e faqih* (Iran's unique religio-political ideology) than the open calls for "Death to the Supreme Leader." Such words would have been inconceivable a year ago, considering that the law forbids any kind of public criticism of the Supreme Leader. But they have become de rigueur in the Iran now being carved out by the Green Movement.

The second pillar upon which the Islamic Republic bases its legitimacy is the will of the people. Despite its autocratic tendencies, the Iranian regime goes to great extremes to maintain popular sovereignty. That is why elections are taken so seriously in Iran. (In a population of approximately seventy million people, more than fifty million voted in last year's election.)

Make no mistake, this is a regime that is deathly afraid of its population. After all, the Islamic Republic came into existence on the heels of a popular uprising. It knows better than anyone the power of the Iranian people, which is why it has thus far learned to bend (but not break) when confronted with the popular will of its citizens, whether on matters of the economy or gas prices, or education, or whatever else Iranians happen to be protesting. It is precisely for this reason that charges of "dictatorship" and comparisons to the rule of the shah are taken so seriously by Iran's leaders. Indeed, there is no more potent criticism of the regime than to say it is "acting like the shah."

Yet explicit comparisons of the current regime to the reviled dictatorship of the shah have become commonplace in post-election Iran, and not just by the opposition. When Mir Hossein Mousavi, Ahmadinejad's vanquished presidential challenger, argued that "stifling the media, filling the prisons, and brutally killing people who peacefully demand their rights in the streets indicate the roots of tyranny and dictatorship remain from the monarchist era," he was echoing similar sentiments made by some of Iran's most reliably conservative politicians, including the conservative Speaker of Parliament Ali Larajani and former foreign minister and current adviser to the Supreme Leader, Ali Akbar Velayati.

Years from now, when the story of Iran is written, the crumbling of these two pillars of legitimacy will be seen as the most lasting legacy of the men and women who took to the streets last year in defiance of the Iranian regime. It is, of course, too early to know what will be the consequences of the success of the Green Movement. What cannot be denied, however, is that Iran is on the verge of the most significant social movement it has experienced in three decades. Whether for good or for bad, the Iran that ultimately rises out of the ashes of last summer's uprising will be unlike the Iran we know today, and for that we should thank the Green Movement.

HOW ISRAEL'S GAZA BLOCKADE AND WASHINGTON'S SANCTIONS POLICY HURT THE GREEN MOVEMENT AND HELPED KEEP IRAN'S HARDLINERS IN POWER

Juan Cole

June 10, 2010

Iran's Green Movement is one year old this Sunday, the anniversary of the first massive demonstrations in the streets of Tehran. Though this day is greeted with great hope in much of the world, a year later the movement is weaker, the country is more repressive, and its hardliners are in a far stronger position—and some of their success can be credited to Israeli Prime Minister Benjamin Netanyahu and the sanctions hawks in the Obama administration.

If, in the past year, those hardliners successfully faced down major challenges within Iranian society and abroad, it was only in part thanks to the regime's skill at repression and sidestepping international pressure. Above all, the ayatollahs benefited from Israeli intransigence and American hypocrisy on nuclear disarmament in the Middle East.

Iran's case against Israel was bolstered by Israeli Prime Minister Benjamin Netanyahu's continued enthusiasm for the Gaza blockade, and by Tel Aviv's recent arrogant dismissal of a conference of Nuclear Non-Proliferation Treaty (NPT) signatories, which called on Israel to join a nuclear-free zone in the Middle East. Nor has President Obama's push for stronger sanctions on Iran at the United Nations Security Council hurt them.

And then, on Memorial Day in the United States, Israel's Likud government handed Tehran its greatest recent propaganda victory by sending its commandos against a peace flotilla in international waters, thereby landing its men, guns blazing, on the deck of the USS *Sanctions*.

Yesterday's vote at the UN Security Council for punishing Iran produced a weak, watered-down resolution that targeted forty companies and lacked the all-important imprimatur of unanimity, insofar as Turkey and Brazil voted "no" and Lebanon abstained. There was no mention of an oil or gasoline boycott, and the language of the resolution did not even seem to make the new sanctions obligatory. It was at best a pyrrhic victory for those hawks who had pressed for "crippling" sanctions, and it is likely to be counterproductive in ending Iran's nuclear enrichment program. How we got here is a long, winding, sordid tale of the triumph of macho posturing over patient and effective policymaking.

Suppressing the Green Movement

From last summer through last winter, the hardliners of the Islamic Republic of Iran were powerfully challenged by reformists, who charged that the June 12, 2009 presidential election had been marked by extensive fraud. Street protests were so large, crowds so enthusiastic, and the opposition so steadfast that it seemed as if Iran were on the brink of a significant change in its way of doing business, possibly even internationally. The opposition—the most massive since the Islamic Revolution of 1978–9—was dubbed the Green Movement, because green is the color of the descendants of the Prophet Mohammad, among whom is counted the losing presidential candidate Mir Hossein Mousavi. Although some movement supporters were secularists, many were religious, and so disarmingly capable of deploying the religious slogans and symbols of the Islamic Republic against the regime itself.

Where the regime put emphasis on the distant Israeli–Palestinian conflict in the Levant, Green Movement activists chanted during "Jerusalem Day" last September, "Not Gaza, not Lebanon. I die only for Iran." They took their cue from candidate Mousavi, who said he "liked" Palestine but thought waving its flag in Iran excessive. Mousavi likewise rejected the insinuations of the Obama administration that his movement's stance on Iran's nuclear enrichment program was indistinguishable from that of Iranian President Mahmoud Ahmadinejad. He emphasized instead that he not only did not want nuclear weapons for Iran, but understood international concerns about such a prospect. He seemed to suggest that, were he to come to power, he would be far more cooperative with the International Atomic Energy Agency (IAEA).

The Israeli government liked what it was hearing; Israeli Prime Minister Netanyahu even went on "Meet the Press" last summer to praise the Green Movement fulsomely. "I think something very deep, very fundamental is going on," he said, "and there's an expression of a deep desire amid the people of Iran for freedom, certainly for greater freedom."

Popular unrest only became possible thanks to a split at the top among the civilian ruling elite of clerics and fundamentalists. When presidential candidates Mousavi, Mehdi Karoubi and their clerical backers, including Grand Ayatollah Yousef Sanaei and wily former president and billionaire entrepreneur Akbar Hashemi Rafsanjani, began to challenge the country's authoritarian methods of governance, its repression of personal liberties, and the quixotic foreign policy of President Ahmadinejad (whom Mousavi accused of making Iran a global laughingstock), it opened space below.

The reformers would be opposed by Iran's supreme theocrat, Ayatollah Ali Khamenei, who defended the presidential election results, even as he admitted to his preference for Ahmadinejad's views. He was, in turn, supported by most senior clerics and politicians, the great merchants of the bazaar and, most significantly, the officer corps of the police, the Basij (civilian militia), the regular army and the Revolutionary Guards. Because there would be no significant splits among those armed to defend the regime, it retained an almost unlimited ability to crack down relentlessly. In the process, the Revolutionary Guards, generally Ahmadinejad partisans, only grew in power.

A year later, it's clear that the hardliners have won decisively through massive repression, the deployment of Basijis armed with clubs on motorcycles to curb crowds, the imprisonment of thousands of protesters, and the torture and execution of some of them. The main arrow in the opposition's quiver was flash mobs, relatively spontaneous mass urban demonstrations orchestrated through Twitter, cell phones and Facebook. The regime gradually learned how to repress this tactic through the careful jamming of electronic media and domestic surveillance. (Apparently, the Revolutionary Guards now even have a Facebook Espionage Division.) While the opposition can hope to keep itself alive as an underground civil rights movement, for the moment its chances for overt political change appear slim.

Nuclear hypocrisy

Though few have noted this, the Green Movement actually threw a monkeywrench into President Obama's hopes to jump-start direct negotiations with Iran over its nuclear enrichment program. His team could hardly sit down with representatives of Ayatollah Khamenei while the latter was summarily tossing protesters in filthy prisons to be mistreated and even killed. On October 1, 2009, however, with the masses no longer regularly in the streets, representatives of the five permanent members of the United Nations Security Council plus Germany met directly with a representative of Khamenei in Geneva.

A potentially pathbreaking nuclear agreement was hammered out whereby Iran would ship the bulk of its already-produced low-enriched uranium (LEU) to another country. In return, it would receive enriched rods with which it could run its single small medical reactor, producing isotopes for treating cancer. That reactor had been given to the shah's Iran in 1969, and the last consignment of nuclear fuel purchased for it, from Argentina, was running out. The agreement appealed to the West, because it would deprive Iran of a couple of tons of LEU that, at some point, could theoretically be cycled back through its centrifuges and enriched from 3.5 percent to over 90 percent, or weapons grade, for the possible construction of nuclear warheads. There is no evidence that Iran has such a capability or intention, but the Security Council members agreed that safe was better than sorry.

When Khamenei's representative returned to Iran in October, the Iranians suddenly announced that they would take a time-out to study the proposal. That time-out never ended, presumably because Khamenei got a case of cold feet. Though we can only speculate, perhaps holding onto the country's stock of LEU seemed to the hardliners like a crucial form of deterrence in itself, a signal to the world that Iran could turn to bomb-making activities if a war atmosphere built.

Given that nuclear latency—the ability to launch a successful bomb-making program—has geopolitical consequences nearly as potent as the actual possession of a bomb, Washington, Tel Aviv and the major Western European powers remain eager to keep Iran from reaching that status. Since the Geneva fiasco left the impression that the Iranian regime was not ready to negotiate in good faith, the Obama team responded by ratcheting up sanctions on Iran at the Security Council, evidently in hopes of forcing its nuclear negotiators back to the bargaining table. Meanwhile, Netanyahu loudly demanded the imposition of "crippling" international sanctions on Tehran.

Washington, however, faced a problem: Russian Prime Minister and éminence grise Vladimir Putin initially opposed such sanctions, as did China's leaders. As Putin observed, "Direct dialogue… is always more productive… than a policy of threats, sanctions, and all the more so a resolution to use force." Moreover, two of the non-permanent members of the Council, Turkey and Brazil, were rising powers and potential leaders of the non-permanent bloc, and neither country was eager to see Iran put under international boycott for, in their point of view, simply having a civilian nuclear enrichment program. (Since such a program is permitted by the Nuclear Non-Proliferation Treaty, any such Security Council sanctions on Iran represent, at best, arbitrary acts.)

By mid-May, Obama nonetheless appeared to have his ducks in a row for a vote in which Russia and China would support at least modest further financial restrictions on investments connected to Iran's Revolutionary Guards. Many observers believed that such a move, guaranteed to fall far short of "crippling," would in fact prove wholly ineffectual.

Only Turkey and Brazil, who lacked veto power in the Council, were proving problematic for Washington. Prime Minister Recep Tayyip

Erdogan of Turkey leads the Justice and Development Party, which is mildly tinged with Muslim politics (unlike most previous secular governments in Ankara). Viewing himself as a bridge between the Christian West and the Muslim world, he strongly opposes new sanctions on neighboring Iran. In part, he fears they might harm the Turkish economy; also, he has pursued a policy of developing good relations with all his country's direct neighbors.

Brazil's President Luiz Inácio Lula da Silva has led a similar charge against any strengthened punishment of Iran. He has been motivated by a desire to alter the prevailing North-dominated system of international relations and trade. Popularly known as "Lula," the president has put more emphasis on encouraging South–South relations. His country gave up its nuclear weapons aspirations in 1980 but continued a civilian nuclear energy program and has recently committed to building a nuclear-powered submarine. Having the Security Council declare even peaceful nuclear enrichment illegal could be extremely inconvenient for Brasilia.

On May 15, Erdogan and Lula met with Ahmadinejad in Tehran and announced a nuclear deal that much resembled the one to which Iran had briefly agreed in October. Turkey would now hold a majority of Iran's LEU in escrow in return for which Iran would receive fuel rods enriched to 19.75 percent for its medical reactor. Critics pointed out that Iran had, by now, produced even more LEU, which meant that the proportion of fuel being sent abroad would be less damaging to any Iranian hopes for nuclear latency and therefore far less attractive to Washington and Tel Aviv. Washington promptly dismissed the agreement, irking the Turkish and Brazilian leaders.

Meanwhile, throughout May, a conference of signatories to the Nuclear Non-Proliferation Treaty was being held in New York to hammer out a consensus document that would, in the end, declare the Middle East a "nuclear-free zone." Unexpectedly, they announced success. Since Israel is the only country in the Middle East with an actual nuclear arsenal (estimated at about 200 warheads, or similar to what the British possess), and is not an NPT signatory, Tel Aviv thundered, "This resolution is deeply flawed and hypocritical... It singles out Israel, the Middle East's only true democracy and the only country threatened with annihilation... Given the distorted nature of this resolution, Israel will not be able to take part in its implementation."

The hypocrisy in all this clearly lay with Washington and Tel Aviv. After all, both were demanding that a country without nuclear weapons "disarm" and the only country in the region to actually possess them be excused from the disarmament process entirely. This was, of course, their gift to Tehran. Like others involved in the process, Iran's representative to the International Atomic Energy Agency immediately noted this and riposted, "The US... is obliged to go along with the world's request, which is that Israel must join the NPT and open its installations to IAEA inspectors."

A windfall for the hardliners: the flotilla assault

With the Tehran Agreement brokered by Turkey and Brazil—and signed by Ahmadinejad—and Israel's rejection of the NPT conference document now public news, Obama's sanctions program faced a new round of pushback from China. Then, on May 31, Israeli commandos rappelled from helicopters onto the deck of the *Mavi Marmara*, a Turkish aid ship headed for Gaza. They threw stun grenades and fired rubber-jacketed metal bullets even before landing, enraging passengers and leading to a fatal confrontation that left at least nine dead and some thirty wounded. An international uproar ensued, putting Israel's relations with Turkey under special strain.

The *Mavi Marmara* assault was splendid news for Iran's hardliners at the very moment when the Green Movement was gearing up for demonstrations to mark the one-year anniversary of the contested presidential election. Around the Israeli assault on the aid flotilla and that country's blockade of Gaza, they were able to rally the public in solidarity with the Iranian theocratic government, long a trenchant critic of Israeli oppression of the stateless Palestinians. Khamenei was then able to fill the streets of the capital with two million demonstrators commemorating the death of Imam Ruhollah Khomeini, the founder of the Islamic Republic, and the Green leaders were forced to put out a statement condemning Israel.

The flotilla attack also gave the hardliners a foreign policy issue on which they could stand in solidarity with Turkey, Iraq, Syria and the Arab world generally, reinforcing their cachet as champions of the Palestinians and bolstering the country's regional influence. There was even talk of sending a new Gaza aid flotilla guarded by Iranian ships. Since Turkey, the aggrieved party, is at present a member of the Security Council, this fortuitous fillip for Iran has denied Obama the unanimity he sought on sanctions. Finally, the incident had the potential to push international concern over Tehran's nuclear enrichment program and their new assertiveness in the Middle East into the background, while foregrounding Israel's brutality in Gaza, intransigence toward the peace process, and status as a nuclear outlaw.

In the end, President Obama got his watered-down, non-unanimous sanctions resolution. There is no doubt that Netanyahu's cowboy military tactics and his reluctance to make a just peace with the Palestinians have enormously complicated Obama's attempt to pressure Iran and has also deeply alienated Turkey, one of yesterday's holdouts. His election as prime minister in February 2009 turns out to have been the best gift the Israeli electorate could have given Iran. The Likud-led government continues its colonization of the West Bank and its blockade of the civilian population of Gaza, making the Iranian hawks who harp on injustices done to Palestinians look prescient. It refuses to join the NPT or allow UN inspections of its nuclear facilities, making Iran, by comparison, look like a model IAEA member state.

IRAN IN DARKNESS AND LIGHT

Nasrin Alavi

June 11, 2010

"My throat smells of hot lead, father
The Ba'athist hit you with two bullets
They... every day
Shoot me in the mouth."

These are the words of Fatemeh, who, like hundreds of thousands of Iranians, lost a family member in the epic Iran–Iraq war of 1980–88 launched by Saddam Hussein. These fallen occupy a special place in the Islamic Republic of Iran's political and moral iconography: almost every official speech on a national theme refers to the sacred blood of "martyrs" who—like Fatemeh's father—are forever exalted. But this is not an innocent act, for this eulogizing involves a posthumous conscription of their loyalty to the revolution of 1979, to Islam, to the Islamic Republic's leaders.

Many descendants of those who sacrificed their lives in the war have come to question the regime's claim on their loved ones and, by extension, on them too; many Iranians who have grown to adulthood since the revolution have been shaken out of any residual bond with Iran's governing system. The ranks of the Green Movement that gathered around the prominent reformist candidate Mir Hossein Mousavi—both before and after the stolen presidential election of June 12, 2009—include many whose parents are esteemed for their bravery in the war.

Which side would these brave men of the Iran–Iraq war—among them Mohammad Jahanara, Mehdi Zeinadin, Mohammad-Ebrahim Hemmat, and the heroic brothers Mehdi and Hamid Bakeri—be on today? Well, the children of these very men have endorsed the Green

Movement. Hamid's daughter Asieh Bakeri, in a speech to her fellow students at Tehran University, said, "Perhaps if my father and uncle were alive today, I would have had to visit them in jail."

The murals of such renowned figures still adorn every street corner in the land. But after the mass protests and demonstrations, and the wave of arrests and show-trials of the post-election months, the honored fallen are less symbols of continuity with today's Iran than of what has been lost, taunting daily reminders of a fracturing ideological state. The children of "martyrs" are now trying to remember history differently in order to create a different future.

In place of fear

They are not alone. Even after the brutal crushing of the protest wave that erupted in June 2009 and lasted for many months, dissent is still everywhere and crops up in surprising places. A small example is a live television interview in May 2010 when the former defense minister, Admiral Ali Shamkhani—an Iranian Arab who lost two brothers in battle against the Ba'athists of Arab Iraq—was asked why he stood against the reformist president Mohammad Khatami in the presidential election of 2001. The interviewer hoped to solicit criticism of Khatami. But Shamkhani's membership in a "martyr" family and his own shining war record no longer offers any guarantees. To the interviewer's visible discomposure, he replied, "Khatami and I are both friends and competitors" and—in a clear reference to the unaccountable clique empowered under Ahmadinejad's presidency—added that he had competed in the elections to show that "the military must only enter [power] through the ballot-box."

Iran has a stable sycophantic system of patronage that maintains, preserves and extends power. Under Ahmadinejad's presidency, many politicians have been empowered, but many people and ministries have also faced upheaval and mass redundancies, such as the extensive restructuring and culling of staff at the Interior Ministry, which was responsible for conducting the elections. Reality inevitably breaks through for these delusional, degraded regimes. On the twenty-first anniversary of the death of Ayatollah Khomeini, there was a live televised screening of the memorial ceremony. Hassan Khomeini, grandson of the Islamic Republic's founder, was jeered at by the crowd with shouts of "Death to Mousavi!" It is a painful reality for regime loyalists who seek to bludgeon their enemies with the mantle of the revolution that most of Khomeini's offspring—including Hassan—are reformists who back the Green Movement.

The clerical hierarchy in Iran's holy city of Qom offers a potent symbol of discontent with the government. A clear majority notably failed to observe the usual protocol of posting official acknowledgments of Ahmadinejad's proclaimed electoral victory. Two grand ayatollahs, Bayat-Zanjani and Saanei, have voiced their "disgust" at the state's ruthless post-election violence. To this day, the list of senior clerics who have openly refused an audience with Ahmadinejad continues to grow.

The political union of the Iranian bazaar and mosque and their persistent strikes are thought to have been critical in the toppling of the monarchy in 1979. This power still exists today, and the general bazaar strike in 2008 against new tax laws forced the usually belligerent Ahmadinejad into a quick policy U-turn. But still, Ahmadinejad's economic mismanagement has led to the near total bankruptcy of century-old trade sectors from commodities such as sugar to textiles. Today it is hard to imagine that he has the traditional backing of Iran's powerful Bazaar merchants.

From the inside

But dissent goes far deeper than conservative terrains or Iran's elite and its scions. A different kind of heckling—unreported inside Iran—was heard at the end of May 2010 in the southern city of Khorramshahr; locals greeted the appearance of Ahmadinejad with angry chants of "We are unemployed!"

In the same week the luxury car manufacturer Porsche officially opened a vast, plush showroom on the outskirts of the capital. Customers queued up to put their names down on a long waiting list for cars that, with the heavy Iranian import taxes, carry price tags of $170,000 or more.

These Porsche-buying Iranians are the true beneficiaries of Ahmadinejad's extravagant, inflationary handouts. National funds have been ploughed exclusively into foreign imports eroding many manufacturing businesses and jobs. With fewer new jobs to be had, local newspapers have recently reported a wave of "pyramid scandals" eerily reminiscent of those that swept through post-communist Europe in the 1990s, schemes that often prey on the financial naivety of the poorly educated. Three decades after the revolution, Iran's economy (supported by one of the world's largest oil reserves) is crippled by corruption and negligence. Ahmadinejad's presidency has not produced employment and prosperity.

The frequent Western media cliché of privileged urban discontent is misleading; most of Iran's prominent student leaders, for example, hail from the very heartland of Ahmadinejad's alleged support base. These students also now have their own "martyred" fallen to honor; on June 1, 2010, hundreds of students at Tehran's Elm-va-Sanaat University commemorated their colleague Kianoush Asa, who was shot a year ago by the security forces. According to the establishment hardliner Morteza Nabavi, the campuses are the "source of the threat" facing Iran, and they remain volatile.

Today the state is grappling with its own demographic "success" and does not seem to know how to come to terms with one of the youngest and most educated populations in the region. Ahmadinejad recently described President Barack Obama's unannounced visit to the front lines of the war in Afghanistan as "cowardly." This gave rise to great deal of online jibes such as, "The guy who used to say that Obama doesn't even have the guts to go to Afghanistan unannounced can't go on a surprise visit to a university in his own country." Another wrote, "This vote thief had to sneak in from fear of the people."

Two out of three people in Iran are under thirty years old and that old George Gallup maxim, "people are always far ahead of their leaders," cannot not be any truer than it is in our demographically youth-dominated Iran.

The revolution of three decades ago has come full circle. It is being undermined from within by the very religious and social factors that brought it to power and sustained its existence. The inner core of the security elite that in chose to side with Mahmoud Ahmadinejad in 2009 has more to fear than the protesters who have been brutally, yet temporarily, silenced.

The student leader Majid Tavakoli wrote a few days ago from Evin prison in celebration of the election of 2009 and the largest street protests in the thirty years of the Islamic republic: "Tyranny... will eventually retreat under the pressure of the people's demands and desires."

Iranian blogger Gistela recently reminded her readers that "in ancient Iran, when a tyrannical ruler ordered an execution, a leather cloth would be used to cover the ground to stop blood from soiling the land, for all our ancient emperors knew that our soil does not absorb the blood of an innocent... it just simmers and simmers and simmers..."

WHAT THE GREEN MOVEMENT NEEDS NOW
Karim Sadjadpour

June 12, 2010

The anniversary of Iran's tainted presidential elections came and went without much sign of life from the opposition Green Movement. Aside from scattered protests, activists were understandably cowed by governmental intimidation and heeded the advice of opposition elders to preserve their power for future battles.

To the optimist, the Green Movement remains the most promising indigenous democracy movement in the history of the Islamic Middle East. To the cynic, it's a flash-in-the-pan phenomenon that peaked last summer. As it enters its second year, there are five key challenges the Green Movement must tackle if it hopes to regain its momentum.

1. Go beyond street protests

Last year, the Green Movement managed to carry out one of the larger spontaneous demonstrations in contemporary world history, drawing three million people by some estimates. But the scale of protests gradually diminished in the face of overwhelming governmental brutality. The movement may have strength in numbers, but when street protests are the lone play in your playbook, what matters is not how many supporters you have, but the percentage of them willing to sacrifice their lives. A movement that espouses principles of democracy, human rights and nonviolence is by definition going to be outmatched by armed government militants who appear ready to die—or at least certainly kill—in order to retain power.

In going beyond street protests, it's imperative that the Green Movement try to enlist the support of key arteries of the Iranian economy—including major industry, labor, transportation unions, government employees, bazaar merchants and, ideally, oil workers—whose sustained strikes could bring the country's economy to a grinding halt. This will require a rigorous effort given that Iran's labor movements, while deeply disaffected, are just as amorphous as the Green Movement itself.

2. Organize abroad

While there are many reasons to be critical of the Green Movement's nominal leadership—opposition presidential candidates Mir Hossein Mousavi and Mehdi Karoubi—both also deserve credit for their obstinacy and composure under tremendous duress. Within the span of a day last June, they were abruptly transformed from long-time regime insiders into opposition leaders. Mousavi's nephew was shot dead, while Karoubi's son was savagely beaten. Both operate under virtual house arrest, and all of their communications are closely monitored.

Under these conditions, they cannot realistically organize and lead an opposition movement. At the same time, they are understandably unwilling to leave Iran or cede leadership to opposition figures abroad. A compromise, one that has long been discussed in Mousavi's inner circle, would be to send a trusted team of senior advisers abroad to join forces with like-minded activists in exile. This was the model used by Ayatollah Khomeini, who spearheaded the 1979 Revolution from suburban Paris.

3. Reach out to "Ali the Plumber"

Economic justice and populism are two incredibly powerful driving forces in Iranian politics. In the late 1970s, Ayatollah Khomeini inspired his revolutionary followers with Robin Hood-esque promises of free electricity, housing and cash handouts if they deposed the crooked shah. Mahmoud Ahmadinejad did the same in the 2005 presidential election, vowing to cut the hands of the corrupt and pledging to put the oil money on people's dinner tables.

To their credit, the Green Movement's leadership has eschewed hollow economic populism in favor of more high-brow talk of democracy and human rights. This year, however, they must redouble their efforts to explain to working-class Iranians, in the clearest possible language, their plans to combat the country's endemic corruption, cronyism and mismanagement. Reminiscent of "Joe the Plumber" of the 2008 US presidential election, Mousavi and Karoubi must show "Ali the Plumber" in south Tehran why his family is suffering under the mismanagement of Ahmadinejad, and how he and his family could thrive in a Green Iran.

4. Steer clear of Khomeini's legacy

Perhaps no other issue accentuates the Green Movement's considerable ideological and generational divides more than the legacy of the revolution's father—the late Ayatollah Khomeini. Mousavi and Karoubi, whose careers were launched by Khomeini, continue to revere him as an infallible icon whose noble revolutionary ideals were perverted by subsequent leaders. For the Green Movement's predominantly younger supporters, however, Khomeini's legacy is considered the problem, not the solution.

Here Mousavi and Karoubi must tread carefully. In order to continue to recruit disaffected members of the traditional classes and create as big a political tent as possible, they will be forced to defend Khomeini's legacy against attack, even among their own supporters. At the same time, however, rather than praising the late cleric and alienating their largest and most vibrant constituency—the youth—they should avoid mentioning Khomeini as much as possible. No matter how you slice it, Khomeini can never be a credible or inspiring symbol for a movement that purports to champion democracy and human rights.

5. Pick up the pace

Mousavi and Karoubi have taken a deliberate rope-a-dope approach intended to wear down the regime over time and gradually recruit a critical mass of supporters—including government officials, traditional classes and Revolutionary Guardsmen—under the umbrella of the opposition. "If the government were to collapse tomorrow," a Mousavi adviser told me several months ago, "we wouldn't be ready to take over. We still need time to prepare."

The Greens' measured approach is complicated by America, Europe and above all Israel's enormous sense of urgency to prevent Tehran's hardliners from acquiring a nuclear weapon. If there is one seemingly universal consensus among the Greens, it's that a military attack on Iran's nuclear facilities would seal their fate. Hence outside powers ask them to pick up the pace. As one Green Movement activist complained to me last fall, "Before the elections they didn't think there was a serious democracy movement in Iran, now they look at their watches impatiently and ask us when we're going to change the regime." Nonetheless, the best way to keep the flame going and deter an outside invasion is to pick up the pace, at least slightly.

In American politics, it's often said that candidates campaign in poetry and govern in prose. In essence, the Green Movement's leadership must focus less on the poetry of opposition—calls for justice and democracy—and more on the prose of it. This means more technocrats who can talk about fixing the fledgling Iranian economy, and fewer intellectuals who spend their time rehashing religious and philosophical debates from centuries ago.

The path to democracy is both delicate and daunting, and not guaranteed. A pessimist might argue, however, that a far more daunting task will be for the Islamic Republic to indefinitely sustain a politically repressive, socially restrictive, economically floundering theocracy in the twenty-first century.

THE GREEN MOVEMENT CHARTER[1]

translated by Khordaad 88

June 15, 2010

In the name of God, the Compassionate and the Merciful

We are still standing tall and proud on the first anniversary of the tenth presidential elections despite our whipped body, which endures bruises and imprisonments. Our demands are the same: freedom, social justice and the formation of a [legitimate] national government. We are confident of victory, hoping for the will and support of God, because we have not demanded anything other than the restoration of our national rights. "All foam on the surface of water will be pushed aside and perish. What remains on earth will be to the people's benefit" (Qur'an 13:17).

The lies, fraud and violations of the law committed during the election prompted a question: "Where is my vote?" You, the people, shouted this question clearly and unambiguously in a nonviolent manner during the historic and unprecedented rally of June 15 [2009]. Everyone, nationally and internationally, heard your voice and saw your message, except for those blinded by superstition, greed and lies. But what was the response [from the ruling elites]? Was it anything other than accusations of treason, murder, imprisonment, shackling the feet of prisoners and attacks on university dormitories?

The atrocities committed in Kahrizak [prison] are now etched in our national memory. We will never forget them. Nor will we forget the killings of June 15 [2009] and June 20 [2009] or the deaths on Ashura [December 27, 2009]. Indeed, they must never be forgotten, lest we betray the blood of the innocents and the martyrs. How can we ever forget the live rounds of ammunition aimed at the people and police cars running over them?

Stains of blood and scars of torment removed the deceitful mask of totalitarians. The people saw through institutionalized corruption and beyond the hypocritical pretense of sacredness. What happened [at that time], and the way that different classes of people were treated by the government, revealed where the problems are rooted as well as the people who are affected by them: laborers, teachers, students, journalists, professors, clergymen, entrepreneurs, women, men, the youth, the aged and all social activists including the oppressed, the poor and the middle class.

Today, our country experiences the greatest number of executions per capita in the world. This is not because our country has the greatest number of sinners. This is because justice, management and good governance have disappeared from our land. The fact that even the most urgent and daily necessities of governing a country have not obliged the totalitarian government to stop spreading lies, corruption and superstition (as well as the fact that they have not stopped undermining the Constitution and other regulations) tells us of the abyss of corruption within the layers of the establishment. It is as if there is a strong structure that solely protects certain special interests funded by hundreds of billions of dollars from oil and other imports. It is a structure that protects unmonitored and unsupervised control over monetary and financial institutions.

Today, taxpayer's money is prone to be pillaged by holy-looking thieves. The nation is still waiting for the government to identify and put on trial those who committed various instances of financial fraud. Whatever happened to that important investigation that began in parliament and was suddenly concluded with a secret barter deal?[2]

Who dares to open investigations into the centers of power regarding the great "privatization schemes," based on Article 44 of the Constitution, to expose the extensive monopolization of our economy? Who has the courage to speak up against this crisis, characterized by the lack of financial supervision over the military, intelligence and quasi-official institutions that have a tight hold on our economy? The question still lingers in the mind of our nation: is this the just Islamic system that we were seeking and we were promised all those years ago? Are there problems that may arise from transparency and are they so terrible that we must seek refuge by promoting secrecy? Have we forgotten the golden rule of that great old wise man of Jamaran, Ayatollah Khomeini, who said, "Do not do something that you cannot justify to the people?"

Dear companions of the Green Path of Hope,

A year has passed since the creation of this unforeseen movement. During this time, the Greens have come a long way on this path, due to losing hope in the ruling establishment. They have come together in their homes and expanded social networks. They have formed lasting and stable bonds among a various strata of society. Strong social networks have been miraculous for spreading information and raising awareness. To see this, it is enough merely to look at the production of art and the democratic spread of analysis, news and information among different social streams. The Green Movement has been responsible for a wave of dialogue about important questions regarding our future. This event is unprecedented with any other moment in our modern history.

Today, people know who has trampled on the basic rights of the nation. People are aware of repeated violations of human rights and the lack of human dignity within the judiciary and the intelligence divisions. People are aware of how far the totalitarians have advanced in desecrating shared national legacies, especially with regards to the value of fundamental human rights. It is because of this very public consensus and dialogue that wisdom and rationality among our people always overcomes emotion, despite all the bitter and bloody events of the recent past. As a result, the troublemakers have failed to move people to violence, although they tried hard to provoke those who had bled, those who lost their loved ones, and those who had been imprisoned. Nonviolent resistance is our strongest weapon against the bullets and electric batons of the uncivilized thugs.

Millions of our people can see today how those with daggers in their hands run after our women and men, old and young. They know those who, due to their debased sensibilities, use the ugliest words against those [participating] in peaceful demonstrations. Our people have responded by creating symbolic artwork instead of using such words. Our people have presented one another with gifts of colorful posters and have distributed countless films and placards based on each other's lives and struggles. This is how our people have made memories of the pain and suffering they had to endure:

> A child by the name of joy
> Eyes bright and glistening
> Hair long as the heights of hope
> Is lost of late.
> Whoever has news of her
> Let us know
> Here between the Persian Gulf
> And the Caspian Sea.[3]

Supporters of the Green Path of Hope,

Based on recommendations made by friends during this year of patience and perseverance, a new program has been prepared for better cooperation and communication between members of the Green Movement and to fortify the common identity of the movement itself.

Clearly, the proposed document cannot meet everyone's expectations and demands. As a humble supporter who was trying to find a solution to this quandary, I was inspired by voters who participated in the human chain that extended from *Rah Ahan* to *Tajrish*[4] during the previous election campaign. Faced with a choice [during the recent election] between bad and worse, they said that they will choose bad. It was only this decision that made the continuity and formation of that memorable human chain possible. True reform begins with this understanding of choice and the ensuing human responsibility for choosing one option over another.

This document is only the first step and during its evolution the Green Movement will create a better and more complete set of guidelines.

"As for that [happy] life in the hereafter, We grant it [only] to those who do not seek to exalt themselves on earth, nor yet to spread corruption: for the future belongs to the God-conscious" (Qur'an 28:83).

Roots and goals

1. Achieving the ideals of justice, independence, freedom, and an Islamic Republic, for which the people won the glorious Islamic Revolution, has encountered numerous obstacles and deviations. Some of these are the emergence of totalitarian tendencies among some government officials; the violations of the basic rights of citizens; insults to human dignity; government mismanagement; a growing gap among economic classes and poverty; neglect and even violation of the law by those responsible for enforcing the law; ignoring our national interests and foreign policy adventurism and the gradual and painful abandonment of ethics. These are what gave rise to the people's protest and the powerful emergence of the Green Movement in the aftermath of the 10th presidential election in 1388 [2009].

2. Based on its commitment to [these] principles and fundamental human, religious, moral and national values, the Green Movement considers itself to be a purifier and reformer of the course taken in the Islamic Republic after the [1979] Revolution. Therefore, it will focus its efforts on bringing about change within the framework of the Constitution and to [ensure] respect for the people's votes and opinion.

3. The Green Movement is an extension of the Iranian people's quest for freedom, social justice and national sovereignty, which had been previously manifested in the [1906] Constitutional Revolution, the 1951 Oil Nationalization Movement, and the [1979] Islamic Revolution.

4. Revisiting the recent history of [our nation's efforts] to achieve enlightened social ideals demonstrates that the goals of the Green Movement can only be realized if we strengthen civil society, expand the

space available for social dialogue, increase awareness, facilitate the free circulation of information, encourage the active participation of parties and associations and generate a [liberal environment] for intellectuals as well as social and political activists who are loyal to our national interests. The achievement of these goals requires an emphasis on common demands, which will facilitate collaboration and coordination among various members of the Green Movement who, despite their own unique identities, have accepted the inherent pluralism of the movement and have gathered side by side under its umbrella.

Fundamental strategies

1. The Green Movement is a broad social movement that does not consider itself infallible. It rejects blasphemous absolutism and stresses the importance of criticism and dialogue both inside and outside the movement. Overseeing the course and evolution of the movement is essential for activists as well as intellectuals and analysts in particular. This will prevent a slide toward totalitarianism and corruption.

2. According to Green activists, the people of Iran want to be part of a proud, honorable and developed country. The Green Movement supports pluralism [in society and in thought] and opposes all attempts to monopolize it. Therefore, we do not tolerate animosity or maliciousness directed at any social group. All individuals who consider themselves part of the Green Movement have a responsibility to try to engage in dialogue (within a healthy atmosphere) with those who are against the movement, in order to make them aware of its goals and principles. We are all Iranian and Iran belongs to all of us.

3. The key issues for activists belonging to the Green Movement include the expansion of social networks, virtual or real, and the initiation of in-depth discussions of the movement's goals as well as its identity.

4. The Green Movement strongly emphasizes the importance of our country's national independence and draws a line at foreign intervention.

However, it does not seek isolation from or direct animosity toward other countries and it is not captive to prejudicial tendencies regarding foreign policy. Justice, freedom, independence and human dignity are universal values. Learning from the experiences of those nations that have struggled to realize such values while accepting criticism and insights from all freedom and peace seeking people who have similarly struggled for human freedom and dignity, is also part of the Green Movement's way.

Green identity: the Iranian-Islamic treasure trove

1. While accepting pluralism within the Green Movement, it emphasizes the necessity of compassionate religion which is characterized by forgiveness, spirituality, ethics and respect for human dignity. Furthermore, it points out that the best way to consolidate these religious values in society is by emphasizing the ethical and compassionate aspects of Islam and the Islamic Republican system. The fundamental principles of the Green Movement draw upon the unity of our Iranian-Islamic heritage for the development and advancement of our country. In the course of doing so it avoids forcing people to follow a specific ideology, sect or clique; it rejects the instrumental use of religion and calls for preserving the independence of religious institutions and clerics from the state as the only way to protect the high moral position of religion [in Iran] and the continuation of its distinguished role in Iranian society.

2. The secret to preserving our Islamic-Iranian culture is the coexistence of our long-lived religious and national values. In this regard, the Green Movement is insistent on preserving the right to promote the highly-held values and lessons contained in the customs of Iranian culture, while breaking taboos that lead to fanatic behavior and publicizing our true national and religious identity.

3. Throughout the history of its struggle for freedom and independence, the people of Iran have repeatedly demonstrated its self-reliance and

unity based on a commitment to a set of principles. Relying on its national heritage and collective reasoning and rejecting narcissism and arrogance, the efforts of the Green Movement of Iran in pursuit of its goals are based on collective agreement and rejecting those elements that seek to create chaos. It believes that this [collective agreement] is possible if it is the result of collective reasoning based on a monotheistic understanding.

4. The Green Movement is an Iranian-Islamic movement that seeks a truly free and advanced Iran. Thus, any Iranian who acts in pursuit of a better tomorrow for his or her nation counts as a Green Movement activist. In our eyes, Iran belongs to all Iranians.

The Right of Popular Sovereignty

1. The right of self-determination is a fundamental principle of the Green Movement. Holding elections is the best way to exercise this principle. It is based on this principle that the movement will continue its efforts to safeguard the people's votes until such time as free, competitive and fair elections, without any vetting [of candidates], can be guaranteed. The people's will and vote are the source of legitimacy for political power and the Green Movement views any vetting of electoral candidates [by the Guardian Council] as unconstitutional and obstructing the right to self-determination.

2. Achieving goals such as freedom and justice are possible only if our national interests and national independence are taken into account. The Green Movement, adhering to this principle, opposes any action that undermines the national interest and which violates our national independence. This is one of our basic tenets.

Values of the Green Movement:
Respect for human dignity and opposing violence

1. The first social value of the Green Movement is defending human

dignity and human rights, regardless of ideology, religion, gender, ethnicity, and social position. The Green Movement emphasizes that the establishment and protection of human rights is one of humanity's most important achievements that emerged as result of collective wisdom. These are God-given rights that no ruler, government, parliament, or power can annul or interfere with. Realizing the protection of such rights necessitates respect for principles such as equality, tolerance, dialogue and peaceful conflict resolution, the realization of which is possible only when there is an environment that allows for a free press, the prevention of censorship, the free activity of nongovernmental organizations and the modification and reform of laws in order to prevent any discrimination between citizens.

2. The Green Movement is a civil movement that is committed to nonviolence. It is committed to working within the framework of the Constitution. It believes that people are the primary victim of any type of violence and so the movement depends on dialogue and peaceful resistance to advance its agenda. Nonviolent resistance is a nonnegotiable value of this movement. The Green Movement will use all the capacities of nonviolent resistance to achieve its goals.

Justice, freedom and equality

3. Justice occupies a special and highly-coveted position among the values and ideals of the Green Movement. A fair distribution of all resources, whether social, political, economic, or otherwise is one of the Green Movement's unalterable goals, for whose attainment it strives for. Spreading justice in society is possible only if the political system and its governing bodies acts independently, both internally and externally, without any kind of servitude toward or reliance on political, economic, and social organizations and power centers, so that it can guarantee the economic development and advancement of the country in such a way that there is social justice for all.

4. Due to the necessity of addressing the needs and demands of all the strata and classes of society, the Green Movement emphasizes the links between the middle and lower classes of society—those that are most vulnerable to social and political pressures. Relying on Article 9 of the Constitution, the movement firmly rejects infringing on the civil rights of citizens in the name of protecting national security, independence and the territorial integrity of the country. While emphasizing the political, cultural, economic, and military independence of the country, it views the recognition of people's right to self-determination as the only way of defending the nation's interests and borders.

5. Establishing freedom and equality was one of undeniable goals of the Islamic Revolution that the Green Movement also emphasizes. Rejecting any form of monolithic or exclusionary thinking, [applying the same] to the press and to political [groups], and opposing the physical elimination of any thinking or viewpoint is at the top of the Green Movement's agenda. In this vein, it is necessary to strive to free the people from any type of domination: political (despotism and authoritarianism), social (discrimination and social inequality), and cultural (intellectual dependency). The Green Movement emphasizes its support for women's rights and its rejection of any type of discrimination based on gender and ethnicity and emphasizes the rights of ethnic minorities.

6. The Green Movement believes that security does not imply security only for the government, but security for every Iranian. Security must be established for all Iranians, so that they can live free of fear under protection of the law. The independence of the judiciary, nonintervention by military forces in political and economic affairs and dealing with the organizers and members of the so-called plainclothesmen are central demands of the Green Movement.

7. The Green Movement calls for the implementation of all articles of the Constitution, particularly those that refer to the rights of the people

(Chapter 3). This is a definite and nonnegotiable demand and goal of the Green Movement.

8. Some of the best ways to achieve this, which deserve special attention, include releasing all political prisoners, eliminating all illegal limitations on the activities of political groups and social movements, such as the feminist movement and the security-oriented framing of their activities, putting on trial the perpetrators of the recent electoral fraud and the torturers and murders of the election protestors and identifying and putting on trial those in the various layers of the government who justify violence against the people.

Moral conduct and respect for personal and social creativity

1. Unfortunately, we have to acknowledge that misguided political, social and economic policies of the government have resulted in a decline in society's ethical standards and in social capital. The Green Movement emphasizes the need to revive our ethics as the common ground and unifying element of the Iranian social life, while pledging to completely abide by ethical and moral principles in its struggle toward upholding the civil rights of the [Iranian] people.

2. The Green Movement is neither an organized political party, nor an unorganized and aimless collection of various people. An overview of the historical experiences of the Iranian people indicates that at key historic turning points they have been able to demonstrate their wisdom, capabilities and discernment by relying on their creative powers which has paved the way for the realization of their goals. The Green Movement relies on its principles and social networks and the wisdom, ingenuity, and civil creativity of the people of Iran. It believes that achieving such ideals as justice and freedom is directly linked with the blossoming of such creativity. The [recent] motto 'Every Iranian is a center [of news and information]' should now be changed to 'Every Iranian is a movement.'

Abiding by the law and negotiating

1. The Green Movement is pursuing the ideals and goals of the Islamic Revolution, relying on a critical rereading of what has happened since the Revolution—particularly in the relationship between the people and the government—and on the national accord of the people of Iran, meaning the Constitution. It seeks a better future for the people of Iran.

2. In this vein, 'the execution of all articles of the Constitution' is the main and fundamental principle of the Green Movement. The movement believes that only through a return to lawfulness, forcing the various state organs to obey the law and confronting those who break the law regardless of their political position, can the people of Iran prevail over the various crises with which it has been grappling with and move toward the path of development and progress. At the same time, the Green Movement asserts that respect for the law does not mean its selective use by the ruling elite. Conditions must be provided to ensure that the laws cannot be used to justify arbitrary violence, baseless accusations and violations of the fundamental rights of the citizens and where violence, injustice, and discrimination become the law instead.

3. The national laws, including the Constitution, are not eternal and unchangeable documents. Every nation has the right to reform its current laws in the quest for redirecting its general political trajectory. However, let it be noted that changing the Constitution is only valid when it is put forth through a process of negotiation and dialogue in society, with the participation of all groups and factions among the people, avoiding any dogmatism, exclusiveness and bullying.

4. Expanding the civil society and strengthening the public sphere are among the main principles of the Green Movement. This movement believes that in order to safeguard our national interests, achieve the goals of the Islamic Revolution, and ameliorate the negative effects of the recent crisis, representatives of various schools of thought and political

groups should engage in negotiations and dialogue. In this regard, we welcome any invitation to transparent negotiations and discourse aiming at defending the rights of the people and solving social conflicts.

5. The Green Movement wants to strengthen the national economy in the international arena and promote investment [in Iran] with the goal of increasing the purchasing power of the Iranian people. The movement advocates a wise foreign policy based on transparent and constructive relations with the world and it rejects adventurism and demagoguery in international relations. The movement seeks the elevation of the dignity of the great and enduring people of Iran.

A humble companion of the Green Movement,
Mir Hossein Mousavi

URBAN MYTHS REVISITED:
THE 2009 PRESIDENTIAL ELECTION

Ali Ansari

July 2010

A year after the disputed Iranian presidential election, the government still has many questions to answer. Although protesting its innocence, the means and motives for fraud were present. Urban myths are not enough to explain what happened.

Iran's tenth presidentail election on June 12, 2009, was the most controversial and contested poll in the thirty years of the Islamic Republic. Far from anointing President Mahmoud Ahmadinejad with a landslide election victory for a second term, the credibility of the result was immediately suspect, unleashing the most extraordinary public anger against the governing elite.

The street protests eventually subsided, but there is still little sign that the widespread anger has dissipated. The situation remains tense, and the ruling elite is no less anxious about the future.

Unlike other disputes which have periodically shaken the Islamic Republic, this one affects and divides the political elite like no other. The government resolutely promotes its historical account of a free and fair election, convinced that it has defeated a "velvet revolution." This defensive position is the reason they provide for the brutal crackdown on demonstrators, journalists and activists, which continues to this day. A year on, it is worth revisiting some of the urban myths which have come to underpin this standoff:

Those who allege fraud must prove their case; the government is innocent until proven guilty.

Not so. In any political system which claims democratic procedures and values, it is the governing elite and holders of power who must answer to the people, not the other way around. Accountability must not be a matter of faith.

Accountability is the basis of any democratic settlement. Without it, the process of "voting" is mere procedural window dressing. In Iran, with its fragile democracy under considerable attack, the situation is more acute.

As a consequence of the election victories of President Mohammad Khatami in 1997 and 2001, a plan was implemented by conservative clerics and politicians to manipulate the electoral system to ensure the desired outcome. As a result, the parliamentary and presidential elections from 2004 to 2008 saw a gradual collapse in turnout, with optimistic estimates for Tehran in 2008 barely reaching thirty percent. For particular reasons, only the 2006 municipal election was an exception.

Last year, all the major institutions of government, including those with oversight of the election were in the hands of the government faction. At least three members of the Guardian Council, the Chief of the General Staff, and the Supreme Leader, all voiced support for Ahmadinejad. In such a climate the burden of proof—and accountability—lies with the government, not the people.

Whatever the faults of the Iranian governing elite, they are not in the habit of defrauding their own people Not so; quite apart from the historical realities of the elections, we have to appreciate the ideological underpinnings of the Principle-ist movement, as defined by Ahmadinejad and his supporters.

Not so; quite apart from the historical realities of the elections, we have to appreciate the ideological underpinnings of the Principle-ist movement, as defined by Ahmadinejad and his supporters.

Ayatollah Mesbah-Yazdi, the movement's chief ideologue is less concerned with democratic integrity than public acclamation. Even this comes a poor second to the self-proclaimed elite's decision about what is right. If the public make the wrong decision it is the 'religious duty' of the elite to correct their error.

Ahmadinejad may be the populist face of an authoritarian movement but this populism is limited to the circle of believers. Everyone else must be guided, or are labelled agents of sedition (*fitna*) or wagers of war against God (*mohareb*).

What is more, in a political system defined by ambiguity, fraud and the ability to perpetrate it becomes second nature. The tendency of government officials serially to exaggerate their academic qualifications is testament to the rottenness of the system. Democracy is meaningless without democrats.

Ahmadinejad is popular with the (devout) poor. The opposition is largely composed of the (effete) "middle class."

This account has been transplanted from other case studies such as Venezuela and China and bears little relation to the social development of Iran in the last century.

The subtext is to suggest that Ahmadinejad's support is authentic—the real Iran—while the opposition is composed of Westward-leaning intellectuals and other culturally uprooted individuals. In the current crisis the distinction may best be described as generational rather than socio-economic.

The argument that the opposition is drawn from affluent 'north Tehran' both ignores the realities of social change over the last thirty years and bears little relation to the widespread disturbances throughout other cities and towns.

The extension of the argument to the specifically "rural poor" does not work either. In the first place they represent about thirty percent of the electorate and therefore could not deliver a majority. And the historical record does not support the argument that they are natural constituents for Ahmadinejad's conservative populism. On the contrary they have been enthusiastic supporters of reform.

Those who argue that Ahmadinejad's extensive provincial tours turned the tide must also explain why at the end of 2006 his political faction was effectively wiped out in the municipal and council elections.

Indeed, if any voting pattern can be discerned it is that, given a choice, the Iranian electorate will vote for the anti-establishment candidate. Khatami was successful in two elections because he was widely seen as 'leader of the opposition'. Ahmadinejad recognised this dynamic last year by pitting himself—somewhat belatedly—against Ali Akbar Rafsanjani.

The administration of Iranian elections is so sophisticated it cannot be manipulated.

Nonsense; the integrity of all electoral systems depends on those administering them and all can to a greater or lesser extent be manipulated. Iran is no exception and indeed has specific problems of its own.

There is no voter registration database and people can therefore cast their vote in any polling booth by producing of their identity card, or in some cases, a passport. This is not a computerised process; there are no barcodes against which identity cards are scanned and no means of relating a ballot to an individual. This is actually an important safeguard; otherwise the ballot would not be secret.

The emphasis on the technical sophistication of the procedure is meant to allay fears of fraud and explain the rapidity of the count. This particular fiction of computerisation appears to have confused the national card—*card-e-melli*—with the identity card.

The barcoded national card is used for activities such as rationing and bank transactions, not at present for elections. It would also seem that the barcode electronic system was only activated in February.[1] Last year's electoral procedure was therefore reassuringly familiar: voters brought a form of identity, took a numbered ballot, wrote the full name of the candidate, along with the corresponding code, folded the ballot and inserted it into the box.

Quite apart from allegations about un-numbered ballots, it is important to understand the procedure and its implications for counting—votes first had to be sorted manually—and of course the likelihood of spoilt ballots.

Given this situation, the speed of the count was remarkable to say the least. The Islamic Republic News Agency announced the result of the first five million ballots counted within an hour of polling stations closing. Subsequent results were announced in blocks of five million votes, each within ninety minutes of the previous announcement.

There was no regional submission, the totals were given in ballot boxes counted nationally, and the percentages remained consistent throughout the night. Opposition observers complained of being excluded from the count, and having their own communication networks shut down.[2]

The speed was all the more remarkable because the Minister of Interior had previously suggested that Iran's experience in managing elections meant they hoped to get the result within 48 hours, and perhaps 24 hours in some rural areas.[3] In the event, the result was effectively known within six hours. The blithe response to this is that the system was "computerised."

Anomalous voting turnout numbers reflect natural patterns of migration.

Even by the standards of Iranian elections, the distribution of voters was strange. The Guardian Council admitted that in fifty towns, voter turnout exceeded one hundred percent, putting this down to normal patterns of internal migration. But these higher turnouts were not matched by lower turnouts in other areas.

It is worth remembering the size of the country and the geographic distribution of the population; it would suggest that some people must have moved extraordinary distances to cast their vote. But here, as in other areas, the devil is in the detail.

The Interior Minister announced that in one district—Shemiran—the number of voters was thirteen times the number of residents.[4] Since Shemiran voted for Mousavi, this example was used to show that he had in fact benefited.

But this example goes to the heart of the regime's mindset. Irrespective of who benefited, the situation is odd. If we assume that Shemiran has fifty thousand residents of voting age, are we to accept that another six hundred thousand moved north on that day to vote?

No "hard" evidence of fraud has yet been provided.

If by this it is meant actual ballots, then this is not surprising, given that the authorities refused to release the ballot boxes. Mohsen Rezaee's request to see them was deemed unconstitutional, and he was refused.[5]

When a modest recount was conducted, it was administered by the very same people who had been accused of mismanaging the election in the first place. Statistical analyses of the data provided does suggest fraud, but it is clearly constrained by lack of direct access to the ballots.[6]

The opposition must pursue their grievances through legal means.

This statement, which may sound right and proper to Western ears, has altogether different implications when one appreciates that, for hardliners, Supreme Leader Ayatollah Khamenei's word is the law. Adhering to the law therefore translates as obedience to the Supreme Leader who, as the replacement of the Hidden Imam, is accorded extraordinary powers for any twenty-first century ruler. This reminds us that the crisis facing Iran is not principally about an election but about the nature of governance and accountability.

The government reaction after the election was a necessary response to an attempted "velvet revolution."

Quite apart from the contradictions this explanation has produced—the threat is alternately extraordinary or irrelevant—no credible evidence has ever been produced to support it. Indeed, this story of sedition has caused considerable unease among many conservative members of the establishment who see opportunities for reconciliation being closed off.

Curiously, the government itself has publicized estimates of the extraordinary size of the crowds mobilized against the election result. It has used these estimates to maximize the threat, mobilize its base, and justify the brutal clampdown.

But at the same time, the existence of such a threat begs the question of government competence, strength and stability. Hence the parallel attempt to downplay the strength of the opposition. Overall, events have exposed the illegitimacy of the government. At a fundamental level, a state whose strength relies on brute force and the disorganization of its opposition is implicitly vulnerable.

The questions that need to be answered are these: was fraud possible and was it likely? The answer to both is an emphatic yes. Both the means and the motivation were present. The government has responded by protesting its innocence, conceding irregularities, and labeling critics as irreligious and/or traitorous. It has refused to be held accountable and failed to answer the case before them. This is simply not good enough.

Perhaps the greatest fraud being perpetrated is Ahmadinejad's chauvinistic belief in Iranian exceptionalism: such things simply could not happen because of Iran's moral and technical superiority. This is emphatically not the case. But then nothing deceives quite as well as self-deception.

THE MOVEMENT HAS GONE UNDERGROUND:
AN INTERVIEW WITH FORMER POLITICAL PRISONER AHMAD BATEBI

Maryam Ny

June 30, 2010

It appears that in the wake of the brutal and widespread crackdown of the June 2009 election protests, a wave of disappointment, pessimism and lethargy has prevailed over the Iranian society. If this wave persists, it could result in missing a historical opportunity to get on the path to democracy. What approaches do you suggest for revitalizing the hope of society in addition to their drive and enthusiasm? What role can the Iranian diaspora play in this regard?

If any social movement does not achieve its goals in a limited period of time, then its government will become immune to the effects. Consider the student uprising in the summer of 1999. The city was in the hands of protesters for nearly a week. Then, [the regime] cracked down and the uprising cooled off. A few years passed and no action was possible, even on the anniversary of the uprising. This is the case for the Green Movement too: the protests did not blossom because the regime is immune.

Now, what can be done?

First, we should analyze the environment of the movement. What feeds it? What does its survival depend on? [The answer is] information and knowledge. For example, if the citizens of Tehran don't realize that people in Tabriz protested the day before, or if Iranians don't receive messages by leaders like Karoubi or Mousavi, or if they are not informed of the protests that occur outside the UN buildings against Ahmadinejad, then they will continue to go on with their daily lives. This is why the regime stifles the flow of information.

On the other hand, we should remember that the Iranian people are dealing with economic difficulties. They have to fight against the regime and put food on the table at the same time. That is a lot of pressure. Outside Iran, we go to work in the morning and come back in the afternoon to devote our time to the Iranian freedom movement. That is our main concern. However, in Iran, people need to fight against the regime and struggle to make ends meet. They are under much more pressure.

So we need to create a structure so that the flow of information and knowledge remains constant in society. Second, we have to raise the price the government has to pay for committing human rights violations. In other words, the Islamic Republic should not dare to throw people into prison so easily. We have to establish a strong information network to spread the news of our compatriots from inside to the world.

Everybody had high expectations for February 11 (22 Bahman). However, big demonstrations did not materialize. Security forces cracked down on a large scale. Why weren't people able to protest as they did on Ashura (December 27) and Student Day (December 7)?

As I mentioned, the more time that passes, the more immune the regime becomes [to protests], and they learn the ways to crack down on and suppress the people. Yet, there were [still] several demonstrations.

One of the developments after the election was that the Ministry of Intelligence, which is the main security establishment, was not able to control people through its traditional methods and operations. This is when the Revolutionary Guards (IRGC) entered the scene. The IRGC practically took control of security operations and also took the Ministry of Intelligence under its supervision. The IRGC operates much more ruthlessly—it beats and kills people.

We saw the events that unfolded on December 27. One of the problems that the IRGC faced was that it had trusted the Ministry of

Intelligence and had accepted the data and statistics that the ministry had provided on the number of people who would be gathering in city squares. It had divided the tasks and its forces based on this data, which was somehow incorrect. Moreover, people had changed their strategy. Those who were leading people from outside Iran had planned to undo all the calculations, and the regime failed to control the people. This resulted in the IRGC acting more professionally the next time. It deployed many more forces and planned to take control on February 11.

The Green Movement does not have [access to] radio, TV or newspapers and cannot spread the news and information as easily as the Islamic Republic. The difference between December 27 and February 11 was that on Ashura [December 27], there were religious ceremonies held all over Tehran, so one could be anywhere in the city. People attended these ceremonies, and therefore, the movement was able to be everywhere. However, on February 11, the routes [of the demonstrations] were predetermined. If the movement wanted to show itself it had to take these routes. [Security forces] had closed all the roads from the day before.

One of my friends who was in Iran said that he was with a friend who had a Basij membership card. They were going to attend the rally. He said, "We saw groups of Basijis who had come from Qom, Mashhad, etc., and they were not letting any of us in. The security was so tight that strangers were not able to enter. The closer we got to Azadi Square, the tighter the security became, and they stopped us before reaching the square. We told them we are Basijis. They asked us for the secret word." This shows they had a password so no outsider would be able to enter.

Now the question is, why is it that the Green Movement could not succeed? [Regime forces] had organized way ahead of time. They had formed teams to prevent any outsider from joining the rally, and they closed all the routes. When the ruling establishment is so powerful, this is the result. Before, people attended protests on twenty to thirty specific days, and they were successful. On this one day, the people were not able to [attend] because of the regime's organization. This was not due to the movement's weakness, but it was because we did not have the same resources that the regime has at its disposal.

After February 11 many supporters of the Iranian Green Movement in the West stepped aside. I do not want to say that we are witnessing a decline, but the situation is calming down. Why has this happened? Is it all because of February 11?

The outside world's understanding of the movement is very different from what is happening inside Iran. The Western world or the media think that movement means demonstrations, and if the latter doesn't exist, neither does the former. However, we know that the culture of the Iranian people is different. The fact that [the Iranian people] write slogans [on walls and banknotes] in the color green and distribute cassettes and CDs demonstrates that the movement is alive. The movement is learning how stay alive without incurring deaths and arrests. The movement is transferring from one form to another.

In all social movements across the world, you see that when a movement goes underground, even for a very short period of time, the activists become slower. This is not sluggishness, but rather a period of transformation. We are passing through this phase. This time, when we have protests in June, we will have fewer people arrested, fewer people killed, and that is how people will learn. It is natural that the government learns how to suppress people and the people learn how to resist.

You mean that the movement is going underground?

Yes, it is, and it should. In the 1979 Revolution, too, the movement went underground. That is why it succeeded.

THE RHYTHMIC BEAT OF THE REVOLUTION IN IRAN

Michael M.J. Fischer

July 2010

Mah, mah-e khun ast,
Seyyid Ali sar negun ast.
[It's the month, month of blood,
Seyyid Ali (Khameinei) will be toppled.]

Montazeri na morde, hokumat morde.
[Montazeri is not dead, the government is dead.]

—slogans chanted in Qom during the funeral
marches for Ayatollah Hossein Ali
Montazeri, December 21, 2009

The beat, the transformation of the public sphere, and the scenarios of the revolution

Coincidence and timing, as in music, are the tricks of politics. Instruments change: the new social media of the Internet, cell-phone cameras, Twitter and Facebook, are all new. But some instruments remain the same: passions, hope and anger. Repetitions emerge, but with a difference, anxiously conjuring up costumes and slogans of the past to act upon a new historic scene. History does not always repeat only twice, the first time as tragedy, again as farce. More often the repetitions, including farce and failure, clear the way for the next movement. The actors need to catch the beat and move in harmonic concert, carrying along the minor notes and the dissonance.

In Iran, religion is part of the music, and so are the ideals of secular constitutionalism. The counterpoint percussion of religion extends into the past as one steady beat all the way to the establishment of Shiism as the state religion in the sixteenth century and, in a different but equally steady beat, back to pre-Islamic Zoroastrian tonalities. The insistent secular-constitutional rhythm is also not new. It goes back more than a century to the Constitutional Revolution of 1905–11 and its antecedent movements. The musicality of Iranian aspirational discourse requires harmonics to proceed. To proceed it cannot mindlessly repeat as if it was an old-fashioned recording with a stuck needle.

Listen first to the passage of the month of Muharram 2009: the doubled *tomback* drum beat of Ashura (tenth of Muharram) and the *dohol* drum beat of the death of Ayatollah Hossein Ali Montazeri (third of Muharram). The goblet shaped tombak played with the fingers has a bass note *(tom)* tapped in the middle of the drum head, and a high note *(bak)* on the edge of the drum head. The two-sided dohol is played with two sticks of different texture, one beat setting a rhythmic pace, the other sending out a beacon signal for those along the lines of march (nomads along their migration routes beat this rhythm to direct the stragglers and to alert the villagers ahead).

Second, listen to the new instruments of our times that have been transforming the public sphere in Iran—the low-tech green armbands and scarves (the green wave, or *moj-e sabz*), and the high-tech Internet and cell-phone cameras, inscribing and filling the spaces of perception. What is new is the decentralized capacities of civil society, recognized in the slogan *resane shomaiid* ("you are the media"), articulating the subjectivity of a new informational flow. These capacities have been in the making for over a decade through the cat-and-mouse game between state censorship and the press, and also through the networking of a student generation marked by the violent repression of demonstrations in 1999 and a growing, determined women's movement partly working under the banner of the One Million Signatures Campaign launched in 2006. Third, listen to the pulse, the long fetch, the waves receding and returning, the long-term respirations of the social revolution (1873, 1905,

1953, 1963, 1979) and the struggles against clerical reaction. In the 1905–11 Constitutional Revolution, Sheikh Fazlollah Nouri insisted that the constitution (*mashruteh*) be conditioned (*mashru'e*) by the veto power of the clerics; this constitutional provision became troublesome after the 1979 Revolution. In the 1920s the clergy opposed Reza Khan's efforts to establish an Ataturk-like republic, causing him to declare himself shah instead. In 1953 Ayatollah Abol-Ghassem Kashani abandoned the coalition with Mohammad Mosaddegh and threw his support behind the young Mohammad Reza Shah. In 1979 Ayatollah Khomeini sidelined not only his liberal-constitutionalist coalition partners (Mehdi Bazargan, Ibrahim Yazdi, Abolhassan Bani-Sadr), but also the clerics (Grand Ayatollah Mohammed Kazem Shariatmadari, Seyyid Mahmoud Taleghani) who warned that the exercise of power among clerics would inevitably lead to the corruption and undermining of Islam.

And yet the social revolution—the slow shifting of power away from the hands of corrupt elites into more participatory and representative government supported by an increasingly educated populace—continues. It is evidenced in years of election processes, however controlled and flawed, at both local and national levels—not in its outcomes, but in the growing insistence on freedom and participation. The social revolution requires not only free elections, but a shift from a dominating rentier economy into a diversified knowledge economy, and the employment of Iran's best and brightest, rather than their exportation to Europe, North America and Australia.

There is the possibility that, as in the 1920s, the social revolution will detour through another Reza Khan before the growing educated middle class makes firm demands for open policy debate and participation in political decision-making, but the long fetch of the social revolution continues. At this moment of writing, the skies are darkening, the outcome is very uncertain, and, at best, a risk-scenario matrix of possible outcomes can be sketched.

Listen to the beat, listen to the call of the reed

Azadi-yet Montazeri, mobarak!
[You are free, Montazeri, congratulations!]

Ashe mazlumen, va mate mazlume
[He lived a *mazlum,* he died a *mazlum*
(wrongfully injured and oppressed)]
—Chants at Montazeri's funeral, December 21, 2009

Listen to the reed, to the separation of the reed,
to the sound of the *ney* (flute)
—Rumi, *Masnavi*

You don't need to be a historian of Iran or a Middle East expert to hear the beat and the sounds in the streets conveyed around the world by cell-phone video uploads to YouTube. You just need, perhaps, a few program notes on the stage set and the actors. The century-long social revolution unfolding in slow bass percussion is one melody line; another important melody line is the yearly passion plays of Muharram, of the death of the third Imam, Ali, who sacrificed himself at Karbala as a call of witnessing against injustice, so that later generations would take up his challenge to establish social justice in this world and not just the next. They articulate together, but not as you might think—not with traditionalists holding the second melody line while the modernists hold the first. There would be no music were it so discordant. Indeed, in the year 2008 (1388 by the Persian calendar), it is precisely the modernists who are calling the Karbala tune, wresting it from a repressive state ideology frozen in the false and unsustainable reconstructions of the revolution of 1979 that are used to legitimize the Islamic Republic of Iran, itself an unstable locution teetering between republicanism and Islamist theocracy. Iran is not the only majority Muslim country struggling with this dissonance, although it is one of the few Shiite ones. There are harmonics (not just similarities, but influences and consequences) for Turkey, Pakistan, Iraq,

Lebanon and Palestine most immediately, and a number of other places more distant. And there are harmonics with revolutionary and religious histories in Europe and the United States, which continue to reverberate in the reception of new migrants from the Islamic world.

Grief, rage, and directed anger

The chants of "Ya Hossein Ali!" are different this year, this Muharram month of 2009. The actors have shifted roles in the annual passion play that expresses itself as national Iranian politics—and not just in the ritual marches and reenactments of the martyrdom of the third Imam (Hossein), son of Ali (the first Imam and son-in-law of the Prophet Mohammad). Ayatollah Hossein Ali Montazeri—once the designated heir to Ayatollah Ruhollah Khomeini—has reemerged in this play as Hossein. And the man who replaced him as Khomeini's successor and isolated him in his house in Qom, and whom Montazeri publicly mocked as unworthy of the role, the "Supreme Leader" Ali Khamenei stands now reviled by the chanting crowds as mere Seyyid Ali, reverting to when he was known in Mashhad as merely a *membari* (sermonizer on the pulpit), Seyyid Ali Pa'in Khiabani (the Seyyed Ali of the Lower Street). Khamenei was elevated to the post of *velayat-e faqih* (rule of the Islamic jurist) or Supreme Leader after the death of Khomeini in 1989 by the Council of Guardians in a move orchestrated by then President Ali Akbar Hashemi Rafsanjani.

The crowds were enraged by Khamenei's "condolences" at Montazeri's death, in which he acknowledged Montazeri only as a teacher (*ostad*) from whom "some" benefited, and prayed that God forgive Montazeri's serious sins: first, disagreeing with the late Ayatollah Ruhollah Khomeini over the execution of thousands of political prisoners in 1988; second, his condemnations in 1997 of the Islamic Republic as neither Islamic nor republic; and third, his rejection of the tenth presidential elections in June 2009 as illegitimate and void (*batel*), and his calls for those who beat, jailed and tortured those who came onto the streets in protest to be condemned as criminals. To Khamenei's lame condolences, the crowds chanted, "We don't want rationed condolences!" Khamenei's condolences are being labeled *kineh*, a form of vengefulness exacted when someone who has done something to you is already down. More generally, the crowds chanted, *"Seyyid Ali qatel-e, velayat-esh batel-e"*: (Seyyid Ali is a murderer, his guardianship is void).

Ayatollah Hossein Ali Montazeri died in his sleep on Sunday, December 20, 2009, the third day of the month Muharram, the month when the third Imam, Hossein, was killed in the Battle of Karbala. Montazeri's *ruz-e sevvom* (seventh-day anniversary; the important anniversaries after a death are the third, seventh and fortieth days and the one year mark) would come on Sunday, the 10th (Ashura) of Muharram, when Hossein was killed by Shemr, the general of the caliph Yazid. Doubly symbolically, Montazeri died on *Shab-e Yalda*, the celebration of the solstice, the slow rebirth of Mithra or Mehr (light, truth, honesty, generosity and the guarantor of promises and contract, symbolized in ancient Iranian Zoroastrian tradition by the sun) and the coming of spring, as the daylight begins to lengthen.

Already at his funeral, in the eulogy by his disciple Hadi Hojatoleslam Qabel, and in the streets, Montazeri was being called by Hossein's honorific, *mazlum* (the wronged one, the oppressed one, the unrevenged slain one): *Montazeri-ye mazlum*. "He lived a *mazlum*, he died a *mazlum*." One does not call the other imams by this honorific. One doesn't say Ali *mazlum* or Hassan *mazlum*, only Hossein, the son of Ali, is *mazlum*, and now Hossein Ali [Montazeri]. Inside the Shrine of Hazrat-e Masumeh (Fatimeh, the sister of the eighth Imam, Reza) where he was buried, the crowd chanted "Ya Hazrat-e Masumeh! Ya Montazeri Masumeh!" according Montazeri the epithet "the pure soul," usually reserved for the imams. In an effort to block his growing centrality, suppress his exposure of Khomeini's execution order against thousands of leftist prisoners, and prevent the circulation of his memoirs and documents, the regime shut down his website the day after his death. But events had already run far ahead.

The transformation of the public sphere

To understand the direction of the revolution, its harmonics, disharmonics and movements—forward and backward, repeats and introduction of new melodic lines, time signatures, out of joint timings, repetitive stuckness or involutions, movements up and down the scales of political involvement and across resonances in local, national and transnational circuits—one must pay attention to the organizational and technical infrastructures within which social and cultural actions happen, and by which the civic spheres have been restructured over the past decade.

In Iran, legacies of women's, labor, and student organizing have been critical, as has been the development of new modes of signification. Two modes of revolutionary signification have been especially important: the color green and the cell phone, with its camera capabilities and its place in the new networked media. One low tech, one high tech; both decentralized and resistant to state appropriation.

The "Green Wave" (*moj-e sabz*) is the confluence of a number of different civil society movements, including the women's movements, the largely but not entirely repressed labor movement, student movements, insistent journalism, and blogging and Internet activism. It might be noted that the names of the presidential contenders of the June 2009 elections, Mir Hossein Mousavi and Mehdi Karoubi, have figured courageously but only modestly in this essay. They occupy places of leadership in a decentralized, evolving movement. The Green Wave has effectively mobilized the Karbala paradigm, the Shiite paradigm of struggle for social justice, against the government, although the government has not given up its own claims to that narrative.

It is important to note, however, that the Green Movement has appropriated the Karbala paradigm differently than during the 1977–79 revolution. The differences are critical indices of the changing structure of the public sphere. The secular "left" factions of the 1977–79 revolution either did not fully appreciate the eschatological discursive power of Shiism, or they wanted to consign it to the past. The Green Movement instead has skillfully deployed the Karbala Paradigm, turning it in a nonfundamentalist direction and contesting the state's capture of its discursive power. In 1977–79, the Karbala paradigm was used as a mobilizing device by the religious factions of the revolution to inject morality and social justice into their political goals; today it is the "secularists" who are using the Karbala paradigm to reclaim both politics and morality from the monopoly control over Islamic interpretation by clerics and their allies, an interpretive control that is explicitly anti-democratic and anti-republican. These clerics view politics as merely plebiscitary affirmation of decisions made by a patronage state based on the control of oil and key economic sectors.

Central among the Green Movement's slogans is the phrase "We are many" (*ma bishomarim*), implying diversity of opinion as well as multitudes that cannot be easily contained. There is also the phrase, "You are the messenger, you are the media" (*resaneh shomaid*), meaning that the message is the act of singular individuals coming together in a diverse multitude, strength composed through the weaving together of diversities. In this phrase, there is both a play upon the "messenger of God" as the spark or voice of the divine in each human being, and a recognition of the multitude in contrast to singularizations of the vox populi.

The Green Wave

It was a stroke of genius to make the color green the symbol of the protest movement. It was at first the campaign device for Mir Hossein Mousavi's presidential bid, but became the symbol of protest against the fraud in the electoral process, and eventually a sign of the protest against the entire authoritarian system (*nezam*) of Khamenei, Ahmadinejad, and the security and economic apparatus of the Revolutionary Guard, Basij, and Ansar-e Hezbollah. The *nezam*, an old Persian political term (dating back to the 11th century Seljuk period), designates what in informal English we call the "system" or the "regime," and in various other tutelary politics, as in Suharto's Indonesia, is called "the order" or "the New Order."

It is a stroke of genius for three very important elements it provides:

evasive visibility, value assertion and open-source, decentralized organization. First, it was something the state could not control yet something that could be made to fill up the visual perceptual arena. Anyone
could find scraps of green cloth to wear as a scarf, armband or patch.
Green body paint and cosmetics also became popular to dab on the forehead and fingers; green nail polish, green eye shadow, green hair ribbons, bandanas and headscarves were also worn. But the cloth could
easily be hidden, either displayed and put away as the need arose. It
required no electricity or other networked infrastructure that could be
interfered with. It could be draped on buildings or statues in visible and
symbolic places. Students in Tehran draped green cloth over the statue
of Ferdowsi, the grand teller of Iran's epic stories from ancient times
(the *Shahnameh*), stories that are used as moral parables, especially
about the fall of rulers who abuse their power.

Green also is the color of Islam and one of the colors of the Iranian
flag. A key strategy of the movement in 2009 was to deny the state its
control of Islamic terms and symbols and reappropriate them for Muslims of all ideologies. For some, it meant a retrieval of the original values
of the revolution, as Mir Hossein Mousavi argued during the presidential campaign. For others, it meant rescuing Islam from the revolution's
coercive nature and reacknowledging Islamic pluralism and tolerance.
And for still others, it signaled a need to move beyond constant reference to Islam. (Pro-regime fundamentalist graffiti soon began to appear
that tried to reappropriate the color green, and there seemed to be some
evidence that the regime's websites modified the color on the flag so
that if it was reproduced the green would become blue.

The effectiveness of the Green Movement soon became clear. It was
an open-source, self-organizing tool, one that didn't need electricity,
computers or networks that the state might disrupt. It was in this sense
a model of and for an expanded open-source set of tools for organizing
overlapping interests, depending more on pragmatism than ideological
uniformity.

Green is a tool for neural media; it is a transformation of the tactics
of the "little or minor media" of the 1977–79 revolution. Graffiti suddenly

appear on walls. Posters with photos call for the release of jailed activists. Anti-regime slogans deface the currency (so much so that the government warned it will not accept such currency as valid tender). Slogan chanting erupts in the subway. Cartoons of Ahmadinejad are circulated with captions such as "enemy of the people." Bureaucrats and employees slip the word "green" into cryptic messages such as, "Copenhagen failed, but we can still look ahead with *green* hopes and *green* ways to a *green* future." The neural media are part of an inventive civil disobedience movement that refuses to grant normalcy to the regime and keeps the sensory field full and active.

Initially, the green was material to fill the visual perceptual arena. It effectively countered the state's assertion that the Mousavi campaign had too few followers to be a serious concern. On the contrary, the flutter of waves of luminous green cloth on the streets and in daily life attracted even more people to the cause, as they began to sense that a vote for Mousavi might not be a fruitless gesture, and this eventually began to worry the state. On June 8, four days before the election, a human chain of tens of thousands held up a huge ribbon of green cloth for some fifteen miles, from north to south Tehran along Valiasr Avenue. It was clear that something momentous was in the air, and it was this threat that perhaps moved the Ministry of Interior apparatchiks into a series of crude attempts to ensure that the election would come out in favor of Ahmadinejad's re-election bid. Indeed, a fatwa from Ayatollah Mesbah Yazdi reportedly gave them permission to do as much, and in the aftermath Yazdi unrepentantly proclaimed that Islamic elections were not to give people choices but to give them a chance to affirm Islamic governments. This is the hardline interpretation of *velayat-e faqih*: the *faqih* (Islamic jurist) or *rahbar* (leader) is not to be questioned and is close to knowing the divine will (even if the actual assertion of that might be heresy for most Islamic scholars). Even more, Yazdi and his allies began a campaign in the fall of 2009 to discredit the grand ayatollahs who sided with the Green Movement and called for summary executions "as in the early days of the revolution."

Undetermined futures

Watching social upheavals unfold in various time frames and through different narrative devices has become the bread and butter of social science over the past two centuries and the tutelary projects of modernization in both the "socialist" and "capitalist" worlds. The unfolding seems more turbulent in recent decades in part because so many more forces are interacting transnationally as well as within the boundaries of nation-states. In the frenzied competition for global positioning, the rhetorical categories of "tradition," "religion" and "modernity" morph into strange new social formations, anxieties, paranoias and emotions that upset the calculations of many political agendas. Nothing is as it seems anymore. In times out of joint, it becomes difficult to adapt to and move beyond grief and anger. It becomes a challenge to negotiate a return to the past or inspire enthusiasms for the future without upset.

To deal with these complex turbulences, I have suggested the need to devise three multidimensional tools, more in the mode of a composer who orchestrates harmonics and dissonances than in the mode of a planner who rationalizes "externalities" into a simple plan. These are the analytic tools of deciphering the aesthetics, technical infrastructures, and scenario-modeling of Persian civil society.

The general aesthetics of politics traces its genealogy through the history of mass politics in Europe. It is not always a pleasing aesthetics, but rather one filled with inversions of the sacred, theatrical methodism, metaphors of contagion, and fantasies of immortalization, of the hardness and purity of the body and of the erotic ecstasy of battle. Many of these aesthetic-political processes operate also in Iran. One need look no further than the IRI's fear of cultural "contagion" and "infection" from the West and its martial language of those who can be killed without judicial procedures (*mohaareb*, "warriors," *mofsed fil arz*, "corrupters of the earth," *monaafegh*, "apostates").

But there is more to the aesthetic of politics in Iran, as I have tried to illustrate not only with the ritual cycles and the Karbala paradigm, but also with the rhythms of repetition and allusion that link events in

sonic and emotional chains over long periods of time, carrying historical memories, engendering grief and rage, as well as determination and
perseverance. Think simply of the chants: "Montazeri is not dead, the
regime is dead"; "Neda is not dead, the regime is dead," Neda as the call
of Iran, the call of the reed separated from its beloved, its roots, its soul
from its body in Rumi's *Masnavi*; Neda and Sohrab, Sohrab and Rustam,
the patriarchal tyranny of fathers killing sons, not allowing independence, succession, maturation and growth (Iran's so-called "Rustam
complex" instead of an Oedipal one).

The aesthetics of politics play upon the instruments provided by
the technical infrastructures of civil society and the public spheres, and
these have been changing. The 2009 movement was facilitated by cell
phones and the Internet just as the revolution of 1977–79 was facilitated
by cassette tapes produced by Khomeini in Paris and disseminated in
Iran. There is no technological determinism here, but there is a determined confluence of social movements of women, labor, students,
journalists and youth, routed through the switches of a technological
infrastructure.

One of the most dramatic emotional aesthetics is generated by the
rapprochement of generations through the events of June 2009. Parents
who had dismissed the Internet as so much frivolity, unnecessarily at-
tracting the evil eye of the regime, suddenly found themselves lauding
their children for having honed their hacking and digital communication skills. Suddenly old songs from the parents' youth of the hopeful
days of revolution thirty years ago no longer seemed unbearably maud-
lin and old-fashioned to their children. The peopling of technologies is
as important as the technologies themselves.

Finally, the future is always underdetermined and dependent on the
political narrowing of choices. This is often not a pretty game. But simu-
lations and scenario-building have become important tools for learning
flexibility toward emergent alternatives. They draw attention to structural forces, pattern configurations, coincident connections, disjunc-
tions and trade-offs. In social science, as in the simulation sciences of

the natural world, they can generate hypotheses, act as shock absorbers, and reveal permutations and patterns that might otherwise be missed

The aesthetics of politics play upon the instruments provided by the technical infrastructures of civil society and the public spheres, allowing the production of alternative future scenarios. Listen to the strange new music transforming the masque of a singular vox populi—one per nation-state, ventriloquized and stolen by a leader—into the harmonics of multiplicities, of *ma bishomarim* ("We are many") and *resane shomaid* ("You are the media"), of subjectivities etched into the new information flows. Listen to the *tombak* and *dohol* drums, the plaint of the ney, the pulse, the long fetch, the respiration, and the ebb and flow of life's restructuring.

THEIR BLACK IMAGININGS:
LETTERS FROM AN EXILED WIFE TO
HER IMPRISONED HUSBAND

Fatemeh Shams
Translated by Erika Abrahamian

Mohammad Reza Jalaeipour had been pursuing his doctorate at Oxford alongside his wife, Fatemeh Shams, when Mir-Hossein Mousavi's presidential campaign began to gain momentum. Though Mohammad Reza was a devout Muslim and had come from a renowned family of martyrs and academics, he believed in Mousavi's more moderate and fair approach to government. He designed Mousavi's website and directed much of his online campaigning from England, before returning with his wife for the elections. When violence erupted on the streets, the couple attempted to leave Iran but were detained on June 17, 2009, at the Tehran airport. Fatemeh was allowed to depart, but Mohammad Reza was sent to the notorious Evin Prison. He was put on televised trial with a group of Iran's brightest minds. During those darkest days, Fatemeh Shams wrote these letters to her husband.[1]

Monday, July 1, 2009

My lovely Mohammad Reza, congratulations on your day!

Six years have passed since the day when you came, with a single branch of tuberose and a small card in hand, to ask me to marry you. The card held these words, in your best calligraphy: "I had entrusted in Ali, but Fatemeh became my fate."[2] I never told you how that day I reread your words and each time interpreted them differently. I concluded that there is indeed a thread that binds you to Ali and that this thread had a

369

hand in our falling in love. When you came to ask for my hand in marriage, you spoke of the kinship that you felt to Imam Ali as a child, and how since then, you had wished to be married on the day of his birth. We were ten days away, and orchestrating a wedding celebration was difficult. But your love for Ali was so pure that despite the obstacles and difficulties, we pulled it off. On our wedding day in Mashhad, the moment when our vows were being read to us and you and I were both fighting back the tears, I looked to you and you were chanting Ali's name. In our life together, whenever there was a knot in your way, you would reach for Ali's hand. This thread of devotion was so profound that unraveling it was impossible.

Today is the day of his birth. I had set all my hopes on today. All my expectations lay on this day, hoping that perhaps a breeze would carry a whiff of Ali's righteousness in their direction and they would allow me to hear your kind voice after three weeks. But they did not allow it . . .

But these days will pass. The day will come when you will push the darkness away and return to my side. The day will arrive when I will recount the tales of your bravery for our child, and he will undoubtedly be proud to have a father like you. The day will arrive when once again, bearing a single branch of tuberose, I will spend this day with you and I will celebrate having you in my life. That day is near. I swear to Imam Ali's reverence that this day is near. He will bestow you with grace and prosperity for spending this day in solitary confinement, praying. I do not worry about your heart; I know it is strong. I swear on my own shaken faith that even if they imprison you unjustly for years, your unbroken faith will be your savior and you will no doubt emerge more devout than before. On that good day six years ago you wrote that you had entrusted in Ali and Fatemeh became your fate. Today I entrust you to Fatemeh so that my Mohammad returns home soon.

• • •

July 16, 2009

My fellow traveler, hello,

I call you my fellow traveler because throughout our years together you have always walked alongside me. Just like that awful Wednesday when we set out together to return home to our studies, to our lives in England. The same Wednesday when they took you from me, and I watched, and I did not even have the chance to scream out: "Hey everyone, look! They are taking my innocent husband without a charge!" I was doomed to silence so you would not worry, so the last image of me in your mind would not be that of a tearful and worried woman.

I stood a few meters away from the place where they were holding you, and watched with incredulous eyes what was happening to you. At 4:30 A.M., exactly one month ago, they took you away from me. They did not even allow me to embrace you, to kiss you, and to bid you farewell. They did not even allow you to tell me, "Don't wait up for me! Be patient and do not get restless!" We were drowning in silence and our empty stares were our only bridge in that instant.

In that last instant, you were on that side of the gate and I was on this side; you were staring at me, and I was frozen with shock. Your face was calm but it held sorrow. Not for yourself, for you were always big-hearted, but for me who was now forced to travel the long way home alone, without you, required to helplessly leave you. You kept on standing there and looking at me from afar until that heartless creature came and took you with him, and they took you away, without a goodbye. Without even showing us the court order for your arrest. What was your crime?

It was difficult. But I had promised you I would go. I had promised you that if they didn't arrest me as well, I would leave so you wouldn't have to worry about me. You knew that if they had arrested me, you wouldn't be able to handle the pressure. That black day, they did not even allow you to see that I had passed through the gates unharmed, and had flown away. I am certain that for the next ten days and your eventual two-minute phone call, your imagination took you down a thousand different paths, so when you called, your first concern was my safe departure. I am sure that they tried to plant the seeds of worry in your heart by telling you that they had me. My love! What went through your mind in those unknowing days? What went through my mind every night and day and what do I go through still? Who can know? Who can understand?

Today is one month and four days since they poured into our home and in front of your mother's unbelieving eyes, shamelessly and with threats of violence took your father from the threshold of his own house and trapped him in a car outside. And then proceeded to ransack our bedroom, looking for you, as your five-year-old sister stood watching. That day the neighbors, disturbed by your parents' shrieks, watched, wondering: where did such savagery descend from and why on this house, with what cause? How naïve of us to think that returning home to our studies was not a crime. How foolish to think that supporting a state-sanctioned, official candidate is a sin and after the inauspicious coup d'état, we should have hidden, escaped, smuggled ourselves out of the country as criminals do. It was with a clean conscience that we packed our bags and hit the road. We were not so afraid of anything that we would want to conceal ourselves, escape, or hide. If the lackeys thought about it for a moment, they would know that if we were guilty, we would not have stepped foot in the airport, unafraid and unconcerned, as we would not deliberately step into their trap. The sad followers are incapable of employing the simplest logic.

In the past thirty days I have done everything I can to bring you to freedom. I have prayed ceaselessly. Not only I but also every member of our families, our friends and acquaintances, have all turned to prayer for your release. You have been so kind to everyone, you've done so much good that now that you are in a bind, the outpouring from friends that I have never even met is overwhelming. Now I understand that whatever good I saw on the surface was only the half of what lay beneath. After your arrest, the vastness of your sacrifices has revealed itself to me.

• • •

My love!

In these thirty days, I have written letters to whomever I can think of. When I tired of appealing to the closed doors of law and (in)justice, where nobody heard my cries, I consulted your three martyred uncles. I told them that these days our youth are charged with defending the honor of our country—the same goal that they, your uncles, sacrificed their lives for—and now our youth are being imprisoned. I told them that your father named you after them so that the memory of their sacrifices and bravery would not escape our minds.

The dead were the first and last place of authority to which I took my complaints. In the visits that the families of the detained had with the authorities, your name was ever present. That day when they visited our dear Khatami, and I was exile-bound, I wrote him and asked him to bow his head on his pure prayer mat and pray for your safe return. I heard back that he is worried from the depths of his heart and will not stop at anything to free you and the others.

But it was not just these letters my lovely! Our families tried numerous times to exercise the fundamental right of obtaining an attorney. But each time, they were met with obstacles. They took away your right to visit with an attorney. Our calls have gone unanswered, and this is my share: no news of you, my own vagrancy, and this worry about your state.

The days that you have been in prison, with no news, have been historic. But the bitterest of these events was the grief of Sohrab's mother.[3] You were not present, you did not see how young Sohrab's mother wept by his graveside. With every ounce of my being, I feel her twenty-six days worth of unknowing, uncertainty, and with each tear, I wish to wash away the blood that she has witnessed. This earth is once again being watered by the blood of its fallen youth, and the green sapling of freedom is growing from its core.

Two nights ago I said a prayer of gratitude because a friend brought word that your singing fills the nights in the solitary cells of Evin, though she had not been to see your face. But just knowing that the songbird of Evin still has his voice calmed my heart. As another friend said, your song tells us of your health and breath and aliveness. I know your heart is strong. I know you are standing strong and that the lack of news is due to your continual resistance. I know that if they had broken you and you had told them what they wanted to hear, I would have heard your voice by now, or even seen you. When at night the grief, stronger and many-rooted, attacks my body and soul, I cry for the weak constitution of your interrogators. Staring into your green, lively eyes and forcing you to write and confess to that which you do not believe. This act must require such a hardened heart. I cry for the repression of those who keep you from sleep for long stretches of time trying to make you give in to their dirty, false confessions, and I ask God to guide them and to give you strength.

• • •

My kind one!

Always, when sleep would overtake you, sitting or standing, you would give into it like an innocent child. I know that when they put you under pressure during the interrogations, you will fall asleep calmly. I curse the dirty, violating hand that wakes you! I also know that when you wake with fear, for a few minutes you will look at your surroundings dumbly. But there is one scene that I can imagine better than any other: faced with this cruelty you will not utter a word, you will rub your eyes with the palms of your hand and, once again, write the truth on the interrogation sheets, making them seethe with all that they cannot get from you. I know that when the hands of that awful creature release you, and you return to your cell, you will once again sing a happy song so that the hearts of those who control these days, upon hearing the pleasure in your voice, will tremble for a moment.

. . .

July 20, 2009

My kind one, hello,

The thirty-fifth day of your detainment has passed, and the hands of the clock are fast moving toward the moment of our reunion. I live for that moment that is yet to arrive.

Three days have passed since my last letter in which I told you how all my letters to the officials have gone unanswered. I've decided that from this day forth I will only address my letters to you. No one but you is worthy of receiving these lamentations, after all. I know that they are much too hardened in the heart, too black in the soul, to allow even a line from my longings to reach you. But I hope for the day when you return to me, hero-like, and read these lines aloud for me. Just like the days when I would write you letters, and you would wait to whisper my words back to me.

So I will tell you of these days of your imprisonment, the days during which they have kept you with no news from the outside and only filled your ears with falsehoods. On the outside, the people have created their own epic poem, and shed much blood in the path of our shared desire. I write for you until the day of your freedom, and so my own conscience will be soothed of my feelings of uselessness, my passions, and my over-indulgent mind. When you arrive, I will tell you such stories and tales that writing of them is not possible. But I shall write these lines so that your name and your memory stay in our collective minds and your im-prisonment and that of your comrades does not become a bitter habit, a perfunctory daily sigh. I write so they won't forget and leave your fate to the hands of time. I write so you know that if you are not here, I am standing and there is a voice that is still alive. Despite their futile at-tempts, they have failed to smother my voice for even a second. I write so they know that if they have tied you up in their tethers of fanaticism and hypocrisy, there is still someone who will reveal the sins of these blood-shedding reprobates and will protest the imprisonment of you: the embodiment of Iran's youthful, Green ideas.

• • •

My purest,

My previous letter to you was written one day before another epic Green day that our people created together. I wish you could've seen how this past Friday, in the same streets that only two days after your arrest wit-nessed the shedding of the blood of our beloveds, green saplings of hope grew all over. It was as if from each drop of Neda's and Sohrab's and other Green martyrs' blood, a creeping, green seedling had grown. People attended the Friday Prayers. But not the same Friday Prayer of our childhood that we watched on the state television. Not the same faces and the same people with their repetitions that we saw for the quarter century of our lives. This time more than any other Friday, the youth of our generation, in their own chosen attire and way, and not dressed to please those in power, attended the Prayers. The same courageous people who with their fervor and intelligence had written the epic poem of Revolution till Freedom, once again chanted their Allah-o-Akbars from the rooftops to the front rows of the Friday Prayers. For many, this was the first Friday Prayer that they had ever attended.

It was a glorious Friday. The elders said that the only other Friday Prayer that was comparable to this one was the Prayer of the now-deceased Ayatollah Taleghani thirty years back. From the same city and the same pulpit.[4]

The Greens showed up because their leader was present as well. Mir Hossein Mousavi came humbly and sat amongst the people and not in the front row. Zahra Rahnavard, his wife, as well. The people came to see what Rafsanjani had decided after thirty years, and in what way he was going to prove his faith to the people. There was much anxiety in our hearts because what he said could be the beginning or the end of many talks and hopes.

But Rafsanjani shone brightly and exceeded all expectations. After thirty years of being in a position of power, he sided with the people and, with honor, left the pulpit of repetitions and flattery. I imagine that the prayer that this giant of Iranian politics said on that afternoon is among the few prayers in his life that he has said with a clean conscience and a solid heart. Rafsanjani did not preach to the undeserving holders of power; instead he showed them how to lead a people, how to rise above the criminals and not give in to their invitations of violence, how to speak of religion and not drag it into the dirt, how to stand politely in front of a gang of slogan-yelling lowlifes and allow them to speak, and how to know when to hold their tongues. He showed the difference between a millennial lump in the throat and alligator tears, and told them how the fake show of piety will no longer convince anyone.

• • •

My dear Mohammad Reza,

How I wish you were here to see how after the historic sermon, people turned the government-scripted slogans in their own favor and in response to the empty cries of yesteryear, instead of Death to America and England, they wished death to Russia.[5] They said louder than at any other time that they would give the blood in their veins not for the Supreme Leader, but for the people of Iran. The response to this sharp-minded alertness was tear gas and batons. I know you know that this is to be expected of such a snake-bitten tribe that is so afraid of the people's wisdom.

This Friday was a historic one in that the people reclaimed the religious excuses for public gathering that this government has used as its own propaganda machine. Be happy, my love, that from now on they will not be able to have even one march where our comrades are not present. They have given the people a great gift with their own two hands, a gift that they can never take back.

I wonder for how long the state television can censor these brilliant scenes? This past Friday, two million people attended the Friday Prayers. What will they do for the month of Moharram, the anniversary of the Revolution, and Qods day?[6] For how long will they paint over our green with their black? For how long will they send hundreds of bruised bodies of our freedom fighters to the graveyards and call their deaths accidents? For how long will they force-feed us tranquilizers so we fall asleep to the nightmares of Sohrab's innocent smile, to his mother's sobs, and to the white bowl of Neda's frozen stare into the camera? For how long will they imprison our dear, ailing Hajjarian[7] and lie to him by saying that his wife and child are suffering and in danger? I wonder how long will they keep someone like you, whose existence has been nothing but benign service to others, in solitary confinement and under psychological torture?

But I know one thing well, that you are firm in your resolve. I wish I could send you word that the people are also firm in their resolve and that they sing the elegy of June each day from rooftops to the streets. Today news came that your interrogators have given up and are angry with you. Angry that you chose solitary confinement and its isolation over their shameful forced "confession" project, and that you are holding your ground. News came that you still laugh like a child and bring hope to the other beloveds who are even more homesick than you. I know this common fight that has made a prisoner of you and an exile of me will be won with patience and hope. I know well that the day will arrive when hand in hand we will take in fresh air and greet the sun anew.

Dawn is close and we are awake.

Forever your love,
Fatemeh

• • •

September 1, 2009, seventy-four days without you.

My kind warrior, my dear Mohammad Reza,

Monday is here once again. I have told you that on Mondays I am a vaga-
bond of a bird, rain-beaten and without a nest, shaking my feathers of
the clouds' tears hourly, only to be rained on once more. When the clock
passes midnight on Sunday, my heart beats in rhythm to the seconds;
one hundred times in each second I fly to that unseen, godforsaken cell
which is alive only in my imaginings.

I imagine this: you come to sit across from me, clad in your gray courtroom attire, lips awash in that sweet smile and of course with your innocent, green eyes. I imagine myself there, standing, and I touch my hand
to the glass window between you and me, and you, as well, touch the
same thick pane of glass that separates us, and the glass fogs up from
the heat of our hands, and we laugh despite the lumps in our throats.
We ignore the fresh cries that are forming inside us. Every Monday, I live
this scene twenty-four thousand times in twenty-four hours and once
again, I am left wanting for your voice and your gaze, here, in the corner
of exile-land where my lot has become aloneness and longing for you.

And I have tired of words. Never did I want my words to herald such
pain; I wanted to write from a place of hope, write with the fervor of
life, but they did not allow it. My occupation has become the chronicling
of my longing for you. You who do not even see my words! And now
they have forced you to send word for me to be silent and not tell of the
injustices against you and me and our generation. What right do they
have to ask you this? A government who is afraid of mere love letters
written by a prisoner's wife, a lovesick and expectant woman whom
they have denied contact with her spouse. Such government should be
read its last rites! What have I written, except of the cruelty against you,
that has them bewildered, this clan of oppressors—so when their own
threats against me have not worked, they send me word through you?
I do not know whether to laugh or cry over their ridiculous fears. Don't
they know that I, your lover, can interpret your voice and your words?
It is for this reason that I will not put down my pen until they let you go.

OPEN LETTER TO AYATOLLAH KHAMENEI

Abdollah Momeni

Abdollah Momeni is a prominent Iranian student leader and pro-democracy activist. He first rose to prominence after the July 1999 student uprising and is currently the spokesperson for the Central Council of the Alumni Organization of University Students of the Islamic Republic (Sazeman-e Danesh Amookhtegan-e Iran-e Islami—Advar-e Tahkim-e Vahdat), Iran's largest reformist student organization. For the past decade he has been in and out of prison, often in solitary confinement, and under constant surveillance by Iran's Ministry of Intelligence.[1] On June 21, 2009, he was arrested at the campaign headquarters of Mehdi Karoubi and was one of the more than 100 people who were brought before a Revolutionary Court as part of a Stalinist show trial. He was charged with spreading "propaganda against the system of the Islamic Republic by transmitting news of street protests, and interviews with anti-revolutionary radios and sites." The evidence produced against him included "contacts with [the] human rights NGOs Amnesty International and Human Rights Watch."[2] His bravery and courage was recently recognized by the Czech human rights group, People in Need, who awarded him and fellow Iranian student activist Majid Tavakoli, the 2009 Homo Homini award "in recognition of a dedication to the promotion of human rights, democracy and nonviolent solutions to political conflicts."[3] Momeni was most recently sentenced to ten years in jail (reduced to four years and eleven months on appeal). In August 2010 he wrote the following open letter from Evin prison to Iran's Supreme Leader, Ali Khamenei.[4]

In the Name of God

God does not like any evil to be mentioned openly, unless it be by him who has been wronged. And God is indeed all-hearing, all-knowing (Qur'an 4:148).

Ayatollah Khamenei, The Leader of the Islamic Republic of Iran

During one of my days in detention at Evin prison, I had the opportunity to hear a televised speech by you. You spoke of the importance of opposing injustice and the need to observe fairness and justice (June 23, 2010). That day, I decided to write a letter addressed to you, thinking that perhaps the news about detention centers does not reach you. So you may not know that besides Kahrizak, at Evin prison too, prisoners are not given even minimal rights, and are subjected to the severest forms of physical and psychological abuse, which are exerted with the aim of character assassination and coercing false confessions. Further, given that I heard that during the time when I and others like myself were facing the worst kinds of torture intent on forcing us to confess to crimes we had not committed, you took the opportunity at prayers on the occasion of *Eid al Fitr*[5] to say that, "Whatever accused persons say about themselves in court is credible." This is why I decided to write a letter and describe the torture and the illegal and un-Islamic treatment which I have received in prison, so that perhaps I can receive an answer to this question: "Are confessions extracted through the use of such inhumane and unethical methods valid in your view or not?" And so, in the hopes of establishing a truth commission to investigate what I have faced during my incarceration, interrogation and court hearings, and as a person accused and imprisoned by the Islamic Republic of Iran during your rule, I will recount my experiences. At the same time, I hope that the recounting of these experiences will not end in increased pressures and difficulties during my stay in prison.

Supreme Leader,

Today, I am in Evin prison because I have been identified as someone who is critical of the Islamic Republic of Iran. As such, it is not irrelevant for me to recount my political views and activities over the last decade. I entered university in 1996 and in the same year joined the Islamic Student Organization and then was elected to the Office to Foster Unity (*Daftar-e Tahkim-e Vahdat*) and was a member of the Central Council and served as the secretary of Tahkim until 2005, when I completed my Masters studies in Sociology at Allameh Tabatabai University. From 2005 to the present I have served as a member of the Central Council of the Alumni Organization of University Students of the Islamic Republic (*Sazeman-e Danesh Amookhtegan-e Jomhouri-e Islami*). I was the spokesperson for this legal organization, which works toward the advancement of democracy and human rights. During my time as a university student, my colleagues and I were most concerned with the independence of the institution of higher education from the centers of power and political parties and groups, as well as providing criticism of the state in an effort to support the people. My friends and I at the Office to Foster Unity believed that the mandate of the student movement was to facilitate the development of an environment where the historic demands for freedom of the people could be articulated and civil rights defended, despite one's political and ideological beliefs and leanings. As such, we believed and continue to believe that the student movement should not sing the praises of the power structures and those in power, rather it must offer criticism of those who take advantage of their power, no matter what their background, and must defend the rights of the people, including women's rights and the rights of ethnic and religious minorities. For this reason over the past decade, I have been targeted by those in power and security forces and as a result have experienced prison and solitary confinement on several occasions. Taking into account this arrest, I have spent nearly 200 days in solitary confinement. While my previous incarcerations were not free of pressure and torture, this recent arrest was a different experience. I believe that informing the public and officials about the atrocities of this latest experience is of greatest importance.

Supreme Leader,

Beatings, verbal abuse and degradation and illegal treatments started at the very moment of my arrest. During my arrest, tear gas was used, which prior to this had only been used in the streets and open air. Breathing tear gas in a confined space made me feel as if I were choking and rendered me unable to move. Still, the security officials did not stop at that. With great spite and hostility they began to beat me, punching and kicking me, so that they could turn me over to their superiors at Evin prison with a bloody nose and mouth, bleeding teeth, and shackled arms and legs. Interestingly enough, when I objected to the treatment I received by vowing to launch a complaint against the approximately twenty security officials [who had come to arrest me], they responded with profanity and vile curses against myself and the judge. Of course this was just a warm-up for the start of my interrogations, where interrogators targeted my body and spirit. From the very beginning, I was faced with this constant proclamation that "the regime has suffered a crack" and the constant promise that "you will all be executed." The anticipation of the realization of this promise haunted me for some time and kept me wondering when and if my life would come to an end, especially on the many occasions either during the day or in the middle of the night when, without any explanation, I would be taken from one cell to another or from one ward to another. During the eighty-six days I spent in solitary confinement, I never saw the color of the sky. During the seven months of my detention in the security wards of 209 and 240 I was only allowed to go into the courtyard on six occasions. After my time in solitary confinement and the end of my interrogations and my court hearing, I was only allowed to contact my family every two weeks—calls that lasted only a few moments and during which my interrogator was present.

Allow me to describe the first days of my detention. After being arrested in the manner described above, I was transferred to solitary confinement—cell 101 in Section 209 of Evin prison. Upon entry into the cell I noticed that there were feces under the carpet in the room, so I objected. I was told, "You are not worthy of anything better than this."

After two days in Section 209, I was taken to Section 240 and transferred to the charge of the Ministry of Intelligence. After this, the conditions of prison became even more difficult and increasingly inhumane. Contrary to the regulations adopted by the Sixth Parliament and the orders of Ayatollah Hashemi Shahroudi,[6] which required that two solitary confinement cells be combined into one to allow for extra space for prisoners, it seemed that in this section each cell was divided into two cells reducing space and measuring 1.6 meters by 2.2. The width of the cell was shorter than my height and I could only lie down in one position. There was a metal bucket placed over a sewage hole, to make a makeshift toilet where we could relieve ourselves. A water faucet was placed over this makeshift toilet so that the prisoner would not have to be brought out of his cell for basic needs. Unfortunately, the positioning of this tomb-like cell, which benefited from the deathly silence of the ward, was such that the *qiblih* [the direction of prayer] was in the same direction as the makeshift toilet and the distance between this toilet and my prayer position was only a few inches. There was also a light which was on twenty-four hours a day, so as to prevent prisoners from even imagining a good night's rest. Enduring solitary confinement and difficult and lengthy interrogation sessions was something I had to become accustomed to. But along with solitary confinement, one also had to cope with repeated sleepless nights resulting from the lengthy interrogation sessions, being forced to stand on one foot for long periods of time, endless beatings and being slapped repeatedly. The pressure and taunts by interrogators for refusing their demands was so great that at times I would pass out during interrogation sessions.

The iron fist of interrogators would also result in my passing out. On several occasions the interrogator in charge of my case strangled me to the point of me losing consciousness and falling to the ground. For days following these strangulations, I suffered such severe pain in the neck and throat, that eating and drinking became unbearable. Of course, the negative impact of torture is not something which prisoners such as I have to contend with alone. At times, the interrogator himself suffers as a result of inflicting torture. I remember during one of my interrogations, after receiving repeated blows to the mouth, the interrogator, who would hit me with the back of his hand, noticed that his fingers had suffered cuts as well.

Interrogators even used my screams and cries which resulted from the beatings I was receiving to taunt other prisoners. Later I heard from some prisoners that during their interrogations, which were purposefully scheduled at the same time as mine [in a different room], they could hear my squealing. It seems that my screams were used to inflict emotional pressure on others.

Based on this account, it is inevitable that the interrogations had only one aim: to break the prisoner and force him to confess to what the interrogator wished. When we asked why it was that they used such methods to extract such confessions, we were told that, "According to the founder of the Islamic Republic the preservation of the Regime is the foremost obligation."

In the first month my interrogators would constantly say that "blood has been shed, the regime has suffered a crack, and many of you will be executed" and "the regime is the plaintiff against you." During interrogations, whenever I did not respond in accordance with the "will of the interrogator," or as he put it, "in line with the interests of the regime," I was told that either I had "to respond as we want you to, or you have to eat and swallow your interrogation form." This was not a threat. After refusing these demands, they would force feed the interrogation forms into my mouth. Once during the month of Ramadan I was forced to eat the interrogation form, while I was fasting. When beatings and cursing are routine during the holy nights of Qadr[7] and these nights are not honored, then it is no wonder that all other behavior is to also be expected.

Ayatollah Khamenei,

From the start of the interrogations, I was forced to write against my friends and those close to me and when I resisted, besides being beaten and slapped repeatedly, I was given this response by the interrogator, "You have to write against others so that your own notorious personality is demoralized." Perhaps this logic, which was intent on demoralizing and breaking me, justified their insistence that I confess to sexual relations and indiscretions which I had not had. When I objected that these accusations were not true, and insisted that I could not implicate myself in a false confession, I would receive beatings and insults and would be told that, "We will bring a prostitute to your court hearing to confess against you and say that she had illegitimate sexual relations with you."

Witnessing the expertise of the interrogators of the Islamic Republic, who are referred to as the unnamed soldiers of the Mehdi (the twelfth Shia Imam),[8] in their use of vulgarities which I could never bring myself to repeat within this letter and some of which I had never heard before, was indeed a painful experience for me. In the continuation of these same interrogation sessions, the interrogator would say, "We will do something to you so severe, that when you hear the name of Section 240 outside of prison, your body will begin to convulse." I would ask myself, how can a security agency utilize such strategies intent on inflicting fear and such threats to ensure the security of a nation, and what will be the end result of such strategies and tactics? How can you reach justice, by relying on the tactics intent on character assassinations of prisoners as a complimenting link in a cycle of torture and repression? How do the standards of forcing false confessions, by any means possible, by the law enforcers, correspond with religion, human rights or ethical standards? In the entire process of interrogation, my interrogators took several opportunities to use derogatory terms and vile language in addressing my late mother, who was a believer and the mother of a martyr [of the Iraq war].They addressed my wife as a [explitive], despite the fact that she has sacrificed much, is devoutly religious and was formerly married to my brother who was martyred in the war [and whom I married in line with tradition and custom]. They addressed my sisters and other female relatives in the most vile of manners, by calling them [explitive], and insulted them on numerous occasions. The constant use of

these derogatory terms and foul language by those who present themselves as the defenders of the Islamic Regime also targeted my martyred
brother—our family's sacrifice for our nation– whom they addressed as
a hypocrite and enemy.

Not only are interrogators disrespectful toward ordinary prisoners, they disrespect former and current government officials. On many
occasions I witnessed how they used insulting and derogatory terms to
address officials such as Hojat ol-Islam Seyed Hassan Khomeini (as a
cheeky child, with morality issues), Ayatollah Hashemi Rafsanjani (as
corrupt), Mir Hossein Mousavi (as the imposter and Islamic Antichrist),
Hojat ol-Islam Mehdi Karoubi (as immoral and corrupt), Hojat ol-Islam
Mohammad Khatami (as immoral, and by naming some pious women,
they would claim that he was involved in relations with them) and
Ayatollah Mousavi Khoeiniha (as seditious). Despite the fact that I had
not even met some of these officials, they wanted me to speak against
them in court. With respect to Mr. Karoubi and Mr. Abdullah Nouri, they
wanted me to use foul language against them in court. With respect to
Ayatollah Mousavi Khoeiniha, they told me to mention him in my court
hearing by name, and say that he had played a central role in the recent
unrest and had served as the main coordinator and director of these
developments. It should be noted that in the most polite of references to
these individuals and figures, the interrogators would still address them
disrespectfully. For example, they referred to Mr. Hashemi (Rafsanjani)
as "Akbar Shah" and vowed to imprison these former and current officials as well. It seems as if the desire of the interrogator preempts the
wishes and will of the judiciary as well and is more powerful than the
law. Interrogators claimed that they were in fact the ones who issued
court rulings. Perhaps it is important to note that the judge in charge of
my case (Judge Salavati) had explained to me that "if the interrogators
are satisfied with you, we will free you." This statement in and of itself
reflects the level of independence enjoyed by judges and court officials.

I pointed to pressures intent on forcing me to confess to sexual
relations and crimes implicating myself. In order to be precise, I will

describe one of my interrogation sessions focused on such issues, which was conducted in a cell. Perhaps this vile example of the pressures I faced can be measured and compared to ethical standards, standards of fairness, and standards of religious piety and the path of Islam. On one occasion interrogators came to me in a small cell and asked, "Have you decided to confess?" "In relation to what issue?" I asked. "Your sexual indiscretions," they replied. "Tell us about all of these indiscretions, and take the pressures off yourself, and also tell us about all the indiscretions of others you know about." They told me untruths about the sexual indiscretions of some of the other prisoners, including former government officials, and claimed that some political activists had confessed to having illegal sexual relations. Later I found out that this was a dirty tactic which the interrogators greatly relied on. These tactics were especially used after the election, and in particular in efforts to pressure the better known figures they had arrested. For example, they claimed that one the leading reformist figures repeatedly had relations with married women.

Under those conditions, where there was intense pressure on me to confess to having illegitimate relations, so that I could help myself, I kept insisting that I had been faithful to my wife. I explained that I had told the head interrogator that these tactics would not resolve any problems, and that you should not enter into these types of allegations in interrogations. They replied by claiming that they wanted me to confess so that I could demonstrate my honesty and willingness to be cooperative. If I write these confessions down on paper, they claimed, I would receive a reduced sentence in court. Otherwise they insisted, "we will intensify pressures." They further claimed that my confession in this respect was of no use to them because, "We know everything already and this confession will only help your own case." They said that they would leave me be for a while, but that they would return, and they advised me to use the time to give their demand some thought while keeping in mind the consequences of not complying and to therefore write what is being requested of me. I explained that my response was clear and so they slapped me forcefully several times. They left the cell, and during my time alone, I vowed to God that I would not succumb to these pressures and would not write anything in contradiction to the truth. I wrote, "I have not had any sexual indiscretions" on the interrogation form they had left behind.

With great anxiety I waited for their return. After a while they returned and asked if I had written what I was asked to write. I explained that I had written what I had previously told them I would write. They took the interrogation form and read it. They stormed toward me and began kicking, punching, and repeatedly slapping me. They cursed at me and my family and after a good beating, while cursing at me and belittling me, they said, "We will prove to you that you are a bastard child and that you are the result of illegitimate relations."

These words made me angry and I responded by fighting. They forced my head down the toilet. They shoved my head so far down the toilet that I swallowed feces and began to choke. They pulled my head out of the toilet and said that they would leave and come back at night and that I had been provided this extra time to confess to my sexual indiscretions. They claimed that I had to "explain fully who I had had sexual relations with, when, how and where." They even demanded that I falsely confess to being raped as a child. On many occasions I was threatened with the prospects of being raped with a bottle or a stick. This was so extreme that for example the interrogator of the Ministry of Intelligence of the Islamic Republic would vow that he "we will shove a stick in your rear so far that even 100 carpenters won't be able to extract it." He would also claim that: "we have informed some web-based sites about your sexual indiscretions and these details will be widely distributed via Bluetooth and CDs."

In this description of what I have endured lies a regretful truth, which demonstrates that the officers and law enforcers of a regime that claims to be based on religious principles, have indeed lost their moral compass. Remembering the details of all of this is indeed a tormenting exercise for me in and of itself and I will not delve further into these details. I only want to demonstrate what kind of pressures a prisoner in

Evin must face before he agrees to confess to crimes that he has never committed. I only want to ask, given these tactics and treatments, haven't the law enforcement officials and the rulers of the current government of the Islamic Republic failed the test of justice, morality, and humanity? This is not the first time such things have happened and public opinion had understood these realities when the tactics used in the interrogation of Saeed Emami's wife were revealed. These latest incidents, however, and the methods used in the interrogation of political prisoners following the elections in 2009, demonstrate that what Saeed Emami's wife[9] endured in interrogation was not an isolated event [by the security system], rather they demonstrate the lack of intent in stopping and ending these illegal actions in our nation. My interrogators would constantly insist that "with the support of the Supreme Leader we are intent on using any means for achieving our goals and we recognize no limits in reaching our aims. We will use all strategies to force critics to accept what we tell them, and we are doing this toward the aim of defending the regime. Not only are these tactics legitimate, they are obligatory."

Supreme Leader,

Just to inform you of the atmosphere of interrogations and the thinking of the team of interrogators, I will relay for you something that my interrogator said in one of our sessions. With a tone filled with hatred and anger he yelled, "I was willing to break Hashem Aghajari's[10] neck with my bare hands after he delivered his speech in Hamedan, and even if I was executed seven times over for doing so, it would have been worth it. But because I did not want this act to be attributed to the regime, I did not commit it." And, still to this day, when praying he explained that he confesses and expresses regret for having failed in carrying out God's will and in sending people like us to hell.

Of course according to my belief, these claims by the interrogator are indeed baseless. It is clear for me that these interrogators do not adhere to any ideology or religion, and it is only their own presence in the power structure and the benefits derived from this presence that motivates them, as well as the hatred they harbor within, which justifies their commitment to carrying out such inhumane assignments.

Leader of the Islamic Republic,

Lies have become customary in our society and they are in service of the rulers. In prison too they are used as tools by the interrogators. Lies and deception serve as the basis for all strategies employed by interrogators. For example, with respect to the situation and atmosphere in society [following the election unrest], the interrogators would feed lies and false analysis to prisoners intent on demoralizing them and their spirits. For example, after the Quds Day demonstrations,[11] they came to us and claimed that "only fifty people had come to the demonstrations and that Mr. Khatami had been beaten up by the public only to be rescued by security officials." Or they would claim that the public was so angry with Mousavi that his security detail had to be expanded that the public would not take to murdering him. In my own court hearing for example, it was mentioned that I had traveled to Germany, to take part in training on how to bring about a velvet revolution designed to overthrow the state. This claim was made despite the fact that my passport had been confiscated by the Ministry of Intelligence several years ago and I have never travelled to any countries in the West.

The interrogators worked hard to claim that the solitary confinement cell was indeed paradise, and their courts, the court of divine justice. They would insist that we should confess to our crimes like we would on judgment day and in the presence of God. The difference is that on Judgment day others speak against the person, but in solitary confinement and under the pressure of interrogation and under physical and emotional pressure it is the prisoner who is forced to falsely confess against themselves so that perhaps the prisoner could free themselves of the iron fists of the interrogators. To recreate such a "paradise," the interrogators would on many occasions beat prisoners in adjoining cells, so that besides our own pressures and beatings and tortures, we would have suffer through the painful screams of those being assaulted—and in this way they wanted to remind us of divine suffering in this "paradise" of theirs.

These are the treatments that are doled out to those who are critical or opposed to the regime. All this treatment is carried out in the framework of a religious regime and is justified by claims of protecting the state. And such a regime, with this type of religious interpretation, does indeed not leave any space for the expression of objection or opposition—even opposition or criticism expressed within the limits of what the law allows. This is happening despite the fact that the rule of the Prophet Mohammad was based on tolerance and kindness toward the public.

Ayatollah Khamenei,

As I have described, I was under great pressure to confess in court against myself, my friends and colleagues within various groups and political institutions with which I was involved or with which I had relations. In particular, I was pressured to provide false testimony in court against Mr. Mehdi Karroubi, whom I had supported during the tenth presidential election.

Following these abuses, eighty-six days in solitary confinement and fifty days of being completely out of touch with the outside world, lack of access to my family, lack of phone privileges or visits (which resulted in everyone outside of prison wondering whether I was actually still alive) and after practicing my lines with the interrogator to ensure I made statements implicating myself, I appeared for my court hearing. I appeared in court despite the fact that I was not allowed to have a lawyer of my own choosing representing me. I was not interested in giving the impression that the court hearing was indeed legitimate by accepting the services of a public defender—a defender who would have to be fully approved by interrogators and whom I would be required to fully cooperate with. This was a court after all, where my testimony was dictated to me by my interrogators beforehand. The interrogators had falsely promised me that if I read the testimony they had prepared during my court hearing, they would release me, by the end of September 2009. But freedom was not my motivation for reading their statement in court and implicating myself in confessions. I was only looking for a way to free myself of the constant physical and emotional torture that was being inflicted upon me in prison. I was seeking to free myself from the iron fists of the interrogators. I was hoping that in this way I could avoid starting each day with the vilest insults launched at me and my family. I was hoping that I would not have my head jammed into the toilet bowl in order to extract a false confession. I was hoping to free myself of the constant beatings, punches, kicks, and slaps of the interrogator. I was looking to free myself of the constant threats of execution and other promised acts of violence against me. I was hoping to put an end to the dirty tactics used to force me to confess to sexual indiscretions I had not committed. It was such that I went to court and read the statement that the interrogators had prepared for me. In court, I tried to read the statement, so it would be readily apparent that it had been dictated to me. I had to confess against myself and read a prepared statement as my defense, a defense which was more like an indictment against me. I did this without believing in what I was saying. Believe me, even those who are guilty do not enjoy confessing in court and in front of the public.

But the experience in Evin and the eventful interrogations orchestrated by the Ministry of Intelligence pushes a person to the breaking point so that he agrees finally to confess against himself, even a false confession. It is a fact that these false confessions are then used by the court system and judges, as a basis for the issuance of verdicts and sentences. This cooperation between the court and interrogators takes place despite the fact that on many occasions I personally witnessed how interrogators insulted and cursed the judges and prosecutors. The interrogators believe that the judge and prosecutors play no role in the issuance of sentences and their opinions do not count. Interrogators believe that they are the ones who decide for the judicial system and for the regime as a whole. With respect to the lack of independence of the judiciary and the judges, I will only point to the first meeting I had with the head prosecutor Mr. Dolatabadi. It should be noted that the crux of pressure and torture I endured occurred during the reign of the former prosecutor, and my meeting with Mr. Jafari Dolatabadi took place five months after my arrest and after my court hearing. As such, I did not expect much to come of the meeting. But still, the interrogator in our interrogation session prior to the meeting with Mr. Dolatabadi insisted that I need not mention the circumstances of my time in detention and interrogation. The interrogator said, "The prosecutor is a nobody and that I am the one who decides." The interrogator told me that in my meeting with the prosecutor I should not demand the services of a lawyer. In the end and to my disbelief, my interrogator was present during my meeting with the prosecutor—the same interrogator who had tortured me, and the experience of this torture over several months was more tangible than all other possibilities. So it was only natural that under these circumstances I did not have much to say to the prosecutor.

Supreme Leader,

Isn't the show of power by the security apparatus in opposing the will of the people, and their elevated position in the decision-making process related to policies of repression and control of political and social developments, a testament to the declining legitimacy of the state? And doesn't it bring to mind the increased dependence of the government on the machinery or apparatus of tyranny?

Haven't our rulers yet reached the belief that the use of force for ensuring their rule is an obsolete strategy? Do they still view repression as the appropriate response to objection, protest, opposition and the demand of rights by the public?

More than 400 days have passed since my arrest. Despite having been released on a heavy bail order for a short period prior to the New

Year's holidays in March, I was returned to prison for refusing to succumb to the demands of my interrogators to continue confessing to
crimes against myself and others while on furlough. I just want to inform everyone that I continue to hold the same beliefs that I had prior
to my arrest and I remain true to those beliefs. As explained earlier, the
statement I read in court and under pressure does not represent my
beliefs.

Our crime has been and continues to be the fact that we believe reform and democracy to be the most appropriate strategies for improving
the conditions of our nation. Our crime is that we advocated limits on
the boundless powers of undemocratic institutions. My question is this:
is the act of supporting the demands of the Iranian nation for democracy deserving of such inhumane and unjust treatment? Have we not
reached the point of accepting that the expression of beliefs of individuals or groups should not be subjected to persecution?

In cases where torture has been proven to have taken place, is the
expectation that the torturer be brought to trial, an unrealistic expectation? If we are to rid ourselves of injustice and those who carry out
injustices, then bringing torturers to trial can be an important step in
promoting effective strategies for implementing justice. Reducing injustice and despotism can facilitate the implementation of justice and the
rule of law.

In the end, what was the aim and logic of the torture inflicted upon
me and my family? I do not even expect a response to this question because the "Elders can discern that which is in the best interest of their
nation." What I do know and believe is that these behaviors do not correspond with the concepts of justice and fairness nor are they justifiable
by law or through religious teachings. I continue to hope that with the
establishment of a truth commission, we will be freed from these clear
examples of injustice and move closer to justice.

Abdollah Momeni
Evin Prison

STRATEGIES OF HOPE:
EDWARD SAID, THE GREEN MOVEMENT AND THE STRUGGLE FOR DEMOCRACY IN IRAN

Nader Hashemi

September 2010

In 1991 Edward Said travelled to South Africa to deliver the prestigious TB Davie Memorial Lecture at the University of Cape Town, which he devoted to the topic of academic freedom.[1] During his visit, he also lectured at other local universities but still found time to immerse himself in the politics of the country. This visit coincided with a transformative period in South Africa's history. Nelson Mandela (whom Said briefly met) had recently been freed, the African National Congress (ANC) was legalized (after a thirty-year ban), and the stage was set for what in retrospect was to become one of the great democratic transitions and emancipatory moments of the twentieth century.

Several years later, Said had a chance to publicly reflect upon his South African experience. In the last decade of his life, he became a regular contributor to the Arabic press, primarily *Al Hayat* and *Al Ahram Weekly*, where he wrote a regular bimonthly column for a largely Arab and Muslim audience. In September 1997 he penned a short essay based on his South Africa trip titled "Strategies of Hope," which sought to apply the lessons from the struggle against apartheid to the struggle for Palestinian self-determination.[2] This important yet generally unknown essay is pregnant with insights. Like much of Said's work, it possesses an enduring quality, and it is especially relevant to those interested in struggles for democracy and human rights in the developing world, where a militarily and politically weaker group confronts a more powerful adversary.

In this essay I seek to illustrate the main arguments Said advanced in his South Africa-Palestine comparison, and then apply them to the case of the Green Movement in Iran and the struggle for democracy inside the Islamic Republic today, while taking into consideration the relevant similarities and differences among the three cases.

According to John Donne, while some "comparisons are odious," relevant similarities do nonetheless exist which merit careful consideration. In his perceptive essay, Said articulated a broad strategy for democratic mobilization that continues to have a transnational and timeless appeal. Leaders and supporters of Iran's Green Movement can benefit from considering this strategy in the aftermath of the 2009 electoral coup, as they begin a protracted, arduous, and momentous struggle for the future of Iran.

The human factor in politics

Said's essay opens with a discussion of the plight of the Palestinians, four years after the 1993 Oslo Peace Process. At that time (as today), Benjamin Netanyahu was in power and the collective plight of the Palestinians was moving steadily from bad to worse. Said lamented that "enough has been said about the economic, social and political deprivations" facing the Palestinians, which have only increased since Oslo, but insufficient attention has been paid to "the human factor" in politics, which "surely [is] the most important." What Said meant by the "human factor" is the paramount importance of individual will and human agency in shaping political struggles. Specifically, the ability during moments of crisis and paralysis to think outside the proverbial box to advance alternative, creative and original ideas in support of emancipatory causes. He reminded readers that "political struggles are always contests of will, in which one side attempts to persuade the other side to give up, to lose the will to resist and fight on. This is not a military but a political and moral matter." His prescription to his fellow Palestinians was "the reactivation of [human] will and, just as important, the revival of belief in the possibility that what human beings do can make a difference."

A specific problem Said identified was the "tendency to think only

in literal terms ... [and] not sufficiently in symbolic and moral ones."
He reminds his readers how the Zionist project in the West was rooted
in a moral claim to be the best response to the Nazi Holocaust and historical anti-Semitism. This is eventually what broadened its appeal after
the horrors of World War II. Surveying the plight of the Palestinians
on the eve of the fiftieth anniversary of their dispossession, Said similarly called for a new collective "human effort ...to demonstrate to the
world the immorality of what was done to us." This, he affirmed, is the
"essential task facing us as a people now" and unless it is pursued "we
can never expect any change in our status as an inferior and dominated
people." In the end he noted that "our struggle with Zionism must be
won first on the moral level, and then can be fought in negotiations from
a position of moral strength, given that militarily and economically we
will always be weaker than Israel and its supporters."

The importance of this general theme was first brought to Said's
realization after visiting South Africa in 1991. The centerpiece of his essay is a conversation he recalled at the ANC headquarters in downtown
Johannesburg with Walter Sisulu, arguably the preeminent figure in the
struggle against apartheid after Mandela.

Said was flummoxed by the changing political landscape in South
Africa, in the Spring of 1991, when only a few weeks earlier the ANC was
viewed by the regime as a banned terrorist organization. What made
such a political transformation possible? Said's recollection of his conversation with Sisulu is worth quoting in full.

> *Said:* What exactly did the ANC do to turn defeat into victory?
> *Sisulu:* You must remember that during the eighties we were
> beaten in South Africa; the organization was wrecked by the po-
> lice, our bases in neighboring countries were routinely attacked
> by the South African army, our leaders were in jail or in exile or
> killed. We then realized that our only hope was to concentrate on
> the international arena, and there to delegitimize apartheid. We
> organized in every major Western city; we initiated committees,
> we prodded the media, we held meetings and demonstrations, not

once or twice, but thousands of times. We organized university campuses, and churches, and labor unions, and businesspeople, and professional groups.

Said: [Sisulu] paused for a moment and then said something that I shall never forget as long as I live.

Sisulu: Every victory that we registered in London, or Glasgow, or Iowa City, or Toulouse, or Berlin, or Stockholm gave the people at home a sense of hope and renewed their determination not to give up the struggle. In time we morally isolated the South African regime and its policy of apartheid so that even though militarily we could not do much to hurt them, in the end they came to us, asking for negotiations. We never changed or retreated from our basic program, our central demand: one person, one vote.

Building on his reflections on South Africa, Said called on his fellow Palestinians to "take our moral presence directly into the Israeli and Western, and even Arab consciousness" and to "show Israel and its supporters that only a full acknowledgement by them of what was done to us can bring peace and reconciliation." The success of this project will gain "moral stature by its human dimensions, its sincere willingness for coexistence, its firm belief in respecting the rights of others." It will also require "a policy of concrete detail, not one of broad, abstract statements that are not fully engaged in the struggle for opinion."

This was a strategy that Said, over the course of decades, repeatedly encouraged Yasser Arafat and the PLO to pursue. Yet despite his close connection to the senior leadership of the Palestinian national movement, there was little interest in engaging with these ideas.[3] His advice fell on deaf ears, and Said resigned from the Palestine National Council in 1991 over the process leading up to the signing of the Oslo Accords, of which he remained a persistent and principled critic.

A comparison with Iran

While the struggles for democracy in Iran today and in pre-1990 South Africa are not identical, relevant parallels do exist. First, a few of the key differences. Iran's political system, notwithstanding its theocratic underpinnings, is not as discriminatory as apartheid South Africa. Until the 2009 presidential election, despite widespread voter dissatisfaction, state repression and elite corruption, the Islamic Republic could nonetheless claim a degree of political legitimacy, as evidenced by the over 80 percent voter turnout in the most recent presidential election (arguably, this was due to the absence of viable alternatives, among other things). Prior to the rise of the reform movement in Iran, elections in the Islamic Republic were never "free," insofar as candidates were screened for regime loyalty—but the they *were* based on universal suffrage and they were basically "fair" in that the announced results closely reflected the number of ballots cast. The case of South Africa was qualitatively different on this score.

Secondly, on a regional level, broad public sympathy and support exists for Iran in its conflict with the United States and the West. The reference here is to the Arab and Muslim populations at large, not the authoritarian regimes (often allied with the West) who rule over them.[4] This can be extended to significant parts of the Third World as well, which similarly resents US pressure and the bullying of Iran and who generally sympathize with its anti-imperial posture. In the case of South Africa, the opposite conditions prevailed. The apartheid regime had little regional support at the elite or the popular level.

Thirdly, in contrast to South Africa, Iran over the last decade has been subject to threats of "regime change" by a global superpower that surrounds its borders with a sizeable military presence. Threats of possible military strikes on Iran by Israel and/or the US are a constant concern and are frequently debated and sometimes advocated in the West by powerful and influential political leaders and constituencies, most recently by Tony Blair.[5] All of this undermines Iran's internal struggle for democracy and sustains Iran's authoritarian rulers by providing them with an opportunity to shift public attention and debate toward external threats and national security issues and away from pressing internal socio-economic and political problems. While South Africa was internationally isolated and quarantined, it never faced a comparable threat of an imminent attack by a global superpower seeking regime change, nor was it surrounded by a hostile and more powerful military force, as Iran is today.[6]

Nonetheless, the similarities remain striking, especially in terms of the internal struggle for democracy. A decidedly authoritarian system struggles to survive and perpetuate itself with increasing brutality and unscrupulousness replete with state censorship, human rights abuses and political chicanery. It draws support from a minority of the population that is deeply loyal and ideologically committed to maintaining the status quo. Both political systems had international pariah status and were subject to broad UN economic sanctions, moral censure and ostracization. Like South Africa this contributes to a siege mentality within Iran that reinforces a sense of moral self-righteousness among ruling elites, which they regularly exploit to solidify their ranks, repel calls for change and pacify their opponents.

These democratic opposition movements—the ANC and the Green Movement—are no match for the power and prowess of the regimes that rule over them. The repressive state apparatuses in both the old South African and Iran have far greater resources to draw upon and are far superior to their rivals in both military and economic terms. Internally, these opposition movements, despite being widely popular, are violently crushed due to state repression and surveillance, and its key leaders are either jailed, placed under house arrest, exiled, or killed. As a result, appeals for international support and solidarity by the ANC and the Green Movement emerged to form a core part of their democratization platforms and strategy (far more so in the case of the ANC, yet it should be pointed out that the Green Movement is still in its infancy).

While other significant differences and similarities exist, these are some of the more salient ones.[7] The lessons here for Iran's Green Movement are several. In many ways the Green leadership has already adopted Said's central point about moral clarity and consistency. At a recent gathering of Iranian journalists, Mir Hossein Mousavi stated that the "Green Movement's strength lies is in its ethics, in calling what is white, white and what is black, black."[8] Since the 2009 electoral coup, Mousavi, Mehdi Karoubi, and to a lesser extent, Mohammad Khatami, have consistently and courageously spoken out against the injustices of Iran's ruling elite. After a meeting in late August 2010, they issued a statement that condemned "the institutionalization of telling lies" in Iran while noting that "they have been so caught up in telling lies that obtaining a true word from this government is like finding a precious gemstone."[9] The plight of political prisoners, the abuse of power, the constitutional and human rights of the people of Iran, and a broad and persistent critique of the policies of Ahmadinejad's "coup d'état government" (as it is called within Iran), have been core features of the Green opposition's strategy. While these criticisms of the Iranian regime are important and provide the movement with necessary leadership, looking ahead there is much more that can be done. Here are some key recommendations.

Saidian recommendations for the Green Movement

The task of "morally isolating" your adversary must be sensitive to context. Generally, advice for democratic movements from those living outside of the country in question often suffers from the trap of "one-size-fits-all" thinking. This is the fallacy of providing prescriptions while ignoring context, background and unique political sensitivities that could be exploited to crush democratic struggles. Thus, for example, what worked in Eastern Europe in the 1980s will not necessarily work in the Middle East in 2010.

In the context of contemporary Iran, morally isolating the Ahmadinejad government on an international level is an easy task in large part because it is already morally isolated by virtue of its own actions. While sympathy for Iran's Green opposition is widespread, it is based more on revulsion for the current Iranian regime than on a clear-cut understanding of internal Iranian politics. At the popular level—especially in the West—there remains widespread ignorance of the Green Movement's basic policies with respect to both internal political developments and especially those issues of global importance such as Iran's nuclear program, the Israel–Palestine conflict and the wars in Afghanistan and Iraq. The Green Movement must do more to publicize its views internationally, especially throughout global civil society, by focusing on how the threat of a US/Israeli military strike undermines the internal struggle for democracy in Iran and generally how Western policy toward Iran, both in the past and in the present, has more often strengthened political authoritarianism than Iranian democrats.[10] A set of clear positions as to how those outside of Iran can best assist the Green Movement would be most helpful. Mehdi Karoubi's advice to Iranian expatriates on the first anniversary of Green Movement is most instructive in this regard, as are his views on UN sanctions.[11]

The more important task, however, with respect to "morally isolating" the Iranian regime lies in the internal dimensions of this endeavor. A small but loyal percentage of the population, for a variety of reasons, still buys into the regime's propaganda, particularly the claim that only Iran's current rulers embody Islamic authenticity and Iranian nationalism. Through its massive propaganda apparatus and tight control of the media, Iran's oligarchs seek to convince the population that the Green Movement is not indigenous and has been manipulated or is on the payroll of foreign powers that seek to subjugate Iran and compromise its political independence; this is a unifying theme shared by Iranians across the political spectrum. Refuting these claims, however erroneous they may seem, remains a pressing task for the Green Movement and its supporters.[12]

Secondly, Said's discussion of "the reactivation of [human] will" and the importance of the "revival of belief in the possibility that what human beings do can make a difference" is essentially a call for new ideas of resistance, ideas that are both nonviolent in nature and morally symbolic in terms of their political impact.

For most of its first year, the Green Movement relied on street protests to express opposition and to rally supporters. After those protests

were brutally suppressed and legal permission to demonstrate was denied, the only option advocated by the leadership was a general and
somewhat vague call to establish "social networks" and spread awareness about the political status quo among Iranians. More can be done
in this regard, and here Iran's Greens need not reinvent the proverbial
wheel. The key is to think in symbolic terms and to follow the lead of
other democratic struggles. One concrete initiative is to keep alive the
memories of fallen heroes and martyrs and to remember the plights of
political prisoners. Neda Agha Soltan and Sohrab Arabi, two students
who were slain in violent crackdown that followed the electoral coup,
immediately come to mind. Their deaths and hundreds of other people
who were killed and tortured should not be forgotten.

Equally important is constantly reminding the world of the plight
of Iran's political prisoners. Recall the important symbolic role Steven
Biko played in the anti-apartheid struggle both during his imprisonment
and after his death. Abdollah Momeni and Majid Tavakoli are similarly
heroic figures, both of them student leaders like Biko, worthy of admiration, respect and global name recognition. This will not happen by
itself; the Greens must make it happen.

Finally, and perhaps most importantly, there is the question of what
Said called the "human dimension" of democratic struggle and the demonstration of a "sincere willingness for coexistence" and "firm belief
in respecting the rights of others." In the context of Iran's democratic
struggle, this necessitates the breaking of a vicious historical cycle of
bloodshed, reprisals and revenge which has characterized Iranian politics for too long.

The Green Movement is best advised to reject this past and chart a
new course rooted in nonviolence with the goal of national reconciliation. To its credit, these themes have already been stressed and repeatedly affirmed by the leadership, but to date no statement has been made
or strategy suggested as to how the Green Movement seeks to deal with
past human rights abuses and injustices such as those that occurred (and
are occurring) at the notorious Evin and Kahrizak prisons. An Iranian

version of South Africa's Truth and Reconciliation Commission is what is needed. This could easily be justified on both secular and Islamic grounds by recalling the general political amnesty given by the Prophet Mohammad when he defeated his rivals and recaptured Mecca in 630 AD.

While some Iranian intellectuals and activists have already made passing references to such a commission, a clear statement by the leadership of the Green Movement on this issue would serve many purposes. Not only would it immediately change the moral language in Iran from "us" versus "them" to a new emphasis on "we"—a united collectivity seeking national reconciliation, forgiveness and justice—but it would also send a strong message to regime loyalists, in particular the Revolutionary Guards and the Basij militia, that a democratic transition in Iran will not lead to political executions and acts of revenge and violent retribution. The Green Movement's non-violent orientation can best be affirmed by continuing to articulate a new future for Iran, one that marks a clear historical break from the violent past and which is rooted in lessons from other political struggles that have universal appeal, such as the anti-colonial movement in India, the African-American struggle for civil rights and the anti-apartheid struglle in South Africa.

Conclusion

Edward Said's advice for the Palestinian leadership as articulated in his "Strategies of Hope" essay was never taken seriously. Rather than investing in their own people and in a global campaign of grassroots mobilization based on an ANC model, Yasser Arafat and Mahmoud Abbas repeatedly chose to compromise with established power along the lines of Mangosuthu Buthelezi, the tribal chieftain and apartheid collaborator. The hope from these Palestinian leaders was always that powerful political forces in Washington, DC could pressure Israel and deliver Palestinian independence from above. Thus, there was little interest in mass mobilization domestically or internationally.

As we approach the twentieth anniversary of the Oslo accords, the collective plight of the Palestinians remains far worse today than when

the Oslo peace process began. The colossal failure of leadership has
been central to this story, in particular its inability or its unwillingness
to mobilize global civil society on its behalf. By contrast, South Africa,
despite its many internal problems, has a far brighter future in large part
because democracy has been consolidated thanks to an effective and visionary leadership. If there are lessons here for Iran's Green Movement,
they are best advised to engage in a careful comparative study of emancipatory struggle for which the ANC and the South African experience
serve as a shining example, and the case of the PLO and the Palestinian
leadership remains a case study in how *not* to lead a successful movement for democratic transition and self-determination.

IRAN'S GREEN MOVEMENT:
AN INTERVIEW WITH MEHDI KAROUBI

Laura Secor

October 12, 2010

When I started visiting Iran, in 2004, Mehdi Karroubi was widely viewed as the most conservative figure among the reformists. He was a white-turbaned, populist clergyman from the agricultural province of Lorestan, and, though he was concerned about protecting Iranians' political rights and freedoms, his voters also tended to be pious, traditional, and oppressed by Iran's rising unemployment and inflation rates. When he ran for president in 2005—the year in which Mahmoud Ahmadinejad rose to power—on the promise to distribute some fifty dollars a month to every Iranian family, some urban reformists called on him to withdraw in favor of a rival reformist candidate, Mostafa Moin, a former minister of higher education who appealed to Iran's burgeoning population of university students.

Karroubi did not withdraw. His allies argued—rightly, it turned out—that his appeal was actually much broader than Moin's. In fact, his rallies looked somewhat like those of his conservative rivals: crowds of mixed ages, women fully enveloped in their garments, men in long sleeves and traditional haircuts. The reformist vote, predictably, split, and neither candidate made it to the second round, though Karroubi, much to the surprise of Moin's supporters, came very close—Ahmadinejad just squeaked by him.

At the time, Karroubi issued a controversial open letter claiming that the election had been stolen from him. He resigned from all his political posts, including one as an advisor to the Supreme Leader, Ali Khamenei. But the newspapers that carried his letter were forbidden to circulate, and almost no one came to Karroubi's defense. Famously, Karroubi said that when he'd gone to bed the night after the election, he was in second place, and when he awoke he was in third. In subsequent elections, Iranians would joke that Karroubi, at all costs, must not go to sleep.

Young Iranians could mock Karroubi all they liked as a perennial presidential hopeful, but once they ran afoul of Iranian restrictions on the press and assembly, it was Karroubi to whom they turned. He was the one reformist politician whose door was always open to the distressed families of prisoners, and who was never afraid to use his connections and his political capital on behalf of vulnerable young people behind bars. He had been a political prisoner himself, under the Shah, but in this he could hardly be distinguished from many hardliners who were brutalized by that experience. In 1988, Karroubi even signed a letter to Ayatollah Khomeini, arguing against clemency for the Revolution's political prisoners. But what Karroubi had exhibited since then was personal decency, strength of character, and a humanitarian instinct that seemed fearless and impervious to pressure.

I met him only fleetingly, in late 2006. He was imposing, in immaculate and finely woven robes, with a manicured white beard and gold-rimmed spectacles. He allowed me one question, to which he provided a cursory answer. By then, he commanded what was practically the only reformist party that could still legally function, *Etemad-e Melli*, or National Trust. He ran a newspaper by the same name which, by the end of Ahmadinejad's first term, was the only reformist media organ that hadn't been banned. Karoubi's party was more centrist, and more dominated by clerics, than Mohammad Khatami's Mosharekat party. But, unlike *Mosharekat*, *Etemad-e Melli* was still a player.

The Mehdi Karoubi who ran for president in 2009 barely resembled the Karoubi who ran in 2005. Now Karroubi emerged as the race's most outspoken proponent of human rights, women's rights, and political freedom. Some of the same young Iranians who scoffed at his campaign in 2005 told me with regret that they would vote for Mir-Hossein Mousavi—they saw him as the more electable candidate, with an appeal that extended from urban youth into Ahmadinejad's constituency—but that their hearts were with Karroubi. In a televised debate, Ahmadinejad displayed chart after chart to defend his claim that the Iranian economy was healthy; Karroubi all but called the President a liar. Although all the opposition candidates derided Ahmadinejad's Holocaust denial (if tepidly), it was Karroubi who indignantly told a rally, "Denying the Holocaust is like defending Hitler. Have we come down so low that we need to defend Hitler's dignity?"

No one expected Karroubi to win the June, 2009, election, or even to significantly split the reformist vote. But when Mousavi disputed the early call for Ahmadinejad, Karroubi closed ranks behind him. The two men, once allies in the revolutionary regime of the nineteen-eighties, became the unlikely leaders of the Green Movement. In the turbulent months that followed—demonstrations crushed by armed militias, thousands placed behind bars, leading reformists paraded in show trials and indicted for conspiracy—Karroubi and Mousavi have been under virtual house arrest, facing periodic violence and persistent rumors of their own detention. Virtually all of their closest colleagues are in prison or silenced.

Still, Karroubi gives the occasional interview by e-mail to the foreign press. I sent him some questions, both about the Green Movement and about some controversies from his past. Excerpts from our exchange are below.

There is a widespread perception outside Iran that the Green Movement has been defeated. We no longer hear about millions-strong demonstrations, and a great many opposition figures have been imprisoned or forced out of the country. Is there still a Green Movement in Iran? Does it have an organized structure and a strategy for achieving its goals?

Because of heavy government suppression, people are not visible in the streets, chanting and demonstrating. But the movement runs very deep. If the government allowed any kind of activity in the streets, the world would see millions of people. The authorities know it, and that is why they have cracked down for the last sixteen months, shutting down any kind of opposition in the most brutal ways. The government has many problems at the moment....The economy and foreign policy are both sources of conflict. All of this makes it very hard for the current administration to accomplish anything. In the first months and days after the election, many officials from the top down were sent to prison, and this has continued. These are clear signs that the movement is still alive.

The Iranian diaspora includes a great many young people who were politically active when they left Iran (many of them very recently), and who wish to be involved with the Green Movement from outside. What role, if any, can these Iranians living abroad play?

Iran belongs to all Iranians, from those who left Iran years ago to all who reside in Iran today. I have always stressed that Iranians outside the country should retain their identity and stay in touch with their homeland. I cannot tell Iranians outside the country what to do, but I can say that it would be good for them to try to convey Iranian public opinion and elite thought to the outside world, to help project the voices of those who are voiceless in Iran.

If it were up to you, what would be the attitude of the United States government toward the Green Movement?

We look to our own people, to our own country and its interests. We try to avoid any dependence on other countries, nor would we suggest any strategy for them. This movement is our own responsibility, and we do not expect other nations or governments to do anything for us. But if they feel a humanitarian obligation to support us, that is another thing.

Do you feel that your safety and freedom are in peril? What is it like to function—and to live—in this environment? How has it changed your daily activities, as a person and as a political leader?

There are many difficulties, and the pressure is intense. I have no security in my home. Recently, for five days in a row, there were rocks
and grenades thrown at my house. Our neighbors have been frightened,
their property burned and destroyed. Our opponents are not afraid of
anything. They closed down the office of my party and even my own
private office. I knew I might face such malicious tactics. From when I
was speaker of parliament to the present, when I have no official position, I have always defended the rights of the people. I am prepared for
any incident or accident, and I am not afraid. But I am concerned about
Islam, and I am afraid that these people who are attacking and harass-
ing people in the name of Islam are doing serious damage to our religion
in the eyes of the world.

*Last year, you publicized allegations of sexual abuse inside Iranian prisons.
To your knowledge, do these kinds of abuses continue to take place, or has
the problem been addressed?*

In our culture, victims of rape suffer deep shame and depression. Moreover, the authorities made the situation very intimidating, such that
rape victims were afraid to speak up. Even so, some of the rape victims
came to see me, and consequently, some of them have been silenced or
forced to leave the country. I do not even know how these people are
doing or if they are recovering. I just documented their claims and made
a film of what they said happened to them while they were in jail, so
that if anyone tried to deny that detainees had been raped, I would have
something in hand. I will say it clearly: they raped people in detention in
the early days of the movement, and they continue to torture dissidents
in brutal ways in prison. I have nothing in hand to indicate recent or
continuous rape in detention.

*What is your opinion of the law that is about to go into effect reducing or
eliminating government subsidies on consumer goods like gas and food?*

I agree in principle with reforming the subsidies, but it should be thought through and analyzed very well by experts. Unfortunately, because of this government's many economic misdeeds, prices skyrocketed before any reform could take place. Now the question is, what happens when the reform laws are enforced? I believe that this government has fatally weakened the economy, such that any subsidy reform might just do further harm.

You were a parliamentary deputy representing Tehran in 1988, when thousands of political prisoners were executed by order of Ayatollah Khomeini. The only political figure to protest this order was Ayatollah Montazeri, Khomeini's designated successor at the time. You co-authored a letter with two other parliamentary deputies, objecting to Ayatollah Montazeri's position for clemency for political prisoners. Many years have passed since those events, and in that time you have come to be seen as a champion of human rights. Do you believe that Ayatollah Montazeri was wrong to object to the killing of political prisoners in 1988? Do you believe Ayatollah Khomeini did the right thing for Iran when he stripped Ayatollah Montazeri of the succession as a result of his objections?

I should answer to this question in two parts. First, in those days I was not aware of executions and neither do I have that knowledge now. I am not sure what happened in the prisons, who ordered it, or if Ayatollah Khomeini was aware of it. Second, the letter you mention had nothing to do with the executions. There was a series of arguments between Ayatollah Montazeri and Ayatollah Khomeini. [Laura Secor notes: i.e., over the treatment of political prisoners even before the executions, as Montazeri argued for greater leniency; others were about the Iran-Contra affair, which one of Montazeri's relatives had leaked to the international press.] These issues between them even caused many of Ayatollah Montazeri's relatives to be imprisoned. In light of these events, we decided to write a confidential letter to Ayatollah Khomeini. This was a very general letter on variety of issues, including some terror attacks and other incidents in Isfahan and Najafabad [Montazeri's home town]. The letter was confidential, and we wrote and sent it before all those things happened. But when it came out and was not confidential anymore, it coincided with those incidents. That letter was about things that happened all throughout that year, and we wrote it to help resolve some points of conflict. If we want to talk about the issues between Ayatollah Khomeini and Ayatollah Montazeri, that takes time. I had no problem with [Montazeri]; I respected him and I respect him still, but there were issues between him and Ayatollah Khomeini.

You recently told Der Spiegel that you advocate free elections, free speech, free assembly, and the release of political prisoners. Do you believe it is possible to institute and safeguard these freedoms without revising the constitutional role of the Supreme Leader? Can you have a democracy whose constitution enshrines velayat-e faqih [the ultimate rule of a cleric as the viceregent of God], and, if not, to which form of government should Iranians aspire?

No comment.

NOTES

Introduction by Nader Hashemi and Danny Postel

1. Larry Diamond, Marc Plattner and Philip Costopoulos eds., *Debates on Democratization* (Baltimore, MD: Johns Hopkins University Press, 2010).

2. For a description of this period see, Section I of this book, and also Scott Peterson, *Let the Swords Encircle Me: Iran—A Journey Behind the Headlines* (New York: Simon & Schuster, 2010), 462–496. Also see the reporting in the *New York Times* by Roger Cohen.

3. Charles Tilly, *Social Movements, 1768–2004* (Boulder, CO: Paradigm Publishers, 2004), 1–5.

4. Robert Fisk, "Symbols are not enough to win this battle," *The Independent*, June 23, 2009; Slavoj Žižek, "Berlusconi in Tehran," *London Review of Books*, July 23, 2009; Hamid Dabashi, "Iran's Green Movement as a Civil Rights Movement," in this volume. For an internal definition of the Green Movement by one of its leading intellectuals, see the eight point description in this volume, "The Key Features of the Green Movement: An Interview with Dissident Cleric Mohsen Kadivar."

5. Timothy Garton Ash, "We can't decide Iran's struggle. But we can avoid backing the wrong side," *The Guardian*, September 23, 2009. Mahmoud Sadri applies Garton Ash's concept of "refolution" to the Green movement in his (unpublished) presentation "'Refolution' Iranian Style" at the conference "The Future of Secularism and the Public Role of Religion in Iran" held at Lake Forest College March 27–28, 2010. Scott Peterson locates the origins of the Green Movement seven months before the June 2009 vote. See his *Let the Swords Encircle Me*, 450–451. For a succinct overview see Abbas Milani, "The Green Movement," in Robin Wright, ed., *The Iran Primer* (Washington DC: US Institute for Peace, 2010), www.iranprimer.usip.org/resource/green-movement.

6. On parallels with the 1979 revolution, see Danny Postel, "Counter-Revolution and Revolt in Iran: An Interview with Iranian Political Scientist Hossein Bashiriyeh," in this volume. On the arc connecting the Green movement to

the Constitutional Revolution of 1906–1911, see Michael M.J. Fischer, "The Rhythmic Beat of the Revolution in Iran," in this volume, and also Ali Ansari, *Crisis of Authority: Iran's 2009 Presidential Election* (London: Chatham House, 2010), 14–16. Also see the interview Ansari gave to Bernard Gwertzman of the Council on Foreign Relations, "Time to Speak Out on Iran," January 13, 2010, http://www.cfr.org/publication/21204/time_to_speak_out_on_iran. html. Mir Hossein Mousavi has also suggested this link. In statement released in August 2010 he noted: "We all know that from the outset of the [1906] Constitutional Revolution, that in a variety of ways, some of the clerics such as [Ayatollah] Na'ini designated religious despotism to be worst form of oppression. Our experiences over the past century, including during the last year, demonstrate that among the enduring concepts of the Constitutional Revolution are justice, freedom, the rule of law, limiting power and making it accountable, all of which are important for shaping our political destiny.... If we look carefully, we would easily notice that there are no obstacles today which could halt the spread of political tyranny. This is why the constitutional movement teaches us that the most important vehicle to restrain power is non-violent struggle—something that our nation has recently started. Some of the demands of the Green Movement clearly reveal this side of resistance." See his "Constitutionalism: The Start of a 100 Year Struggle to Limit Political Power," *Jaras* (Persian) August 5, 2010, http://www.rahesabz.net/ story/20847/. A fairly accurate English translation can be found at: www. khordaad88.com/?p=1730.

7. Hamid Dabashi, "Iran's Green Movement as a Civil Rights Movement," in this volume.

8. The Leveretts have been the most vocal mainstream critics of the Green Movement. Their writings on Iran can be found at www.raceforiran.com. For a representative sample of their views on the Green Movement see Flynt Leverett and Hilary Mann Leverett, "Iran's Green Movement Approaches Irrelevance: Why Does Washington Continue to Gamble on It?" *Foreign Policy*, March 17, 2010, www.mideast.foreignpolicy.com/posts/2010/03/17/iran_s_ green_movement_approaches_irrelevance_why_does_washington_continue_ to_gamble/ and "Who's Really Misreading Tehran?" *Foreign Policy*, June 14,

2010, http://www.foreignpolicy.com/articles/2010/06/14/whos_really_mis-reading_tehran. For a thorough refutation of their interpretation of internal Iranian politics, especially their spurious claim that "Ahmadinejad won. Get over it" (the title of their notorious screed on Politico.com, June 15, 2009), see Ali Ansari, "Urban Myths Revisited: The 2009 Presidential Election," in this volume, and his book *Crisis of Authority: Iran's 2009 Presidential Election* (London: Chatham House, 2010), 1–12, 47–53, 56–59 and Peterson, *Let the Swords Encircle Me*, 488–489, 520–531, 554–556, 684–686.

9. This is a direct quote from the memorandum issued by Iran's Ministry of Culture and Islamic Guidance, dated August 16, 2010 and reprinted on opposition websites. For a copy of this document see "The Name and Image of Mousavi, Karoubi and Khatami in Newspapers and News Agencies is Forbidden," *Jaras*, August 22, 2010, www.rahesabz.net./story/21941/ and William Yong and Robert F. Worth, "Iran Clamps Down on Reporting on Protest Leaders," *New York Times*, August 25, 2010.

10. "Iran: US Funded Sedition Leaders," Press TV, August 26, 2010, http://www.presstv.ir/detail/140105.html.

11. Edward Yeranian, "Iran's Supreme Leader Says He Represents Prophet Muhammad on Earth," *Voice of America*, July 21, 2010, www.voanews.com/english/news/middle-east/Irans-Supreme-Leader-Says-He-Represents-Prophet-Muhammad-on-Earth-98945624.html; "Khamenei: You Must Obey Me," Rooz Online, July 22, 2010, http://www.roozonline.com/english/news/newsitem/article/2010/july/22//khamenei-you-must-obey-me.html. Full Farsi text is available from Khamenei's website at: http://farsi.khamenei.ir/treatise-content?uid=1&tid=8. This is not the first time Khamenei has demanded total obedience. In January 2000, at the height of the reform period, when Khatami and his allies were on the ascent and hardliners were desperately trying to block their reformist agenda, Khamenei delivered a similarly worded speech. See Scott Peterson, *Let the Swords Encircle Me*, 532.

12. Responding to the charge that the Green Movement is dead, Mir Hossein Mousavi replied that if the government allowed us one day to organize a peaceful demonstration, this issue could be settled. In his own words: "It is very easy to test this claim [that the Green Movement is dead]. Instead of

filling with streets with security forces like they did on December 7 [Students Day] and June 15 [anniversary of the Green Movement's largest rally] allow the people to express their views based on Article 27 of the constitution [which guarantees freedom of assembly]. "Let Us Put the Current Destructive Policies to a Referendum," October 5, 2010, http://www.kaleme. com/1389/07/13/klm-34012.

13. For a moving personal account of this period see Afsaneh Moqadam, *Death to the Dictator!: A Young Man Casts a Vote in Iran's 2009 Election and Pays a Devastating Price* (New York: Farrar, Straus and Giroux, 2010). On the show trials, see Laura Secor, "The Iran Show," *The New Yorker*, August 31, 2009, http:// www.newyorker.com/talk/comment/2009/08/31/090831taco_talk_secor. Evan Siegel has translated the indictments by the Islamic Revolutionary Court. They are available at: http://www.qlineorientalist.com/IranRises/ the-indictment/ and http://www.qlineorientalist.com/IranRises/the-complete-text-of-the-indictment-of-the-second-group-of-accused-in-the-project-for-a-velvet-coup/.

14. Amnesty International, *Iran: Election Contested, Repression Compounded* (December 2009), 9, www.amnesty.org/en/library/asset/MDE13/123/2009/ en/1e69a8fb-dcf1-4165-a7fc-a94369e364bf/mde131232009en.pdf. By far the best and most up-to-date analysis on the status of human rights in Iran has been produced by the New York-based International Campaign for Human Rights in Iran. For a broad overview on the post-election crackdown see the following two reports they have produced: *Campaign Report on Human Rights in Iran since 12 June 2009* (September 21, 2009), http://www.iran-humanrights.org/2009/09/report09/ and *Men of Violence: Perpetrators of the Post-Election Crackdown* (June 2010), http://www.iranhumanrights.org/ wp-content/wp-content/menofviolence/Men-of-Violence-English.pdf. Also see Human Rights Watch, *The Islamic Republic at 31: Post-election Abuses Show Serious Human Rights Abuses* (February 2010), www.hrw.org/en/ reports/2010/02/11/islamic-republic-31and Amnesty International, *From Protest to Prison: Iran One Year After the Election* (June 2010), http://www. amnesty.org/en/library/asset/MDE13/062/2010/en/a009a855-788b-4ed4-8aa9-3e535ea9606a/mde130622010en.pdf.

15. "Tehran Police: Mir Hossein Mousavi's Nephew was Assassinated," BBC Persian Service, December 29, 2009, http://www.bbc.co.uk/persian/iran/2009/12/091229_op_ir88_police_basij_kayhan_mousavi_assassination.shtml and Borzou Daragahi and Ramin Mostaghim, "Mousavi's nephew had received death threats, friends say," *Los Angeles Times*, January 1, 2010, http://articles.latimes.com/2010/jan/01/world/la-fg-iran-nephew1-2010jan01.

16. Alan Cowell, "Blast Kills Physics Professor in Tehran, *New York Times*, January 12, 2010. "Audio File of a Lecture by the Martyr Professor Ali Mohammadi and the University of Tehran Students' Communiqué," January 13, 2010, http://www.kaleme.com/1388/10/23/klm-8214.

17. Amnesty International, "'Shocking' Executions of Iran Protesters Condemned," January 28, 2010, http://www.amnesty.org/en/news-and-updates/news/shocking-execution-iran-protesters-condemned-20100128.

18. "Iranian cleric urges more executions of protesters," Reuters, January 29, 2010; "Jannati: You Executed Two People and I Thank You," BBC Persian Service, January 29, 2010, www.bbc.co.uk/persian/iran/2010/01/100129_l17_jannati_execution.shtml. For background and context as it relates to the Green Movement, see International Campaign for Human Rights in Iran, "Unprecedented Remarks by Ayatollah Jannati for More Protester Execution," January 31, 2010, http://www.iranhumanrights.org/2010/01/unprecedented-remarks-by-ayatollah-jannati-for-more-protester-execution/.

19. "Iran to hang nine more over election unrest," Reuters, February 2, 2010. Beyond these deaths, widely believed to be the work of operatives from Iran's Ministry of Intelligence, two doctors who worked at the notorious Kahrizak prison, which was shut down due to the harsh treatment of prisoners, have mysteriously died. Ramin Pourandarjani, who told a parliamentary committee that jailers were torturing and raping prisoners, was found dead on November 10, 2009. His death was called a suicide. On September 21, 2010, before he was scheduled to leave Iran, Dr. Abdolreza Soudbakhsh, an Associate Professor at the University of Tehran Medical School, was killed by an assassin's bullet outside of his clinic. He treated inmates suffering from infections to the urinary tract and reproductive systems—in other

words, medical problems as a result of rape. The day after Soudbakhsh's assassination, Gholamreza Sarabi, a heart specialist, was shot in front of his office in Tehran's Narmak district but was not killed. On September 28, 2010, the Islamic Students Association at the University of Tehran Medical School issued a statement of protest at the targeting of their professors. The full text (in Persian) can be obtained at www.anjomaneslami.com/index. php?option=com_content&view=article&id=77:6-7-89&catid=1:2010-08-12-12-50-56&Itemid=26. For background on these developments, see Farnaz Fassihi, "The Doctor Who Defied Tehran," *Wall Street Journal*, December 21, 2009; "Dr. Soudbakhsh: The Second Victim of the Kahrizak Tragedy from the Medical Society," *Jaras* , September 27, 2010, http://www.rahesabz.net/story/24268/; "The Assassination of Two Iranian Physicians in Two Days," BBC Persian Service, September 23, 2010, www.bbc.co.uk/persian/iran/2010/09/100923_l07_iran89_assassination_university_professor_sarabi.shtml.

20. For critical analysis of this event see Juan Cole, "How the Iranian Regime Checkmated the Green Dissidents on a Crucial Day," February 12, 2010, http://www.juancole.com/2010/02/how-iranian-regime-checkmated-green.html and Muhammad Sahimi, "Were the Greens Defeated?" *Tehran Bureau*, February 12, 2010, http://www.pbs.org/wgbh/pages/frontline/tehranbureau/2010/02/-opinion-many-had.html.

21. Scott Peterson, *Let the Swords Encircle Me*, 527.

22. For attacks on the home of Mehdi Karoubi, including video footage see www.pbs.org/wgbh/pages/frontline/tehranbureau/2010/09/headlines-5.html. For the increasing intimidation and threats against Mousavi see Muhammad Sahimi, "Hardliners Close In on Mousavi," *Tehran Bureau*, September 13, 2010, http://www.pbs.org/wgbh/pages/frontline/tehranbureau/2010/09/report-hardliners-close-in-on-mousavi.html. For an English translation of some of the most important statements and interviews by the Green Movement leadership see www.khordaad88.com/ and http://www.princeton.edu/irandataportal/.

23. Hamid Dabashi, "White moderates and greens," *Al Ahram Weekly*, January 21–27, 2010.

24. Akbar Ganji, "The Latter-Day Sultan: Power and Politics in Iran," *Foreign Affairs* 87 (November-December 2008), 45–66; Hossein Askari, "Iran's slide to the bottom," *Asia Times*, September 15, 2010.

25. A persistent pattern that has emerged from the testimony of political prisoners is that their torturers are motivated by a dogmatic interpretation of Islam whereby the future of Islam is tied to the survival of the Islamic Republic in its current form. In other words, the interrogators and the tortures of the Islamic Republic have internalized the regime's propaganda line out of a solid ideological devotion to the regime as being the embodiment of God's will on earth. For details on the ideological devotion of regime loyalists see Scott Peterson, *Let the Swords Encircle Me*, 545–546 and Abdollah Momeni's open letter to Ali Khamenei in this volume.

26. The figure twenty-eight comes from Peterson, *Let the Swords Encircle Me*, 577 and refers to both inside and outside of Iran. Speaking to reporters after he defected to Norway, Farzad Farhangian affirmed: "I describe myself as a soldier for my country, for my nation, not for my regime. Actually this is a regime I don't belong to at all." He added: "I'm apologizing to the Iranian people. During the last 30 years I was of service to the Iranian people, 23 of them in the diplomatic service, but the deviation that the Iranian republic has reached leaves me no choice. I hope to be a voice of the opposition" (Borzou Daragahi, "IRAN: Another Europe-based Tehran diplomat defects, seeks asylum," *Los Angeles Times* blog, September 14, 2010, http://latimesblogs.latimes.com/babylonbeyond/2010/09/iran-iranian-diplomat-quits-post-in-brussels-applies-for-asylum-in-norway.html). Also see "Iran diplomat Farzad Farhangian defects to Norway," BBC News, September 14, 2010.

27. The Reporters Without Borders 2010 Press Freedom Index ranked Iran 175 out of 178 countries (only North Korea, Turkmenistan and Eritrea obtained a lower ranking). See http://en.rsf.org/press-freedom-index-2010,1034.html.

28. One example of how the Iranian regime has lost the battle of ideas can be discerned from its attack on the university system (which already had been ideologically overhauled after the 1979 revolution). On August 30, 2009, Khamenei gave a revealing speech which laid out the basic problem – the study of humanities and the social sciences. He complained that there were

too many students enrolled in these disciplines. "Teaching humanities in universities will lead to the spread of doubt with respect to foundations of religion and faith," he observed. "Many subjects in humanities are founded on the basis of philosophies that deal with materialism and rejection of monotheism and Islamic teachings. Educating students in these fields causes them to lose faith in Islamic teachings. Teaching students these topics [humanities] leads to spreading doubt and disbelief for the basics of religion and faith." For the full text of his remarks (in Persian) see, "Remarks at a Meeting with Academics," http://farsi.khamenei.ir/speech-content?id=7959. For an English summary see www.persian2english.com/?p=142 and for more details see "Iran's Minister of Science reaffirms the need to 'Islamicize' the Universities," BBC Persian Service, September 1, 2010; "Iran Launches New Crackdown on Universities," Radio Free Europe/Radio Free Liberty, August 26, 2010, www.rferl.org/content/Iran_Launches_New_Crackdown_On_Universities/2138387.html and see Charles Kurzman, "Reading Weber in Tehran," *Chronicle of Higher Education*, November 1, 2009, www.chronicle.com/article/Social-Science-on-Trial-in-/48949/.

29. Mehran Kamrava, *Iran's Intellectual Revolution* (Cambridge: Cambridge University Press, 2008) and Farhang Rajaee, *Islamism and Modernism: The Changing Discourse in Iran* (Austin, TX: University of Texas Press, 2007). For deeper theoretical background see Nader Hashemi, *Islam, Secularism and Liberal Democracy: Toward a Democratic Theory for Muslim Societies* (New York: Oxford University Press, 2009), 67–102 and Farzin Vahdat, *God and Juggernaut: Iran's Intellectual Encounter with Modernity* (Syracuse, NY: Syracuse University Press, 2001).

30. Robert Tait, "Iran bans election protest footballers," *The Guardian*, June 23, 2009; "TV Black List Produces More Victims," *Mardom Salari* [Tehran], August 15, 2010; Meris Lutz and Ramin Mostaghim, "IRAN: Newspaper says actors, singers, poets and writers banned from television over support for opposition" *Los Angeles Times* blog, August 20, 2010, www.latimesblogs.latimes.com/babylonbeyond/2010/08/iran-newspaper-says-actors-singers-poets-and-writers-banned-from-television-over-support-for-opposition.html; Steve Inskeep, "Mohammed Reza Shajarian: Protest Through Poetry," National

Public Radio (NPR), September 27, 2010; Robert Mackey, "An Iranian Direc-tor's Impassioned Defense," *New York Times* blog, The Lede, November 17, 2010.

Why Are the Iranians Dreaming Again? by Ali Alizadeh

1. The title is a reference to Michel Foucault's 1978 essay "What Are the Iranians Dreaming About?"

Cultural Jiu-Jitsu and the Iranian Greens by Charles Kurzman

1. I thank the organizers of the conference on "Iran: The Politics of Resistance," held at the New School in New York City, where this essay was first presented. I thank Ali Kadivar for his help in preparing this work, and I thank and salute Kian Tajbaksh and the thousands of other political prisoners in Iran for their courage, their endurance, their intellectual, cultural, and political contributions.

2. www.facebook.com/mousavi. The official campaign website, www.mirhus-sein.com, was shut down after the election.

3. Iranian Ministry of the Interior, www.moi.ir, June 24, 2009.

4. *UNESCO Statistical Yearbook* (Lanham, MD: Bernan Press, 1999), p. 11–31; and World Bank, *WDI Online: World Development Indicators* (Washington, DC: World Bank, 2009).

5. Charles Kurzman, "A Feminist Generation in Iran?" *Iranian Studies*, 41, no. 3, (June 2008), 298.

6. Gene Sharp, *The Politics of Nonviolent Action* (Boston: Porter Sargent, 1985), vol. 3, 658.

7. Gene Sharp, *"The Political Equivalent of War": Civilian Defense* (New York: Carnegie Endowment for International Peace, 1965); *National Security Through Civilian-Based Defense* (Omaha, NE: Association of Transarmament Studies, 1985); *Making Europe Unconquerable: The Potential of Civilian-Based Deterrence and Defence* (London: Taylor & Francis, 1985); *Civilian-Based Defense: A Post-Military Weapons System* (Princeton, NJ: Princeton University Press, 1990).

8. Gene Sharp, *From Dictatorship to Democracy: A Conceptual Framework for*

Liberation (Boston, MA: Albert Einstein Institution, 2003); *Waging Nonviolent Struggle: 20th Century Practice and 21st Century Potential* (Boston, MA: Extending Horizons Books, 2005); and other materials published on the website of Gene Sharp's organization, the Albert Einstein Institution, www.aeinstein.org.

9. Khuzestan TV, February 5, 2008, translated by MEMRI TV, www.memritv.org/report/en/2567.htm; the video is posted at www.youtube.com/v/6rGRY7p_s00.

10. Fars News Agency, July 1, 2009, www.farsnews.com/newstext.php?nn=8804091439. The same author, Payam Fazlinezhad, published a five-part series with similar allegations in the *Kayhan* newspaper, July 4–9, 2009, www.kayhannews.ir.

11. I am pleased to credit Professor Negar Mottahedeh for this insight.

12. Among other sites, the video was available on YouTube at www.youtube.com/watch?v=bbdEfoQRsLM.

13. Charles Kurzman, *The Unthinkable Revolution in Iran* (Cambridge, MA: Harvard University Press, 2004), 50–56.

14. *"Negahi tahlili beh shabih-sazi-ye masaleh-ye Iran va Falastin: Ta Ruz-e Qods"* ("An Analytical Look at Analogizing Between the Problems of Iran and Palestine: Toward Jerusalem Day"), September 2009, www.mowjcamp.ws/article/id/32687.

15. greenway1388.files.wordpress.com/2009/12/117.jpg, December 27, 2009.

16. www.youtube.com/watch?v=ieX1gYojwyQ, January 18, 2010.

17. Simon Critchley, opening remarks at the conference "Iran: The Politics of Resistance," New School, New York, February 12, 2010.

18. Kurzman, *The Unthinkable Revolution in Iran*, 163–172.

19. media.farsnews.com/Media/8803/ImageReports/8803121479/14_8803121479_L600.jpg, June 2, 2009.

20. GlobeScan, telephone survey of Iran, June 2009.

21. WorldPublicOpinion.org, telephone survey of Iran, August 27–September 10, 2009. I thank the Program on International Policy Attitudes at the University of Maryland for sharing the dataset with me.

Iran's Green Movement as a Civil Rights Movement by Hamid Dabashi

1. Abbas Amanat, "Middle-Class Uprising," *New York Times*, June 16, 2009, roomfordebate.blogs.nytimes.com/2009/06/16/where-will-the-power-lie-in-iran/#abbas.

2. Djavad Salehi-Isfahani, "What if Ahmadinejad Really Won?" *New York Times*, June 16, 2009, roomfordebate.blogs.nytimes.com/2009/06/16/where-will-the-power-lie-in-iran/#djavad.

3. Eric Hooglund, "Iran's Rural Vote and Election Fraud," *Tehran Bureau*, June 21, 2009, www.pbs.org/wgbh/pages/frontline/tehranbureau/2010/06/irans-rural-vote-and-election-fraud.html.

Slaps in the Face of Reason by Kaveh Ehsani, Arang Keshavarzian and Norma Claire Moruzzi

1. For details, see an English-language summary at the feminist website Meydaan, www.meydaan.com/english/.

2. For instance, see Ali Ansari, Daniel Berman and Thomas Rintoul, "Preliminary Analysis of the Voting Figures in Iran's 2009 Presidential Election" (London: Chatham House, June 2009); and Walter R. Mabane, Jr., "Note on the Presidential Election in Iran: June 2009," online at www-personal.umich.edu/~wmebane/note24jun2009.pdf

The Key Features of the Green Movement: An Interview with Dissident Cleric Mohsen Kadivar

1. For more background see: Ahmad Sadri, "Mohsen Kadivar," in John L. Esposito ed., *The Oxford Encyclopedia of the Islamic World* (New York: Oxford University Press, 2009), vol. 3, 288–290; Farhang Rajaee, *Islamism and Modernism: The Changing Discourse in Iran* (Austin, TX: University of Texas Press, 2007), 208–221 and Yasuyuki Matsunaga, "Mohsen Kadivar, An Advocate of Postrevivalist Islam in Iran," *British Journal of Middle Eastern Studies* 34 (December 2007), 317–329. For access to his most recent writings see www.kadivar.com.

"Multiplied, Not Humiliated" by Ziba Mir-Hosseini

1. See Nayereh Tohidi, "Women and the Presidential Election: Iran's New Political Culture," *Informed Comment*, September 3, 2009, www.juancole.com/2009/09/tohidi-women-and-presidential-elections.html.

2. The film, We Are Half of Iran's Population, is accessible online at www.monthlyreview.org/mrzine/bani-etemad120609.html.

3. The interview with "Seyyed," the refugee Basij man, is available at www.channel4.com/news/articles/world/middle_east/iran+basij+member+describes+election+abuse/3466142.

4. The known women political prisoners are listed at www.feministschool.com/spip.php?article3828˜. [Persian]

5. See for instance the writings of Fatemeh Sadeghi (www.alborznet.ir/Fa/ViewDetail.aspx?T=2&ID=259); Nasrin Afzali (jensemokhalef.blogspot.com/2009/12/blog-post_15.html); Sarah Laqaie (www.meydaan.info/Show-article.aspx?arid=934); and Masih Alinejad (chrr.us/spip.php?article7307). [Persian]

6. Ebadi's commentary is posted at www.iranfemschool.com/spip.php?article3916. [Persian]

Delegitimizing the Islamic Republic of Iran with a Fatwa by Ahmad Sadri and Mahmoud Sadri

1. The first Caliph of the Umayyad Dynasty and an opponent of Ali. Among Shia Muslims, due to his conflict with Ali, he is a detested figure.

The Regime's Pyrrhic Victory by Mr. Verde

1. This refers to June 5, 1963 when Ayatollah Khomeini first emerged on the national stage opposing the policies of the Pahlavi monarchy. After a series of speeches, a summer uprising ensued which many scholars consider to be a prelude to the 1979 Islamic Revolution.

A Winning Strategy: Principles for Effective Civil Disobedience in Iran by Hamid Farokhnia

1. Hamid Farokhnia is a pseudonym of a journalist in Iran.

"If a Nation Wants to Change Its Destiny..."

1. A technical term of Islamic law that describes the process of making a legal decision by independent interpretation of the legal sources.

The Green Movement Charter

1. Also known as Mir Hossein Mousavi's Eighteenth Statement, June 15, 2010. This translation is taken from Mousavi's official website: www.kaleme. com/1389/03/25/klm-22913, originally translated by www.khordaad88.com and edited for this volume. Muhammad Sahimi has also translated this document for *Tehran Bureau*: www.pbs.org/wgbh/pages/frontline/tehranbureau/2010/06/the-green-movement-charter.html.

2. According to Muhammad Sahimi, the secret "barter deal" refers to a widely rumored arrangement where the judiciary will not prosecute Mahmoud Ahmadinejad's first vice president, Mohammad-Reza Rahimi and his chief of staff, Esfandiar Rahimi Mashaei, for corruption, in return for Ahmadinejad not pushing for the prosecution of the head of the judiciary, Sadeq Larijani, who is believed to be involved in his own corruption scandal. For background see Reihaneh Mazaheri, "Corruption Without End," *Tehran Bureau*, April 23, 2010, http://www.pbs.org/wgbh/pages/frontline/tehranbureau/2010/04/corruption-without-end.html.

3. Mohammad-Reza Shafiei Kadkhani, a celebrated Iranian writer, poet and literary critic.

4. Two landmarks that span the length of Tehran, from south to north.

Urban Myths Revisited by Ali Ansari

1. "The National Card Will Not Be Abolished," BBC Monitoring Online, December 31, 2009.

2. "The Social Intelligence and Enthusiasm of the Iranian Nation Will Not Believe So Much Injustice and Violation of the Law in Its Historical Memory," *Qalam News*, BBC Monitoring Online, June 20, 2009.

3. "Interior Minister: Presidential Elections Vote Counting To Be Manual," *Jomhuri Ye Eslami*, BBC Monitoring Online, February 9, 2009.

4. "Sadeq Mahsuli: The People's Votes Are Similar All Over the Country," *Resalat*, BBC Monitoring Online, June 27, 2009.

5. "Rezaee Denied Iran Ballot Box Details," *Press TV*, BBC Monitoring Online, June 18, 2009.

6. See in this regard Walter Mebane's comments quoted in "Statistical Tests Suggestive of Fraud in Iran's Election," *U.S.News & World Report*, July 14, 2009, www.usnews.com/science/articles/2009/07/14/statistical-tests-suggestive-of-fraud-in-irans-election.html.

Their Black Imaginings by Fatemeh Shams

1. This is an edited version of the letters written by Fatemah Shams to her husband. For background see Nazila Fathi, "To Reza in Jail: Love and Unity," *New York Times*, May 15, 2010.

2. Ali is a revered figured in Islam (especially Shia Islam). He was both the first Shia Imam, first cousin of Prophet Muhammad and his son-in-law. Fatemeh is also revered figure in Islam. She was the Prophet Muhammad's daughter.

3. Sohrab Arabi was a nineteen-year-old high-school graduate who was detained at Evin Prison after the elections. His mother waited for him outside of the prison, even posted bail, only to be told weeks later that her son had died during a torture session. Sohrab and Neda Agha-Soltan, gunned down in the streets, became the poster-children of the Green Movement.

4. Ayatullah Mahmud Taleghani (1911–1979) was a popular, progressive and charismatic cleric, second only to Ayatullah Khomeini in political prestige. For background see: Mahmud Taliqani, *Society and Economics in Islam: Writings and Declarations of Ayatullah Sayyid Mahmud Taleghani*, translated by R. Campbell (Berkeley: Mizan Press, 1982) and Forough Jahanbakhsh, *Islam, Democracy and Religious Modernism in Iran* (1953–2000) (Leiden: Brill, 2001), 69–80.

5. This was due to close Russian support for the Iranian regime.

6. Qods day or Jerusalem day falls on the last Friday of every Ramadan. It was declared by Ayatollah Khomeini as an annual day of solidarity with the Palestinians that is marked by a public demonstration.

7. The reference is to Saeed Hajjarian, a leading Iranian intellectual and pro-democracy activist. For back on him see Muhammad Sahimi, "Reformist Strategist: Saeed Hajjarian," *Tehran Bureau*, July 8, 2009. www.pbs.org/wgbh/pages/frontline/tehranbureau/2009/07/reformist-strategist-saeed-hajjarian.html.

Open Letter to Ayatollah Khamenei by Abdollah Momeni

1. Azadeh Moaveni, "In Iran, Student Activist Pays Price for Democracy Pursuits," *Los Angeles Times*, June 21, 2003.

2. Amnesty International, "Abdollah Momeni, prisoner of conscience," www. amnestyusa.org/all-countries/iran/abdollah-momeni-prisoner-of-conscience/page.do?id=1221014.

3. Available at: www.clovekvtisni.cz/index2en.php?id=548.

4. This letter was translated and distributed by the International Campaign for Human Rights in Iran in early September 2010, www.iranhumanrights. org/2010/09/letter-momeni-khamanei. For more background on Abdollah Momeni see "Exiled Ally Talks About Jailed Iranian Activist's Torture Allegations," Radio Free Europe/Radio Free Liberty, September 11, 2010. Available at: www.rferl.org/content/Exiled_Ally_Talks_About_Jailed_Iranian_Activists_Torture_Allegations/2155029.html.

5. The celebration and holiday that marks the end of Ramadan.

6. Head of the Judiciary at the time.

7. These are the last ten odd nights of Ramadan, considered by Muslims to be the most holy days of the year.

8. In Shia eschatology the twelfth Shia Imam is Muhammad al-Mahdi, a prophesied redeemer, who went into occultation in the 9th century and will return at the end of time with Jesus Christ to establish a reign of justice and peace.

9. Saeed Emami was a high-ranking member of Iran's Ministry of Intelligence who was involved in the serial murders of Iranian political dissidents in the late 1990s. Following the murder of a prominent opposition figure, Darioush Forouhar, and his wife in 1998, public outrage led to his arrest. He mysteriously committed suicide in prison before his trial, an event widely viewed as a deliberate attempt to silence him. His wife was subsequently interrogated and forced to confess to illicit sexual liaisons as well as being an Israeli spy. A tape of her interrogation was leaked and circulated on the internet. It prefigured the type of interrogations that are now routine in Iranian prisons and which Abdollah Momeni was subjected to.

10. Hashemi Aghajari is an Iranian historian and university professor who gave a famous speech in 2002 on "Islamic Protestantism" in which he famously stated that Iranians "are not monkeys who merely imitate" what clerics tell

them. He was charged with apostasy but after public outrage and international condemnation he was given a lighter sentence and eventually freed.

11. Annual demonstration in solidarity with Palestine that occur on the last Friday of Ramadan.

Edward Said, the Green Movement and the Struggle for Democracy in Iran by Nader Hashemi

1. Edward W. Said, "Identity, Authority and Freedom: The Potentate and the Traveler." University of Cape Town TB Davie Memorial Lecture, May 22, 1991.

2. The essay first appeared in Arabic in *Al Hayat*, September 25, 1997 and in English in *Al Ahram Weekly*, September 25-October 1, 1997. It was republished in Edward Said, *The End of the Peace Process: Oslo and After* (New York: Pantheon, 2000), 193–199. All quotations are from this version.

3. For details see, "The Incalculable Loss: Conversations with Noam Chomsky," in Adel Iskandar and Hakem Rustom eds., *Edward Said: A Legacy of Emancipation and Representation* (Berkeley: University of California Press, 2010), 381–383.

4. Shibley Telhami, "A Shift in Arab Views on Iran," *Los Angeles Times*, August 14, 2010. Also see the 2010 Arab Public Opinion Survey by Shibley Telhami at www.brookings.edu/reports/2010/0805_arab_opinion_poll_telhami.aspx.

5. Mark Tran, "Tony Blair: West should use force if Iran 'continues to develop nuclear weapons'," *The Guardian*, September 1, 2010. Also see Jeffrey Goldberg, "The Point of No Return," *The Atlantic*, September 2010 and Newt Gingrich's speech "America at Risk" at the American Enterprise Institute, July 29, 2010.

6. The claim that South Africa was internationally isolated is not entirely correct. During the 1980s under the Reagan Administration, US trade actually increased, despite Congressional sanctions. There was also US support for South Africa policy in the region and as late as 1988 the ANC was officially viewed as a terrorist organization. Nelson Mandela was only recently taken off the US terrorism list.

7. A critical difference is that in the Iranian case the opposition leadership was formerly part of the ruling regime and still supports the ideals of the 1979 Revolution and the political theology of Ayatollah Khomeini (properly

understood). As a result, they adopt a policy of reform, not a comprehensive overhaul of the Islamic Republican system leading to a revolution. On this point the South African case is qualitatively different. Also, the ANC supported sanctions against South Africa while the Green Movement leadership opposes existing UN sanctions against Iran.

8. Mir Hossein Mousavi, "The Multiplicity of Imprisoned Journalists Speaks to the Legitimacy of the Green Movement," August 4, 2010, www.kaleme.com/1389/05/13/klm-27824.

9. "Meeting between Karoubi and Mousavi on the Eve of Quds Day," September 2, 2010. From Karoubi's personal website available at: www.sahamnews.org/?p=7153.

10. "Toward a Green Foreign Policy for Iran," *Tehran Bureau*, September 4, 2010, www.pbs.org/wgbh/pages/frontline/tehranbureau/2010/09/toward-a-green-foreign-policy-for-iran.html.

11. Masih Alinejad, "The Green Movement at Year One: An Interview with Mehdi Karoubi," *Jaras*, May 26, 2010, sahamnews.org/?p=2969. An English translation can be found at www.khordaad88.com/?p=1619. Saeed Kamali Dehghan, "Iran sanctions strengthen Ahmadinejad regime—Karroubi," *The Guardian*, August 11, 2010.

12. The leadership of the Green Movement is acutely aware of this propaganda tactic. See Mousavi's Iranian New Year message in March 2010 on "patience and endurance" in which he specifically speaks to and repudiates these accusations while recognizing that respecting the religious sentiments of society and reaching out to the pious are important goals that will push the movement forward. In Mousavi's own words, "Another point is to take into account people's religious inclinations. The government has embarked on negative propaganda against us in order to make the society believe that we have changed our religious views. We have to convince people these are merely lies and accusations. We have to strengthen our bonds with the grand ayatollahs and the clergy in a bid to thwart their legend." "IRAN: Opposition leader Mousavi calls upcoming year one of 'patience and endurance'," Babylon & Beyond (the Middle East blog of the L.A. Times), March 16, 2010, www.latimesblogs.latimes.com/babylonbeyond/2010/03/iran-opposition-leader-mousavi-calls-upcoming-year-one-of-patience-and-endurance.html.

CONTRIBUTORS

ERVAND ABRAHAMIAN is Distinguished Professor of Iranian and Middle Eastern History and Politics at Baruch College, City University of New York (CUNY). His books include *Iran Between Two Revolutions* (1982), *Khomeinism* (1993), *Tortured Confessions: Prisons and Public Recantations in Modern Iran* (1999) and *A History of Modern Iran* (2008)

SOHRAB AHMARI is a law student at Northeastern University and an organizer in Boston's Iranian and Muslim communities. He has written on democratic reform in the Muslim world for the *Boston Globe*, *The Guardian*, *Tehran Bureau* and *Huffington Post*.

PAYAM AKHAVAN is Associate Professor of Law at McGill University in Montreal. He was Legal Advisor to the Prosecutor's Office of the International Criminal Tribunals for Former Yugoslavia and Rwanda and is co-founder of the Iran Human Rights Documentation Center.

NASRIN ALAVI is the author of *We Are Iran: The Persian Blogs* (2005), a book that showcased the explosion of blogging in Iran and illuminated the complexities of life for young people under theocratic rule. She writes frequently for *openDemocracy* and blogs for the *New Internationalist*. She lives both in London and Tehran.

ALI ALIZADEH is a Researcher at the Centre for Research in Modern European Philosophy at Kingston University (formerly at Middlesex University).

ALI ANSARI is director of the Institute for Iranian Studies at the University of St. Andrews. His books include *Confronting Iran: The Failure of American Foreign Policy and the Next Great Crisis in the Middle East* (2006), *Iran Under Ahmadinejad: The Politics of Confrontation* (2007) and *Crisis of Authority: Iran's 2009 Presidential Election* (2010).

SAID AMIR ARJOMAND is Professor of Sociology at Stony Brook University and is the editor of the *Journal of Persianate Studies*. His books include *The Shadow of God and the Hidden Imam* (1984), *The Turban for the Crown: The Islamic Revolution in Iran* (1988) and *After Khomeini: Iran Under His Successors* (2009).

REZA ASLAN is a contributing editor at the *Daily Beast* (thedailybeast.com). His books include *No god but God: The Origins, Evolution, and Future of Islam* (2005), *Beyond Fundamentalism: Confronting Religious Extremism in a Globalized Age* (2010) and *Tablet & Pen: Literary Landscapes from the Modern Middle East* (2011).

GOLBARG BASHI teaches Iranian and Middle Eastern Studies at Rutgers University and is a frequent contributor to *Tehran Bureau*. Her writings can be found at golbargbashi.com.

HOSSEIN BASHIRIYEH is one of post-revolutionary Iran's key political thinkers. His books include the monumental *State and Revolution in Iran, 1962–1982* (1984). He taught political science at the University of Tehran from 1983 until 2007, when he was fired for political reasons. He now teaches political science at Syracuse University.

AHMAD BATEBI became an iconic figure amid Iran's 1999 student protests when his photo appeared on the front cover of *The Economist* holding a bloodstained shirt. Thereafter, he was sentenced to ten years in prison. Now living in exile in the US, he is widely regarded among Iranians as an icon of democratic struggle.

ASEF BAYAT is Professor of Sociology and Middle East Studies at the University of Illinois. His books include *Workers and Revolution in Iran* (1987), *Street Politics: Poor People's Movements in Iran* (1997), *Making Islam Democratic: Social Movements and the Post-Islamist Turn* (2007) and *Life as Politics: How Ordinary People Change the Middle East* (2010).

CHRISTOPHER DE BELLAIGUE has worked as a journalist in the Middle East and South Asia since 1994. His books include *In the Rose Garden of the Martyrs: A Memoir of Iran* (2005), *The Struggle for Iran* (2007) and *Rebel Land: Unraveling the Riddle of History in a Turkish Town* (2010). He lives in Tehran.

ROGER COHEN is a columnist for *The New York Times* and the *International Herald Tribune*.

JUAN COLE is Professor of History at the University of Michigan. His blog, *Informed Comment* (juancole.com), is one of the most widely-read sources on the Middle East. His books include *Sacred Space and Holy War: The Politics, Culture and History of Shi'ite Islam* (2002), *Napoleon's Egypt: Invading the Middle East* (2007) and *Engaging the Muslim World* (2009).

HAMID DABASHI is Professor of Iranian Studies and Comparative Literature at Columbia University and the host of *The Week in Green* (www.weekingreen.org). His books include *Close Up: Iranian Cinema, Past, Present, Future* (2001), *Iran: A People Interrupted* (2007) and *The Green Movement and the USA: The Fox and the Paradox* (2010).

SHIRIN EBADI is Iran's most prominent lawyer and human rights activist. She was awarded the Nobel Peace Prize in 2003. Both she and the Defenders of Human Rights Center, of which she is director, have been subjected to harassment and repression by the Iranian government. She is the author of *Iran Awakening: A Memoir of Revolution and Hope* (2006).

KAVEH EHSANI is Assistant Professor of International Studies at DePaul University. He is a member of the editorial committee of *Middle East Report* and serves on the editorial board of the Tehran-based journal *Goftogu*. **NORMA MORUZZI** is Associate Professor of Political Science and Gender & Women's Studies and Director of the International Studies Program at the University of Illinois at Chicago. She is the author of *Speaking through the Mask: Hannah Arendt and the Politics of Social Identity* (2000). **ARANG KESHAVARZIAN**

is Associate Professor of Middle Eastern Studies at NYU and a member of the editorial committee of *Middle East Report*. He is the author of *Bazaar and State in Iran: The Politics of the Tehran Marketplace* (2007).

MORAD FARHADPOUR AND OMID MEHRGAN are translators and writers based in Tehran. Together they co-translated Adorno and Horkheimer's *Dialectic of Enlightenment* into Persian. Farhadpour's books (in Persian) include *Depressed Reason* and *Paris-Tehran*. Mehrgan's books (in Persian) include *Theology of Translation: Walter Benjamin and the Translator's Prophetic Mission* and *Urgent Thinking*. On February 3, 2010, Mehrgan was arrested in Tehran and taken to an undisclosed location. He was released later that month.

HAMID FAROKHNIA is a pseudonym for a writer in Tehran who is a staff writer at *Iran Labor Report* (iranlaborreport.com) and writes for *Tehran Bureau*.

MICHAEL M. J. FISCHER is Professor of Anthropology at MIT. His books include *Iran: From Religious Dispute to Revolution* (1980), *Debating Muslims: Cultural Dialogues in Postmodernity and Tradition* (1990), *Mute Dreams, Blind Owls, and Dispersed Knowledges: Persian Poesis in the Transnational Circuitry* (2004) and *Anthropological Futures* (2009).

AKBAR GANJI is one of Iran's leading dissident voices. He spent six years in a Tehran prison for exposing government involvement in the so-called Chain Murders, the assassination of intellectuals critical of the Iranian regime. His books include (in Persian) *The Dungeon of Ghosts* (1999) and (in English) *The Road to Democracy in Iran* (2008).

FRED HALLIDAY (1946–2010) was Professor of International Relations at the London School of Economics and Political Science. His books include *Iran: Dictatorship and Development* (1978), *Rethinking International Relations* (1994), *Revolution and World Politics* (1999) and *100 Myths about the Middle East* (2005).

NADER HASHEMI teaches middle east and Islamic politics at the Josef Korbel School of International Studies at the University of Denver. He is the author of *Islam, Secularism and Liberal Democracy: Toward a Democratic Theory for Muslim Societies*.

ZIBA MIR-HOSSEINI is Research Associate at the London Middle East Institute, School of Oriental and African Studies (SOAS), University of London. Her books include *Islam and Gender: The Religious Debate in Contemporary Iran* (1999) and *Islam and Democracy in Iran: Eshkevari and the Quest for Reform* (2006). Her films include *Divorce Iranian Style* (1998).

RAMIN JAHANBEGLOO is Professor of Political Science at the University of Toronto and a Research Fellow at the university's Centre for Ethics. His books include *Conversations with Isaiah Berlin* (1992), *Gandhi* (1999), *Iran: Between Tradition and Modernity* (2004), *The Clash of Intolerances* (2007) and *The Spirit of India* (2008).

MOHSEN KADIVAR is a leading Iranian dissident cleric. Currently in exile, he is Visiting Research Professor in the Department of Religion at Duke University. In 1999, he was convicted and sentenced to eighteen months in prison on charges of spreading false information about Iran's "sacred system of the Islamic Republic" and helping enemies of the revolution.

MEHDI KAROUBI emerged as one of the leading figures in the Green Movement in the aftermath of Iran's 2009 presidential election, in which he stood as a candidate. A former speaker of Iran's parliament, he has incurred the wrath of Iran's hardliners by exposing a systematic campaign of rape against political prisoners following the 2009 election.

STEPHEN KINZER is Visiting Professor of International Relations at Boston University and a columnist for *The Guardian*. His books include *All the Shah's Men: An American Coup and the Roots of Middle East Terror* (2003), *Overthrow: America's Century of Regime Change from Hawaii to Iraq* (2006) and *Reset: Iran, Turkey, and America's Future* (2010).

CHARLES KURZMAN is Professor of Sociology at the University of North Carolina at Chapel Hill. His books include *The Unthinkable Revolution in Iran* (2004), *Democracy Denied, 1905–1915: Intellectuals and the Fate of Democracy* (2008) and *The Missing Martyrs: Why There Are So Few Muslim Terrorists* (2011).

SCOTT LUCAS is Professor of American Studies at the University of Birmingham and the editor of EA WorldView (enduringamerica.com). His books include *Divided We Stand: Britain, the US and the Suez Crisis* (1991), *Orwell* (2003) and *The Betrayal of Dissent: Beyond Orwell, Hitchens, and the New American Century* (2004).

ABDOLLAH MOMENI is the spokesperson for the Central Council of the Alumni Organization of University Students of the Islamic Republic, Iran's largest reformist student organization. For the past decade he has been in and out of prison, often in solitary confinement, and under constant surveillance by Iran's Ministry of Intelligence. Momeni is in Evin Prison.

IAN MORRISON is an editor of the *Platypus Review* and writes for *Tehran Bureau*. He lives in Chicago.

DANNY POSTEL is the author of *Reading "Legitimation Crisis" in Tehran: Iran and the Future of Liberalism*. He is the editor of *The Common Review* and also works as communications coordinator for Interfaith Worker Justice.

HOMAYOUN POURZAD is a pseudonym for an organizer with the Network of Iranian Labor Associations in Iran and a contributor to *Iran Labor Report* (iranlaborreport.com).

ZAHRA RAHNAVARD is a leading figure in Iran's feminist movement. A political scientist, she was fired as chancellor of Tehran's exclusively female Al-Zahra University. *Foreign Policy* magazine named her one of the Top 100 Global Thinkers of 2009. She is the wife of Mir Hossein Mousavi and widely considered the brains behind his presidential campaign.

KARIM SADJADPOUR is an Associate at the Carnegie Endowment for International Peace and was chief Iran analyst at the International Crisis Group based in Washington, DC, and Tehran, where he conducted interviews with senior Iranian officials, intellectuals, clerics, dissidents, paramilitaries, businessmen, students and activists.

AHMAD SADRI AND MAHMOUD SADRI are the co-editors and co-translators of *Reason, Freedom, and Democracy in Islam: Essential Writings of Abdolkarim Soroush* (2000). Ahmad Sadri is Professor of Sociology and Islamic World Studies at Lake Forest College. Mahmoud Sadri is Professor of Sociology at Texas Woman's University.

GARY SICK is a Senior Research Scholar at the Middle East Institute, School of International and Public Affairs, Columbia University. He is the author of *All Fall Down: America's Tragic Encounter with Iran* (1985) and was the principal White House aide for Iran during the Iranian Revolution and the hostage crisis.

MUHAMMAD SAHIMI is Professor of Chemical Engineering and Materials Science and the NIOC Chair in Petroleum Engineering at the University of Southern California. He is the lead political columnist for *Tehran Bureau*, blogs at *Huffington Post*, and contributes regularly to antiwar.com.

LAURA SECOR is an independent journalist who writes frequently about Iran for the *New Yorker*. She has been a staff editor of the *New York Times* op-ed page, a reporter for the *Boston Globe*, an editor of *The American Prospect*, and a senior editor and writer for *Lingua Franca*. Her book *Fugitives from Paradise*, about Iran, is forthcoming in 2011.

FATEMEH SHAMS was born in the city of Mashhad, Iran. She and her husband, Mohammad Reza Jalaeipour, both doctoral students at Oxford University, attempted to leave Iran amidst the post-election crackdown but were detained on June 17, 2009, at the Tehran airport. Fatemeh was allowed to depart, but Mohammad Reza was sent to Evin prison, where he was put on televised show trial.

ABDOLKARIM SOROUSH is widely considered as Iran's preeminent religious thinker and philosopher. Forced into exile, he is currently living in the United States, where he has been a visiting professor at Harvard, Princeton, and Yale. The collection *Reason, Freedom, and Democracy in Islam: Essential Writings of Abdolkarim Soroush* was published in 2000.

MOHAMMAD AYATOLLAHI TABAAR is a Scholar at the Middle East Institute in Washington, DC, a Visiting Scholar at George Washington University's Elliott School of International Affairs and a broadcast journalist for the BBC World Service, writing articles and producing radio programs on American, Middle Eastern and international politics.

"MR. VERDE" is a pseudonym for a journalist in Iran who is a correspondent for the online forum Enduring America World View (enduringamerica.com).

CORNEL WEST is University Professor in the Center for African American Studies at Princeton University. His books include *Prophetic Fragments* (1988), *The American Evasion of Philosophy: A Genealogy of Pragmatism* (1989), *Race Matters* (1993), *Democracy Matters* (2004), *Hope on a Tightrope* (2008) and *Brother West: Living and Loving Out Loud* (2009).

ROBIN WRIGHT is Senior Fellow at the United States Institute of Peace and the Woodrow Wilson International Center for Scholars. Her books include *In the Name of God: The Khomeini Decade* (1989), *The Last Great Revolution: Turmoil and Transformation in Iran* (2000), *Dreams and Shadows: The Future of the Middle East* (2008) and *The Iran Primer* (2010).

SLAVOJ ŽIŽEK is a Slovenian philosopher and cultural critic. He is a professor at the European Graduate School, International Director of the Birkbeck Institute for the Humanities, Birkbeck College, University of London, and a senior researcher at the Institute of Sociology, University of Ljubljana, Slovenia.

This page constitutes an extension of the copyright page.

"The Gandhian Moment" by Ramin Jahanbegloo was first published in *Dissent,* June 20, 2009. "Iran's Green Movement as a Civil Rights Movement" by Hamid Dabashi was first published at CNN.com, June 22, 2009. "A Specter Is Haunting Iran—The Specter of Mosaddegh" by Stephen Kinzer was first published at the *Guardian* online, June 22, 2009. A Movement Centuries in the Making" by Hamid Dabashi; and "The Decade's First Revolution?" by Gary Sick were first published in *The Daily Beast.* "Slaps in the Face of Reason" by Kaveh Ehsani, Arang Keshavarzian, and Norma Claire Moruzzi; and "Broken Taboos in Post-Election Iran" by Ziba Mir-Hosseini first appeared in *Middle East Report Online,* published by the Middle East Research and Information Project (www.merip/org). "Feminist waves in the Iranian Green Tsunami?" by Golbarg Bashi; "The Green Path of Hope"; "Turning Point?"; "A Raging Fire Under a Heap of Ash"; "The Political Evolution of Mousavi"; and "Statement by Five Religious Intellectuals" by Muhammad Sahimi; "Steps Ahead on May Day" and "A Winning Strategy" by Hamid Farokhnia; and "From Birmingham to Tehran" by Sohrab Ahmari all first appeared in PBS/Frontline's *tehranbureau:* pbs.org/wgbh/pages/frontline/tehranbureau "Iran: a green wave for life and liberty" by Asef Bayat; "Iran's Tide of History" by Fred Halliday; "Iran in darkness and light" and "Iran's coming of age" by Nasrin Alavi were all first published by *openDemocracy.* "I am not a speck of dirt, I am a retired teacher" is reprinted from the *London Review of Books,* July 23, 2009, by permission of the LRB. "Berlusconi in Tehran" by Slavoj Žižek first appeared in the *London Review of Books,* July 23, 2009. Reprinted by permission of the author. "Counter-Revolution and Revolt in Iran" first published in *Constellations,* Volume 17, Issue 1, pages 61–77, March 2010. "The people reloaded" by Morad Farhadpour and Omid Mehrgan first published in *Red Pepper,* September 14, 2009. "The Hinge of History" by Roger Cohen first appeared in *The International Herald Tribune;* reprinted coutesy of the author and The New York Times Company. "Ayatollah Montazeri's Brave Struggle for Justice" by Payam Akhavan was first published in *The National Post,* December 22, 2009. "The goals of Iran's Green Movement" by Robin Wright first appeared in the *Christian Science Monitor,* January 6, 2010. Against the status quo" by Ian Morrison first appeared at *The Platypus Review:* platypus1917.org, January 8, 2010. "This Magic Green Bracelet" by Nasrin Alavi first appeared in *New Internationalist,* Jan/Feb 2010. www.newint.org/features "The Struggle for Iran's Soul" by Christopher de Bellaigue was first published in *Prospect,* January 27, 2010, Issue 167. Copyright © Christopher de Bellaigue by kind permission of the author c/o Rogers, Coleridge & White Ltd., 20 Powis Mews, London W11 1JN. "Iran's Revolutionary Echoes" by Said Arjomand first appeared at project-syndicate.org, February 2, 2010. "The Regime's Pyrrhic Victory" by "Mr. Verde" first appeared at *enduringamerica.com* "Laying Low but Not Gone" by Mohammad Ayatollahi Tabaar first appeared in *Foreign Policy,* April 30, 2010. "The Harsher the Repression, the Stronger the Movement Grows" by Shirin Ebadi first appeared at the *Guardian* online, June 8, 2010. "How Israel's Gaza Blockade and Washington's Sanctions Policy Helped Keep the Hardliners in Power" by Juan Cole first appeared at *TomDispatch.com* "Urban Myths Revisited" by Ali Ansari was first published by *The World Today,* Volume 66, Number 7. "The Movement Has GoneUnderground" by Maryam Ny first appeared online at Persian2English.com "The Rhythmic Beat of the Revolution in Iran" by Michael M.J. Fisher first appeared in *Cultural Anthropology,* Volume 25, Issue 3, pages 497–543, August 2010. "Their Black Imaginings, translated by Erika Abrahamian: Originally published in the *Virginia Quarterly Review.* English translation copyright © 2010 by the Virginia Quarterly Review. "Iran's Green Movement: An Interview with Mehdi Karoubi" by Laura Secor, originally published at *The New Yorker* online, October 12, 2010. Unless otherwise noted above, pieces are reprinted by arrangement with the author.